PLANNING
BEYOND 2000

PLANNING BEYOND 2000

edited by
Philip Allmendinger
and
Michael Chapman

Images by
Joe Gilmore

JOHN WILEY & SONS

Chichester • New York • Weinheim • Brisbane • Singapore • Toronto

Copyright © 1999 by John Wiley & Sons Ltd, Baffins Lane, Chichester, West Sussex
PO19 1UD, England

National 01243 779777. International (+44) 1243 779777

e-mail (for orders and customer service enquiries): cs-books@wiley.co.uk.

Visit our Home Page on http://www.wiley.co.uk or http://www.wiley.com

Philip Allmendinger and Mike Chapman have asserted their right under the Copyright, Designs and Patents
Act, 1988, to be identified as the editors of this work.

OTHER WILEY EDITORIAL OFFICES

John Wiley & Sons, Inc., 605 Third Avenue, New York, NY 10158-0012, USA

WILEY-VCH Verlag GmbH, Pappelallee 3, D-69469 Weinheim, Germany

Jacaranda Wiley Ltd, 33 Park Road, Milton, Queensland 4064, Australia

John Wiley & Sons (Asia) Pte Ltd, 2 Clementi Loop #02-01, Jin Xing Distripark, Singapore 129809

John Wiley & Sons (Canada) Ltd, 22 Worcester Road, Rexdale, Ontario M9W 1L1, Canada

LIBRARY OF CONGRESS CATALOGING-IN-PUBLICATION DATA

Planning beyond 2000 / edited by Philip Allmendinger and Michael Chapman
; images by Joe Gilmore,
    p. cm.
  Includes bibliographical references and index.
  ISBN 0-471-98441-8. — ISNB 0-471-98442-6 (pbk.)
  1. City planning. I. Allmendinger, Philip, 1968–   .
II. Chapman, Mike.
HT166.P523 1999
307.1'216—dc21   98–49776
                                                            CIP

BRITISH LIBRARY CATALOGUING IN PUBLICATION DATA

A catalogue record for this book is available from the British Library

ISBN 0-471-98441-8 (hardback)
ISBN 0-471-9442-6 (paperback)

Typeset in 9/12pt Caslon 224 from authors' disks by Mayhew Typesetting, Rhayader, Powys
Printed and bound in Great Britain by Bookcraft (Bath) Ltd.

This book is printed on acid-free paper responsibly manufactured from sustainable forestry, in which at
least two trees are planted for each one used for paper production.

CONTENTS

CHAPTER 1

PLANNING IN THE MILLENNIUM

Philip Allmendinger and Michael Chapman

INTRODUCTION

It is tempting to think that we are living in new and different times – an era that marks us out from previous ages. This feeling itself is not new and has been around at various times. But what we are experiencing now, as we approach the millennium, is a remarkable nexus of significant factors that could be seen to at least hint at the prospect of 'newness' within an atmosphere of uncertainty. First, at the global level, we have what could be described as the fall-out from the end of the cold war. The impact of changes in Europe and the former Soviet Union in the late 1980s and early 1990s cannot be overemphasised. As Alex Callinicos (1991: 8) has put it:

> Far beyond the countries directly affected, people shared a sense of suddenly widened possibilities. Parts of the furniture of the post-war world that seemed irremovable suddenly disappeared – literally in the case of the Berlin wall. Previously unalterable assumptions – for example, that Europe would be permanently divided between the superpowers – abruptly collapsed.

As a consequence we have had a resurgence of the 'end of history' idea (again, something that seems to have cropped up throughout history). Most (in)famously, Francis Fukuyama (1989) has pointed to the global ideological convergence towards liberal democracy. For him, the end of the cold war heralded the end of ideology – we all were, or at least eventually would be, liberal democrats. But the certainty this provides needs to balanced with the uncertainty created by another form of convergence in the form of the European Union (EU). The economic implications of European Monetary Union (EMU) and the loss of national sovereignty through the European Parliament require new governance and institutions as a consequence.

Second, after 18 years of New Right rule in the UK (and increasingly the rest of the world), we now have New Labour. This change of government underestimates the sea change that occurred on 1 May 1997 which witnessed the ousting of John Major's government with the biggest post-war landslide victory. With this election came a new mood of optimism accompanied by some widely welcomed immediate changes – an independent Bank of England, referendums on devolution for Scotland and Wales, incorporation of the European Convention on Human Rights into UK law, 'Welfare to Work', a commitment to join the European single currency and a focus on social exclusion. The Prime Minister Tony Blair (1998) seeks to focus on inclusion rather than the harsh realities of exclusion as experienced under the Thatcher years:

> . . . it (Labour's vision) is to find a new way, a third way, between unbridled indi-vidualism and laissez-faire on the one hand; and old-style Government intervention, the corporatism of the 1960s social democracy, on the other. To find the route to social justice in a modern age. Traditional goals; modern means. We know ever-higher tax and spending by government isn't on. We know Government running industry or state subsidies doesn't work. We know protectionism and isolationism won't deliver lasting prosperity in a global economic age.

Third, we have recently marked 50 years of the UK planning system and according to Cullingworth (1997: 130), this landmark should be celebrated:

> A remarkable feature of this legislation is that it has survived largely intact over the fifty years since it was passed. . . . This is quite different from the position in most areas of public policy, where there has been transformation, as with education, health, transport, and what used to be called the public utilities.

Finally, there is the millennium itself. The millennium is not confined to Christianity, and other religions such as Islam and secular movements have all exhibited elements of millenarianism. What they all have in common is a mixture of reflection, celebration and hope that underpins and adds most to the feeling of change.

Overall, the time would seem to be ripe for confident reflection in an era of optimism and increased uncertainty. We would argue that the time *is* right for such an exercise, but there is a danger in being sucked into the millenarian and largely Western complacency about new times. Of most danger is the 'end of ideology' idea. While there is undoubtedly a convergence of ideologies towards liberal democracy at a macro scale, we should be wary in accepting it at face value and its implication of consensus. There are inherent tensions and contradictions between the liberal and democratic in liberal democracy. As David Held (1992: 23) has also pointed out:

> Contemporary democracies have crystallised into a number of different types – the Westminster, Federal and consensus models, for example – which make any appeal to a liberal position vague at best.

This 'new world order' (or 'disorder' as some have termed it) masks continuing issues such as poverty, social exclusion and environmental degradation, but presents the solutions as either technical fixes to the operation of the market or without hard choices. The idea of consensus and inclusion has been taken forward and heralded by New Labour. The general goodwill they have enjoyed (with some exceptions) combined with the nationwide relief in removing the previous stale government seems to have led to a renewed trust in government to solve problems.

Obviously values such as trust should be welcomed, but this should not emasculate genuine debate concerning means and ends. Perhaps the biggest question is 'will they deliver?' Early analysis does not bode well as the government have committed themselves to the tight spending plans of the previous Tory administration.

As far as the environment is concerned, planners and others should be particularly wary for two reasons. First, Labour has never been the natural party of the environment; it was the party of production and was circumspect of anything that might inhibit this. Trade Union and constituency MP pressure concerning, for example, nuclear power has meant that the party's record on the environment has been 'wretched' according to Robin Cook (Anderson and Mann, 1997: 168). This may have changed in recent months with the publication of a plethora of White Papers on everything from regional guidance to 'modernising' planning but these are only consultation documents. As was shown in the debate over new homes in the countryside and the rural lobby's march on London in February 1998, New Labour is not ideologically set in its ways. It is open to persuasion not least because of the second reason to be wary. Labour has had to widen its appeal and woo 'middle England'. It is precisely this same constituency that has taken to the environment and NIMBY-type attitudes (Allmendinger and Tewdwr-Jones, 1997). A tension therefore emerges. The government has said it wants to be one of the great reforming and radical governments – but it has to please disparate interests. Tension is something politics deals with; the New Right had important tensions of their own most notably between the free market liberals on the one hand and the strong state authoritarian Conservatives on the other. But it does raise a question mark over optimism that this government can and will address important issues that face the environment and planning.

Not that planning and planners are pushing for any great change or re-evaluation of their role. After 50 years, the message emanating from academics and professionals seems to be 'business as usual, please'. The 1997 Royal Town Planning Institute (RTPI) members' survey found that the main reasons for becoming a member was career progression while central government was seen as the main source of thinking about planning (RTPI, 1997). The technocratic professional seems alive and well.

Planning has travelled from the halcyon days of 'positive planning' in the 1950s and 1960s that included new towns, urban regeneration, betterment and industrial location to the current relief that it survived the Thatcher years and is once again seen as valuable if only to take on board sustainability and the exclusionary NIMBY notions of shire voters. This is not to say that we should return to the 'command and control' approach of the post-war years. That would not be possible or desirable. But it does reflect a lack of debate beyond the complacency: a nip here, a tuck there. Nobody is asking whether we *need* planning or what its role should be in society. Planning, like democracy or environmental protection, has become a meta-narrative that everyone can agree on but not pin down and say what it actually means. What this points to is the need to debate the role of planning.

4
—

Finally, there is the wrapping paper for all of this: the millennium. There is a certain smugness about the whole genuflection of millennium fever underpinned by a self-righteousness that you could dub the 'Sinatra syndrome' – 'we did it our way'. The significance of what is essentially an arbitrary, artificial and predominantly Western method of time keeping seems at the same time to be both compelling and bizarre (Thomson, 1997). The problem is that (quite naturally) attention is being focused on the future not the past. The past is a patchwork of achievements both good and bad, but it got us here, so it must essentially be 'all right'. The view is a typical 'if it's not broken don't fix it'.

We take a different perspective. Our personal view is that there are serious problems with planning that need to be addressed. There are also some very important debates and questions that remain unresolved. This nexus of opportunity provides a useful way of packaging a debate that should have been held anyway. The book tries to address some of these questions in a provocative and thoughtful way while at the same time 'mapping out' a future direction for planning.

It might be as well to set out here what we mean by 'planning' and thereby define the scope of this book. In 1947 the answer to that question would have been much easier. Planning was a technical activity aimed at making a more pleasant, healthy and efficient environment – the 'art and science of town planning' as the RTPI puts it. Fifty years on, in our politically fractured postmodern landscape there is little such agreement. Like most people, we take an inclusive view. Planning now encompasses such a variety of issues that one could include everything from saving the planet to where swings should go in a children's playground. This in itself poses new problems and challenges. Planners themselves are having their technical and apolitical stance challenged by the increasingly political and inclusive nature of the subject. Whereas the formerly narrow scope of the profession in a time of growth and public acquiescence lent itself to simple choices, the modern planner is faced with a myriad of competing claims and difficult if not irreconcilable options. The implications are of resentment from the 'losers' and those excluded. The problems for planners are of a questioning of their role – are they mediators or technical experts? Should they be open about their values? These are hardly new problems but are exacerbated by the increasingly fraught and conflict-ridden nature of the world and planning. These problems, among others, add to the challenge of planning in the twenty-first century. As an introduction to the questions it is worth while focusing upon the contexts and processes that will influence planning. We have already touched upon two main factors, others include the following.

GLOBALISATION

There has been and will continue to be a reduced role for the nation state for three main reasons. First, governments have shown themselves not to be adept as direct providers of services as the command economies of the former Eastern bloc demonstrated. Privatisation is now the norm as governments seek to raise revenue and (as importantly) shed responsibility for services over which they are increasingly losing control because of increased demands and falling resources. Second, the increasing importance of global capital in dictating foreign and domestic economic policy has been emphasised by the mobility of skilled workers to minimise taxes and maximise benefits. Information on the kinds and success of policies is now more freely available, allowing investors to compare regions and nation states in reaching their decisions. This is particularly so as a previously fragmented world begins to fuse into trading superblocs that seek to realise barrierless internal competition and economic power on the world stage. As Robin Cook said in his speech to the General Affairs Council in Brussels as Britain started its presidency of the EU, the momentum towards enlargement is partly to do with increasing 'clout in international talks on trade'. Finally, the EU is decanting power and influence in a variety of fields including economic policy, work standards and tax. Two of the criteria for joining the European single currency, that is, limits on the level of national debt as a proportion of gross domestic product and the underlying inflation rate, effectively dictate economic policy. As power shifts away from national to supranational bodies or the market, what are the implications for domestic policies that aim to intervene in the operation of the market such as planning? What are the implications for local economic development and other local strategies?

COMPLEXITY

As we have seen, it seems that making things 'happen' or 'not happen' is becoming increasingly difficult even though society seems to be becoming more sophisticated. Governments no longer have total control over their economies; workers, capital and information can move freely around the world undermining mere national initiatives. Issues such as homelessness, poverty and pollution are still very present despite (or because of?) attempts to resolve them. Can we really 'solve' problems such as these or are they inherently too complicated? On the planning front there are expectations that planning can 'solve' the problems of town-centre decline while granting permission for popular out-of-town developments, provide adequate amounts of housing while protecting the countryside. How can planning resolve these deeply complex and apparently contradictory objectives? On another level there seems to be an increasing complexity in who does what. The plethora of government and non-government organisations and initiatives seems to confuse rather than clarify. Have the attempts at solving problems led to a bureaucratic quagmire that impedes rather than facilitates progress?

EUROPE

Britain's future will increasingly be dominated by Europe. Whatever party comes to power in the next decade or so there will be little to challenge to political hegemony of further European integration. As it is, the Labour Party have tied their colours to the mast and presented a more positive view of Europe than we were perhaps used to in recent times:

> We willingly pay the price of pooled sovereignty in defence, for the greater prize of collective security through NATO. We should be ready to pay a similar price in the European Union for the prizes of political security and stability, liberal and open markets, higher incomes and more jobs. Security used to come from self-reliance and defensive barriers. Today, it comes increasingly from openness and the removal of barriers (Blair, 1998).

Three main themes dominate the future of the EU and of each member state. First, there is economic and monetary union. Britain will not be joining the first wave of a single currency though its economy is inextricably linked to the future prosperity and success of it. But large issues and questions remain. The creation of EMU will undoubtedly cause significant economic adjustments as price differentials become more transparent to consumers and economies of scale throughout Europe become potentially more realisable. Following EMU, exchange rate adjustments will no longer be possible and neither will realistic labour mobility in the short term. The EU is addressing the potential for structural instability through increasing pressure for greater macro-economic convergence, e.g. reducing barriers to trade, controlling inflation, improving labour mobility. Two scenarios need to be allowed for: the possibility of 'economic shock' and the move towards greater economic and social integration. As Lowe and Ward (1998) point out, economic integration has been the motor behind environmental integration and the growth in EU environmental legislation.

Second, under Agenda 2000, which established the criteria for EU enlargement, agreement has already been reached to admit 10 central and eastern European countries and Cyprus as well as continuing discussions with a further 6. This will undoubtedly have major ramifications for future European and British interests. Enlargement will require reform of the Structural and Cohesion funds as well as the Common Agricultural Policy. Britain is likely to be a net loser in any future change to the Structural Fund as the needs of the new member states are comparatively greater.

Third, since the mid 1970s and increasingly throughout the 1980s and 1990s Europe has been concerned with environmental matters (Figure 1). This has been one of its most popular roles in the UK even as EU legislation brought us into conflict with the European Court throughout the antagonistic anti-European Thatcher years. As we stated above, economic factors have remained the driving force behind environmental legislation and this is likely to continue to force more

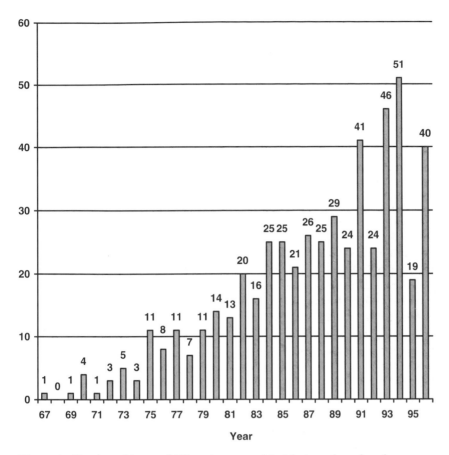

Figure 1 Number of items of EC environmental legislation adopted each year.
Source: Haigh (1997)

change. The British government have shifted from a position of open hostility to one
of acceptance under the Major governments to almost leading the fight at Kyoto. As
John Gummer concluded in 1994, 80% of UK environmental legislation has its
origins in Europe. In planning we are still to fully realise the impact of the European
Spatial Development Perspective (ESDP) and the 'balanced development' objectives
of Europe 2000+. It remains to be seen what the implications are of the latter's aims
of reducing the tendency towards excessive growth of major conurbations. The
ESDP aims to be more 'prescriptive' than the earlier 2000+ document which will
require greater EU powers to force change upon member states (Williams, 1996).
The UK presidency of the EU in 1998 made completion of the ESPD one of its main
objectives. But there are other challenges to planning. The more prescriptive and
codified approach provides a contrast to the more flexible and pragmatic administrative concerns of the UK planning and environmental process.

POLITICAL CHANGE

8

The referendums on devolution for Scotland and Wales both returned 'yes' votes. A Parliament for Scotland and a Welsh Assembly will both be running on 1 January 2000. The government also has proposals to hold referendums on regional assemblies in England as well as an elected Mayor for London. The Scottish Parliament will undoubtedly have the potential to make radical changes to the face of planning. As a legislative body with the authority to pass its own planning laws and policies we could see the emergence of a distinctly Scottish approach. In recent years the Scottish Office has been commissioning a number of 'blue sky' studies on the future of planning north of the border that have come up with distinctly different and in some cases radical approaches to planning and regulation. The Scottish Labour Party has always had a stronger environmental emphasis than their English counterparts. Could this mean a greater emphasis on sustainability and a breakaway from the English approach to planning regulation? The Welsh Assembly's powers will have less of an impact than its Scottish counterpart as it will not have legislative power. Nevertheless, through policy guidance it will still have the potential to make radical changes to the shape the direction of planning. What will these directions be and what are the implications?

SUSTAINABILITY AND THE ENVIRONMENT

The renewal of planning following the dark days of the 1980s undoubtedly came with the resurgence of interest in environmental matters. At all levels of government (United Nations, European Community and UK) there is a clear commitment towards sustainability and sustainable development. Planners and planning have latched on to this with enthusiasm as it fits well into their 'expert' technocratic nature. But serious difficulties dominate. Most fundamental are issues of definition concerning whether a 'deep green' preservationist, 'techno-green' technical fix or 'shallow green' growth-based strategy are employed. Further, as a consensus-building exercise on the need to tackle global environmental issues sustainability has been spectacularly successful – but this masks the difficult choices that will and are emerging, such as the balance between environmental protection and economic growth. Planning practice has been ill-equipped to deal with these issues – can a local plan effectively resolve issues of jobs and environmental protection? If brownfield development is now the priority, how will developers be encouraged to reuse land and who will pick up the costs of restoration?

LOCAL GOVERNANCE

Any discussion on local governance will not be complete without reference to four significant proposals by government. First, there is the proposal for 'Best Value' announced in March 1998. The idea is to extend and localise the Citizen's Charter approach to performance indicators by introducing a compulsory survey of local opinion that will inform published service targets. External audits will then assess the level of performance against these targets and, in the words of Local Government Minister Hilary Armstrong, 'Star performers will get credibility. Poor performers will have to brush up their acts' (DETR Press Release, 3 March 1998). This shift must be taken in conjunction with the Labour Party's embarrassment over corruption in authorities such as Doncaster and Peterborough and may have influenced the Prime Minister's announcement that local authorities have to justify current existence: 'If you are unwilling to work to the modern agenda then the Government will have to look to other partners to take on your role' (*Independent*, 4 March 1998).

Second, there are the wider institutional and structural requirements needed to introduce Regional Development Agencies (RDAs) proposed in Partnerships for Prosperity (DETR, 1997d). Nine RDAs are proposed covering the existing areas of the government offices, with London having its own one. Each agency will have a board comprising of appointed persons who will be responsible for promoting sustainable economic development and co-ordinating the work of existing regional bodies such as English Partnerships. RDAs have been criticised for lacking any clear relationship with the existing regional chambers of local authorities and the role of the Secretary of State in directing them. But as John Prescott made clear at their launch, RDAs will have a close relationship with elected regional government which the government is committed to introduce in some form.

Third, and related in some ways to RDAs, there are the proposals to devolve greater power to regional bodies for the responsibility in drawing up regional guidance. Accepting some of the criticism aimed at them in the past, the government proposes to widen their scope to introduce more non-land use matters, transfer the main responsibility for preparation to regional planning conferences, introduce greater public involvement and carry out a 'sustainability audit'.

Finally, there is the *Modernising Planning* consultation paper (DETR, 1998b). This takes an incremental and limited view of the future of planning that focuses on more explicit central planning guidance, emphasises speed and efficiency with shorter plans incorporating 'better targeted consultation', speeding up major inquiries and introducing some economic instruments to complement planning controls. As is to be expected from such a minor adjustment of planning controls, the RTPI welcomed it wholeheartedly.

A number of issues arise from these changes. But perhaps the most significant and obvious is the degree of decentralisation (though with appropriate safeguards remaining) *and* the willingness of the government to bypass local government altogether if necessary. Despite the warm words for a planning system that the Labour Party consider is rightly 'theirs' there is obviously some dissatisfaction with its slowness and local accountability (specifically, and within the government's general criticism of local government). Planning seems slow to respond to this. Of the 37 'Best Value' pilot schemes only 5 local authorities included planning. The government seems to be concerned with an efficient and open planning system that is accountable. Planners themselves figure little if at all and are merely the 'implementers' of the system. How should planners react to this? What are the implications for professionalism? Could planners be bypassed if they do not meet the government's aims?

SOCIAL EXCLUSION AND THE CONNEXITY OF PROBLEMS

There are presently 150 000 homeless people in the UK, 100 000 children do not attend school in England and Wales and half of all crimes take place in one-tenth of the neighbourhoods with a higher proportion of single-parent families than anywhere else in Europe. These are some of the bare facts behind what the government and others have termed 'social exclusion'. The establishment of the Social Exclusion Unit in December 1997 sought to improve understanding of the key characteristics and promote solutions through encouraging co-operation and recommending changes in policy mechanisms. What it has done is raise two important considerations. First, is what Geoff Mulgan has termed 'connexity' (1997): the intricate and ever closer relationship of issues often beyond national and traditional institutional boundaries. But just as there is an appreciation of a greater connectedness to problems there is also a recognition of an increasing individuality spreading around the world. From the freedom of consumers to the codified guarantees of human rights people are becoming more atomised and individually empowered. The challenge is to fuse or temper the tensions of individuality and the cohesion of issues that face us. This brings us to the second point. Unlike the Tory governments of the past, New Labour has chosen a decidedly interventionist route. This may mean breaking down traditional hierarchies, professional groupings and institutional frameworks and promoting a more fluid, dynamic approach. Planning has a lot of lessons to learn from this. It is still a 'traditional' professionally based discipline within a 'comfortable' framework of government. If problems are becoming more connected and unresolvable (and looking at issues such as town-centre decline it appears that planning is no different) then how can planning take these issues forward? Will it break out of its reticence for change and be proactive rather than reactive?

HOUSEHOLDS AND HOUSING DEMAND

There has been a recent and seismic shift in the government's approach to housing provision that has been dominated by the debate over the role of green belts and the outcry from shire authorities who have reacted against the imposition of housing targets. Replacing the old 'predict and provide' approach we now have an emphasis on forecasts as 'guidance' to be taken into account together with other factors. Rather than the Secretary of State and Regional Government Offices the emphasis will be on regional planning conferences to take greater responsibility for deciding how communities will meet their needs. Local needs will take priority over other demands. So have the NIMBYs won? This may have been the case but for the simultaneous emphasis backed up with fiscal measures upon brownfield (or as John Prescott prefers to call them 'recycled') sites. The government aims to increase the achievement of the Conservatives who managed an average of 42% of development on reused sites and aim for 60% over the next 10 years. The challenge this presents planners and others is not insignificant. Government has recognised this and appointed the architect Richard Rogers to co-ordinate a national database of potential sites. Other changes include the introduction of a sequential test for housing sites similar to that for retail development. This has all been launched in the midst of many development plan reviews. What will the impact be upon plan preparation? Are the targets achievable? How should local authorities and others go about bringing sites forward?

INCREASED DEMANDS FOR PARTICIPATION

The last 25 years or so have witnessed the growth in a more active and political citizenry. From a largely passive post-war population who were happy on the whole to leave decisions to the all-knowledgeable technocrat or the 'man from the ministry' we have witnessed the rise of single-issue politics and demands for greater involvement if not participation in decisions that affect people. Although changes were made in the 1960s following the Skeffington report, input into planning processes is still largely based on a statutory minimum with individual local authorities enhancing this in eclectic and patchwork ways. Again, this growing demand will create tensions especially with the introduction of service charters. The 1980s witnessed the emergence of NIMBYs. With the 4.4 million new homes required nationally by 2016 issues of 'where?' are now becoming more locally sensitive, particularly in the overcrowded south-east of England. How can planning accommodate more voices while at the same time 'plan'?

COMMODIFICATION

This is covered by Mark Tewdwr-Jones in Chapter 8 and Rob Imrie in Chapter 7. Suffice to say here that both chapters chart the proceduralisation of planning that is increasingly concentrating on means rather than ends – losing the 'big picture' – and a contraction of planning objectives towards meeting market criteria and facilitating development. This has been re-emphasised by the current Labour government who seem to have a similar concentration on quantity (though with a hint at quality as well). The consultation paper on modernising planning issued in January 1998 clearly emphasises speed in development control and plan preparation. The problem which has long been identified revolves around the trade-off between quantity and quality. Local authorities could refuse to carry out pre-application discussion, minimise public involvement in plan making and delegate more decisions to officers, thereby improving their chances of meeting eight-week figures. But the obvious implications are of a more bureaucratic rather than open and inclusive system. There are no easy answers to this and it remains to be seen what impact the government's 'Best Value' approach will have, and how planners will react to its challenges.

These factors provide the broad influences and concerns of planning as it enters the twenty-first century. Different authors in the book place different emphases on different aspects and come to different conclusions. But without doubt the biggest influence that runs through each of the chapters is the legacy of the New Right. From the deregulation of public policy to the emphasis on performance and efficiency of what remains, the influences upon planning and the environment into the twenty-first century will be found in the changes introduced at the end of the twentieth.

Macnaghton and Pinfield explore sustainability and identify it as the most urgent and potentially radical factor that will shape the future direction of government policy. They argue that for planning to come to terms with such a radical shift in thinking will require profound institutional and cultural changes which, unless forthcoming, will mean that planning is bypassed as a mechanism to deliver sustainable development. Particularly, planning's top-down approach does not fit with the more 'bottom-up' agenda of sustainability. In a related chapter, Macdonald and Heaney criticise planners for accepting the idea of sustainability uncritically and trying to integrate it within existing structures and processes.

Dave Shaw tackles the other politically contested area of rural planning in the shadow of the Countryside Alliance and BSE. He believes it is a contested and misunderstood area of planning with tensions arising between land use policy and agricultural support being unresolved. As a Cinderella area of planning attention was focused upon urban issues such as regeneration making a more co-ordinated and strategic approach necessary if the rural is not to lose out. The urban aspect of planning and regeneration is covered by Rob Atkinson who traces the development and legacies of the market-led property approach of the 1980s and 1990s into current New Labour thinking. Far from tackling the problem, he claims that deprivation and exclusion are becoming increasingly concentrated and severe, requiring more radical solutions than are currently on offer. In a similar vein, Jones and Watkins look at the reliance and implications of market-based systems though focus on the interface between housing and planning. Like urban regeneration, tensions are emerging from a government committed to its inheritance of a project-led planning and the need for a more positive approach to enforce the preference for 60% of new housing to be built on brownfield sites.

Another legacy of the 1980s and 1990s that has widespread implications for planning is the 'new managerialism' as Rob Imrie terms it. Part of the market orientation and focus on efficiency under the Conservatives and continued under Labour's 'Best Value' is a move away from discretion and towards more account-able 'people' orientation. Obviously, with a profession such as planning that is used with discretion this is going to raise problems. Mark Tewdwr-Jones also reflects on these problems but concentrates on image and the profession. Do we still need one in the light of a much more open approach? If the context and content of planning are changing rapidly, what values and attitudes are needed in the twenty-first century?

High on the political agenda at the moment is the issue of transport, especially following the merger of the departments of Transport and Environment after the 1997 election. Julian Hine continues the questioning of the present and future role of planning by exploring the changes required if planning is to meet the demands of a more public and less privately orientated society.

Colin Williams examines the changing nature of local economic development and the emergence of what he terms a 'new localism' which planning has either failed to recognise or chosen to ignore. Williams argues that the changing nature of production and consumption from manufacturing to services requires new thinking from planners. Etherington and Chapman echo some of Williams's concerns about the changing nature of the economic base of urban areas and the ways in which planning ameliorates global economic processes in different locales. Planners as urban managers need to recognise and contribute towards combating the spread of poverty and social exclusion in deprived urban communities. Cities need to remain competitive and adapt to the changing economic, social and environmental circumstances associated with moves towards greater European economic and monetary integration. The way cities respond to such challenges and how urban economies perform and restructure as a consequence of these processes have far-reaching implications, not only for successful city-wide regeneration strategies, but for the successful implementation of policies designed to tackle the spatial concentration of poverty and exclusion. Further evidence of this is provided by Kettle and Moran in their examination of housing and social exclusion in Leeds. Tackling exclusion will not be addressed by the mechanisms and attitudes inherited from the deregulatory and market-dominated era of the 1990s.

Michael Chapman then examines the European context to spatial planning and land use policy in the UK by arguing that, even under the more pro-European stance taken by the Labour government, there is still a great deal of confusion and misunderstanding over the influence of the EU on the planning system and how the European policy agenda will increasingly shape future developments in spatial policy and planning. Any attempt to review the planning system in the new millennium has to take on board the role and significance of the EU. It is still far from certain if a European spatial planning framework will emerge which every

14
—

member state can adhere to, but this does not mean that British planners should neglect the wider objectives of the EU and assess the impact of the EU through its own actions and policies, on the planning system.

Finally, Philip Allmendinger provides an abstract and reflective exploration of how different factors of influence will provide new challenges and agendas for planning. Using an eclectic mix of postmodern and chaos theory he tries to outline the shape of a 'new' planning based on flexible, local responses to global and localised pressures.

CHAPTER 2

PLANNING AND SUSTAINABLE DEVELOPMENT: PROSPECTS FOR SOCIAL CHANGE

Phil Macnaghten and Graham Pinfield

INTRODUCTION

The concept of sustainable development now clearly provides the new context for framing public policy on land use and environment as we approach the new millennium. The official endorsement of the term by the international community and the signing of the global plan for its implementation, Agenda 21, by national governments at the 1992 United Nations Conference on Environment and Development (UNCED, 1992) at Rio marked a watershed in the institutional conception of the environmental problematic. The full implications as to what changes are necessary for human society to achieve the integration of social, environmental and economic policy-making at all levels of government is a significant challenge for us all.

However, the 'millennial shift' that may be required from the current paradigm, and the prevailing imperatives that drive policy within the international community and national governments (e.g. the promotion of economic growth, trade liberalisation, deregulation) to the new paradigm of sustainable development, cannot be achieved without profound institutional and cultural change. This is reflected in Section 3 of Agenda 21 which deals with the role of major groups, and is also partly reflected in the reform of the United Nations itself, a process currently under way with Maurice Strong – who organised the UNCED conference – appointed as Under-Secretary General responsible for UN reform.

The UK played a leading role in responding nationally to the international challenge posed by Rio. One key policy response was to produce the strategy document *Sustainable Development: The UK Strategy* in 1994 (UK Government, 1994). More recently, a revised strategy formulated under the incoming Labour government has been produced for consultation (UK Government, 1998). However, both documents failed to address the institutional and legislative reform that may be necessary to promote sustainable development. Government departmentalism remains significantly unchanged (apart from the merger of the Department of Environment and Transport in 1997) and there is little material evidence to date that the concept of sustainable development has moved to the 'heart of government policy' as often stated by the Deputy Prime Minister, John Prescott and the Environment Minister, Michael Meacher. Significantly, the issue of social exclusion and the recent setting up of the Social Exclusion Unit to bring government departments together to tackle poverty, seems closer to the centre of the new Labour government machinery and thinking.

In terms of planning, an area which is firmly in the brief of the Department of the Environment, Transport and the Regions, the frameworks underpinning the UK planning system remain much as they were laid down in the original Town and Country Planning Act of 1947 and there are currently no proposals in the UK Strategy or in the government's parliamentary programme to introduce new legislation. Under the previous government consultants were commissioned to look at how the planning system should change to better promote sustainable development but the report has yet to be published. Meanwhile, the Town and Country Planning Association is to hold a Commission of Inquiry, under the Chairmanship of Baroness Hamwee, to look at the future of the planning system.

In this chapter we set out some dilemmas for the planning system if it is to meet the challenges posed by the emerging sustainable development discourse. For town and country planning, over 50 years after the 1947 Act, this is a particularly opportune time to assess what changes may be necessary to the planning system such that it can become more closely aligned with the principles and values of sustainable development.

Indeed, we need to ask some searching questions about how we plan for a sustainable society in the new millennium. For instance, what potential has the political rhetoric and discourse of sustainable development to shift the long-standing institutional inertia that is present at all levels of government? Furthermore, how might the principles of sustainable development be best operationalised within the practice of town planning? What is the relationship of planning to Local Agenda 21 (LA21) initiatives in local government and what are the main obstacles for planning in terms of embracing sustainable development in a comprehensive manner?

To address these questions we begin by focusing on the origins and principles of sustainable development discourse and the challenges these offer town planning. We then examine in more detail a key tenet of sustainable development, that of public participation, examining the cultural barriers to participation and what this may imply for the practice of planning. This we explore by looking at two recent qualitative studies on the public understanding of, and identification with, sustainability initiatives. Through such studies we find that the task of encouraging participation raises wider questions concerning the position of planning in retaining the status quo, and the radical opportunities provided by the sustainable development discourse to provide an outlet for the expression of people's needs and desires for a better 'quality of life' *and* a healthy environment.

To illuminate the degree to which radical change may be required we explore the recent phenomena of the direct action environmental protest. We examine the recent growth of this movement in the UK particularly in the context of anti-road protests and what it may imply for sustainable development planning initiatives. Finally, we conclude by drawing out some suggestions as to how planning can contribute to wider programmes of sustainable development.

SUSTAINABLE DEVELOPMENT AND PLANNING

The 1992 United Nations Conference on Environment and Development (UNCED) at Rio, otherwise known as the Earth Summit, is where the discourse of sustainable development was formally endorsed by national governments. The UNCED conference was the largest and most complex conference ever organised by the United Nations – attended by 178 governments, over 120 heads of state, and thousands of interested parties, from environmental non-governmental organisations (NGOs), business interests, aid agencies, trade unions to academics.

While perhaps not as radical as environmentalists had hoped, it still contributed to an impressive array of outputs, including two global conventions (on climate change and biodiversity), an Earth Charter, a programme of action for sustainable development named Agenda 21, and a new UN Commission on Sustainable Development (CSD) set up to monitor progress. Moreover, through the conference national governments became committed to the principle and broad programme of sustainable development including a requirement to produce national sustainable development strategy to implement Agenda 21, and encouragement for local governments to produce LA21 plans in partnership with local communities.

One very real effect of the Rio process was to provide a common term – sustainable development – whereby states and corporations have to analyse their policies and practices in relation not only to their current and potential environmental impacts but also their putative impact on future generations. The repercussions of Rio have extended into all areas of society. No longer is environmental rhetoric the preserve of environmental organisations. Now multinational corporations routinely express the need for sustainable development, as do aid agencies, government departments, insurance firms, major corporations, the EU, local government and citizens' organisations.

Since Rio, working definitions of sustainable development have come to be broadly accepted by governments, NGOs and business and there has been a growing impetus within the *practitioner* community to move beyond questions of principle and definition (Macnaghten and Jacobs, 1997) to practical implementation in policy and action. Considerable effort has been invested by national and international bodies to develop tools and approaches which aim at translating the goals of sustainable development into specific actions, and which seek to assess whether real progress is in fact being made towards achieving them. In this regard the development of sustainability indicators has proven to be popular (see

Adriaanse, 1993; Department of the Environment, 1996c; Lancashire County Council, 1997; OECD, 1993; Pinfield, 1996; WWF and NEF, 1994).

But what precisely is meant by the term 'sustainable development'? Can we develop prescriptions which encompass diffuse social, cultural and economic circumstances? Can we approximate core values or principles which underpin the discourse and which can help in the development of policy initiatives?

In formal texts the Brundtland definition of sustainable development has been more or less universally accepted and endorsed in such documents as Caring for the Earth, the EC *Fifth Action Programme* and *Agenda 21* (see CEC, 1992a; IUCN, 1991; UNCED, 1992; WCED, 1987). The thesis is that continued economic and social development is only possible when it safeguards the natural resources on which all development depends, and when such development is focused on meeting current needs and the needs of future generations. Nature becomes formally recognised as the resource of human economic activity, and the project of sustainable development becomes one of incorporating this concept (previously forgotten in the project of modernity) into the project of development.

Haigh (1995) suggests that in contrast to the doom-laden debates that characterised the limits to growth debates in the late 1960s and 1970s, the more attractive proposition, originating from Brundtland, is that sustainable development can at the same time improve environmental quality *and* human welfare. Finger (1993) analyses the particular configuration of 'environment' as used in the Brundtland report in more depth. He suggests that the political credibility of the report in the international arena arose, in part, from how it presented sustainable development as an apparent 'win–win' situation where environmental sustainability came to be seen as good for economic development, and economic development as good for environmental sustainability. Such reasoning led to highly optimistic expectations as captured, for example, in one early passage of the report:

> We have the power to reconcile human affairs with natural laws. And to thrive in the process. In this, our cultural and spiritual heritage can reinforce our economic interests and survival imperatives (WCED, 1987; cited in Finger, 1993: 42–43).

In this context what does sustainable development imply from a planning perspective? In many respects the roots of planning provide a good foundation for sustainable development: planning grew out of the need to protect public health, to prevent unplanned (physical) development, to protect nature as a refuge from modern life, to provide for the public interest, to manage the environment, and to find a balance between competing demands (Abercrombie, 1933; Hall, 1973; Healey and Shaw, 1994; Newby, 1979). Many of these traditional aspirations have clear resonance with the ideas and principles behind sustainable development more recently elaborated.

However, there are other factors and new imperatives that need to be incorporated into planning. To analyse this it is useful to remind ourselves of the Brundtland definition (WCED, 1987):

> Sustainable development is development that meets the needs of the present without compromising the ability of future generations to meet their own needs.

Although such a definition is open to multiple and contestable interpretations (see Jacobs, 1998; McManus, 1996; Owens, 1994; Redclift, 1993; Sachs, 1993), a nascent consensus appears to be emerging in official documents concerning the various elements of the sustainable development discourse. These include an incorporation into policy of the principles of environment, quality of life, future generations, equity and participation (see Blowers, 1993; LGMB, 1993; UNCED, 1992). In what ways do such principles impact on planning? What are the implications in practice of UK Planning Policy Guidance notes 1 and 12 (DoE, 1996a, 1992e) which state that planning and development planning in particular must be guided by the principles of sustainable development?

The notion of environmental limits and the carrying capacity of ecosystems has to some extent been embraced by the planning profession. However, the precise identification of limits and the carrying capacities of ecosystems has remained a matter of some considerable debate (Breheny and Hall, 1997). The matter concerns not simply what constitutes an environmental capacity but also what weight should be attached to such limits in providing constraints on economic activity. Owens (1994) distinguishes two broad themes in the literature which she terms a weak definition of sustainability and a strong one. She suggests that whereas a weak definition merely amounts to 'giving environmental capacities greater weight', a strong definition regards 'environmental capacities . . . as placing some ultimate constraints on economic activities' (Owens, 1994: 442; see also CPOS, 1993; Healey and Shaw, 1994; Jacobs, 1993; Williams, 1993). She submits that whereas a weak definition of sustainability can be fairly easily accommodated within current planning practice, a strong definition requires a more fundamental ethical change for the planning profession, in which nature is valued for its own sake independently of its instrumental value to human beings.

'Quality of life' and the discourse of 'needs' following from the Brundtland definition are central to formal prescriptions of sustainable development. Yet such terms are sometimes problematic for planners whose profession traditionally has been concerned with analysing the quantitative aspects of development as suggested above, in terms of household growth and the need for residential and industrial land. Developing more detailed understanding of what might constitute people's needs, and of what constitutes their 'quality of life', is a new arena for the profession. Such sensitivity may require not simply adopting new processes of listening to what people want or need in their day-to-day lives, but also the formation of partnerships between planners and health professionals, community groups, community development professionals and social scientists. Through such partnerships the planning profession may offer innovative ways to reconfigure policy towards 'quality of life' concerns over and above their traditional land use and physical development remit.

Equity is another principle frequently included across the various accounts of sustainable development (Wagle, 1993). Agenda 21, for example, argues that over-riding priority should be given to the needs of the poor (UNCED, 1992). Such considerations pose extra demands on the planning system in terms of, for example, the siting of toxic waste dumps, or the sustainable regeneration of poverty-stricken communities. However, analysis of the 'equity commonplace' in diverse sustainability leaflets suggests an inherent tension between the need for fairness in apportioning the costs of environmental damage, and the need for common action in response to a common threat (Myers and Macnaghten, 1998). Planners will need to be extra-sensitive to considerations of equity not least because of the new government's commitment to social inclusion. This may involve an analysis as to whether planning policies seek to redistribute the benefits of resource use and development and reduce the impact of adverse developments on poorer communities.

Concern for the well-being of future generations is perhaps the most well-understood feature of sustainable development and one, it could be argued, that planning is well placed to deliver. Certainly the development plan-led system that has been in place since the UK Planning and Compensation Act 1991 came into force has enabled planning to be forward-looking. However, sustainable development requires policies oriented towards a long-term future. Incorporation of long-term time-frames (typical LA21 'visioning' exercises are geared to the year 2020) presents a considerable challenge for the profession. It requires a leap mentally but also in terms of information and projections. It is all the more difficult in a world apparently governed more and more by short-term considerations (for accounts of the 'glacial' long-term dimensions of environmental issues, see Adam, 1998; Castells, 1996; Grove-White, 1997a; Macnaghten and Urry, 1998: ch. 5).

These are some of the challenges and dilemmas that planning may have to face if it is to deliver policies aimed towards sustainable development. In some respects the incorporation of the above-mentioned principles are already well advanced (e.g. the more precise definition and incorporation of the idea of environmental limits). However, organisational and institutional changes may be required. One major area in which there may be a substantial need for change is in terms of public involvement and participation. Sustainable development implies a new and more direct relationship with the public in policy-making that was not envisaged in the original 1947 Act. In the next section we examine the issue of public participation.

PLANNING AND PUBLIC PARTICIPATION

Involving local communities in programmes of sustainable development and particularly LA21 has become an issue of paramount importance for planners, policy-makers and politicians across the party political spectrum. Involvement of the public is seen to be vital to ensure there is a robust constituency of popular support and political commitment in what are at times difficult and controversial decisions. Agenda 21 itself recognised that environmental and social change cannot be prescribed from above; rather, support would need to be stimulated at a local level. For these reasons the idea of LA21 was conceived and introduced to help foster public participation.

However, the notion of *participation* as conceived in LA21 goes beyond the usual forms of consultation familiar in the current planning system. The current and fairly limited provisions for public involvement in the planning process can be traced to the 1968 Town and Country Planning Act, later consolidated into the 1971 Act. The details of how this was to be done were made in the 1969 Report of the Skeffington Committee entitled *People and Planning* (Ministry of Housing and Local Government, 1969), and the new system of structure and local plans set out in the Town and Country Act 1971. Although the Skeffington report stressed that the public had to play a full part in the plan-making process, in practice this has been much limited. Hill (1994) characterises current forms of participation as being broadly consultative in nature, and as being centred on the eliciting of people's views through surveys, exhibitions and so on.

The development plan preparation process provides the most scope for public involvement in planning, yet despite changes brought in with the Planning and Compensation Act 1991 it remains – apart from a few more creative approaches described below – an obscure, technical and inaccessible process for most of the public. The public inquiry system, and examinations in public into development plans as introduced in the Planning and Compensation Act, provides much of the framework for public input into the planning system. The public inquiry ostensibly constitutes an arena in which the public can express their views on proposed developments. But, in practice, particularly in the environmental sphere, the inquiry system has been criticised as biased in favour of development, as excluding many critical criteria from debate, and as marginalising local people through the use of overly technical language (for various critiques, see Tyme, 1978; Wynne, 1992). Indeed, although Grove-White (1992) argues that the public inquiry system became a key vehicle through which, in the context of Britain's administrative culture, an environmental agenda was able to become defined and made explicit throughout the 1970s and 1980s, most environmentalists have viewed the system more cynically, as a exercise of maintaining the status quo while giving the appearance of demo- cratic debate. In this respect the renewal of calls for wider participation *vis-à-vis* LA21 constitutes an opportune moment for the planning profession.

So how do we go about encouraging wider public participation in sustainable development planning? In order to address this we need to examine first the wider cultural context in which environmental concern and protest now take place, in order to search for clues as how best to promote public participation in sustainable development.

It has long been recognised that although the discourse of sustainability has been shaped through its origins in global institutions as a way in which governments and intergovernmental fora can talk about a common environmental agenda, its success will depend on its ability to mobilise local responses to global imperatives (Redclift, 1992). Agenda 21, for example, argues that only if ordinary members of the community, particularly those in disadvantaged groups, take part in decision-making processes can the outcomes of those processes be regarded as good. And as a recent review of LA21 in the UK put it, the goal is an 'active democracy with more people involved in developing and implementing solutions to the problems that society faces' (UNA and CDF, 1995: 45).

But the crucial question is of course whether people will in fact participate. It is likely that participation will occur only if the public accept or 'believe in' the project in which they are being asked to take part. Do they? It would also seem that people must in some sense identify with the discourse of sustainability. That is, they must in general terms accept the argument being presented, concerning the undesirability and/or unsustainability of the present situation, the desirability of the proposed future, and the practicability of the suggested means of getting from one to the other. In other words, people must identify with global environmental concerns in their daily lives, accept the need to live in ways which respect the finite limits of the planet, be prepared to change unsustainable aspects of their personal lifestyles, and support government and business sustainability initiatives.

In recent years a number of studies have sought to examine the extent to which such assumptions bear resemblance to everyday life. For this section we focus on two such research projects, one addressing how 'citizens' in Lancashire perceived sustainability issues in daily life (for a full account of the research findings, see Macnaghten et al., 1995), the other undertaken to examine the social and institutional factors which influence public definitions of, and responses to, global environmental issues (see Harrison et al., 1996). Both studies used in-depth focus group discussions with lay publics, focusing on how people understood environmental issues and concerns in day-to-day life. Both indicate that the project of encouraging public support and participation in formal programmes of sustainability may be more difficult than hitherto conceived.

Firstly, the studies found how people's receptivity to knowledge, as provided by scientific or policy bodies, is strongly shaped by their sense of agency – that is by their implicit sense of their own power or freedom to act upon or to use that knowledge. The significance of this is that people's inability or unwillingness to assimilate information may frequently be due to tacit political or cultural structures of empowerment or disempowerment which may have no apparent connection with the particular environmental issue in question. Thus Harrison et al. (1996) note a general tendency towards greater public awareness and understanding of environmental issues in the Netherlands than in the UK, apparently connected to the greater sense of public agency and involvement within the former.

Equivalent groups in the UK appear to feel more disconnected from political and policy institutions, and this general sense of relative alienation and disempowerment may contribute to a correspondingly diminished sense of active involvement in, or responsibility for, policies connected with such issues, or with information relating to them. In such circumstances it is hardly surprising to find people apparently less 'informed' about, or attuned to, environmental problems and responses. The crucial point is that it would be misleading to attribute such apparent ignorance to a lack of information, awareness, concern or intelligence. The significant factor lies within the structuring of social relations within different societies. This research shows that the more general characteristics which affect the quality of people's identification with public institutions are fundamentally important in explaining the apparent fluctuations in people's attitudes and behaviours towards the environment.

Secondly, the studies showed the need to situate sustainability concerns within a framework of wider social and economic change. The Lancashire study especially found a strikingly familiar and shared picture of uncertain lives, insecure jobs, unsafe streets, and loss of community and neighbourliness (Macnaghten et al., 1995). Especially pronounced and prevalent in discussions was the sense of existing trends intensifying and accelerating. Pessimism of a deteriorating future was widespread, and here environmental problems featured alongside crime, job insecurity and family breakdown. Importantly such perceptions were themselves connected to a lack of personal agency, where people felt disempowered from structures of power and democracy. For some, this was explained as the result of the apparently intractable forces of globalisation, of a market system uncontrollably spreading into more and more aspects of daily life. For others, this was seen as the consequence of current practices of corporations and public institutions, who appeared out of touch with the long-term concerns of the public. And such views permeated the environmental sphere, contributing to the general perception that those 'in control' were neither likely nor willing to respond to environmental problems.

Thirdly, for many people, especially among the younger and better-off groups, there was considerable latent support, although unfamiliarity with, the concept of sustainability. Sustainability appeared to provide people with a vocabulary to talk about the long term in a culture which appeared remarkably short term and self-serving. Indeed, many people felt themselves personally responsible for environmental problems, even though there was much confusion over how serious the problems really were, and how indeed to obtain trustworthy and credible information. Experts, especially those working for governments or corporations, were perceived to produce largely biased and self-serving information, again fuelling a propensity for non-involvement. As one of the unemployed participants drily said: 'they keep you in the dark and come up with terms like sustainability' (Macnaghten et al., 1995: 63).

How do such findings impinge on the formal models of sustainability as promoted by government? Official discourses of sustainability assume relationships of trust between citizens and institutions, based on a view of the state as benign. They assume that people accept official information as credible, as heightening concern and as leading to personal responsibility and lifestyle change. But these studies suggest that few of these assumptions can be sustained. Institutions of the state were generally seen as part of 'the system' which generates environmental and social problems rather than as benign agents committed to solving them. The lack of faith in the institutions of the state was held across all focus group discussions. These institutions were regarded as theoretically responsible for developing sustainability, but were thought to be very unlikely to do so since they were run for the vested interests of their own members and 'big business'.

What we are suggesting, in other words, is that people's non-involvement in sustainability initiatives may be simply due not to ignorance or apathy, but to their more general sense of powerlessness, itself a product of their largely negative first-hand experience of public institutions. In such circumstances, as a largely top-down process tied very much to legislation and institutionalised processes and procedures, planning would appear not to be currently well placed to successfully encourage wider public involvement. But can Agenda 21 help to restore public trust in the planning process? Are the principles of participation as embedded in LA21 likely to prove credible and empowering?

In Agenda 21 it was suggested that: 'by 1996 most local authorities in each country should have undertaken a consultative process with their populations and achieved a consensus on a "Local Agenda 21" for the community' (UNCED, 1992: Section 28.28). While the mention of consultation again emphasises a passive type of engagement the idea of building consensus indicates the desire for more active involvement of the public in sustainable development. Indeed, at the recent United Nations General Assembly Special Session (UNGASS) meeting in New York in June 1997, set up to examine progress five years after Rio, UK Prime Minister Tony Blair noted that all local authorities should produce a local sustainable development strategy for their areas by the year 2000. In practice however, it is evident that many local authorities are seeking to develop LA21s through existing consultative methods of public involvement.

Does the preparation of local authority LA21 plans offer the opportunity for developing widespread public participation? Certainly there are a number of interesting and creative processes taking place around the UK within the LA21 plan preparation process, and these may provide arenas in which trust can be built between local communities and public institutions for inclusive and widespread partnerships of sustainable development. Indeed, there may be more general lessons that could be applied to the statutory development plan preparation process. Some of the most innovative experiments include:

- *'Life in Hertfordshire' and 'Whole Settlement Strategies'*. As part of the development of their Structure Plan, Hertfordshire County Council carried out a public consultation exercise that included the running of 'focus groups' of stakeholders to identify aspirations for the future of the county and more specifically for individual towns, for example, Hitchin and Potters Bar. These two towns are being used as pilots to test the idea of 'Whole Settlement Strategies' which look at the town as a whole and what needs to be done to improve the quality of life there (LGMB, 1997).

- *'Blueprint for Leicester'*. This Leicester City Council sponsored initiative, undertaken with the help of an independent charity Environ, has involved a comprehensive community consultation exercise throughout the city as a basis for developing LA21 strategy for the city.
- *Going for Green Pilot Sustainable Communities Project*. These neighbour- hood-based projects, sponsored by UK government and including communities in Lancashire and across the UK, are currently exploring conditions for grass- roots local involvement in sustainable development.
- *Hyndburn Borough Council Neighbourhood Panels*. These panels of local people are exploring new forms of local decision-making on sustainability issues as part of the Hyndburn Council's LA21 called 'Prospects'.
- *Citizens' Juries and Panels in Manchester and St Helens*. These initiatives, undertaken by the Centre for the Study of Environmental Change (CSEC) at Lancaster University, are exploring the potential for new avenues of civic engagement in which communities can directly influence decisions which impinge on them, including those which stem from global environmental issues such as climate change.

Such experiments in public participation have become fairly commonplace in recent years and come under what are being generally called 'deliberative insti- tutions'. The context for such initiatives is that currently few people feel that they can influence the wider world through personal action. Deliberative processes involving citizen juries, citizen panels, town meetings and focus groups may offer new ways in which communities can become involved in decision-making. Indeed, there is a critical need for the planning profession to learn from these experiments. Sensitively handled, they offer the scope to explore the rich complexity of attitudes and perspectives which people hold about sustainability matters, and the potential for achieving wider support in making difficult and controversial choices.

However, it is currently unclear as to whether experiments such as those highlighted above, involving new patterns of engagement between civic society and the polity, can renew the bonds of trust that appear so fragile. For many there will remain scepticism about any engagement with local authority or central government run initiatives. In such circumstances the option for direct action may remain a more viable and credible way of promoting more sustainable lifestyles. In the next section we briefly examine whether the direct action anti- road protest may reveal clues as to how to encourage wider involvement in environmental initiatives.

Planning and the New Protest Movements

Since Rio we have witnessed the emergence of new and more direct patterns of environmental protest within Britain and elsewhere. The most dynamic of such protests have been those directed against the construction of new roads, fuelled not least by the sensed failure of the planning and public inquiry systems in the eyes of the public, and supported by particular pressure groups, notably Earth First! They reflect also a growing mood of disenchantment with formal institutions and the beginnings of locally organised action and self-help.

By February 1994 Geoffrey Lean (currently environmental correspondent for the *Independent on Sunday*), described the estimated 250 anti-road groups in the UK as 'the most vigorous new force in British environmentalism'. The institutional context was the government's £23 billion proposed roads programme named 'Roads to Prosperity', which was actively opposed by a wide consortium of environmental groups. But by contrast with previous campaigns, the tactic of non-violent direct action came to be used by the anti-roads grass-roots protesters.

The first of these protests occurred at Twyford Down, a highly symbolic and protected landscape threatened by the M3 extension, at a time when the more established and professional movements were accepting the end of a hotly fought but unsuccessful campaign including a lengthy public inquiry. A new form of protest emerged, centred on 'tribes' of people living on the site, comprising a loose coalition of activists taking part in active non-violent direct action over many months. One such tribe, the 'Dongas', soon became a focal point of the protest, coming together as a group to do something about the threatened destruction of the site. But instead of becoming involved in existing mainstream environmental groups, such as the hitherto radical groups like Greenpeace and Friends of the Earth, campaigners decided to innovate 'do-it-yourself' campaigns.

Since Twyford such protests have taken more diverse forms, from roads to open-cast mining to leisure developments to the proposed second runway at Manchester airport. The array of direct actions has also diversified as protesters have become more expert, through the use of mass trespass, squatting in buildings and living in trees or tunnels threatened by road programmes. They have become more sophisticated in the use of new technologies, including mobile phones, video cameras and the Internet. This has enabled almost instantaneous dissemination to the media, as well as information about actions for a growing band of protesters prepared to travel up and down the country to protest against proposed developments.

There is thus a newer generation of environmentalists who are bypassing conventional environmental groups (often perceived to have been co-opted by the state and industry and whose commitment to the environment is perceived as mere rhetoric) to engage in more radical direct action. For such individuals it is not merely traditional environmental groups who are bypassed, but also the usual planning consultation and decision-making processes which are largely seen as 'rigged'. Such newer environmentalists employ various kinds of non-violent direct citizens' action in the face of the intransigence of what is perceived to be 'the system'. Such protest appeals particularly to young people who become directly engaged and personally involved in working for a better future.

Such protests share common themes: they often appeal to young people, they have been formed partly in reaction to the professionalism and growing elitism of the more established environmental groups, they emphasise inventiveness in method including the surprising use of new technologies, they emphasise too a sense of fun and self-expression, and perhaps above all else they demonstrate a heightened cynicism with official organisations and processes (for more detail on this, see Macnaghten and Urry, 1998: ch. 2).

Generally, such protests have been tolerated by local planning authorities. They are often seen as lying outside the formal planning processes and hence not a matter for concern. Protesters against the Department of Transport's M65 extension in Lancashire in 1995, for example, left their tree camps in Blisworth Woods and marched to the nearby examination in public into the Lancashire Structure Plan carrying branches from the woods. The protesters were allowed in by the inspector to make their protest against further road-building schemes in the draft plan, but the event went largely unrecorded in the proceedings and the meeting was conceived on both sides as merely symbolic. Such an event demonstrates the mismatch between the formal inquiry system, viewed as self-serving and largely irrelevant to the protesters, and the direct action protests, seen as undemocratic and naïve by planners and others involved in the inquiry system.

What do the above examples say about the role of formal sustainability initiatives to achieve widespread popular support? Strikingly, they suggest that arenas in which people have expressed most passion and commitment for long-term environmental improvement have arisen in spheres bypassing formal bodies and procedures. And in many such cases official bodies have been surprised by the scale of protest, with little available vocabulary to make sense of the commitment or passion invested. Yet such protest remains the site where considerable numbers of people are involved, and where many more identify with the aims and practices of such protesters. Indeed, there has been, in recent years, a flourishing of 'civic society' going on outside conventional politics and political institutions, in the form of self-help networks, therapy and counselling networks, sport, craft, alternative health practices and so on (Grove-White, 1997b). Parallels exist too with other arenas of direct action, with Greenpeace's campaign against Shell over the dumping of the Brent Spar, and with direct action protest against the transport of live animals. In such cases official bodies have failed to realise that the public does not really care about the technical arguments of costs versus benefits; they just 'don't like shit being dumped in the oceans' (Ghazi et al., 1995).

These examples point to a new moral framework in which people now expect business and public bodies to operate, beyond the more limited concerns of shareholders and specialist interests. How long-lived these new protest movements are likely to be remains to be seen. The challenge for the planning system concerns how to harness such energies in the grass roots as prime opportunities for officially endorsed programmes aimed at more sustainable lifestyles.

PROSPECTS FOR CHANGE

At UNGASS, dubbed 'Earth Summit II or Rio+5', the urgency to meet the global and collective environmental challenge that was so apparent at Rio appeared to have dissipated. Notwithstanding many high-powered delegations, including the presence of UK Prime Minister Tony Blair and three of his cabinet in his newly elected Labour government, there was little evidence that much had been achieved at the international arena, nor that there was the political will for radical common action.

Many of the environmental and other trends identified at Rio continued to worsen in the five years up to New York, and many of the agreements of the Earth Summit simply have not been implemented. Disputes erupted between the developed and developing world, represented by the G7 group of nations, about development assistance and funding of the Global Environmental Facility set up to benefit poorer nations. Agreements could also not be reached on reduction of energy consumption, in part due to lobbying by oil-producing nations, or on the need for a forest convention. How do we understand such a dismal state of affairs? Why have governments apparently achieved so little in the five years since Rio? Why is the rift between North and South as wide as ever? Why indeed, has there been so little public uptake and identification with the global challenge of sustainable development?

One reason, Tom Burke former special advisor to the UK DoE suggests, is that the agenda has shifted from an easy and familiar set of issues where environmental progress can be achieved in politically favourable contexts, to one where pro-tecting the long-term future is far more hazardous, long term and politically unpopular (Burke, 1997). He characterises the new agenda in terms of the declining state of ecological systems – croplands, rangelands, forests, fresh water, oceans and the atmosphere – on which the global economy rests, and points to how ameliorative action is likely to be both expensive and intrusive, especially on the poor and those less able to adapt. His answer is that action by governments alone is insufficient, and that any hope for a truly sustainable society will depend on the active participation of the business community, voluntary organisations and local communities.

What this illustrates is an emerging context for debates on public participation and the extent of the challenges for states and corporations to enter into active partnerships with the public through processes of renewal. If the state is to pro-mote environmental initiatives which engage the public, it will have to prove exemplary intent to a highly sceptical public. And such partnerships will have to recognise too that plans for a sustainable future cannot rely on existing methods of consultation or on existing reliance on expert knowledge but that everyone has to be involved and has to have a say.

A rare bright spot in the UNGASS process was the stated success of LA21 which was singled out for particular praise. One United Nations report went so far as to state: 'the efforts of local authorities are making Agenda 21 and the pursuit of sustainable development a reality at the local level' (Bigg, 1997: 13). However, as we have argued above, the success of local authority inspired LA21s needs to be balanced with a public apparently ever more mistrusting of official bodies to deliver environmental commitments in the long term. Processes of renewal remain in their infancy and will constitute an agenda of mounting significance for planners and other professions well into the coming millennium.

CONCLUSIONS

Over fifty years since the Town and Country Planning Act of 1947 and the onset of the new millennium is a good opportunity to take stock of where we are and what still remains to do in terms of planning and sustainable development. As a recent concept, sustainable development throws down many new challenges: the need to consider environmental limits, quality of life, equity and the needs of future generations. There is also the need to embrace more comprehensively the need for greater public participation. In these areas the planning system is seen to be in need of updating, even reinvention. One of the key areas is public involvement, yet here we find a public sceptical of the institutions of government responsible for promoting sustainable development and an unwillingness to engage in the processes of planning. The opportunities for engagement through the formal planning system in terms of consultation on development plans or through examinations in public or public inquiries appear increasingly dated when set against the more creative processes now being driven forward under the LA21 umbrella.

As a reaction against such unsatisfactory experiences with the planning system and with government institutions, the new protest movements provide some interesting insights into how far things may need to change in order to satisfy the demands of many (young) people. For these protesters the idea of 'balancing' competing interests is no longer adequate when valuable landscapes and habitats are at stake and the system is 'rigged' in favour of the developer.

So what needs to be done? First, there would appear to be a good case for a thorough review of the planning system in the context of sustainable development and other factors such as European integration. The Town and Country Planning Association's Inquiry into the Future of the Planning System would appear to reflect the mood that could perhaps be taken up by government. Certainly there would be an argument for a comprehensive review of environmental and town and country planning legislation to reflect the principles of sustainable development.

This then leads to the relationship of planning with LA21 planning and with the growing number of community plans that are being produced by local authorities (see Redditch Borough Council). The new government has already suggested that it may introduce a new power of community initiative for local authorities and a new duty of care on local authorities to promote the environmental, social and economic well-being of local areas. Should such a duty be combined with a statutory duty to produce local sustainable development plans in the form of LA21 plans and should these be combined with land use development plans?

Thirdly, what might be done to improve public participation in the planning system? One of the determinants of any initiatives here must be to re-establish bonds of trust between the public and political institutions. This may involve wider attempts to open up government decision-making and take government closer to the people. Could planners contribute to the re-empowerment of civil society through programmes of democratic accountability by public institutions? Is there a role for further decentralisation of decision-making down to very local level in ways that do not merely replicate existing structures at a more local level? Should new techniques of public participation be used hand in hand with this process and how can we ensure that proper account is taken of the wishes of local people? How can local government in particular contribute to such a process through developing skills of listening to local communities and through devolved decision-making? These are challenging questions that go beyond the boundaries of the profession.

The town and country planning system has been one of the pioneering pieces of legislation of the twentieth century on a par with the development of the welfare state. However, like the welfare state it is in need of review and updating to take it into challenges that lie ahead in the new millennium.

CHAPTER 3

Environmental Policy in the New Millennium – Does Planning Have a Role in Achieving Sustainable Development?

Roderick Macdonald and Donna Heaney

Introduction

This chapter examines the role of land use planning in addressing environmental policy issues and particularly considers the potential of land use planning in delivering the much-debated concept of sustainable development. The chapter:

- Briefly reviews the sustainable development and environmental policy debate
- Assesses where planning fits into this debate, in terms of government policy, development plans and development control
- Asks whether planning is being sidelined by other initiatives such as Local Agenda 21 and European-wide strategies
- Examines the key issue of location of development

The chapter concludes by assessing the mechanisms needed to allow the planning system to make a more responsive and meaningful contribution to the environmental debate as we go into the new millennium, particularly in terms of implementing the concept of sustainable development.

Sustainable Development and the Environmental Debate

In the first four post-war decades policy-makers regarded environmental issues as secondary to economic growth and consumer spending. An interest in the environment was regarded as the preserve of a minority – radicals, dreamers and those seeking an alternative lifestyle. Political interest in the environment was low, resources continued to be exploited, car use encouraged and economic development promoted at all costs. Emerging environmental concerns were, however, brought to the fore by the Brundtland Commission in the celebrated report *Our Common Future* which defined sustainable development as '. . . development that meets the needs of the present without compromising the ability of future generations to meet their own needs' (WCED, 1987: 43 1–1).

The Earth Summit in Rio de Janeiro in 1992 adopted the principles of sustainable development, demanding a change in attitude – that people should think globally and act locally. Five years on in 1997 world leaders met again to review progress, this time in New York, with a particularly high profile contribution from Britain, and Prime Minister Tony Blair who attacked the failure of the United States to tackle car emissions (*Guardian*, 1997). A further gathering occurred in Kyoto in the same year to agree an international treaty to stabilise emission levels. Despite such initiatives it has been argued that the global environmental situation has worsened (Dennis, 1997). Much of the debate at these high-profile gatherings is not new, being previously debated by the aforementioned radicals and dreamers, but what is new is the emerging urgency and political legitimacy attached to environmental issues. In parallel, a new business interest is emerging in terms of the environment, with some companies suddenly adopting 'green credentials'.

Despite positive words and apparent political commitment, such as the establishment of the UK Round Table on Sustainable Development, the general approach of government to environmental policy has been that of seeking voluntary action (Agyeman and Tuxworth, 1996). At one level this is related to a continued reluctance to view environmental policy with the same importance as economic policy. Equally, the long-term nature of environmental policy does not necessarily square with the short-term nature of national and local political processes. But as Buckingham-Hatfield and Evans (1996: 5) have argued:

> The goals of environmental policy including sustainability are overwhelmingly political. These goals are informed, or confused, by scientific or technical evidence, but the process of identifying and establishing the goals is political and conflictual, and quite rightly so.

At the individual level it seems people are concerned about the environment in principle, but are less likely to voluntarily change established habits. But why should they change? In reality government has given little guidance to the general public on how to act in more environmentally sustainable ways, instead promoting economic growth and consumer spending. It has, however, been argued that the pursuit of sustainable development is not an option but an imperative obligation as there is real potential for major climatic problems leading to loss of food production and natural disasters (Southwood, 1997). As Myerson and Rydin (1996: 25) have noted, sustainable development '. . . is an, affirmative sounding way to utter dire warnings that would be too demoralising if phrased in more negative ways'.

Early 1998 saw the launch of a consultation paper, *Sustainable Development: Opportunities for Change*, which is intended to lead to a revised version of the national sustainable development strategy which was first published in 1994 under the Conservative administration. This document highlights four key objectives for sustainable development: social progress which recognises everyone's needs; effective protection of the environment; prudent use of natural resources; and maintenance of high and stable levels of economic growth and employment. The document then identifies five key ways of achieving sustainable development: developing sustainable goods and services; building sustainable communities; managing the environment and resources; communicating sustainable development principles, and through international co-operation and development. These are admirable intentions which few would disagree with, but the document fails to consider how potentially conflicting aims will be dealt with and how day-to-day implementation will occur.

Equally, the sustainable development debate is in danger of remaining superficial unless connections are made into everyday life. Cynically, one could argue that sustainable development is a smokescreen to allow people, businesses and governments to carry on as before in the pretence of protecting the environment. For most people environmental issues are overshadowed by concerns relating to poverty, poor housing conditions, crime and employment. Importantly, however, all of these issues are integral to achieving sustainable development; reflecting a move from physical environment issues, covering flora, fauna, landscape and such like, to a more holistic approach to the environment involving social and economic concerns (Dennis, 1997). The integration of complex socio-economic issues with environmental aspects is, however, no easy task.

However, sustainable development is clearly well intentioned and in principle well supported, but can it actually be brought about and does it mean making politically untenable decisions? It appears consciences can be easily appeased by using unleaded fuel to drive to the bottlebank and buying so-called 'green' products. As Naess (1993: 329) argued:

> . . . environmental measures which are popular are those which are not perceived as a threat to the consumption and behavioural pattern of each individual. Policies which may be perceived as negatively affecting the individual's level of consumption or opportunities for personal choice appear to be considerably more controversial.

The voluntary approach has limitations and stronger actions in terms of both incentives and penalties ('carrots and sticks') are required from government in order to begin to achieve sustainable development. The difficult task is, however, ensuring such mechanisms do not further disadvantage the most vulnerable groups in society.

LAND USE PLANNING AND ENVIRONMENTAL POLICY

A key issue for this chapter is to question whether the statutory planning system actually has a role to play in the implementation of sustainable development. This is discussed in the following section in terms of government policy, development plans and development control as the key operational aspects of the system.

GOVERNMENT PLANNING POLICY

The UK government views the planning system as one of the key mechanisms for implementing sustainable development. Department of the Environment (DoE) (now Department of the Environment, Transport and the Regions, DETR) Planning Policy Guidance Note 1, *General Policy and Principles* (PPG 1), emphasises the contribution of the planning system to achieving sustainable development; including providing for economic needs while respecting environmental objectives, using existing developed areas, conserving resources and shaping new development (DoE, 1997a). This is a consistent theme which runs through much current planning guidance. In Scotland National Planning Policy Guideline (NPPG) 1, *The Planning System*, notes the main activities of the planning system '. . . relate to the global need to guide today's development in ways which can sustain our environment for the future' (Scottish Office, 1994c: 5). Department of the Environment PPG 12, *Development Plans and Regional Planning Guidance*, was a particular step forward as it specified the need for environmental appraisal of development plans and the integration of environmental aspects into plans (DoE, 1992b). PPG 9, *Nature Conservation*, was also important in raising the profile of nature conservation issues in planning (DoE, 1994a). On the ground PPG 6, *Town Centres and Retail Development* (DoE, 1996d), has perhaps had the most impact by controlling the amount of car-dependent out-of-town retail development allowed.

Recent government planning policy now gives the environment much greater priority than in the past, but this has been criticised as belated in terms of European thinking and for lacking a regional dimension (Davoudi *et al.*, 1996). Government policy documents have also been criticised as being expressions of intent rather than real tools for the implementation of sustainable development (Roger-Machart, 1997). There has been a call for more government guidelines, but cynically some argue that guidelines would only provide additional strategies for planners to gloss over conflicts (Myerson and Rydin, 1996). Increased debate involving local communities and business is seen as more important than guidelines, but it is generally agreed that practical advice on how sustainable development might be applied locally is required (Agyeman and Tuxworth, 1996). The consultation paper, *Sustainable Development: Opportunities for Change*, has stressed it is in the task of building sustainable communities that planning has a key role to play in encouraging employment, housing, access to services and recreation; however, details on how to achieve this are missing. Positively, the document notes that the government intends to publish good practice guides to help local authorities to incorporate more fully sustainable development principles in development plans and in urban design.

DEVELOPMENT PLANS

The Planning and Compensation Act 1991 increased the importance of development plans in making development control decisions, therefore enhancing the
potential for the application of sustainable development principles through plans.
Winter (1994) noted that most early 1990s plans appeared to be giving only
minimal consideration to sustainability but considered newer plans could potentially provide an important framework for environmental decisions. Theoretically,
plans should integrate different aspects of sustainable development, but in practice
local authorities and others appear uncertain how actually to operationalise the
concept of sustainable development in development plans, especially when faced
with demands for growth and development in their areas (Morgan *et al.*, 1993).
When Davoudi *et al.* (1996) examined the oft-quoted Lancashire Structure Plan
they found the document less than radical with long standing aspects of the
planning system, such as protecting the sanctity of agricultural land and green
belts, accepted as environmentally sustainable without question.

It has been argued that tensions between environment and development in the
land use planning system may be procedurally resolved by the strategic environmental assessment of development plans (Therivel *et al.*, 1992). However, as
Marshall (1994) argued, environmental assessment of plans is much more difficult
than the more common environmental assessment of individual projects. The
process of environmental appraisal of plans as advocated in the Good Practice
Guide, *Environmental Appraisal of Development Plans* (DoE, 1993c), can be
criticised as relying too much on ticking boxes and not enough on public
involvement.

DEVELOPMENT CONTROL

Implementation in the planning system essentially comes through the process of
development control – the granting or refusing of planning applications. Rowan-
Robinson *et al.* (1995: 283) concluded that in terms of sustainable development,
the development control process has some problems, but dramatic change is not
required, arguing that '. . . planning powers are wide enough and the tools of
control are sufficiently versatile to ensure that land use and development objectives are compatible with sustainable development – if local authorities can be
persuaded to use them'. Rowan-Robinson *et al.* (1995), however, noted constraints
on the development control process in achieving sustainable development included
the slow adjustment of the courts to permit material planning considerations wider
than 'traditional' planning, the once and for all nature of development control with
little scope for monitoring and review, and perhaps most importantly, determining
at an operational level whether an individual development control decision will
actually contribute to the wider aim of achieving sustainable development. A

research report for the Local Government Association and the Local Government Management Board agreed with the view that the mechanisms for development control to contribute to the achievement of sustainable development are in place (CAG Consultants, 1998). However, it advocates a sustainability checklist approach for development control officers and developers to ensure sustainable development issues are taken into account in everyday planning practice. This checklist would cover aspects such as aesthetics, waste, energy, local needs, employment, poverty, health, education and public participation – issues that sustainable development espouses but also issues the planning system has long been attempting to address.

Owens (1997) noted that the planning profession has clearly aligned itself with the notion of sustainable development albeit with an element of scepticism and frustration. She considers the actual capacity of planning to deliver sustainable development is likely to be severely tested over the next decade. However, Selman (1995) noted planning is a useful tool for government in seeking to achieve sustainable development, but argued this cannot just be traditional land use planning but must begin to address wider issues such as protection of critical natural capital and issues of equity. The concept of sustainable development has undoubtably given the planning system enhanced purpose and credibility, but a particular problem is that the planning profession's interpretation of sustainable development is narrow, still focused on economic development as opposed to environmental and social impacts (Beardmore, 1997). The planning system does not appear to be open to radical change, indeed Marshall (1996: 142) highlighted that despite some good words and actions Britain does not really engage in environmental planning *per se*. He argued:

> So far there has been little firm development of a new form of 'environmental planning' in some wider senses, despite the often heroic efforts of civil servants writing annual reviews and local planners revising structure and local plans. Such a new form of planning would need a social and economic refocusing as much as an ecological one, and that is incompatible with the main current drives at British government and EU levels.

On the other hand, it can be argued that planners have been engaged in promoting sustainable development for many years – but now need to take a step further. The much-quoted paper *Sense and Sustainability* noted that the achievements of the planning system over the last 50 years must be built on, but planners must go beyond the safe haven of balancing development and the environment into the rather more difficult task of actually realising environmental objectives and, most controversially, identifying environmental limits to development (Jacobs, 1993). Owens (1997) has argued that planners often define sustainable development as 'balance' which means that environmental capacities will not always be respected, although she notes in practice environmental capacity will be socially and politically defined.

In summary, planning clearly has a major role in working towards sustainable development and has an important contribution to make. Some aspects will only require minor changes to current operations, other aspects will require more radical overhauls, for example public participation needs to engender more meaningful involvement from a wider range of people than at present. Despite some very positive moves by individual local authorities the real potential of planning, however, appears to be held back by a lack of clear direction as to how development plans and development control can actually operationalise concepts of sustainable development in everyday planning practice.

LOCAL AGENDA 21 AND EUROPEAN INITIATIVES: PASSING PLANNING BY?

LOCAL AGENDA 21

Land use planning is not the only policy process seeking to achieve sustainable development. Key to the process of moving towards sustainable development has been Local Agenda 21 (LA21). Agenda 21 emerged from the 1992 Rio conference and expanded on the work of Brundtland by recognising five major issues: carrying capacity, intergenerational equity, intragenerational equity, quality of life and consultations, and partnership (Bennett and Patel, 1995). Of the 2500 action points within Agenda 21 two-thirds relate to action by local authorities, hence one of the key objectives of Agenda 21 is for each local authority to draw up its own LA21, particularly by fully involving its local population. The Audit Commission (1997) found that such progress is patchy, but highlighted excellent work by some authorities. Their report was followed up with government guidance urging all local authorities to draw up LA21 strategies.

Local Agenda 21 has a much wider remit than the statutory planning system. It is much more related to an overall improvement in quality of life and offers an opportunity to take radical and innovative action (Freeman *et al.*, 1996). Projects undertaken under the banner of LA21 are extremely varied, including crime prevention, journeys to school and environmental improvement. More recently LA21 has involved debates regarding citizenship, local democracy and social equity. However, as Dennis (1997) noted, there is some evidence that LA21 has not really changed the status quo and is not involving 'real' communities. There is also some evidence that local authorities are struggling to implement LA21 strategies because of lack of resources and a difficulty in engaging local businesses and the private sector (Groundwork, 1997).

The key issue here, however, is whether statutory planning and LA21 are combining to develop effective environmental policy and practice. It is worth stressing the fundamental difference between planning and LA21. Land use planning is essentially a top-down process with its statutory background, whereas LA21 is very much a bottom-up community-based process (Carter and Darlow, 1997). Beardmore (1997: 14) argued considerable differences exist between planning and LA21, asking:

> . . . is it really credible that the current chasm between LA 21 and planning policies will be allowed to remain? Once that connections have been made, many (if not all) of our entrenched land-use planning principles will have to be revised or even discarded.

Although good examples of links between planning and LA21 can be found, such as subjecting all planning applications to environmental appraisal at Woking Borough Council (Morphet and Hams, 1994) and the introduction of LA21 principles into regeneration strategies (Bennett and Patel, 1995), others echo the concerns of Beardmore. As Carter and Darlow (1997) have argued, central government could play a greater role in clarifying relationships between the LA21 process and land use planning which would raise the credibility of both processes in attempting to achieve sustainable development.

EUROPEAN ENVIRONMENTAL INITIATIVES

It was only in 1992 that the Maastricht Treaty gave equal weight to environmental protection and the economy within the European Union. The Fifth Environmental Action Programme *Towards Sustainability* then stressed the need for more proactive environmental policy, with the interim review of this programme subsequently emphasising the need to reconcile environment and economy. *Europe 2000+: Co-operation for European Territorial Development* (CEC, 1994c) has also attempted to provide a more strategic orientation to policy. However, it has been argued that *Europe 2000+* is disappointing, concentrating on traditional environmental concerns such as water, open space and traffic congestion rather than actually integrating initiatives from different sectors (Gibbs, 1996). The continued drive towards Europe-wide spatial policy has continued with *European Spatial Development Perspective*, the physical plan for Europe, under preparation. The problem is that many British planners, and more importantly planning authorities, will not perceive these plans and programmes as relevant. The aspect of European policy most prominent in British planning is not spatial development policy, but the Structural Funds. There have been recent attempts to integrate environmental aspects into these funds, including environmental appraisal of programmes and funding job creation schemes related to the environment. It appears such requirements will drive integration of environmental and economic aspects much more than physical plans.

It could be argued that the European environmental agenda may generate major change in planning with a cross-national boundary perspective ultimately bypassing the UK planning system. As Marshall (1996) has argued, the British system is still nationally guided even though Europe has affected it. He notes that planners should be aware of European initiatives but not to the detriment of local forms of planning, and stressed it would be going too far to say that British planning has been Europeanised although aspects such as environmental assessment have been '. . . stapled onto the existing system with uncertain and variable results' (Mitchell, 1996: 135). It does appear, however, that British environmental policy and practice on pollution and nature conservation have been transformed by European influences, for example the production of the National Air Quality Strategy of 1997, but the same cannot be said of land use planning.

Is it the case, therefore, that LA21 and European initiatives are resulting in a bypassing of land use planning in the environmental debate? It does appear that unless there is more co-ordination between planning and LA21 there is indeed a danger that planning initiatives to achieve sustainable development will be upstaged by LA21, with its potential for addressing a much wider range of concerns and its ability to take a more holistic approach to sustainable development. In reality, however, planning and LA21 should operate together; both processes are required and should be seen as complementary. More work is needed at central and local levels to ensure this happens. In terms of European environmental policy the planning system has not yet been bypassed and in reality this is not likely in the near future. European initiatives have helped prioritise the drive towards sustainable development and formulate UK environmental policy in some key areas. However, it is the requirement to incorporate an environmental component into Structural Fund applications which will really drive European-wide environmental policy rather than remote physical plans which, unfortunately so far, appear unconnected with local attempts to move towards sustainable development.

LOCATION OF DEVELOPMENT: PLANNING'S KEY CONTRIBUTION?

Much debate on how to plan for sustainable development has focused on where development should be located in the future. This debate has been particularly linked to concerns to reduce the need to travel by car, thereby reducing CO_2 emissions entering the atmosphere. Government forecasts indicate that 4.4 million new households will exist by 2016 which has raised the profile of this debate. According to the government, 80% of these new households will consist of only one person, reflecting societal trends of increased divorce rates, fewer people marrying or marrying later and people living longer. Henderson (1997) suggests an additional 169 000 ha of land, an area equivalent to that of Surrey, is required to meet this demand.

The Government has indicated that it wishes to see 60% of these new houses built on brownfield (that is previously developed) sites. This view is supported by the UK Round Table on Sustainable Development which considers the use of existing urban areas for the majority of this housing as the more sustainable option. More recently the UK Round Table on Sustainable Development has argued this figure should rise to 75% of new housing locating on brownfield sites (*Planning*, 1998). It has, however, been stressed that such brownfield utilisation would only be achievable with government financial help, as considerable resources are needed to enable building on contaminated and derelict land (Henderson, 1997). A greenfield tax has been advocated as a way to encourage brownfield development. This is currently under government consideration.

The key problem with seeking to utilise brownfield sites is that developers most commonly wish to use greenfield sites because of ease of building and market-ability reasons. They do not want to build on problematic brownfield sites which will often be located in inner-city or former industrial areas. Related to this is consumer demand for new housing in rural and semi-rural areas as opposed to inner-urban locations. Despite this issue government and many planners consider that use of brownfield sites and general maintenance of existing patterns of development, in particular utilising existing settlement boundaries, is the key to sustainable development. By comparison greenfield development is seen to have a number of disadvantages including increasing car dependency, irreplaceably damaging natural resources and leading to disadvantaged groups becoming more disadvantaged, for example as more shops locate out of town with a subsequent reduction in facilities that non-car owners can access.

ALTERNATIVE DEVELOPMENT PATTERNS

There is, however, an alternative view that achieving sustainable development is not necessarily synonymous with maintaining compact cities and building in existing urban areas. The Town and Country Planning Association (TCPA) consider high brownfield development targets will mean more houses of lower quality squeezed on to sites. They argue sustainable urban living should not be confused with so-called town cramming as this creates poor urban environments with higher-income groups leaving the city as in the North American situation (Hall, 1997). The TCPA stress that cities need to be places people actually want to live in (like many European cities), arguing for more decentralised 'sustainable city regions' combined with measures such as social housing and land assembly powers for public bodies. Importantly they stress that so called town cramming is often less sustainable than well-conceived greenfield development (TCPA, 1997).

It is also argued that many people in urban Britain are living in poor housing conditions and that this will be made worse by increased city cramming. Stewart (1997: 11) has stressed that government is ignoring the housing circumstances of the vast majority of people and contends proposals to concentrate new development in urban areas offer '. . . little comfort to Britain's hard pressed urban majority'. Similarly, MacDonald (1997) has argued that local authorities should think hard before refusing to permit housing development on 'environmental grounds' when so many people do not have adequate and affordable housing in both urban and rural areas.

A basic argument in favour of the densely developed city is that compact cities assist in reducing car use. Gordon (1997) argues, however, that there are no published travel data, including the National Travel Survey, to support the idea that urban form significantly affects travel behaviour and therefore reduces car use. Gordon notes that the compact city argument ignores consumers' demands which are much more sophisticated than the basic needs approach of planners, whom he has accused of ignoring the reality of market trends. Gordon argues that increasing fuel prices would have a much more direct effect on reducing car use, particularly as it has the advantage of working with, rather than against, market forces. However, the Scottish Consumer Council in a report for the Scottish Office argue that while price mechanisms are important in influencing travel behaviour in urban areas, other measures such as accessible and acceptable alternatives to the car are equally important (Scottish Consumer Council, 1998).

A range of other possibilities do exist to merely locating new development in existing settlements: including building new settlements, expanding country towns and using corridors of high-quality public transport as the focus of development. Owens (1991b), for example, has stressed the advantages of 'decentralised concentration' involving clusters of high-density, mixed land use, small to medium-sized settlements. There has also been a call to move away from traditional urban containment measures, such as green belts, and a move more towards more flexible green wedges or similar, especially linked to high-quality public transport corridors. Recently green belt policy has been criticised for the way it artificially maintains the compactness of cities. The planning adviser to former Secretary of State for the Environment John Gummer (David Lock) has argued that the compact city is neither desirable nor achievable. Similarly, Keyner (1997) suggested green belts may be contributing to urban sprawl and damaging countryside, particularly as they encourage 'leap-frogging' of development into countryside beyond the green belt. Green belts have also been accused of leading to unnecessary urban intensification and increases in housing land prices, while failing to act as proper regional planning mechanisms (Cherry, 1992; Elson et al., 1993). Most green belts date from the 1950s and it would be timely to consider the functional needs of cities related to sustainable development rather than maintaining an arbitrary ring around them which has very little to do with current development and movement patterns.

Is location of new development therefore planning's key contribution to achieving sustainable development? If government predictions are correct the sheer amount of development required over the next 20 years would suggest this is going to be a fundamental issue for planning in terms of sustainable development. However, questions arise as to whether this development should be located in existing centres, perhaps the obvious choice in terms of sustainable development, or whether other forms of development are required, in particular recognising the effect of town cramming on cities and the sophisticated locational and travel demands of the population. Both camps, however, do agree that cities must be made more 'liveable' if they are to be sustainable (in terms of better quality housing, varied local services, efficient public transport and a safe, clean environment), but disagree whether the majority of new development should be accommodated within cities. Clearly, planning has a key role in ensuring optimal locations are chosen for new development to ensure it is sustainable in social, economic and environmental terms but also in terms of the particular locality in question. It is also crucial for planning to reconsider traditional spatial planning tools, such as the green belt, which in reality may not be all that valuable in attempting to achieve sustainable development, especially as commuting from development areas beyond green belt boundaries is often encouraged and artificial limits on city growth imposed.

Conclusions

Sustainable Development and the Environmental Debate

The last 10 years have seen a heightened environmental awareness from the public, government and business, although (not surprisingly) the most popular environmental actions have been those which do not radically affect consumer demand for goods and services, the ability of politicians to get re-elected and the economic performance of businesses. The short-term nature of politics and the dominance of business interests have meant a proactive agenda has not been pursued. The achievement of sustainable development, however, does require some fundamental changes in everyday life. Government particularly is required to give the public more information about environmental costs (for example, the real cost of using a car) to allow more informed consumer choice related to the environment.

Sustainable development is a challenging concept to implement as it requires difficult political decisions to be made as well as consideration of multiple and often conflicting issues. Although clear progress has been made, the mainstream environmental policy debate cannot be described as radical and hence the frustrations of both 'eco-warriors' and, increasingly, ordinary members of the public driven to take direct action. Government needs to consider more radical solutions to achieving sustainable development – a reliance on the voluntary approach is clearly not enough. Politically difficult decisions must be made for the long term. Development of greater public awareness in relation to the environment will, however, make such decisions easier as the electorate realise the importance of considering environmental costs. Equally, a holistic policy approach considering more carefully social equity and economic aspects as well as the physical environment is urgently required. Increased consideration of social equity issues is particularly important as government and others must ensure that policies to achieve sustainable development do not impact unjustly on the most vulnerable or poorest members of society.

LAND USE PLANNING AND ENVIRONMENTAL POLICY

Planning has generally been guilty of not moving the environmental debate on to a more radical and proactive plane, including taking the key step into making difficult decisions about environmental capacity, as opposed to constantly seeking to achieve a balance between environment and economy. However, it could be argued that achieving consensus and balance is a key aspect of a more holistic approach to sustainable development. Government policy has made some welcome statements and has considerably strengthened the role of planning in the sustainable development debate. Government, however, needs to take the next step of indicating exactly how planning should operationalise the concept of sustainable development in development plans and development control, and allow planning to take a more holistic approach but without extending the remit of planning so wide that it becomes meaningless.

LOCAL AGENDA 21 AND EUROPEAN INITIATIVES

Local Agenda 21 is, however, able to take a holistic approach by drawing different interests and issues together. It could, therefore, be suggested that LA21 will mean the bypassing of planning. While this is not likely, especially given the statutory basis of planning, there must be closer integration of planning and LA21. Land use planning and LA21 must be complementary with both systems working together.

The UK planning system is also not likely to be subsumed by European directives in the immediate future. While there is a place for pan-European plans they cannot replace locally derived and delivered plans. The European Union (EU), however, has a key role in driving the environmental debate and enforcing compliance in individual countries which may be reluctant to address environmental concerns. This will be particularly important as the Union widens with the entry of Eastern European countries with poor environmental records. The EU also has the ability to take a longer-term perspective than individual countries which may seek to respond to shorter-term political agendas. Care must be taken, however, to ensure that such European strategies have relevance to implementation at the local level, including through planning systems, otherwise they will be ignored.

LOCATION OF DEVELOPMENT

Where new development should be located in the future has become a key issue for planning. The debate over whether this should be in existing towns and cities or on greenfield sites has attracted professional, media and public interest, particularly fuelled by concerns about excessive loss of green belt land. The obvious solution is compaction of existing settlements which uses derelict and underused land, supports public transport and maintains town centres. Negative aspects are, however, increasing congestion, loss of open space and poor space standards in housing. Such concerns have fuelled a more radical debate related to the need for alternative forms of new development including new settlements, development along public transport corridors and the replacement of green belts with more flexible urban growth management designations. In reality the solution will be a mixture – good new development on carefully selected greenfield sites combined with the regeneration of cities, both combined with improvements to public transport and locally available services. It will be vital for planning to involve local people in formulating the best way forward for their area in a positive way.

IMPLEMENTING SUSTAINABLE DEVELOPMENT

Protecting the environment and working towards sustainable development is clearly important in principle. Actually implementing the concept is, however, the key challenge for the statutory planning system. Indeed the national policy context can be criticised as not enabling successful operationalisation of good intentions. The following general principles are key to the implementation of sustainable development through the planning system:

- A *holistic approach* needs to be taken considering social equity and economic aspects as well as the physical environment.
- There is a need to *get beyond the short term*, in politics, community involvement and in business.
- *Clear long-term strategies* are required in order to bring different aspects of policy together, particularly to integrate environmental, economic and social issues.
- Planning must go *beyond balancing* environmental and economic aspects and must make tougher decisions as to whether environmental capacity has been reached.
- Tensions and difficult decisions must be exposed with a *more proactive agenda* pursued with more incentives and penalties utilised. This will require more regulation and intervention in the free market but also more public information and education to allow people to make more informed decisions about the environmental consequences of their actions.

- Environmental policies must not *further disadvantage the disadvantaged* by their implementation.
- A *wide range* of public and private organisations and businesses must be involved in achieving sustainable development. Strategies which do not have the support of businesses and community organisations in an area will not succeed.
- *Democracy and equity* must be enhanced through increased community involvement and engaging individuals and groups who do not usually get involved in planning.
- The *localised needs* of different types of areas and people must be recognised, including avoiding applying universal solutions to all areas; for example, policies for sustainable development will clearly be different in rural as opposed to urban areas.
- *Co-ordination* is required between tiers of government including the Scottish Parliament, Welsh Assembly and the new Regional Development Agencies.

In terms of the day-to-day planning system such broad aims need to be linked to tangible actions. It is suggested that the following are required if planning is to make a full contribution to the achievement of sustainable development:

- The production of good *baseline information* is required, covering social, economic and physical environment issues. In some cases this simply may mean reassessing existing information. In other cases new surveys are required to help ensure planning policies and decisions are compatible with the principles of sustainable development.
- Appropriate *development plan polices* need to be in place to guide the achievement of sustainable development. Meaningful participation and consultation in the formulation of these polices will be crucial to ensure their successful implementation, as will central support in the planning appeals process.
- Improved *public involvement* in policy-making and in development control, in particular targeting groups not usually represented in the process, is required. Planning documents and decision-making processes must be made more open and accessible to the public.
- Ensuring *involvement of developers* in achieving sustainable development is important, particularly as many changes will be to their advantage, such as creating more liveable housing environments.
- *Explicit consideration* of sustainable development issues is required in development control decisions with a checklist approach potentially aiding this.
- *Environmental assessment* of a wider range of projects is required. Simpler forms of environmental assessment could be adopted for less complex developments. Equally, strategic environmental assessment of development plans must

be developed into an integral part of the planning process as opposed to being an 'added extra' as at present.

- Improvements to the sustainability of development can be achieved through *negotiation, conditions and planning obligations* achieving planning gain, but linked to clear development plan policies and good baseline information.
- Enhanced *monitoring and enforcement* will ensure successful implementation of policies and planning permissions while protecting the environment from damaging breaches of planning control.

Positively, many of these activities are already being undertaken by planners, but as CAG Consultants (1998) have contended, there needs to be a more conscious, structured recognition of sustainable development issues in everyday planning practice, ensuring integration of environmental issues throughout the planning process and that the achievement of sustainable development is not marginalised or confined to words in glossy policy documents. Combined with a more proactive environmental policy from government, particularly raising public awareness and making environmental costs and social equity issues more explicit, planning can clearly play a positive role in achieving sustainable development as we go into the new millennium.

CHAPTER 4

WHITHER RURAL PLANNING?

Dave Shaw

INTRODUCTION

> The enduring character of England is most clearly to be found in the countryside. Yet the pace of change has quickened and much of what we most value about the rural scene seems threatened by increasing mobility, pressures of leisure and recreation, the decline of jobs in rural industries and the demands for new jobs and businesses which once would have been found only in the towns (DoE and MAFF, 1995).

This is the opening paragraph of the former Conservative government's White Paper entitled *Rural England: A Nation Committed to a Living Countryside*. It clearly indicates how complex and contested planning for the rural economy actually is. Recognition is made of the rapid and dynamic restructuring, which is part of the new global order, yet paradoxically, the popular public perspective is of a countryside that is intrinsically valuable, and in need of protection. A Countryside Commission survey of 1995 suggested that 95% of the British public has a strong affinity with the countryside, even if they did not use it, and a 91% felt there was a moral duty to protect the countryside for future generations (reported in DoE and MAFF, 1995).

The first nine months of a new Labour government have been noticeable for the way that countryside matters have been so prominent. Major concerns are being voiced as to the viability of many of our farming communities. The strength of the green pound has once again helped to plunge farming in general into a crisis reminiscent of the late 1980s. In particular sectors the stresses and strains have been even more pronounced. There have been angry scenes as beef farmers have literally fought for compensation in the light of the protracted BSE crisis. While this has inevitable implications for the viability of particular farms and farming communities, there will be also impacts on the wider rural economy. Similarly, the debates surrounding the proposed ban on fox hunting have been polarised between moral and ethical arguments of the anti-hunt campaigners and the countryside lobby, who argued that such a ban would not only destroy a rural tradition but would have enormous impacts on local rural economies. Furthermore, there has been a heated debate concerning access to the countryside between landowners and those wanting greater freedom to roam. At the same time the conservationist lobby is heightening the debate as to where new developments, particularly residential, should occur and the extent to which the countryside should be consumed. To some extent, all these perspectives coalesced in March 1998, when an estimated 250 000 joined a rally in central London organised by the Country-side Alliance. It focused media attention on the fact that there was considerable public support for rural policy, but what form it should take, and whose concerns should be protected in the 'public interest', were by no means clear among the multifarious range of interests represented at the march.

The rural environment is clearly a contested arena and a plethora of perspectives, policy initiatives and programmes impact on rural areas with spatially discriminating effects. However, from a planning perspective it is an area that has been sadly under-researched. Much of the limited research into countryside planning is often sectorially based, with an emphasis on the dominant land use, i.e. agriculture. The White Paper *Rural England* was therefore anticipated as a timely, if not a long overdue attempt to recognise a wider and changing rural perspective (Lowe, 1995). The academic literature on rural change, much of which has emanated from geographers, has increasingly emphasised the diverse nature of the rural economy, thus implying the need for a subtle and well-informed approach to rural planning. Regulation theory is being used as a conceptual framework to try to understand how the forces of capitalism vary over time and space (Goodwin and Painter, 1996). As a result rural areas are being characterised by their diversity reflecting the importance of locality. It is not just the macro frameworks produced by the national or supranational levels of governance that are important in under-standing rural change in particular localities, but in addition 'the dimensions of . . . cultural and political power are currently changing dramatically in rural areas, and the shape and form of their particular dynamic will help to produce and sustain different norms and customs of regulation in different rural places' (Goodwin *et al.*, 1995: 1250). For Murdoch and Marsden (1994) this manifests itself in four idealised types of countryside which reflect the complex interplay between prescribed frameworks from national governance or above and local social, econ-omic and political processes. The 'preserved countryside' is characterised by an anti-development perspective and preservationist attitudes. Such concerns are usually expressed by new, frequently middle-class, social groupings who often bring with them a perception of what the countryside should be like. Limited, high-quality residential development or appropriate leisure developments so that the countryside can be enjoyed, may be permitted. The 'contested countryside' is where agricultural and development interests may be politically dominant but there is increasing conflict between old and new rural residents. Third, the 'paternalist countryside' is less contested from an external development perspective, but falling income may encourage large private estate owners to diversify their activities. Finally there is the 'clientist countryside' whereby farming still has a predominant role, but this is only sustained by state support. In all of these areas the importance of farming as the dominant land use is diminishing, and the countryside is increasingly being commodified for urban pleasure.

What is clear from this brief discussion is that rural areas are extremely dynamic and have been subject to considerable change. In looking forward to the new millennium I want to suggest that the pace of this change is likely to accelerate. There is perhaps nothing new in this, indeed Curry and Owen (1996) note that most books on rural policy claim that they are written in a time of unprecedented change. However, despite renewed interest in rural affairs there is a real threat that rural places will become even more subsumed by an urban agenda based on need. I want to argue that what is needed to face this challenge is the ability to think more strategically about the future of the rural economy, and in so doing so it will be important to recognise that this is characterised by enormous diversity rather than homogeneity. Such an approach is likely to be promoted by policy and institutional reform which sees broad frameworks being established which should be complemented by strategies developed to suit local conditions. After nearly two decades where decision-making has been increasingly centralised (Thornley, 1993, 1996) there are signs at least that there is a new desire once again to decentralise if not devolve responsibility to regional or local governance. However, at the same time there are threats which perhaps suggest that the rural dimension of policy-making might be dissipated still further. The chapter begins by briefly reviewing the current position of rural policy, with particular reference to economic development policies. Rutland's approach to strategic integrated rural development will then be used to examine the extent to which this offers an appropriate model for the management of rural change in the new millennium.

PLANNING THE RURAL ENVIRONMENT

Traditionally, planning in rural areas has seen the emergence of two distinctive management systems (Curry and Owen, 1996). The Town and Country Planning system has largely been confined to the management of the built environment, and then predominantly through development control mechanisms, which has at best limited or controlled the amount of new building in the countryside. For many groups advocating a conservation or preservationist perspective, most notably the Council for the Protection of Rural England (CPRE), far too much development has been permitted and is likely to be allowed within the countryside under this system (CPRE, 1997). The second area of countryside planning relates to agricultural production. Since the days of post-war reconstruction both national and European policy has emphasised the maximisation of yields. Growing environmental concerns during the 1980s and 1990s have led to a plethora of designations and schemes designed to ameliorate some of the worst excesses of agricultural overproduction. In addition to these core management systems, a range of agencies have grown up with particular responsibility for aspects of the rural environment. The Countryside Commission is principally concerned with aesthetic matters, promoting the conservation or enhancement of the countryside from a perspective of recreational use and general public enjoyment. English Nature's remit is wildlife conservation and the Rural Development Commission focuses on social and economic development in the countryside. Such an *ad hoc* and incremental approach has resulted in a long-standing call for a more co-ordinated approach to rural planning (see for example Cherry, 1976; Davidson and Wibberley, 1977; Gilg, 1978). As the recent rural White Paper was awaited, Curry and Owen (1996) hoped that it would herald a more concordant set of policy objectives and intentions for the countryside. As it transpired they were to be disappointed, for despite its wide-ranging and comprehensive review of rural policies, programmes and initiatives, it failed to establish a radical new policy agenda, provide a clear strategic direction or make new resource commitments.

Evidence of policy evolution did, however, come subsequently in a revised Planning Policy Guidance Note for the Countryside in 1997 (DoE, 1997b). This replaced the 1992 version of PPG 7 and set a new national context within which planning and development in the countryside should occur. The Guidance Note, which was interestingly subtitled *Environmental Quality and Economic and Social Development*, reaffirmed the long-established commitment to protecting and enhancing the character of the countryside, but indicated that rural prosperity was an integral component of the policy. Underlying the new policy were six principles for the future of the countryside planning:

- The pursuit of sustainable development
- Shared responsibility for the countryside as a national asset, which serves people who live and work there as well as visitors
- Dialogue to help reconcile competing priorities
- Distinctiveness, approaching rural policies in a way which is flexible and responds to the character of the countryside
- Economic and social diversity
- Sound information as the basis for effective policies (DoE, 1997b, para 1.2.3)

Three key dimensions of this new approach are worthy of comment. First, greater emphasis appears to be given to development, especially if it helps to diversify the rural economy and create rural prosperity. The reuse and adaptation of existing buildings are encouraged to meet both commercial and industrial needs as well as tourism and leisure pursuits. Second, there is a tacit acceptance of the diversity of rural areas and the need for distinctive policy responses which recognise local circumstances. Third, in developing and implementing strategies at a variety of scales there is a need for flexibility and dialogue between different groups. This not only helps to reconcile the inevitable conflicts between different groups but also leads to a collective understanding of the interconnections between economic and social problems in rural areas, and collective action can lead to synergy between policy-makers and practitioners from differing disciplines.

DIVERSIFYING THE RURAL ECONOMY

One of the long-standing problems bedevilling many rural communities is that poverty and deprivation remain essentially hidden. 'The influx of seemingly wealthy and mobile migrants to many areas linked either with retirement or commuting to existing jobs in urban areas has served to cast a cloak of prosperity during the 1980's' (Cloke *et al.*, 1994: 168). Such perspectives are not new (see for example Shaw, 1979) but the scale of the problem, in absolute rather than relative terms, and its dispersed geographical nature mean that it underlies this façade of affluence. Enormous economic restructuring is occurring. Farming has continued to shed jobs throughout the twentieth century and there is no reason to suspect that the trend will not continue. In terms of local rural services, long-established trends of closure persist. For example, the Rural Development Commission (RDC) reported in 1998 that 82% of parishes with a population of less than 10 000 have no food shops and 45% of all village food shops have closed in the last seven years (RDC, 1998). In some parts of the country, dependency on a dominant employer has made local economies additionally vulnerable to change. Closure and downsizing in the extractive industries or the implications of the peace dividend have led to substantial job losses in some cases.

What is apparent is that the impact of these changes have been felt very differently in different rural locations and what has grown up is a series of *ad hoc* policy responses that respond to individual crises in particular policy sectors (Gilg, 1996). Furthermore, during the 1980s, government attempts to engender economic restructuring have become embedded in questions of efficiency. The particular characteristics of a place and its needs have become less significant in terms of the rhetoric of public policy. Thus, it has been increasingly difficult to distinguish rural from urban-based initiatives, with regenerative activities in all areas based on notions of competition, partnership and leverage rather than on needs-based allocations and an understanding of the variability of local circumstances. Having said that, most rural policy remains targeted at a minority of the rural populars, namely the agricultural sector.

In response to the farming crisis of the late 1980s, incentives were introduced to diversify the income source to farming. These were of two types. First, attempts were made to encourage farmers to develop alternative sources of income by either diversifying their activities on the farm or by using their skills in off-farm employment. While the take-up of associated incentives was not as widespread as anticipated, some studies suggest that by the mid 1990s farm diversification was generating £675 million per annum and was providing around 80 000 employment opportunities (DoE and MAFF, 1995). With only 430 000 employed in farming, diversification activities therefore represent a considerable proportion of the agricultural labour force. The emphasis here was very much on reusing surplus farm labour (whether family or employed) as a resource. The ways in which farmers have sought to diversify by capitalising on their assets by using land or buildings is largely under-researched. However, a study by Shaw and Hale (1996) indicated that while the majority of applications from farmers were for residential conversions, over 30% were for commercial and industrial purposes. In general there is also evidence that many local authorities were not unduly restrictive when it came to promoting diversification in rural areas (Elson *et al.*, 1995). The second type of incentive, initiated through reforms of the EU's Common Agricultural Policy, involved a shift from production-based support towards more environmentally sensitive agricultural management systems. Here farmers were supported for taking land out of production (set aside) or adopting less intensive farming practices (e.g. in Environmentally Sensitive Areas).

During this period, the RDC, formed in 1909 and probably the oldest of the government quangos, continued to focus its resources for rural regeneration on the remoter peripheral and disadvantaged rural areas. The bulk of the RDC's regeneration portfolio is targeted at the rural development areas. These were introduced in 1984 and revised in 1994, using quantitative measures of need. They currently cover parts of 29 counties in England, some 109 districts, 35% of the area of England and about 2.75 million people (RDC, 1993). In partnership with the relevant local authorities, community councils, and other interested partners the RDC prepares a Rural Development Programme which identify needs and priorities in the designated rural development areas. Research in the early 1990s, albeit for the RDC, suggested that there was widespread support for the Rural Development Programme. They had helped to highlight the particular problems of the area involved, had helped create inter-agency dialogue between those wishing to address rural problems and had helped lever out new resources for local communities (Bovaird *et al.*, 1990).

Part of this additional support has come through the EU's Objective 5b programme. The areas designated for this Structural Fund support have been largely con-terminus with the rural development areas. Under this European programme some £410 million of European funding is available to rural areas in the UK for the period 1994–99. In addition a further £21 million is available under the LEADER Community Initiative designed to develop innovative rural development projects. In addition the rural economy, and in particular the farming economy, has been supported by massive public subsidy through the EU's Common Agricultural Policy (CAP). Despite these support mechanisms rural poverty remains in relative terms very significant, with 20% of the rural population being on or near the margins of poverty (Cloke *et al.*, 1994).

More recently there has been a shift in emphasis in rural regeneration policy away from a spatially targeted needs-based approach to one where greater emphasis is given to efficiency criteria, value for money and competitive bidding. This of course is not unique to the rural areas and reflects the orientation of the previous government's regeneration programmes across the UK. As a result rural areas have been able to bid for Single Regeneration Budget (SRB) money, and in addition, paralleling the success of the urban City Challenge experience, in 1994 the RDC launched Rural Challenge, whereby six prizes of up to £1 million would be awarded annually to what were judged to be the best proposals. Much has been written about the impact of competitive bidding in urban areas, but within the rural context the literature is noticeable for its absence. An exception has been Little *et al.*'s analysis (1998) of the implications of Rural Challenge on both the winners and losers in the competition. As well as reiterating many of the concerns expressed in relation to urban partnerships, for example the temporary and convenient nature of the partnership, a number of perspectives that added a distinctive rural dimension to the debate were highlighted (Little *et al.*, 1998). First, the institutional capacity in rural areas is limited. The local authorities are inevitably the main body able to co-ordinate the required partnership and bidding, but they frequently experience difficulty in finding appropriate partners. For example, the private sector in rural areas often comprises a large number of small and diffuse units that are unable to make an effective contribution to such initiatives. Second, the local authorities themselves, given their small scale, frequently felt that they neither had the time, resources nor expertise to develop effective bids. If such feelings are expressed by project officers for competitions that are specific to rural areas, then it is possible to argue that the more universal competitions, such as SRB, will place the rural areas at a relative disadvantage to their more urbanised competitors.

INSTITUTIONAL AND FUNDING REFORMS

But what of the future? Despite the limitations highlighted above, there is currently a relatively transparent rural programme with specific institutions and agencies responsible for its delivery. However, it is clear that significant changes are on the way both in terms of institutional and funding arrangements. It is perhaps too early to be too definitive about what will occur, but there is a very real danger that the rural dimension of policy will become even more diluted. At the same time I would argue in parallel to what is occurring across planning in general, the need for a more strategic approach which is flexible and responsive to change, is likely to become more important. This will provide the necessary framework for accessing any funding.

As we have already seen, one of the most significant fiscal support mechanisms for rural areas comes from the EU. Any changes in such funding mechanisms are, therefore, likely to have profound impacts on the rural economy. The Commission's proposals for reform were published in July 1997 in *Agenda 2000: For a Stronger and Wider Europe* (CEC, 1997a). This document considers three main areas: reform of the European Structural Funds, continued reform of the Common Agricultural Policy and preparations to accommodate further eastern expansion of the EU. It is important to recognise that *Agenda 2000* is a negotiating document which will inevitably be subject to compromise and change as the various member states become embroiled in detailed discussion as to the precise nature of the reforms. However, the intention is that by 1 January 2000, the new operational programmes for those areas to be assisted by European funding will have been agreed. This document and the subsequent negotiations will therefore have important implications for the level of European funding directed towards the rural economy from 2000 to 2006.

In relation to the Structural Funds the Commission accepts that through prudent financial management, it will able to fund the proposed reforms without expecting an increase in the overall level of contribution from member states. Consequently there is an expectation that 1.27% of member states' gross domestic product (GDP) will continue to be allocated to the Structural Funds. This will raise the necessary extra revenue to fund enlargement by virtue of an anticipated economic growth rate of 2.5% across the existing EU members and of 4% growth in the accession countries. It is estimated that such contributions will generate some additional 20 billion ecu by 2006.

As well as dealing with enlargement, two key themes which underpin the proposed Structural Fund reforms are concentration and simplification. Based on a 1994 evaluation of the value of European Structural Funds, the Commission has concluded that there is a need to concentrate resources in a more targeted way, directed at those areas of particular need (CEC, 1996b, 1997b). Hence the original proposal is to concentrate the spatial component of Structural Funds into areas containing 35–40% of Europe's population rather than the current 51% (CEC, 1997b). Moreover, it is increasingly felt that the complex arrangement of Structural Fund programmes needs to be simplified. Instead of the current seven objectives, four of which are spatially targeted (Objectives 1, 2, 5b and 6), and 13 different Community Initiatives, it is proposed that in the future there should be only three key objectives and three Community Initiatives. The Objective 1 areas would continue to be the main focus for targeted resources, but there would be a strict adherence to the requirement that the eligible areas must have a GDP that was less than 75% of the EU average. Under such criteria therefore the Highlands and Islands Objective 1 status would be expected to disappear. The new Objective 2 programme would become a general 'catch all' for every other spatially targeted measure. It would deal with declining areas, areas facing major urban restructuring, areas with high unemployment or suffering depopulation and would encompass the former Objective 5b or rural designations. Furthermore, many of the other Community Initiatives designed to address particular problems (URBAN, RECHAR, RENAVAL, etc.) would be incorporated within this new Objective 2 programme. The Objective 3 programme would be a horizontal measure designed to improve human resources and would support programmes dealing with such issues as retraining to accompany economic and social changes, lifelong learning and training, active labour market policies to fight unemployment and programmes to combat social exclusion. It is not intended that this programme would be spatially targeted, but would deal with some of the more widespread issues associated with economic restructuring. Within the Community Initiatives, the principles of simplification and concentration have led to only three programmes being proposed. Again two have a spatial dimension, INTERREG, the cross-border transnational programme, will be retained, as will LEADER, specifically designed to help diversify the rural economy, and a new initiative designed to promote equal opportunities is proposed.

From a rural perspective, these reforms of the Structural Funds cannot be seen in isolation from the proposed reforms of agriculture support. It is expected that the CAP reforms of 1992 will continue, with a further move away from price support mechanisms, particularly in relation to cereals, oilseed rape, beef and dairy cattle. These changes result from a complex interplay of factors including the GATT negotiations, intended to liberalise global agricultural markets and reduce public policy expenditure, a desire to reduce the proportion of the EU budget devoted to agriculture, which is allied with an increasing public desire to see a closer association between environmental and agricultural policy (Ilbery and Bowler, 1998). How these reforms will manifest themselves is open to debate. But is important to recognise the importance of this subsidy to the rural economy. The East Midlands region, for example, received £453 million of subsidy through CAP in 1996 (Enterprise PLC, 1998). To date, the much heralded McSharry reforms have, in practice, been largely cosmetic, with price support mechanisms or compensation payments still accounting for the vast majority of agricultural support (Potter, 1998). To offset declining farm incomes from production subsidies it is proposed to enhance a variety of agro-environmental schemes, perhaps with a geography dimension to reflect the different types of agricultural economies in rural areas and the specific problems they face (Fischler, 1998).

At the same time there are changes taking place at the national level in relation to both the institutional framework and funding for rural policy. First, the new Labour government has set in motion legislation to create regional development agencies (RDAs) throughout England. Shadow agencies should be established during 1998 and they are expected to be fully operational by 1999. The idea is to bring a fresh approach to regional development based on the notions that: power should be decentralised from Whitehall; regional structures should be based on partnerships; regional issues are diverse and need to be addressed in an integrated and co-ordinated manner; and there is a need for regional vision and leadership (DETR, 1997c).

It is emphasised that the new RDA's should have a strong rural perspective, but it is recognised that the priority and emphasis given to rural issues are likely to vary from one region to another. Hence, for example, it has been acknowledged that through the consultation process the geographical characteristics of the South West RDA are likely to lead to a strong focus on rural issues and sustainable development (DETR, 1997c). However, this rural dimension to policy may be less evident elsewhere.

As well as institutional reform the government also proposes to revise and simplify regeneration policies and programmes. Regeneration is now seen as a comprehensive package of measures designed to address social, environmental and economic problems in an integrated and robust manner. This idea was embodied in the Single Regeneration Budget (SRB) of the previous Conservative government. To date some 500 schemes across the country are being supported under the first three years of the SRB Challenge Fund (DETR, 1998c). A fourth round was announced in July 1997 and the results of this competition are due in the spring of 1998. As the residual programmes such as the Urban Development Corporations and City Challenge wind down, more resources appear to be drawn into the SRB Challenge Fund. In setting its own policy stamp, the government's consultation paper *Regeneration Programmes: The Way Forward*, and the supplementary guidance to the fourth round of SRB Challenge Fund both seek to place greater emphasis on areas of need and opportunity, and promote a more strategic approach to the bidding process (DETR, 1998c). In this respect it is likely that there will be greater scrutiny of the ways in which proposals contribute to regional and local regeneration strategies and calls for greater collaboration between government offices in the regions and the bidders themselves. The question is the extent to which rural areas are able to develop effective and coherent strategies to enable them to compete.

It is clear therefore that at the level of European and national government considerable change is taking place. The real question is what are the implications of such policy shifts for the rural economy? Predicting the future is analogous to a young child doing a jigsaw for the first time. It is not certain if all the pieces are there and whether the pieces are likely to be put together in the wrong order. However, for many there are real concerns that rural areas will lose out. This centres on the fact that rural deprivation, while being highly significant, is dispersed throughout the rural areas and indicators of need are likely to portray rural areas in a relatively good light in comparison with the undoubted pockets of need within the urban context. Furthermore, the way that national policy shifts are possibly just as important in helping to determine the availability of European funding during the early years of the new millennium. Suffice to say, echoes of the early 1970s, 1980s and 1990s, where rural deprivation was perceived as a hidden and ignored problem, are once again resurfacing, as a potential urban focus to policy reasserts itself.

From a European perspective, the reforms of production subsidies have, to date, amounted to little more that rhetoric. While such proposals are still being pushed strongly by the Commission, the extent to which powerful political lobbies within the member states will dilute such proposals is still open to debate (Gilg, 1996; Potter, 1998). Nevertheless some reforms seem inevitable with CAP beginning to revert to one of its origins of supporting vulnerable rural populations through various agro-environmental measures, some of which may be geographically specific (Fischler, 1998). From a broader rural diversification perspective the European picture is still more confused. Simplification and concentration of regenerative initiatives, whether urban or rural, into a 'catch all' Objective 2 programme have led to the fear that the rural dimension of policy might be subsumed by an urban agenda, particularly given the powerful lobbying at the European level on behalf of metropolitan authorities. Furthermore, the eligibility criteria for EU Objective 2 funding is still subject to much debate. Fothergill (1997) identifies two key areas for negotiation. First, while the eligibility criteria themselves still have to be finalised and there may be scope for separate criteria for industrial, rural and urban areas, unemployment levels seem critical in the standardised approach the Commission wishes to adopt across the EU. Because, in the UK, there has been a long-standing policy for the long-term unemployed to be directed towards sickness rather than unemployment benefits they have effectively been lost from the UK's unemployment count. If such flawed data are used, Fothergill (1997) argues that a disproportionate number of the 35–40 million people across Europe currently living in areas eligible for structured funds, and likely to lose out through these reforms, are inevitably going to be concentrated in the UK. Furthermore, with rural areas generally recording lower unemployment rates than the national average, then the fate of Objective 5b areas hangs precariously in the balance. Second, and perhaps more seriously from a rural perspective, is the extent to which national governments will have a role in drawing up the eligibility maps for their own countries. Fothergill (1997) suggests that through this process we might be witnessing the renationalisation of European regional policy. Whatever the outcome, it seems more likely that action by national governments themselves, in the field of regional policy, will have a significant impact on the areas eligible for EU Structural Fund support. The Commission has called for greater coherence between EU and national regional development funding regimes (CEC, 1997b). In this case coherence means that any region enjoying Structural Funds after 1999 must also be eligible for national state support, with a clear regional development purpose. Once again ideas of greater concentration and synergy between funding sources are being promoted with the corollary that resources should not be spread too thinly over large areas in a fragmented manner.

It is within this context that proposals for reforming the institutional and funding regimes in England have greater resonance. As part of the promotion of a regional dimension to policy-making there would be a rationalisation of institutions responsible for regeneration activities. Most notable among these will be the RDC. The staff are expected to be subsumed within the new RDAs, but in many parts of England it seems likely that an urban perspective or agenda will predominate. So angry was the President of the RDC at this proposal that he resigned. What will happen to the funding and the policy frameworks established by the RDC to focus its regenerative work is still debatable. As we have seen, the Rural Development Areas which are the focus of RDC activities were redefined in 1994 and were intended with perhaps some minor modifications to remain until well into the next century. The delivery mechanism, the Rural Development Programme, with its emphasis on partnership and consensus, has been acknowledged a useful implementation tool and the new RDAs will be expected to develop similar programmes targeted at their most deprived rural areas (DETR, 1997c). Whether this equates to retaining the existing rural development areas and the level of support available is still unclear, but any further concentration of resources will limit the extent to which rural areas may be able to benefit from any revisions to the Structural Funds outlined above.

The proposals to target regeneration money through the SRB Challenge Fund still further into those areas of greatest need are even more worrying for rural areas, especially, as if seems likely, there is closer coherence between EU and national regional funding programmes (DETR, 1998c). Using the DETR's index of local conditions (ILC) even those rural authorities with particular problems, Penworth and Kerrier in Cornwall, Copeland in Cumbria and Fenland in Lincolnshire, fall outside the 100 worst local authorities in England, and even here deprivation is concentrated in particular wards. Using national indices disadvantages rural areas in a number of ways. Often the indices are urban biased. Thus, for example, car ownership which might be seen as a surrogate for low income in an urban context is often an unaffordable necessity with a rural context. Furthermore, the nature of deprivation in rural areas is by its very nature dispersed, often within a community dominated by inward migrant affluence. Thus because of both the scale of analysis and the nature of the indicators used there is a possibility that rural areas might lose out.

Together these policy shifts suggest that there is a need for special pleading for rural areas. What might happen is that concentration and simplification of policy at both the European and national levels of governance may lead to the further watering down of an already weak rural policy framework. While special pleading may produce a residual rural regeneration strategy it is clear that a coherent, co-ordinated and integrated strategic approach is going to be a necessary prerequisite to lever resources out of regional, central or pan-European governance. Within Rutland County District Council such threats have a degree of resonance, and in conjunction with their local neighbours they are attempting to ensure that a coherent rural strategy remains. Their activities provide a good example of the way other rural authorities might need to develop rural strategies and alliances to counteract the threat of a more urban-orientated policy approach.

A NEW RURAL STRATEGY FOR THE EAST MIDLANDS

On 1 April 1997, Rutland County District Council, as it is known for legal purposes, was formally established as a new and uniquely rural unitary authority. It has a total population of only 34 000, which is concentrated in the two market towns of Oakham, population 9000, and Uppingham, population 3000, and some 50 small villages. Despite giving the outward signs of affluence, house prices are among the most expensive in England, and there is immigration to the area.

Rutland faces many of the classic issues facing rural areas, access to affordable housing, services and a range of well-paid and sustainable jobs. Yet because of its small size and apparent well-being the authority faces the challenge of how to ensure its rural agenda is heard and articulated. This involves taking action at a local level as well as playing an active role as partner in the wider regional debates while thinking strategically about the future rural agenda. The objective is not to guarantee access to funding sources, whether that be from Europe, national or regional sources, but that there is a coherent and consistent framework which provides a means of relating Rutland's own objectives to a wider policy debate and provides a springboard for generating bids. The evolution and development of Rutland's strategy provide some useful pointers for other rural authorities.

The creation of Rutland as a unitary authority was in some ways more frantic than elsewhere. Final agreement that Rutland's autonomy should be increased was not reached until February 1996, leaving less than 15 months before the new unitary authority came into existence. The main arguments in favour of Rutland being granted unitary status were that, it was popular at the local level among the citizens, and it could demonstrate an ability to deliver its statutory services effectively and efficiently through an enabling model. This was set out in a document *Blueprint for Success* (Rutland District Council, 1996) which described how the new authority would deliver its services. The enabling model involved the continued expansion of service purchase from other authorities. Housing revenue and contract work had been contracted out several years ago and social services, education, highways and some of the new authority's planning functions were bought mainly from Leicestershire County Council (Rutland District Council, 1996). However, inevitably during the preparation for unitary status much effort was spent ensuring that the appropriate internal structures, mechanisms and procedures were in place so that the council could be fully operational from 1 April 1997.

Once this had been achieved, more effort and emphasis are now being placed on involving the community in decision-making and delivering their identified priorities. The starting point was to identify the priorities of the people through a MORI survey of some 820 residents and a series of eight community fora, some subject based (e.g. economics, social, education, environmental and youth issues) and some geographically orientated (e.g. Oakham town centre, Uppington town centre and the parishes). This then has provided a thorough understanding of the communities' priorities and preferences, which is intended to contribute to a business plan. This is seen as being an important strategy document that will enable bids for funding to be made. It will, for example, show how Rutland's objectives meet regional, national and European priorities. While this business plan still has to be written, the information gathered is already aiding local decision-making, for example in the field of transportation. The MORI survey and discussion groups unsurprisingly highlighted access and the availability of public transport as a key area of concern. Rutland has already taken steps to improve provision in accordance with community wishes. They have begun to re-engineer bus routes, altering both the routes and the timetables following consultation with parish councils. Early evidence suggests that at least in the short term the income generated by this new 'Rutland Flier' has gone up dramatically (Morphet, 1998). Travel passes for the elderly have been switched from Leicestershire County Council passes to national ones. This was particularly important for those in the east of the county who would more naturally travel to the local market towns of Northamptonshire or Lincolnshire. Finally all the authority's transport expenditure whether for education, social services, bus passes or transport subsidies has all been pulled together to ensure greater co-ordination and integration of effort. These are laudable efforts to improve the delivery of local services, but the important point to note is that the authority is preparing a coherent strategy which is wide-ranging in its scope and content, and is intended to ensure that Rutland is able at least to compete for access to resources. By its very nature, Rutland's policies are inevitably rural, though there are social and economic issues such as social exclusions, enhancing business competitiveness, improving the communications for people and goods and of information, and sustainable development that all have more universal applicability. The challenge for Rutland and other rural authorities is how to maintain or enhance a rural dimension to policy. Rutland, as a small authority, is a small voice which needs to work together with others to ensure that there is strong, rather than residual, rural agenda.

This partnership approach is operating at a number of levels. At the regional level there is the East Midlands Rural Forum which was established in 1995, in response to the rural White Paper. This body in conjunction with others is developing a 'Rural Strategy and Action Plan' which is designed to 'ensure that the proposed RDA has a rural voice and recognises the priorities of the East Midlands Rural Strategy in programme funding and the promotion of local forms of governance' (Enterprise PLC, 1998: 3). At the moment this new partnership is little more than a lobbying organisation designed to ensure that the East Midlands has a coherent rural voice. One of its key objectives is to ensure that there is a single 'corporate rural budget' (Enterprise PLC, 1998). At the moment in the face of much uncertainty and repositioning the Rural Forum is at least providing a voice for rural issues in the East Midlands. This in part may be interpreted as a defensive response to perceived threats, but not only does this partnership want to act as a strategic forum which facilitates and ensures a strong and commonly held position is taken forward to the regional level but also there appears to be strong support for the partnership to evolve into a 'doing agency' which speaks for and 'delivers on behalf' of their respective organisations, perhaps as a subregional 'Economic Development Agency' (Enterprise PLC, 1998).

At the same time the region and the local authorities are taking every opportunity to lobby with national and European policy-makers to ensure a rural voice continues to be heard. In addition many of the local authorities surrounding Rutland are working together to develop a subregional rural agenda. Already they work together on a joint marketing campaign to promote tourism, but within a rapidly emerging regional agenda there is a general perception that there is a need to think more coherently about what they want and ensure that their voice is heard. Thus a 'best value network' has been established to exchange information, share ideas and possibly collaborate with bidding for resources. Initially established as a group of local government officers, with political support, it is further evidence of an attempt to promote a rural agenda.

It is clear from the brief review of what is happening in the East Midlands that there is a clear appreciation of the threats to rural policy from the current reorganisation of institutions and programmes. The response has been to try and establish a partnership of organisations to promote the rural dimension of policy at the rural area and at the same time developing broad-based strategies for promoting the social economic well-being of the area. This goes beyond land use into a wider community-based approach, perhaps even integrated into the Local Agenda 21 (LA21) process.

WHITHER RURAL PLANNING?

So is there a future for rural policy? It is paradoxical, and in many ways ironic that, at a time when rural issues are so prominent in the minds of the public, there might be so much which potentially undermines rural policy. The issues are likely to remain the same, associated with economic restructuring, access to jobs, services and housing, conservation or preservation versus development, how to maintain or enhance countryside character while improving access. The way of doing things is likely to very different. This would appear to be the main challenge facing officers and members from rural authorities. What is clear is that the institutional and policy framework, which has never really been stable, is undoubtedly in a period of very rapid flux. This is not just happening in rural areas, but more widely throughout all levels of governance. Nevertheless in focusing on rural policy it seems clear that local authorities will have an important function in developing appropriate strategies which will need to focus on facilitating and enabling the delivery of appropriate services to local people. This will require the development of more holistic and integrated strategies, often in partnership with neighbouring local authorities. As a more coherent regional dimension to policy emerges this partnership will be particularly important to ensure that policies in rural areas address and tackle problems particular to localities. What will all this mean for rural planning in the new millennium? If the challenges are taken up now it may lead to a co-ordinated and integrated approach to rural planning where policies and programmes are designed to address particular locally determined problems.

CHAPTER 5

URBAN CRISIS: NEW POLICIES FOR THE NEXT CENTURY

Rob Atkinson

INTRODUCTION

During the 1980s Britain's cities were the laboratory for an experiment which prioritised the role of the private sector as the motor force for change and renewal. By the end of the decade serious questions were being posed about the market in general and its capacity to regenerate urban areas in a manner which did not increase social polarisation and inequality. At this point the Conservative government began to rethink some of its own conventional wisdom on urban policy. The outcome, north and south of the border, was urban regeneration based on a strategic approach with integrated, multi-sectoral partnerships allocated a central role.

This chapter will review the developments which led up to these new initiatives, discuss the initiatives and the role of partnerships before considering what, if any, effects the new Labour government will have on urban regeneration policy as we move into the new century. More specifically, it will examine the extent to which a genuinely strategic approach has been adopted or is likely to be developed in the future, the role of local government and the community in urban regeneration and the resources available to urban policy.

URBAN POLICY IN THE 1980s

This section will provide an overview of urban policy in the 1980s and the criticisms directed at policy and its outcomes. The section will function as a backcloth to the emergence of new policies in the 1990s and indicate the issues which the new initiatives would attempt to tackle. One point should be made at the outset; urban issues never figured significantly on the policy agenda during the Thatcher years and it is quite likely that had there not been persistent outbreaks of 'urban unrest' they would have fallen off the agenda altogether. More specifically, urban policy abandoned any concern with issues of social justice, poverty and inequality, indeed the generation of inequality was seen as a necessary stimulus to regeneration while poverty and social justice were simply defined out of existence.

The basic assumption underlying 1980s urban policy was that the problems to be found in Britain's cities were the result of too much state intervention and bureaucratic planning systems which had discouraged private investment and caused the private sector to disinvest in urban areas. At the same time there was a tacit assumption that urban problems were residual, the result of not allowing the market to operate freely and the presence of populations who had become dependent on the welfare state. The solution was to allow markets to work and the benefits would eventually 'trickle down' to those at the bottom of the pile (for overviews see Deakin and Edwards, 1993; Atkinson and Moon, 1994a).

Despite this generalised faith in the market it took several years before a clear 'policy' emerged; initially the emphasis was on localised and spatially defined market-based experiments perhaps best expressed in urban development corporations (UDCs) and enterprise zones (EZs). In both UDCs and EZs the emphasis was on limited deregulation and the creation of an environment in which the private sector could flourish. Initially EZs were more prominent, but by 1987 the emphasis switched to UDCs, which were viewed by the Thatcher government as the 'jewels in the crown' of urban policy. This new emphasis derived from the apparent success of one of the first UDCs (London Docklands Development Corporation (LDDC)), established in 1981, in regenerating a run-down area close to central London. As a result other UDCs were created between 1987 and 1992 (see Imrie and Thomas, 1993b for overviews).

The apparent success of LDDC seemed to point the way forward; the private sector could not only act as the motor of economic growth in cities but also provide the leadership which local government had failed to give, thus breaking the spiral of decline that had developed in many parts of Britain's cities. LDDC's success was largely based around the efforts of property speculators who were primarily concerned with the physical renewal of areas by the erection of large-scale office complexes, retail outlets and dwellings for the upper end of the owner-occupied sector. The belief was that relatively small amounts of public sector funds could be used to lever in large amounts of private sector investment, as a result gearing ratios became the principal criteria for assessing the effectiveness of urban regeneration. This approach was reproduced within many cities as the British economy began to boom in the second half of the 1980s and became known as the property-led approach (see Turok, 1993; Imrie and Thomas, 1993b, for overviews). In policy terms this approach reached its zenith in the 1988 document *Action for Cities* (1988) which extolled the virtues of private initiative and failed to even mention the role of local authorities. However, this key role for the property development sector was not the product of any deliberative reflection on the part of government, it simply resulted from a series of largely uncoordinated circumstances created by changes in the financial markets and the availability of large quantities of speculative capital searching for investment opportunities in the booming British economy in the second half of the 1980s.

It is perhaps one of the great ironies of 1980s urban policy that within 18 months of UDCs being defined as pivotal to regeneration the very conditions which laid the basis for their success began to crumble as the British economy entered into a major downturn in 1989/90 and the property development sector was decimated. Within the space of a few years the policy that had 'emerged by accident' was in tatters. In this uncertain climate the criticisms that such an approach to urban regeneration was ephemeral, largely bypassed those in need and accentuated social polarisation began to be heeded. These criticisms were given added weight when the Audit Commission (1989) and National Audit Office (1990) criticised urban policy as both incoherent and lacking direction. Thus by the end of the 1980s the stage was set for the emergence of new initiatives to tackle the problems of Britain's cities.

INTO THE 1990s – A NEW ROLE FOR LOCAL GOVERNMENT AND THE COMMUNITY?

As we have seen, by the late 1980s the tide had begun to turn against property-led urban regeneration and a gradual recognition was beginning to emerge that local government and communities affected by regeneration had a role to play. This section will focus on the initiatives that emerged during the 1990s and the idea central to them – i.e. a strategic, integrated partnership between public, private, voluntary and community sectors. The most notably examples are City Challenge, SRB and the Scottish partnerships.

CITY CHALLENGE

The notion of partnership[1] has become increasingly central to urban policy in the 1990s and seems likely to be the cornerstone of policy in the first decade of the twenty-first century; City Challenge is one of the first examples of this approach (for overviews of City Challenge see Atkinson and Moon, 1994b; De Groot, 1992; Oatley, 1995; Russell *et al.*, 1996). City Challenge appears to represent the reappearance of Victorian ideas of self-help and paternalism combined with internal market notions of competition and a belief in the superiority of private sector management methods. In this latter sense it was very much in tune with wider changes in the structure and management of British government that had been taken during the 1980s (see Atkinson and Cope, 1994). These views were clearly summarised by Heseltine (1991: 9) in a speech announcing the City Challenge initiative:

> . . . when I speak of the need for a sense of partnership in our modern cities, it is today's equivalent of that Victorian sense of competitive drive linked with social

obligation. Success and responsibility go hand in hand today just as surely as they did a hundred years ago. . . . Men and women will compete with one another and give of their best. People will set the pace and exercise their discretion. And by enriching themselves, their lives and their communities, they enrich society as a whole.

City Challenge's aims and the criteria bids were required to meet (see DoE, 1992c: 2–3) were ambitious and wide-ranging, above all stressing the importance of adopting a strategic approach to an area. According to the *Bidding Guidance* (DoE, 1992c: 2), areas chosen for City Challenge may:

- Offer substantial economic opportunities
- Be significantly deprived or
- Be a combination of the two

On the one hand the *Guidance* stressed aims typical of 1980s initiatives such as the need to attract additional inward investment, adding value to existing public and private investment, stimulating wealth creation and an enterprise culture. But there was also reference to widening social provision, ensuring that those who lived in the selected area were among the beneficiaries of regeneration and improving the quality of life in targeted areas. In addition the idea of a multi-sectoral, integrated partnership, including the local community, was given a central role in the development and delivery of the strategy. The clear intention was '. . . to develop the capacity within the areas selected for self-sustaining regeneration and self-help which will continue after the period of funding' (DoE, 1992c: 2).

Initially only 15 of the 57 Urban Programme Authorities (UPAs) were invited to bid for funding, but, as result of protests from excluded authorities, an additional six were added. In the first round 11 of the 21 authorities were successful, each receiving £7.5 million per year for five years. In total the 11 authorities received £412.5 million over the five years; however, this money was seen as a way of levering in additional public and private sector monies. A second round began in early 1992 and 54 of the 57 UPAs took part, each bidding for a share of £750 million over a five-year period; once again each successful authority received £7.5 million per annum over the five years. There were 20 winners, taking the total of beneficiaries over the two rounds to 31 (see Table 1) and involving £1165.5 million.

While the sums involved were not insignificant they hardly represented a major input of resources, and the projects were heavily dependent upon the 'levering-in' of additional funds from other public and private sources. Indeed, winning authorities were expected to 'bend' their own programmes to benefit the selected areas, thereby removing resources from other equally, if not more, deprived areas. In addition the City Challenge was funded by top-slicing seven other DoE national inner-city and housing programmes (DoE, 1992c: 9) thereby depriving some

Table 1   *City Challenge winners by round and deprivation ranking*

Authority	Deprivation ranking	Successful round
Hackney	(1)	2
Newham	(2)	2
Tower Hamlets	(3)	1
Lambeth	(4)	2
Brent	(8)	2
Manchester	(11)	1
Leicester	(12)	2
Wolverhampton	(13)	1
Lewisham	(16)	1
Birmingham	(14)	2
Liverpool	(14)	1
Kensington and Chelsea	(17)	2
Sandwell	(19)	2
Nottingham	(20)	1
Blackburn	(21)	2
Middlesbrough	(23)	1
Bradford	(26)	1
Kirklees	(31)	2
Walsall	(34)	2
Hartlepool	(35)	2
Bolton	(36)	2
Newcastle	(37)	1
Sunderland	(38)	2
Derby	(41)	2
Stockton	(46)	2
Wirral	(48)	1
Sefton	(50)	2
Wigan	(53)	2
North Tyneside	(54)	2
Barnsley	(55)	2
Dearne Valley	(*)	1

* = indicates a joint bid by three UP authorities – Rotherham, Barnsley and Doncaster. (Source: Atkinson and Moon, 1994b.)

authorities of Urban Programme funds they would otherwise have received. Moreover, City Challenge did little to make up for wider cuts in local authority finance; for instance Jeremy Beecham, leader of a council which made a successful bid, estimated that his local authority would lose £200 million from central cuts in other programmes over the five-year life of City Challenge (Beecham, 1993).

Perhaps one of the most surprising aspects of City Challenge was the explicit statement by government that partnerships were to be led by local authorities, although it was made very clear that the private, voluntary and community sectors should be closely integrated into the process. In some ways City Challenge appears to represent the rehabilitation of local authorities after the prolonged and bruising conflicts between central and local government during the 1980s. On the other hand it may also be seen as a recognition by the centre that it had largely 'won' these battles and that it no longer needed to engage in a highly interventionist strategy. Local authorities, in terms of rhetoric if not in reality, had become more in tune with the ethos of the Conservative government and could be largely trusted to run projects such as City Challenge without a great deal of direct oversight. Simply by setting the rules of the game, to which bidders had to conform, and by utilising a series of key output indicators which would structure the development of projects and to which partnerships could be held to account, the centre could exercise control at a distance. City Challenge should also be seen in terms of the ongoing attempt to restructure local governance in the direction of the facilitate or enabling state (Ridley, 1987; Brooke, 1989). Russell *et al.* (1996: 41) make this point well when they note City Challenge '. . . aimed to change the way in which different interests in cities related to each other. It was concerned not only with *what* was done but *how* it was done.'

Another innovative element in City Challenge was its apparent willingness to allow the local partnerships to select which area they would focus on and the nature of the projects developed. As the DoE's *Guidance* notes stated (1992c: 5):

> The mix of objectives will depend on the area selected. However they should tackle the problems which are perceived by the residents of the area and by potential investors as being crucial to its regeneration.

The selection of area was crucial and it would appear that DoE regional officers gave '. . . a clear steer to local authorities about the kinds of areas they should be targeting for the bid. Some councillors felt the decision had been imposed on them' (Russell *et al.*, 1996: 12). There was thus a clear tension between whether to select areas on the basis of need or on the basis of (economic) development potential, and while a compromise frequently emerged the freedom to select areas was clearly circumscribed by the centre. There was also some concern that all winners received exactly the same funds regardless of the problems faced.

Other aspects of City Challenge which attracted some criticism were the bidding process (see Oatley, 1995) and the level of community participation. Firstly, many authorities felt that the bidding timetable was too tight and did not allow for proper consultation with other partners, particularly the community, thereby potentially undermining one of the central mechanisms of the programme. Secondly, many bidders questioned the use of competitive bidding as a means of allocating scarce resources. Questions were raised regarding the openness of the bidding process and the clarity of the bidding criteria. Others saw it as little more than a 'beauty contest' inappropriate for dealing with deep-rooted problems (Beecham, 1993). Thirdly, there was considerable criticism that City Challenge failed to actively engage the community. Many critics felt it failed to provide either the time or resources necessary to build the community capacity essential for deprived communities to participate as equal partners (see MacFarlane and Mabbott, 1993; MacFarlane, 1993). We will return to these points later in the chapter when considering SRB and the system developed in Scotland.

City Challenge can in one sense be seen as yet another in the long line of urban experiments going back to the late 1960s (see Atkinson and Moon, 1994a). At the same time it also represented an attempt to respond to criticisms that urban policy was lacking in focus, was uncoordinated and ignored disadvantaged areas and people (for a generally positive assessment see Russell *et al.*, 1996). However, at the time of its launch City Challenge still remained one, not particularly generously funded, urban initiative among many. By 1993 government had decided to initiate a major review of urban policy and not to have a third round of City Challenge; this review was to be perhaps the most significant event in urban policy since the 1977 White Paper *Policy for the Inner Cities* – the outcome was the Single Regeneration Budget (SRB).

THE SINGLE REGENERATION BUDGET

In 1993 the DoE received the results of a wide-ranging report on urban policy – *Assessing the Impact of Urban Policy* (Robson *et al.*, 1994) – which was then 'sat upon' for almost 18 months before being published. The report confirmed many earlier criticisms of urban policy and raised doubts over the appropriateness of this policy. Its main conclusions questioned: (1) the overall coherence, both in policy and organisational terms, of the large numbers of urban initiatives which existed; (2) the overemphasis on the private sector; (3) the marginalisation of local government; (4) the failure to direct the benefits of regeneration to communities and individuals that had suffered the worst effects of urban decline; (5) the lack of participation in, and accountability of, regeneration schemes to local people (Robson *et al.*, 1994)[2]. The outcome of the DoE's review brought together 20 programmes from five central government departments (see Table 2) under the overall control of the DoE to ensure greater organisational co-ordination between departments with programmes that had implications for urban areas. At the same time a cabinet committee known as EDR (or Economic Development and Regeneration) was set up to ensure greater co-ordination at central level and to decide on the allocation of funds (this role was later taken on by the cabinet's Economic Competitiveness Committee).

This central restructuring was complemented in each of the 10 English regions by the creation of integrated regional offices, later renamed government offices for the regions (GORs). Each GOR is composed of the regional offices of the DTI, Department of Employment (subsequently amalgamated with the Department for Education), DoE and DoT plus a senior representative from the Home Office, while contacts with other departments that lack a regional office were also established.

Table 2 *Programmes contributing to the Single Regeneration Budget*

Department of the Environment	*Employment Department*
Estate Action	Business Start-up Scheme
Housing Actions Trusts	Teacher Placement Schemes
City Challenge	Compacts
UDCs	Education Business
Inner City Task Forces	Partnerships
City Action Teams	TEC Challenge
	Local Initiative Fund
Home Office	Programme Development Fund
Safer Cities	
Section 11 Grants (part)	*DTI*
Ethnic Minority Grant/	Regional Enterprise Grants
Ethnic Minority Business	
Initiative	*Department for Education*
	Grants for Education Support
	and Training (GEST) (part)

Source: DoE, 1994a.

In addition each GOR established contacts with local authorities, chambers of commerce, TECs, etc., in its region. A single regional director oversees the operation of each GOR, the director's role being to ensure that the individual programmes of the departments comprising each GOR do not operate along narrow departmental lines but take into account local needs and interests. Originally it was intended that each GOR should produce a regional regeneration strategy; however, this idea was subsequently dropped.

The SRB acknowledged the need for greater clarity of thought regarding the regeneration process; like City Challenge its objectives explicitly stated that local people should benefit from regeneration. *Bidding Guidance* (DoE, 1993a: 5) stated that bids would be expected to meet one or more of the following objectives:

- Enhance the employment prospects, education and skills of local people, particularly the young and those at a disadvantage, and promote equality of opportunity
- Encourage sustainable economic growth and wealth creation by improving the competitiveness of the local economy, including business support
- Improve housing through physical improvements, greater choice and better management and maintenance
- Promote initiatives of benefit to ethnic minorities
- Tackle crime and improve community safety
- Protect and improve the environment and infrastructure and promote good design
- Enhance the quality of life of local people, including their health and cultural and sports activities

The intention was that resources gained through SRB be used in a strategic manner, either as part of a wider strategy or targeted on a particular local area, thereby moving away from the previous situation where a multiplicity of unrelated schemes operated within a locality. By taking a strategic approach, achieving greater coherence of spend and integrating a range of players into the regeneration process it was hoped that much more could be achieved with the same (or less) resources (i.e. synergy).

SRB came into existence on 1 April 1994, although there was no allocation of funds through the competitive bidding mechanism in the first year. The SRB Challenge Fund came into being on 1 April 1995 with partnerships developing and presenting their bids during the second half of 1994 (for detailed discussions of SRB in the first two rounds see Mawson *et al.*, 1995; Hall *et al.*, 1996). This points to what for many was, and continues to be, a serious limitation on SRB. In the first year (1994/95) of its operation all SRB funds were committed to ongoing programmes (e.g. UDCs, the Urban Programme, Estate Action, City Challenge, section 11 grants, etc.), it was only in 1995/96 (Round 1) that £125 million, out of a total budget of £1.4 billion, was made available with £225 million per annum being made available to round 1 winners in 1996/97 and 1997/98. In 1996/97 round 2 bidders had only £40 million available with £200 million in 1997/98. According to the House of Commons Environment Committee (HoC, 1995b: 2) over the period 1995/96–1997/98 £800 out of an SRB total of £4 billion was competitively allocated to new schemes. In total some 370 schemes were funded in rounds 1 and 2 with a further 182 schemes being approved for round 3, beginning in April 1997. Additional resources for the Challenge Fund element of SRB only become available as other programmes wind down and terminate. In theory these funds should then be moved into the Challenge Fund and the latter will take up an increasing proportion of total SRB expenditure. However, there is no guarantee that as existing programmes terminate their funds will be transferred, given that public expenditure operates on a three-year cycle (e.g. 1995/96–1997/98) and all new allocations have to be negotiated with the Treasury.

According to the DoE's own expenditure plans (DoE, 1997c, Figure 4a: 52) the Challenge Fund element will increase from zero in 1994/95 to a planned total of £625.5 million in 1999/2000, but over the same period total SRB expenditure is planned to decline from £1.458 billion to just over £1 billion, a drop of almost £450 million (or just over 32%). This would seem to confirm that SRB involves a reduction in the resources available to urban regeneration (see Nevin and Shiner, 1994, 1995). These figures were prepared by the 1992–97 Conservative government which clearly assumed that other funds from within the public sector (including the European Structural Funds) and the private sector (including the Private Finance Initiative (PFI)) would make up for any reductions. However, this seems extremely unlikely given the PFI's lack of success to date and the estimate that mainline programmes relevant to regeneration will be cut by around £6 billion over the period 1993/94–1997/98 (Mawson *et al.*, 1995: 32). Thus SRB, while entailing significant reduction in regeneration funds, is part of a wider process of cuts in public sector resources relevant to urban regeneration.

There are two other crucial elements of SRB which have already been mentioned – competitive bidding and partnerships, both of which are also central to City Challenge. The following discussion will therefore refer to the experience of both City Challenge and SRB. I will deal with competitive bidding first, although the two are clearly related.

While City Challenge restricted bidding to the 57 UPAs, SRB allowed all areas in England to bid for funds. At one level this clearly made sense as it has long been recognised that urban deprivation is not confined to UPAs and that other urban and rural areas also contain deprivation, albeit often less concentrated and more widely dispersed than in UPAs. The first two rounds of SRB (for a more detailed analysis see Mawson *et al.*, 1995: ch. 6; Hall *et al.*, 1996: ch. 5) appeared to move funds away from the larger cities with the worst levels of deprivation; unfortunately these were precisely the cities *Assessing the Impact of Urban Policy* (Robson *et al.*, 1994) had identified as doing least well in terms of regeneration under previous urban regimes. Moreover, there was a clear relationship between the chance of a bid being successful and regional location, and this was determined by the amount each region was allocated.[3] In other words bids in different regions, even if they were of the same 'quality', did not have the same chance of success. Within regions GORs played a key role in the bidding process, it was they who bidders turned to for advice and guidance and thus they who could steer bids in certain directions. In the absence of a regional regeneration statement bidders were forced to engage in a process of 'second guessing' what their GOR wanted and of interpreting feedback from GORs. The position of GORs is also somewhat ambiguous in that they partner regeneration within their region while at the same time acting as the centre's representative and judging bids (see Hogwood, 1995).

It should therefore come as no surprise to find that there has been considerable criticism of the bidding process (see HoC, 1995a, b; Mawson *et al.*, 1995: ch. 4; Hall *et al.*, 1996: ch. 3). In particular bidders perceived the process as one without clear rules, over-bureaucratic and generally lacking in transparency. It is perhaps best to describe the process for the allocation of funds as 'managed competition'. This 'managed competition' takes place within the 'rules of the game' whereby bidders have to meet certain basic conditions regarding what they bid for (e.g. there is a tacit recognition that schemes should contain a strong emphasis on economic growth/wealth creation and employment/education[4] and the organisational form for developing bids and delivering them.

Bidders for funds are expected to be partnerships between public sector bodies (e.g. local authorities, TECs), the private sector, voluntary bodies and local communities. In SRB, unlike City Challenge, local authorities are not allocated an automatic lead role. In theory organisations from any sector can take the lead role, although in practice local authorities have led the majority of partnerships, with TECs coming in a rather distant second. Very few bids have been led by the private sector and even fewer by the voluntary or community sectors. It is the partnership which prepares and submits the bid and is then responsible for delivering the scheme. As already noted, the integration of all the partners into a coherent organisational form is regarded as crucial to SRB's success.

The House of Commons Environment Committee (HoC, 1995a, b) highlighted the problems of private, community and voluntary participation, problems which were acknowledged by the government in its response to the Committee's report (see Cmnd 3178, 1996: 6–9). Indeed in later versions of the SRB *Bidding Guidance* the term 'real participation' is used with reference to the community and voluntary sectors' involvement in partnerships. However, there are a number of 'structural' problems relating to community and voluntary sector participation. One problem has been the speed at which bids are prepared; sufficient time is not allowed for anything other than superficial forms of consultation and in some cases not even that. Even where well-organised voluntary and community organisations exist the agenda appears to have been largely set by the lead bidder, usually local government, TECs and to a lesser extent the private sector. Furthermore, SRB remains relatively new and many existing community and voluntary bodies simply do not understand it. Nor will the passage of time necessarily solve this problem; given their small size and lack of resources many community and voluntary bodies may well choose to invest their resources in the concrete issues they were developed to tackle rather than learn how to take part in the uncertain processes of SRB.

Nor is this simply an issue of more time being needed to allow greater participation; additional resources are required to enable communities to organise themselves (i.e. develop community capacities) and put forward suitably detailed proposals. This is something which government has explicitly refused to provide, assuming that as time passes these capacities will automatically develop. Overall there is a risk that participation will be seen by local communities as largely symbolic, a way of meeting bidding conditions without giving local people any real control over the process of regeneration (see Atkinson and Cope, 1997).

It has also been suggested (see Clark, 1995) that cuts in public expenditure have produced a situation in which local authorities and TECs view SRB as a means to recoup some of their losses. In such a situation community groups and the voluntary sector may appear as an unaffordable luxury, particularly in the case of TECs who have a contractual remit which strongly emphasises economic and training issues to the detriment of social issues. From this brief discussion it is clear that real participation by the community and voluntary sectors in SRB partnerships requires a fundamental rethink of attitudes by politicians and officials in central and local government.

In addition other problems remain. SRB schemes will run for between one and seven years, and after (although preferably before) a scheme terminates the remaining organisations and projects will have to find funds. This will not necessarily be an easy task and there must always be a danger that once funding is withdrawn there will be a slow (or rapid) return to the status quo ante. It is not difficult to envisage former SRB areas requiring remedial treatment within a decade of a scheme's termination. Moreover, there is no guarantee, particularly in a competitive allocation process, that the most deprived areas will be targeted; bids may focus on areas with significant development potential to attract private sector investment, thus maximising leverage and economic development. Such an approach would run the risk of reproducing the problems of the property-led approach. In addition strong reservations have been expressed over the decline in projects directed towards housing and the problems facing ethnic minorities (see Mawson *et al.*, 1995: ch. 8; Hall *et al.*, 1996: 27–38).

THE SCOTTISH EXPERIENCE

In Scotland local authorities were able to maintain a more significant role in regeneration activities and the community sector's role was recognised somewhat sooner. For instance *New Life for Urban Scotland* (1988) was less hostile to local government than its English counterpart *Action for Cities* (1988), and its follow-up document *Urban Scotland into the 90s* (1990) signalled the importance of the community somewhat earlier than south of the border. Perhaps the best examples of this approach are to be found in the four partnerships initiated by the Scottish Office in Castlemilk, Ferguslie Park, Wester Hailes and Whitfield where the bulk of urban resources have been targeted. Each of these initiatives is based on the adoption of a strategic, integrated approach (over a period of up to 10 years) in which partnership, involving the private and community sectors, is intended to be a central organising principle, source of finance, basis for innovation and mechanism of service delivery. However, Scottish experience with partnerships has not necessarily been any more positive than in England (Barr, 1995; Hastings and McArthur, 1995; McArthur, 1993). For instance Kintrea (1996) in a study of housing regeneration in Ferguslie Park noted how the Ferguslie Park Partnership imposed its own management structures to which the local community was expected to adapt. Later the partnership actually replaced a long-standing community organisation with forms of representation more amenable to its aims. Thus he concluded (Kintrea, 1996: 304):

> . . . not just the official and politicians in Ferguslie needed more experience in the techniques of participation, but that the whole process of identifying and progressing the Partnership was antipathetic to effective community involvement.

As in England there is a real danger that community participation is seen by local communities as a form of symbolism and incorporation.

What is most interesting about recent developments in Scotland is the method of selecting partnerships. Emerging out of a major review initiated in 1993 (Scottish Office, 1993) it was decided to adopt a broadly similar approach to that of SRB which shifts the emphasis from '. . . individual projects to strategies which form part of a concerted and co-ordinated effort to assist and improve a deprived area' (Scottish Office, 1994a: 4). Here too the role of the private sector is a key factor in decisions over the allocation of resources. Where it differs from its English counterpart is that local authorities are allocated the lead role (see Scottish Office, 1994a, 1994b). The new regeneration regime is based around four priority partnerships areas (PPAs), which will receive around two-thirds of Urban Programme funding, and cover council-wide areas with second-tier regeneration programmes targeted at smaller areas. Decisions will be made not on the basis of competitive bidding as in England, but after the submission of proposals from partnerships to the Scottish Office and subsequent discussions between the Scottish Office and the partnerships. The Scottish system resembles the 'contract system' in France (e.g. the *Contrat de Villes*) whereby the central state enters into integrative 'contracts' with local authorities which identify priorities for action and guarantees additional finance for a three-year period (see Le Gales and Mawson, 1994; Parkinson and Le Gales, 1995). Although as Turok and Hopkins (1997) have argued, the Scottish system has replicated many of the problems found south of the border.

Thus within Britain we have two distinct modes of allocating public resources to urban regeneration. It would be naïve to suggest that the Scottish method is necessarily any more open and transparent than its English counterpart, but it does appear to allocate a more central role to dialogue than the SRB Challenge Fund 'beauty contest'. However, in Scotland partnerships still 'compete' with one another but through a process of negotiation, thus it could be argued that City Challenge and SRB have brought this competition out into the open. The simple fact is that resources are always going to be scarce and a method of allocating them has to be found; under the Conservatives the vogue was for methods which attempted to replicate markets on the assumption that this would improve the quality of proposals. Whether the quality of schemes developed under a competitive resource allocation system are better or worse than those developed in Scotland's (or the French) more dialogue-based system is a moot point (for a 'positive' view of competition see Russell *et al.*, 1996: 42–45; see Turok and Hopkins, 1997 for a critical assesment of the new Scottish system). However, the election of a new Labour government in May 1997 will lead to changes in the method of resource allocation south of the border and the Scottish experience may well be relevant, as we shall see in the next section.

URBAN POLICY IN THE FUTURE

Will the election of New Labour lead to any fundamental changes in urban policy? The short answer is no. Prior to the election campaign the Labour Party committed itself to observing the Conservatives' public expenditure totals during its first two years in government, thus urban regeneration can expect no new funds. Nor will SRB be abandoned, broadly speaking the bringing together of 20 separate programmes was welcomed by the Labour opposition (*Hansard*, 4.11.93, col. 517). As we shall see, change will mainly be limited to the context in which SRB operates and its internal allocation system.

In July of 1997 the newly created Department of Environment, Transport and the Regions (DETR) issued supplementary guidance for round 4 of the SRB Challenge Fund (DETR, 1997b). The supplementary guidance advised partnerships that their bids should complement the new government's manifesto commitments and take account of proposed programmes (e.g. Welfare to Work and Action on Drugs). The emphasis was very much on '. . . a concerted attack against the multiple causes of social and economic decline . . .' (DETR, 1997b: 1) which tackled '. . . the needs of communities in the most deprived areas' (DETR, 1997b: 2). Furthermore GORs would simultaneously issue 'Regional Regeneration Frameworks' for round 4 to guide bidders and engage in closer co-operation with partnerships in the framing of bids. As a result the outcome of round 4 will not be known until March/April 1998. A consultation paper on the future of regeneration policy (DETR, 1997c) was also published which reflected the new priorities signalled in the supplementary guidance and sought new ways to develop urban regeneration. Perhaps the most important aspect of this paper relates to the method by which SRB Challenge Funds will be distributed in future. While no decision on the distribution methods and formula will be reached before the late spring/early summer of 1998, it would appear that the 'managed competition' already evident under the previous government will be intensified, with clearer allocations being made to each region, funds distributed according to '. . . clear regional criteria and frameworks, . . . ensuring the bulk of resources go to the areas of greatest need . . .' (DETR, 1997c: 10; see also the Milan Report, 1996: ch. 6). There was also an indication that the contractual framework found in Scotland and France might be adopted.

The most contentious issue is likely to be over the definition and measurement of 'need'; experience with the various systems used to distribute funds to local authorities has shown that relatively small changes in distribution formulae can produce large and unexpected results. If a needs-based allocation system is developed to distribute SRB funds we should not expect controversy to be removed from the system. Nor will the allocation of funds within regions be straightforward, it too is likely to be a highly political and conflictual process. The establishment of a regional strategy will be subject to competing pressures and demands given that there is no inherent coherence within regions, they are after all administrative creations. Intraregional competition will also be expressed over the allocation of SRB funds and it is likely that such a process will be every bit as opaque and unaccountable as the current competitive allocation system.

The new government published another consultation paper in the summer of 1997 (DETR, 1997c) which announced that regional development agencies (RDAs) would be established in the English regions from April 1999. This was followed by the publication of a White Paper – *Building Partnerships for Prosperity* (DETR, 1997a) – in December 1997. Initially RDAs will be created by the centre and accountable to Parliament, although in the future they may also be accountable to elected regional chambers/assemblies. The exact status and role of these chambers remain somewhat vague, in some cases where regional 'feeling' requires it they could be elected, although any moves in this direction would be during a second Labour term of government. According to the White Paper, RDAs,

> . . . will take a wide view of economic development. They will address the creation of inclusive, sustainable growth based on greater productivity and leading to new employment opportunities and to strengthened local communities (DETR, 1997a: 21, for more detail on their roles see ch. 9)

Furthermore they will take over the running of the SRB within each region and eventually the role of English partnership within each region. While the 'partnership ethos' will be central to their operation it is also intended that their ethos be essentially business orientated (see DETR, 1997a: 10). This appeared to be modified somewhat by John Prescott in the House of Commons where he stated:

> Regional development agencies will be business-led, but board members will include representatives not only of industry but of local authorities, further and higher education, the voluntary sector, rural interests and tourism (*Hansard*, no. 1769, col. 358, 3.12.97).

However, the White Paper made it clear that the boards of RDAs will have no more than 12 members, of whom the chair will normally have a private sector background and '. . . overall, those with a business background will predominate' (DETR, 1997d: 49), leaving relatively little space for representatives of the organisation listed in the previous quote.

It would appear that the creation of RDAs and reform of SRB are unlikely to resolve the contradiction between economic development and the needs of the deprived so long present in British urban policy. Moreover, both consultation documents, the White Paper and a speech by the Minister for the Regions, Regeneration and Planning (Caborn, 1997) made clear no new funds will be forthcoming and that yet again the primary focus will be on achieving better value for money from existing funds, improving service delivery and thereby increasing outputs.

CONCLUSION

Is there an urban crisis in Britain? There is no easy answer to this question. The DoE-commissioned *Assessing the Impact of Urban Policy* (Robson *et al.*, 1994) suggested that there had been improvements in the relative position of UPAs and other deprived urban areas. However, in the largest cities and many inner-urban areas the situation remains bleak, and in many central and peripheral social housing estates deep-rooted problems of bad housing, unemployment, poverty, etc., remain (see Power and Tunstall, 1995). This would indicate that there is considerable unevenness both between and within urban areas and that polarisation is increasing '. . . between the most deprived wards and those with fewer problems' (Robson *et al.*, 1994: 32) resulting in an increasing concentration of urban problems. Writing in 1992 Willmott and Hutchinson (1992: 82) noted:

> After 15 years, and many new initiatives, surprisingly little has been achieved. Given the record so far, it is difficult to have much confidence in more of the same or to feel at all hopeful about the future prospects for deprived urban areas.

While subsequent changes in urban policy, notably SRB, have attempted to address problems such as the lack of co-ordination, unresponsiveness to local needs, etc., it remains the case that the resources available to urban policy are overshadowed by the scale and depth of the problems that exist. Nor has SRB tackled the question of strategy; the Conservative government maintained that priorities were to be determined at local level, which while appearing laudable may also be seen as an abrogation of any strategic role. Moreover, despite the apparent openness of the SRB bidding guidelines it became increasingly clear that there was a heavy bias in favour of bids prioritising economic/wealth creation and training objectives over more socially orientated objectives (e.g. housing, provision of community facilities). Subsequent changes in SRB instituted by the new Labour government appear unlikely to change the situation fundamentally.

It is, however, unreasonable to expect urban policy on its own to solve the problems associated with deprived urban areas. There has long been a debate over the extent to which urban policy should be directed at people or places. This is a false dichotomy, policy has to aid both people and places. The way forward is to ensure that urban policy is integrated into a wider policy approach which includes economic, industrial and welfare policy; the simple fact of the matter is that these policies command infinitely greater resources than does urban policy. The problem is that for too long urban policy has acted as a 'filler in of gaps', mopping up the worst cases of fallout produced by wider economic and policy changes. It has functioned as both a form of symbolism and crisis management (see Atkinson and Moon, 1994a). As a result urban policy itself has been incoherent and it is debatable if it deserved the appellation 'policy'. SRB appeared to be a step towards developing a more internally coherent urban policy, although one severely limited by a lack of resources and based on the belief that it is always possible to extract more from the same, inadequate, resources. The review process instituted by the new Labour government appears likely to take this process a step further, holding out the possibility that urban policy will be integrated into a regional development strategy. What remains unclear is how this will fit into wider national strategies on the economy and welfare. There is a real danger that different policy strands will not complement and reinforce one another but work against one another. The problems of co-ordination and coherence remain. In this sense one is reminded of the debates surrounding the 1977 White Paper (see Atkinson and Moon, 1994a: ch. 4) and a rather fatalistic sense of *déjà vu* is engendered; it is to be hoped lessons have been learnt from past mistakes.

While the Blair government has at least been prepared to talk about poverty, inequality and social exclusion, how far this will affect urban policy and resource availability is difficult to divine. My own, pessimistic, view on the future development of urban policy is that 'everything changes and nothing changes', a view encouraged by Labour's relatively low profile of urban issues prior to and since the general election. Government proposals that new policies be assessed for their impact on families have no urban counterpart, i.e. an 'urban impact analysis'. To anyone of a sceptical frame of mind these silences suggest that urban issues still remain relatively low down the government's policy agenda and that urban policy will remain very much a case of 'muddling through'.

If things are to improve the first step should be to bring urban policy much closer to the centre of government policy-making. As suggested in the previous paragraph, when new policy proposals on economic policy, social security, education, health, etc., are being developed their implications for deprived urban areas should be assessed and policies modified accordingly. Such an approach would help ensure that more general policies do not operate to the detriment of these areas. There is also a need to 'bend' these wider national programmes to ensure that they reinforce regional and locally based regeneration programmes. Co-ordination could potentially be achieved through a body similar to the recently established Social Exclusion Unit (or in collaboration with it); however this will require a senior minister with the political clout at cabinet level to force Whitehall departments to rethink their priorities and take urban issues into account.

In addition the government should immediately restore the cuts in urban expenditure instituted by the last Conservative government in its final public expenditure statements (see DoE, 1997c) and pledge to at least double, in real terms, the funds available for urban regeneration over the period 1999–2004. Taken together this would provide the basis for a sustained attack upon urban problems.

The provision of additional funds is unfortunately not the end of the story. Government needs to ensure that not only are additional monies used to meet the needs of deprived communities but that they are also used to enhance the capacity of deprived communities to participate in regeneration partnerships. A significant portion of any new funds would need to be channelled in this direction. The enhancement of local community capacities to represent and articulate their interests would seem all the more important with the likely dominance of RDAs by business interests.

The creation of RDAs also raises additional problems, at the moment they represent an enhanced level of regional governance. However, if they are to be successful it seems to me that this requires a considerable decentralisation of power (and functions) from Westminster and Whitehall; assuming the willingness of the latter to allow this, then the creation of powerful, representative regional chambers/assemblies becomes all the more important. Linked to this last point is the question of local government boundaries, and with enhanced regional government it may well be necessary to rethink the current local government boundaries and create smaller unitary authorities which are closer to and more responsive to local communities. In such a context local urban regeneration programmes may well be able to reflect the needs of the deprived more closely and regional assemblies articulate them more effectively both within the region and to the centre.

NOTES

1. However, it should be noted that the idea of partnership is by no means new. In the 1970s (e.g. in the 1977 White Paper *Policy for the Inner Cities*, Cmnd 6845) partnership essentially meant a partnership within the state between central government departments and local authorities. During the 1980s partnership referred to the relationship between the state and the private sector whereby the state essentially underwrote the activities of the private sector (e.g. UDCs).
2. What part this particular report played in the review of urban policy is open to question. DoE officials tended to play down the report's significance, often strongly criticising aspects of it and arguing that, by the time of its publication, the report had been overtaken by events, i.e. the announcement of SRB. However, the outcome of the review strongly reflected many of the issues highlighted by the report.
3. According to the DoE officials giving evidence to the House of Commons Environment Committee (HoC, 1995b: 19) regional allocations were determined by two factors: 'The first element is based on regions' share of population in areas with above-average deprivation nationally; and the second element is based on the score in the Index of Local Conditions . . . of district-level deprivation.' These were then combined on a 50/50 basis to give a rough regional allocation, the intention being to prevent any major shifts in funds compared to the previous distribution.
4. Page 1 of all the annual editions of the *Bidding Guidance* for SRB contains a footnote which states: '. . . regeneration is used as a shorthand term for sustainable regeneration, economic development and industrial competitiveness . . .'. Moreover, successful bids '. . . will be expected to maximise the leverage of private sector investment and intensify the impact of public sector resources by achieving greater coherence of spend' (DoE, 1993a: 5). Such advice clearly prioritises economic issues over, say, housing issues.

CHAPTER 6

PLANNING AND THE HOUSING SYSTEM

Colin Jones and Craig Watkins

INTRODUCTION

Since 1979 a strong market oriented ideology has dominated both planning and housing policy. In the 1980s the primacy of the market over the planning system was asserted through the 'project based' approach where local political control was reduced through enterprise zones, UDCs and simplified planning zones (Thornley, 1996). More recently, although environmental and social issues have moved up the agenda with the move to a locally oriented 'plan-led' approach, planning policy has continued to be subject to an unmistakable market orientation (Allmendinger and Tewdwr-Jones, 1997). At the same time housing policy has been dominated by a range of initiatives designed to promote homeownership and deregulate the private rented sector (see Whitehead, 1993 for a review). For example, it is only recently that the mechanism for allocating dwellings has become more fully (re)commodified. As the scale of commodification (marketisation) continues to expand, it seems clear that further spatial and structural changes will be felt in the housing system (see Forrest and Murie, 1995; Pawson and Watkins, 1998). Taken together the reliance on market-based policy measures in the planning and housing policy arenas represents a vastly important departure from the ways in which the state has traditionally sought to influence the housing system. Recent evidence suggests that Tony Blair's New Labour government are unlikely to depart from the market orientation of recent years (DETR, 1998b). Driven by these recent policy trends, in this chapter we seek to review the relationship between planning and the housing system. We argue that although the most important challenge for the planning system appears to be the need to resolve the question of where and how to accommodate between 4.4 and 5.5 million new households by 2016, these published projections are only part of the problem. The growth of homeownership, radical changes to the tenure structure and the changing spatial relationships which will be experienced with continuing decentralisation from the cities will continue to combine to represent formidable challenges in the early part of the next millennium. Furthermore, while it is clear that the private sector can and will provide most of the housing required, it is less clear how the planning system can facilitate the provision of at least 40% of these homes for social housing.

As Cullingworth (1997: 946) argues:

> . . . the land use system was never designed to cope with growth and change on the scale which has been experienced over the last fifty years.

While acknowledging Allmendinger's view that the brunt of this change has, in fact, been dealt with by changes to the planning process (Allmendinger, 1998), it is clear that, in order to cope with the next 50 years, the system of housing land allocation requires a major overhaul. In our view there are fundamental problems with the current system. Not least, if planning for housing is a technical exercise, as planners like to claim, then those involved in the system need to be better equipped for the task. Unfortunately, as Cullingworth (1997) notes, there is a total absence of economic analysis in planning which is particularly marked in the area of land allocation. This is an issue we will explore as our discussion proceeds. The starting point for this chapter, however, is an attempt to put the current system of planning for housing into the context of the radical change to the housing system and urban economic structures since the inception of the system. It is clear from this analysis that the current passive approach which is increasingly dominated by well-organised environmental interest groups and electorally important suburban and county interests who seek to deny market forces is ill equipped for today's challenges.

This discussion precedes a brief summary of the current system, the treatment of housing need and the provision of affordable housing, and the techniques which dominate the allocation of housing land for the private housing market. From this analysis, two issues emerge. First, we argue that the system would be improved by augmenting current planning techniques. Specifically, we suggest that improvements in the efficacy of allocating land for private housebuilding would be achieved by a better understanding of the economics of local housing markets. As the economic arguments for planning are based on the control of externalities, the mitigation of market extremes, the provision of (quasi) public goods such as open spaces, the enabling of a speedy (re)development process, and by ensuring the co-ordination of land use and transport communications a better and more efficient pattern of economic activity, this is significant. We do not deny the existing role of market signals in the planning process, but a clearer understanding of the structure and operation of housing markets can help planners better accommodate the market. The need for improvement in this area is evident in the continuous debate about the suitability of land sites identified to meet housing requirements. Second, we argue that the current token provision of affordable housing in local plans (Barlow *et al.*, 1994) needs to be reconsidered in the light of the large shortfall in social and affordable housing currently predicted.

PLANNING FOR HOUSING IN CONTEXT

SPATIAL CHANGE, HOUSING AND PLANNING

The growth and decline of British cities are perhaps not surprisingly intertwined with the history of planning. The high densities and appalling housing conditions in the cities in the late nineteenth century were a major catalyst for the germination of first planning ideas; the garden city movement saw planned decentral-isation to model communities as a solution (Hall, 1989). In fact decentralisation of the urban population began in the last century with the introduction of tramways in the 1870s (Jones, 1979). The early part of the twentieth century saw the beginnings of urban sprawl encouraged by suburban railways and the motor bus as cities spread out from their confined Victorian cores. The intellectual reaction against this occurrence spurred the incorporation of the Town Planning Institute incorporated in 1914 and the formation of the Council for the Protection of Rural England (CPRE) in 1925, and a series of inter-war planning Acts designed to (but unable to until the 1935 Act) control ribbon development.

Around 1940 the population of most British urban core cities reached a maximum. They had spread out from the centre and grown by annexing land. The inner parts of industrial towns were largely unchanged from the mid-nineteenth century. There was a planning consensus that the solution to the congestion and housing problems of these urban cores lay in planned decentralisation. For example Abercrombie's Greater London Plan of 1944 foresaw the planned decentralisation of over a million people in an overcrowded city, and the creation of new planned communities (with only 250 000 via spontaneous migration).

The 1946 New Towns Act included eight new towns to serve London overspill as Abercrombie had planned, and with the 1952 Act provided the mechanism for the planned overspill from all the major cities. In many ways this scheme followed faithfully the visions or blueprints of the original planners – new towns as garden cities. These new towns were physical 'solutions' provided by the state in which virtually all the original housing was provided by a public agency, a new town corporation. New towns continued to be established through the 1950s and 1960s. An essential element of this strategy was the creation of green belts surrounding the cities and containing their growth. This was made possible by the 1947 Town and Country Planning Act with its strong negative powers of control on development.

The final component of the planning strategy was the rebuilding of the cities. Once the immediate housing shortage following the Second World War had been alleviated, slum clearance began in earnest in the 1960s, unleashing a juggernaut which reached its zenith in the early 1970s. It was a unique and massive upheaval to the cities involving a major displacement of communities. Unfortunately the rebuilding of the cities primarily in the form of mass-produced council housing did not meet the aspirations of the residents. The curtain was effectively drawn on this era with the 1974 Housing Act which switched the emphasis of housing renewal from slum clearance to (subsidising) improvement of the housing stock. There remained a crisis in planning: the profession's claims for the wholesale modernisa-tion of the built environment of cities enthusiastically championed since the 1940s had failed (Brindley et al., 1989). The post-war planning consensus was destroyed.

Throughout this reshaping of the cities by planners, underlying decentralisation pressures were continuing to influence the urban form. After 1961 the populations of conurbations began to decline as growth in the suburban rings did not keep pace with population loss at the centre. As we have seen this was, of course, partly planned, but decentralisation accelerated through the 1970s and 1980s. The principal underlying force behind this long-term trend is falling intra-urban transport costs and higher incomes. This initially led a movement to the suburbs, and with the continuing growth of car ownership commuters are travelling further and further to work. The population of at least parts of surburban rings stagnated in the 1980s as decentralisation continued beyond their boundaries.

A further major factor on these urban trends has been the relocation of industry. The continuing decline in the nation's manufacturing base has led to virtually all centres suffering a net loss of manufacturing jobs. The statistics reflect the persistence of the deindustralisation process which began in the 1950s. Its effect is especially severe on the core cities with their concentration of traditional heavy industries. The pattern of change to a degree also reflects the decentralisation pressures, stimulated by new production techniques, containerisation and an improvement in inter-urban road networks. As a consequence Parr and Jones (1983) argue that the urban system has moved into an urban dispersal stage. The decline of the traditional core cities as manufacturing centres has been balanced by the rise of small free-standing centres.

The decentralisation of employment and the increased flexibility provided by the car have led to larger and larger travel to work areas and housing market areas. In 1977 the White Paper, *Policy for the Inner Cities*, recognised for the first time the economic decline of the core cities. It was the beginning of policies designed to revive the cities, policies which were reinforced by strict adherence to the surrounding green belt. At the same time it spelled the end to new towns as resources were channelled into the inner city.

The flight of manufacturing industry from cities left much derelict and vacant space in its wake. These brownfield sites have provided the opportunity for new housebuilding, especially for sale. Local authorities have actively promoted these sites to speculative housebuilders as a means of redressing local tenure 'imbalance' and as the only 'viable' use for the land. Such initiatives have included the conversion of derelict redundant buildings such as warehouses, and central government has supported them through grants to developers where necessary. This policy has been so successful that almost half of all new housing was on brownfield sites by 1995 (although this figure varies considerably by region). Yet there remains uncertainty over its continuance at least in some areas: some commentators argue that there are emerging shortages in some areas and the easy sites, i.e. the cheapest, may have been developed, leaving highly contaminated ones remaining (Breheny and Hall, 1996). These views seem unduly pessimistic for large parts of the country, given also the current level of obsolescent office blocks.

The development of the urban system and housing problems have therefore provided major impetus to the formulation of planning structures and ideas. In the discussion above the focus has been on the policies, but urban change also stimulated the creation of strategic planning with the establishment of structure plans machinery in 1968. The analysis above further suggests that planning, in terms of both policies and structures, cannot ignore fundamental spatial economic forces. In particular urban dispersal will continue. The emphasis of planning towards inner cities cannot be all encompassing; the shifting of the optimum location of manufacturing industry has to be embraced, for example inward investment invariably requires greenfield sites. Similarly the use of the car continues to support the decentralisation of population. There may also be physical and financial limits to the redevelopment of cities via the recycling of brownfield sites for housing, although recent proposals to tax greenfield sites acknowledge this to some extent.

GROWTH OF HOMEOWNERSHIP AND THE DECLINE OF COUNCIL HOUSING

In 1945 homeownership represented 26% of all households in Great Britain; private rented was the predominant tenure, accounting for 62 per cent, while public sector tenants were very much a minority, only 12 per cent of the total (Malpass and Murie, 1994). The subsequent three decades saw the growth of both public sector and owner occupation. By 1979 public sector tenants represented 32% of the total and owner occupation had risen to 55% of all households. The growth of homeownership was then given a further stimulus by the introduction of the right of council tenants to buy their home in 1980. The demise of public sector housing had begun: few council houses have been built for general needs since that date and the right to buy policy has led to 2.7 million dwellings being sold by 1997, just over 30% of the 1979 stock.

By 1989 homeownership had reached 66%. Despite the jolt of record levels of repossessions and negative equity in the recession of the early 1980s there is continuing survey evidence to suggest that the vast majority of households aspire to homeownership. Perhaps the only consequence of the last recession is that house purchase has been delayed until later in life, a trend which has been reinforced by increased debt levels incurred by recent graduates with the move from student grants to loans.

All studies conclude that the level of homeownership is close to its ceiling and the rate of growth of homeownership has slowed. The government (DoE, 1995c) has forecast that owner occupation will reach 70% by the year 2005. Looking further ahead Meen et al. (1997) estimate that homeownership will grow by only 0.3% per annum to nearly 72% by 2016 with tenure differences being maintained.

Part of the reason homeownership is so attractive are the alternatives. Social housing rents have been driven up since 1980 redrawing the financial balance between owning and renting. The housing opportunities in social renting are also limited with many housing estates suffering severe problems and unlettable. The solution to these 'surplus' estates has become partial or wholesale demolition with the cleared land then offered to private housebuilders. The number of new council houses since 1980 has been reduced to a trickle as a consequence of central government's reduction of capital allocations for housing.

The development of housing tenure contrasts with the perceived wisdom at the time of the 1947 Town and Country Planning Act, the foundation of the current planning system. It was thought that the era of the private speculative builder had gone and that most new building would be undertaken by the public sector within an orderly planning framework. The passive nature of the planning controls in the Act was to be balanced by the positive physical development to be undertaken by public agencies. Indeed between 1946 and 1950 the public sector, local authorities and new town development corporations built four out of five of all new homes (Hall, 1989).

The Conservative governments of the 1950s placed a greater reliance on the private sector: housebuilding split equally between the public and private sectors during this period. This position was endorsed by Labour when it returned to power in 1964, and broadly remained unchanged through to the end of the 1970s; the public sector contributed 47% of new building in the decade to 1980. In the 1980s the demise of new council housebuilding, only partly replaced by housing association building programmes, meant that four out of five homes in the 10 years to 1994 were built by the private sector for sale.

The new Labour government is releasing sales receipts from council house sales for spending on public sector housing, but much of this will be used to refurbish the existing stock. While there is likely to be some reawakening of houses built for social renting, the speculative housebuilder is likely to have the dominant role in housing provision for the foreseeable future. And those houses built for social renting are likely to be built by housing associations with mixed public and private funding. The role of a local authority is changing from direct provision of subsidised housing to that of strategic (housing) planning and enabling.

Thus the roles of the private sector housebuilder and the local authorities are almost the reverse of that anticipated when the planning system was conceived 50 years ago. The planning system has to directly address the demands of private builders and consumers. Further, with growing affluence and car ownership house buyers are travelling longer distances to work and insisting on better-quality environments. The nature of work has also changed. The increasing reliance on successive short-term employment contracts in the next millennium is likely to mean people putting greater reliance on cars, not moving when changing jobs and travelling potentially long distances to work. This will reinforce decentralisation pressures as central regional locations accessible to major road networks will become even more attractive.

CURRENT PLANNING SYSTEM

The two-tier structure of the planning system set up in England and Wales by the 1968 Town and Country Planning Act has remained intact despite the trends outlined above and the Conservative proposals to unify them in the 1980s (Moore, 1995). Only in the major conurbations are there unitary plans (to date) covering the constituent councils. Until the recent reorganisation of local government elsewhere, structure plans were prepared on a county basis, setting out general lines of development and the policies which will be applied. Local plans cover the administrative area of district councils who have a duty to produce one in conformity with the structure plan. These local plans are more detailed, concerned explicitly with land use – allocating sites for particular purposes and forming the basis on which the (re)development of an area can proceed.

An important function of the planning system is to ensure sufficient provision of land for new development. A critical input is the assessment of local housing land requirements. The approach to this task is top-down with the results fed into the statutory development plan system, and local authorities are obliged to take account of the findings in structure/unitary development plans. Ultimately the government requires that local plan policies provide for a five-year supply of housing land with two years ready for immediate development.

This five-year supply is derived as part of a structure plan or a unitary plan. The first step in the process is essentially technical and involves a simple extrapolation of the past. National household projections for household types are estimated, taking into account the (changing) demographic structure of the population. The results are published for regions, shire counties, metropolitan districts, districts in Scotland and London boroughs. These local forecasts, which are crucially dependent on identifiable previous migration patterns, are essentially trend based.

In England, the next stage is the preparation of a Regional Planning Guidance (RPG) statement by the Secretary of State which after consultations with local bodies takes into account policy considerations such as environmental constraints, the state of the current housing stock, previous over/undersupply and land availability. The output is a local housing requirement for a local authority set in terms of an average annual housing provision, but with no indication of size, density, house type or tenure. These housing requirements are then fed into the structure plans. This procedure has been subject to considerable debate and criticism at a technical level (Baker and Wong, 1997). Much of this has centred on the forecasting approach and the data sources.

With the recent introduction of RPG, county councils in England now adopt their own structure or unitary plans, without the necessity of explicit approval by the appropriate Secretary of State (who can object by calling in the proposed plan before it is formally adopted). In Scotland the preparation of structure plans is broadly the same: the Secretary of State publishes local population projections which provide guidance to local authorities, but there is no RPG and plans are still subject to formal acceptance by the Secretary of State. The lack of RPG possibly reflects the lower demand pressure on land: Scotland's population has been broadly stationary in recent times, although there has been an increase in the number of households. A further difference in Scotland is the use of local plans at the subdistrict level. The process is similar in Wales.

In summary the structure plan process in England and Wales via the 'imposition' of an RPG constraint involves a top-down approach in which population forecasts are translated into land allocations for each district council. Scotland and Wales, on the other hand, approach the same task from the bottom with no formal attempt by the Scottish or Welsh Office to ensure the achievement of an overall control figure. In Northern Ireland there is as yet no formal strategic land use planning but following criticism by the House of Commons Northern Ireland Select Committee a framework is now in preparation.

Irrespective of whether the top-down or bottom-up approach is applied, the system is heavily dependent on forecasting accuracy which is in turn dependent on an understanding of market trends and social needs. In the next section we examine the relationship between the planning system and estimates of housing need, and consider the efficacy of current techniques in relating housing land provision to the local market.

HOUSING NEED, HOUSING POLICY AND PLANNING

In 1951 there were 6.5% more households than dwellings with three-quarters living in substandard or overcrowded conditions. The solution was clear-cut: build more houses, and up to the end of the 1960s governments used to compete to build the most houses (Whitehead, 1997). By the 1960s there was a crude national surplus, but the empty houses were often in the wrong place. Perhaps encouraged by the crude surplus of housing or no longer seduced by the 'numbers game', there was no government statistical national estimate, of housing need from 1977 until 1994.

The government's approach to calculating national housing need employs a basic model. It calculates housing need by subtracting the increase in the number of dwellings expected to be provided by the private sector from the expected increase in the number of households. Housing need is therefore a residual; it represents the number of households without the financial means to make a demand for housing effective in the market. Housing demand is made effective by a household's own resources.

Using this simple net flow model, and based on the household projections described above, the government estimated that there was a need to build homes for social renting toward the bottom of the range, 60 000–100 000 per annum until 2001 (DoE, 1995b). Independent studies presented to the House of Commons Select Committee on the Environment's investigation on housing need forecast somewhat higher figures – Shelter 85 000–90 000, Holmans 90 000 and the Chartered Institute of Housing 120 000. The differences stem from the underlying assumptions and the use of a variant on the basic model (HoCSCE, 1995).

The essential model has been criticised on a number of points. It does not take economic considerations into account (Bramley and Watkins, 1995). This view is endorsed by Malpass (1996) who argues that with the reduced role of public sector housing in the late 1990s, housing need is crucially dependent on the state of the economy. A further problem is the one-dimensional view of housing need in terms of the lack of reference to the quality of housing (CIH, 1995).

The most consistently quoted criticism to the Committee was the backlog of housing need caused by the low levels of building for social housing in the 1980s, at a time when there was a record increase in the rate of household formation. Holmans argue that the backlog was the order of 480 000 with the major components comprising 110 000 concealed households, 140 000 sharing households and 100 000 single people homeless or in hostels who want, and would be better off in, a flat (Holmans, 1996). The House Builders Federation claim that the backlog is even higher.

A more fundamental point arises about the research method utilised in these assessments of housing need. As noted earlier, this approach gives great prominence to national population forecasts and trends rather than economic factors. It also relates to changes in broad aggregates at the national level, ignoring the components of housing need at the local level. Just as the national housing surplus of the 1960s hid shortages at a local level so this national needs study also suffers from the lack of a 'bottom-up approach'.

The 1977 Housing Green Paper (DoE, 1977; Scottish Office, 1977) identified local needs assessments as logically the most appropriate base to calculate the scale of the housing problem (within a national housing policy framework). Such studies would take into account the nature and conditions of the local housing stock, the scale of homelessness and overcrowding, specific household groups, housing market conditions and land availability. Unfortunately the housing investment plans (housing plans in Scotland) set in place to assess local needs after the Green Paper were quickly adapted to form local authority bids to central government for capital allocations (Malpass and Murie, 1994).

The discussion above highlights the scale of housing need that requires to be met by social housing. This in itself has significant implications for land use planning. But planning constraints can be a source or cause of local housing need. In particular, restricting development land, say for environmental reasons, not only reduces the opportunities for social housing but also by constraining private development forces up land and house prices (Hancock et al., 1991; Monk and Whitehead, 1996; Bramley and Watkins, 1996). This has become most acute in rural areas, and the Rural Development Commission (RDC) noted in its evidence to the HoCSCE (1995: 309) on housing need that

> . . . without an adequate supply of housing people on low or modest incomes are denied the opportunity to live or remain in the countryside . . .

Hull (1997) argues that historically there has been confusion over the responsibility of housing need between planners and housing departments. Some witnesses to the

HoCSCE on housing need proposed that planning should take an explicit role in the resolution of housing need by ring-fencing land for 'affordable housing'. This would be achieved by the creation of a new land use subcategory for this purpose only. This has been rejected by the government as mitigating against mixed developments. Instead the government suggested, in National Planning Policy Guideline 3 (NPPG 3) issued in 1992, that planning authorities may take account of the need for affordable housing when formulating their development policies. However, a government definition of affordable housing was delayed until 1996, when it was ultimately defined as

> . . . to encompass the range of both subsidised and market housing designed for those whose incomes generally deny them the opportunity to purchase on the open market as a result of a local relationship between income and market price (DoE, 1996b: 4).

The National Housing and Town Planning Council (NHTPC, 1995) argues that the 1992 NPPG 3 formed a watershed in the bringing together of social/affordable housing provision and the planning system. However, while it may have stimulated a more corporate approach within local authorities there still remain considerable hurdles to this integrated approach. While the land use planning system operates within a 5–15 year time-frame with regard to the allocation of housing land, housing policy has a much shorter time horizon geared, as noted above, to its bids to national government for investment funds. At present this often means that land zoned for housing with the anticipation that social housing will be built on can lay empty for years while the funds are found.

In summary there is strong need for a significant social housing programme which will have direct implications for the planning system. In some locations planning constraints have exacerbated housing need. There is a case for integrating the land use planning system with housing policy, but at present this has reached only an embryonic stage. Major barriers are the different time horizons of the two systems and the fact that the planning system does not distinguish between tenures when allocating land for housing. Further, the retreat of local authorities from direct social housing provision will shift local housing policy towards a passive approach similar to the present planning system.

PLANNING TECHNIQUES

The 1960s saw the development of mathematically sophisticated system-modelling techniques, but over-reliance on their forecasts brought disillusionment with this approach in the mid 1970s. Very often the sophistry of the mathematics hid the theoretical limitations of the models (Field and MacGregor, 1987). Recent planning techniques are less ambitious, but still in many ways suffer from theoretical weaknesses in economics, together with data deficiencies.

Today forecasting techniques for planning and housing are very often a combination of trend extrapolation and the use of assumptions about the future within a 'physical' accounting framework. This is evident from the local population forecasts considered above which are crucially dependent on identifiable previous migration patterns. These population forecasts are normally based on National Health Service data on households moving to a new doctor in another family health service authority area. This leads to a number of criticisms of the under-lying economics (Baker and Wong, 1997). Like most planning forecasts these are tied to the administrative boundaries of local authorities which take no cognisance of local housing market structures discussed below, and perhaps most importantly there is the lack of any reference to tenure.

Bramley and Watkins (1995) have also queried other economic fundamentals of the population projections. The result, they argue, is that population projections to a degree are circular: household projections determine land allocation which determines the number of households living in an area. However, the lack of reference to economic forces may lead to projections underestimating actual out-comes. In particular, it is not clear whether these projections represent effective demand or normative measures of 'need'. In a follow-up paper Bramley (1996) re-examines previous household projections with hindsight to reaffirm his arguments.

These criticisms suggest that a rethink is required about housing/population forecasts. Techniques require us to take account of a more behavioural approach to analysing and forecasting the housing market. The HoCSCE (1995) recommended further development of behaviourally based methods for the assessment of housing demand and need at the national level. In fact the logical starting point for such research is at the local level. Local housing market studies are able to examine the scale and characteristics of specific demand and supply flows crucial to forecasts of housing needs and land requirements. In this way, for example, it will be possible to gauge the size of houses required by the expected surge in small households.

LOCAL HOUSING MARKET STRUCTURES AND PLANNING

A logical starting point to the analysis of local housing structures is the definition of a local housing market area (HMA). An HMA is the most appropriate functional area rather than the *ad hoc* administrative boundaries of a local authority. Only in Scotland are local authorities expected to allocate land within an HMA framework. Unfortunately, advice issued by the Scottish Office in Planning Advice Note 38 (Scottish Office, 1996b) on housing land requirements does not define an HMA. Rather it states:

> These are ideally areas in which a self contained housing market operates. A prag-
> matic test is that a substantial majority of people moving house and settling in an area
> will have sought a house only in that area (Scottish Office, 1996b: 9).

This advice suggests the likelihood of overlapping HMAs across district council boundaries around conurbations, and advises local councils to refer to a recent research manual by Scottish Homes (1993). This manual notes that the labour market and its locational structure within a region is critical in shaping HMAs, although it recognises that it is not the only factor. It concludes:

> Thus, in terms of housing and labour markets, a self contained housing market would be an area in which the majority of those moving house (migration), without changing jobs, would stay, and an area in which the majority of the employed population both reside and work (Scottish Homes, 1993: 20).

The logic of this analysis is that households will move to meet their individual domestic requirements with changing income or as they pass through the family life cycle without changing employment. Both the Scottish Office note and the Scottish Homes manual suffer from vagueness of definition and proposing the basic unit of analysis as a local authority.

Jones and Mills (1996) derive a system of HMAs for the former Strathclyde region based on the criterion of spatial containment of buyers, and operationalised by reference to migration patterns. They apply an algorithm which groups settlements in HMAs so that there is a majority of buyers who move from within its boundaries. This 50% benchmark derives 23 HMAs. Increasing the containment criterion to 60% reduces the number of HMAs to 15 and removes all but one small HMA. These results show that the region is dominated by an HMA based on Glasgow, encompassing much of the conurbation. Yet there are also relatively small communities (within the boundaries of district councils) in rural and even in some urban areas which have relatively closed HMAs.

The significance of their findings for planning policy is that any assessment of demand based on a local authority's administrative boundaries is likely to be inaccurate. The HMAs identified for Strathclyde do not in all cases conform to these areas. In many cases individual local authority areas are either too large or too small. And while HMAs are not strictly closed entities it is possible to develop a national system of HMAs just as there is for travel-to-work areas (TTWAs). A framework of HMAs (rather than regions) is also a more appropriate way to account for long-distance moves such as those subject to the economic cycle or through retirement. Within each HMA the planning system will be able to manipulate supply and demand.

The large-scale nature of some HMAs suggests that such manipulation may have (ideally) to take account of the arguably neighbourhood-specific nature of housing demand (Maclennan, 1992), especially with regard to local plans. Where even moderate size HMAs exist, a full assessment of local demand requires submarket analysis within the HMA or analysis of housing demand in a particular settlement set within the wider context. This conclusion mirrors recent debate about the usefulness of TTWAs as the appropriate level of analysis for assessing localised unemployment (Turok, 1997). In both labour and housing markets the definition of the extent of a spatial market represents normally only the first essential prerequisite for more policy analysis.

Housing submarkets stem from the inefficient nature of the housing market. Maclennan and Tu (1996: 390) describe them as

. . . fault lines along which the market may fracture or suffer disjunctures.

They arise where demand by a group of households is confined by the requirement for a particular housing characteristic, perhaps a neighbourhood or a house type. In addition the lack of close substitutes and long-term supply constraints means that their choice is restricted, so that excess demand in any submarket will lead to a price premium in that submarket.

The use of submarkets as the basis for local plan/policy analysis has so far been constrained by limitations in our knowledge of housing market structures. Submarkets could be defined as neighbourhoods or house types, or a combination of both. A number of approaches have been considered to identify them (see for example Ball and Kirwan, 1977; Maclennan et al., 1989; Adair et al., 1996; Watkins, 1998), but there is no universally accepted nor simple method. For example, Maclennan and Tu (1996) set out a three-stage process which begins with the collection of information on the characteristics of individual dwellings, this data set is then subject to a cluster analysis, and these clusters are then tested for price differences using multiple regression analysis. The data requirements alone of such a process are extremely daunting especially outside Scotland where price information on individual housing transactions does not exist. The more practical alternatives are the use of surveys of household search patterns when moving or consultation with local estate agents.

HOUSING CHALLENGES FOR PLANNING IN THE NEXT MILLENNIUM

The debate in the late 1970s and 1980s about the importance of planning versus the market (see Brindley et al., 1989) may appear to have been resolved, but the task for planning is no easier. It is no longer a question of planning being subservient to the market, but it also clear that planning cannot evade the underlying market influences on the pattern of land use. In particular, housing-led urban dispersal and high levels of owner occupation are set to continue.

The original physical planning solution approach is no longer possible in an era where 7 out of 10 households are owner occupiers and 4 out every 5 new houses are for sale. The planning system will be expected to be responsive to the demands for owner-occupied housing in quality environments and decentralised locations.

The anticipated 23% growth in households by 2016 magnifies this challenge especially in the high-demand areas of the South West, East Midlands and East Anglia.

At the same time there is a consensus that planning should intervene in or regulate the market to protect and conserve the environment, and promote urban regeneration. Regulative planning has been at the heart of planning system – project demand, draw up plan for future development and land use then grant/ refuse planning permission to meet plans – but it now faces potential meltdown. Trend planning will be less and less possible in high-demand areas of the country. Regulative planning has to reinvent itself.

How is the planning system to cope with the 4.4 million new households (in England) expected to be formed by 2016? We saw some of the potential fallout from this in late 1997 and early 1998. Planning constraints in high-demand areas have already exacerbated housing problems by crowding out local people from the housing market. Beneath the surface of the apparent planning consensus, there-fore, lie significant equity issues. Negative planning control intervenes between competing interests for the good of all; but if it is applied to arrest the potential mass movement to rural areas facilitated by the car, then some interests lose, for example the country dwellers who do not own a home.

With the projected increase in households, the current passive approach will not be able to impose constraints on rural development without high-density development and unacceptable piling up in some cities, especially those where brownfield sites are now dwindling, and an increase in housing problems for local country dwellers. Preserving rural amenity will be at a cost to already dis-advantaged groups in rural and urban areas. Thus the CPRE's concept of 'environ-mental capacity' to limit new housing development in rural areas is a very partial view (Green Balance, 1994). To address the whole picture planning has to take a more positive approach and integrate with housing policies.

Breheny and Hall (1996) argue that at least 50% of demand created by house-hold formation will have to be met beyond conurbation boundaries on greenfield sites. In the absence of positive planning market forces are likely to prevail and households will decentralise into the countryside. However, in achieving their personal goals, the scale of development will destroy the countryside environment so much sought after. Breheny and Hall (1996) argue that this will also lead to inefficient long-distance commuting. Their solution includes the creation of new settlements and consideration given to green belts around cities being bodily lifted outwards. Any revival of new towns, unlike previous generations, will have to be led by private sector development requirements.

With the high level of owner occupation combined with the dramatic rise in the number of households, to achieve its consensual goals planning requires an efficient interface with market forces. If planning is to manipulate the market it has to understand it and work within the constraints it sets. For example, it will be possible to deflect demand within a local HMA, but to do so requires identification of the boundaries. Similarly migration is not to a region but to specific locations within a region. There is therefore a strong case to develop strategic planning policies underpinned by research and monitoring of the housing market within the framework of a national system of local HMAs. Such a system would link into the existing national network of TTWAs.

Within a local HMA there are similar arguments that planning, in any manipulation of demand, should take as much cognisance as possible of residents' preferences. This is especially true for cities which generally wish to retain their population and attract inmigration. Hence local plans need to be drawn taking into account the structure of local housing submarkets. This will also avoid unnecessary constraints and provide a clearer analysis of the negative trade-off of particular planning decisions.

In meeting the demands of owner occupiers, the majority tenure, the role of social housing and housing need should not be overlooked by the planning system. Holmans (1996), for example, argues that if the backlog of housing need is added to the extra 4.4 million households projected by 2016 then the total becomes 5 million. This is particularly true given that planning policies can be part of the problem. And with the postulated growth of households the pressures on planning could easily make the position worse. Any failure by the planning system to resolve the growth of households will be felt worst by the lower income groups.

There is an evident requirement for a rethink about the administration and formulation of policy in planning and housing, not least in a more corporate approach in terms of research and implementation, but also at the strategic level. If we are to fully address the household growth 'timebomb' then there is a case for positive planning. However, many local authorities are operating a rearguard action against inward migration with a passive NIMBY approach. At the same time the responsibility of local authorities for social housing is being eroded through existing stock transfer to housing associations, and new building is also predominantly being undertaken by housing associations. With the move to regionalisation in the UK, consideration should be given to a regional housing/planning strategy perhaps through public agencies drawing on the experience of the Scottish Homes and Tai Cymru Housing models.

In conclusion, the planning system will continue to come under pressure in the next millennium. The planning system and its predictive techniques are driven by demographic trends and needs. These techniques were developed when planning essentially involved physical solutions. Now, however, planning for housing needs to reappraise itself taking into account the operation of the housing system and, given the radical change in the tenure structure, the preferences of owner occupiers in particular. To do so efficiently requires the development of economic behavioural models which incorporate tenure and the structure of local housing systems. There is an immediate imperative with the clash between continuing urban dispersal and planning policies aimed at maintaining the rural environments and reviving the cities. These conflicts are magnified in the South West, East

Midlands and East Anglia. In both the social and market sectors of the housing system there is a strong case for a more corporate positive and strategic spatial approach which addresses these issues.

In fact, a recent policy statement by the government appears to recognise the limitations of the current passive planning system (DETR, 1998b). It indicates a willingness to consider economic instruments as part of positive planning. This suggests a superstructure of financial incentives and taxes operating above a reformed planning system within which the old system of 'predict and provide' will be replaced. The ideas are embryonic and to be effective they will need to be developed within a clearly defined framework.

CHAPTER 7

THE IMPLICATIONS OF THE 'NEW MANAGERIALISM' FOR PLANNING IN THE MILLENNIUM

Rob Imrie

INTRODUCTION

> Where champions of the managerial state have celebrated its dynamism . . . what we
> see is the unstable oscillation of a form of state that cannot reconcile the social
> contradictions and conflicts of contemporary Britain within a managerial calculus
> (Clarke and Newman, 1997: 159).

The 1990s have witnessed profound and, potentially, deep-rooted transformations
in the nature of social, community and other, government services in the UK. Public
expenditure cuts, combined with political antipathy to state-controlled and
delivered welfare services, have seemingly stimulated the emergence of a 'mixed
economy of care' (Clarke and Newman, 1997; Cochrane, 1993). For some,
decentralised welfare systems, characterised by private sector suppliers attentive to
users' needs, are emerging (Nocon and Qureshi, 1996). For others, the emergent
context is being driven by quasi-markets which emphasise 'value for money' criteria
or a balance sheet mentality in determining spending priorities (Hadley and Clough,
1996; Hoggett, 1996; Leach *et al.*, 1996). In particular, many commentators talk
about changes in governance in terms of what Clarke and Newman (1997: 140)
characterise as a 'shift from a regime dominated by bureau-professionalism to one
dominated by managerialism, embedded in processes of both the dispersal and
concentration of power' (also, see Cochrane, 1993; Hoggett, 1996; Lowndes, 1996).

Managerialism in local governance is connected to Margaret Thatcher's initial
drive in the 1980s towards the debureaucratisation of local government. Organisational change in local government was seen as a key mechanism in facilitating her
political objectives, based on an agenda to free up markets, challenge the power of
the trade unions and organised labour, while dismantling the cornerstones of the
welfare state. In particular, the emergent managerialism of the late 1990s reflects the
legacy of a period which, in seeking to reinvent local government, introduced
stringent, centrally imposed, financial targets, devolved systems of service delivery
and organisational forms designed to produce flexible, responsive, modes of governance. In turn, such transformations have become part of the new organisational
landscapes of local governance which are, so some claim, dominated by accountants,

business or corporate values, and technicist procedures and discourses (Cochrane, 1993; Hoggett, 1996). Indeed, as Clarke and Newman (1997: 148) suggest, the new managerialism is one which places a premium on 'goals and plans rather than with intentions and judgements. It is about action rather than reflection.'

In turn, the new managerialism in planning, and other service functions, has been translated into practices with a performance-based orientation. Thus, for example, the policy emphasis in local governance is increasingly connected to prioritising efficiency over other forms of output. For planners, for instance, efficiency is characterised by the speed of turnaround of planning applications, the completion of local plan preparation, the facilitation of development objectives and the streamlining of procedures, such as public consultations, which, potentially, slow down the attainment of operational objectives. The primacy of efficiency over other objectives is, in particular, focused on 'short term goals since those are the ones against which outputs and performance are measured' (Clarke and Newman, 1997: 147). Moreover, planners are increasingly subjected to a managerialist culture within local governance which seeks to divide and disperse functions, while focusing on the attainment of narrowly defined intra-organisational goals rather than a wider public purpose. This, then, is an emergent governance culture of target setting, performance management and the 'building of a corporate commitment . . . linked to survival in a competitive environment' (Clarke and Newman, 1997: 147).

The wider implications of such changes in local governance, for planning practices and procedures, is the focal point for this chapter. I divide the chapter into three. First, I provide a brief outline of the broader transformations in local governance by developing aspects of Clarke and Newman's (1997) thesis concerning the managerialisation of local government. Second, I draw out some of the wider procedural and policy implications of Clarke and Newman's (1997) analysis for the future of local governance and, in particular, for planning theory and practice. In doing so, I shall argue that planning practice, into the millennium, is likely to be characterised by a range of interrelated, and possibly irresolvable, tensions concerning the governance of urban and regional systems. These include, among others, the continuing struggle between central and local levels of governance over the control and direction of planning policy, and the emergent pressures for the democratisation of planning in a context whereby counter-pressures, in pursuit of procedural efficiency, make democratic procedures in planning highly unlikely. I conclude by assessing the possibilities for the emergence of new modes of planning practice with the potential to transcend the depoliticising strictures of a managerial logic.

THE MANAGERIALISATION OF LOCAL GOVERNMENT

A range of commentators concur that the remaking of local government is occurring with a shift towards what Clarke and Newman (1997) term the managerial state (also, see Clarke and Newman, 1993; Cochrane, 1993). Clarke and Newman's (1997: 155) analysis is based on the understanding that politics has shifted to the right and that the 'centre ground is now contested around a series of issues established by Thatcherism in relation to economy, state, and social welfare'. Such issues revolve around the break-up of the post-war consensus on state-delivered welfare, including the drive towards the marketisation of public service provision and the trans-formation of the alleged inefficiencies of the bureaucratic and/or technical pro-cedures of the state. For Clarke and Newman, then, the new managerialism is premised around Hay's (1996) contention that the UK is characterised by a single vision democracy with the main political parties competing with each other to see who can best consolidate the post-Thatcher settlement. In this sense, manage-rialism is no less than 'a cultural formation and a distinctive set of ideologies and practices which form one of the underpinnings of the political settlement' (Clarke and Newman, 1997: ix).

In particular, one of the key roles of the emergent local governance is the facilitation of the operations of the enterprise state by making local government more businesslike. For local government, since the early 1980s, streamlining pro-cedures and cutting waste and bureaucracy have been clarion calls. Targets and performance measures have become commonplace, mission statements have proliferated, while, as Cochrane (1993: 107) notes, the issuing of contracts and monitoring of service provision and performance are part of standard procedures. Indeed, as Heseltine (1980, quoted in Pollitt, 1993: vi), former Minister for the Department of the Environment, has argued:

> . . . efficient management is the key to the national revival . . . and the management ethos must run right through our national life – private and public companies, civil service, nationalised industries, local government, the National Health Service.

For Heseltine, and others, managerialism is premised on new methods and modes of accounting, 'with costs attributed to outputs not inputs and outputs measured by quantitative performance measures' (Clarke and Newman, 1997: 147; also, see Cochrane, 1993; Skelcher, 1996; Stewart and Ranson, 1994). Indeed, such managerialist imperatives have been reaffirmed by Tony Blair who, at the annual (1997) Trades Union Congress conference, noted that, 'in a modern welfare state the role of government is not necessarily to provide all social provision but to organise and regulate it most efficiently and fairly'.

This scenario, then, conceives of the market as supreme and managerialisation as the key in the pursuit of a 'particular form of calculus which privileges efficiency goals' (Clarke and Newman, 1997: 155). Downsizing welfare is critical to the overall project, characterised by what Clarke and Newman (1997: 146) have termed the replacement of 'previously unified planning and provision structures' by the disaggregation of service functions into quasi-contractible or quasi-market forms. Thus, in a context of fragmenting, or dispersing, levels of governance, notions of enabling, integrating, linking or, in short, managing, policy processes become paramount. Moreover, the language of corporate business is everywhere in public services with, for example, the quality of the product being stressed in terms of policy decisions. Responsiveness to the consumer or customer, within tightly defined limits, is also seen as a central objective of the emergent managerialist state, while external evaluations, monitoring, audits, appraisals, and reviews of policy procedures, and staff and institutional performances, have become commonplace.

Moreover, for some observers, the managerialisation of local governance is increasingly connected to the pursuit of process over substance and, by implication, the reduction of social and political issues to technical and/or procedural matters (Cochrane, 1993; Hoggett, 1991). As Clarke and Newman (1997) note, conflicts and contradictions in the operations of the welfare state, such as, for example, who gets what resources and where, are being 'managerialised' or, in Clarke and Newman's (1997: 159) terms, being 'redefined as problems to be managed'. In this sense, substantive policy questions, concerning 'efficiency for whom', or 'why efficiency', or 'who will gain and lose from policy', are being recast as operational and/or procedural issues (or of how to manage within the pre-existing, and predefined, series of socio-political values). Indeed, for planning practice, the 1990s have witnessed the reaffirmation of a process-led, or procedural-managerialist, approach (see Healey, 1996, 1997). Increasingly, then, planning functions are perceived of as the development of reticulist and negotiation skills, networking, resource management and the management of processes of change.

Indeed, the managerialist ethos is powerful, yet problematical, for the socio-political consensus it claims can be attained through the development of the appropriate socio-institutional relations, networks and policy (process) procedures (Healey, 1997). In particular, managerialisation underpins the emergence of a potentially new orthodoxy in planning theory and practice which is premised on a Blairite vision of a welfare-pluralist society, in which all can share in the fruits of society (see Imrie and Raco, 1997, 1998). While such visions have been, to date, shrouded in vague political statements by New Labour, the underlying tenor is the development of consensus through collaboration, change through negotiation, and the inculcation of shared values and objectives. For planners in practice, in a changing context of a fragmenting policy arena, and where their ability to engage in the substantive policies arenas is limited, a managerialist perspective on planning is, therefore, seductive for reaffirming the legitimacy of planning's process-based credentials. In this sense, managerialisation provides a potential, yet problematical, source of legitimation for the (continuation of the) planning profession.

TRANSFORMATIONS IN LOCAL GOVERNANCE AND THE CHALLENGES FOR PLANNING PRACTICE IN THE MILLENNIUM

The emergence of the managerial state in the UK has tended to reinforce the myopic focus of local planning practice with the detailed, day-to-day, management of land use development and change, or what Thomas (1997) refers to as 'the sucking of the substance out of what planners do'. In this sense, it is difficult to discern significant changes to planning procedures but more of an intensification of long-established traditions and practices (see also, Tewdwr-Jones, 1995a; Thomas, 1995, 1998). These include, among others, facilitating the objectives of the market, and reinforcing the role of planners as technicians and/or managers of change. In particular, one can identify three interrelated challenges for planners in practice in the context of the emergent systems of local (managerialist) governance. First, the managerialisation of local governance is connected to a redrawing of central–local government relations which, at face value, appears to be underpinned by decentralising tendencies. However, the managerialisation process, I would argue, is connected to tighter central state controls over the content of planning policy strategy and substance, while decentralising the operational, or implementation (the managerial), aspects of the planning process.

Second, calls for the democratisation of local governance is occurring in a context whereby the efficiency ethos of managerialism is implicated in counter-trends towards de-democratisation (see Imrie and Raco, 1997; Offe, 1996; Wolmar, 1997). Indeed, pressures for community involvement in planning policy processes, and the democratisation of policy practices, are heightening in a context whereby planners are increasingly having to justify their actions by recourse to measures of efficiency and value for money. How, then, should, or could, planners seek to resolve some of the underlying tensions and contradictions that this situation poses? Third, the seemingly fragmenting nature of social groups, collectivities and local governance institutions, is posing a challenge for planning practitioners to develop new mechanisms for the (re)combination of such disparate elements. Increasingly, planners are being encouraged towards management practices premised on the development of associative and collaborative networks to enable the attainment of planning objectives (see Healey, 1997). In this sense, managerialisation is, potentially, providing one of the impetuses towards emergent planning theories and practices which, problematically, prioritise the pursuit of process over substance. I discuss each theme in turn.

CENTRAL–LOCAL RELATIONS AND PRIMING THE MARKET BY REINVENTING PROCEDURAL EFFICIENCY

The emergent forms of local governance, as we move towards the millennium, are characterised by the dispersal of functions from hierarchies and the development of decentralised systems of policy-making and implementation. Indeed, recent moves towards regional governments in Scotland and Wales have been heralded by Tony Blair, and other commentators, as indicative of the development of locally responsive, people-based government (DETR, 1997c). Moreover, the Nolan Committee, appointed in 1994 to investigate standards of public behaviour and accountability, reaffirms a move towards generating more open government in recommending opacity and accountability on the part of public service departments, officers and politicians. Others talk of the emergence of community-based planning, through policies such as City Challenge, and the possibilities of less centrally directed policy agendas (Oatley, 1998). Yet, there is much contention over the precise direction and substance of changes in local governance systems and, as Taylor-Gooby and Lawson (1993: 133) suggest, the central state is still a dominant figure in that 'power over the essentials is retained centrally while management of the inessentials is decentralised'.

Indeed, the optimism of the early 1990s, whereby the Planning and Compensation Act (1991) was seen by some as the restoration of a plan-led system, with the capacity to bring local planning to the forefront in determining patterns and processes of urban and regional development, has more or less dissolved (Tewdwr-Jones, 1995b; Thomas, 1995; Thornley, 1995). This has been occurring over a period which has witnessed the diminution in scope of local planning powers through the use of central government directives seeking, first and foremost, to reinforce the primacy of the market and the efficiency of service functions. For example, as Williams (1997: 11) comments, in relation to the development plan process:

> We must also recognise that the production and adoption of a development plan is not
> an end in itself. The more fundamental goal – which we should not lose sight of – is to
> ensure that the time taken to prepare and adopt local plans and then determine major
> planning applications which are consistent with the plan should be shorter.

Such concerns, with speed, efficiency and turnaround, continue to underpin the drive towards a managerialist approach to local planning practice with the central state key in disciplining and directing local policy and strategy. Indeed, central state direction, through national planning policy guidance (NPPG), has intensified, with 36 Planning Policy Guidance notes in England, and 13 in Scotland, being issued since 1992.[1] However, as some commentators suggest, the guidance notes tend to be characterised by the inability 'to accept that restriction may be a legitimate community goal' (Hayton, 1997: 208; also, see Healey, 1996, 1997). Thus, for Hayton (1997: 208), the NPPG system is problematical for reinforcing a pro-development emphasis 'with the planning system being seen as less about regulation and restriction and far more about facilitating development'.

In particular, Hayton (1997), like others, also recognises the potential stranglehold of central directives over local discretion (also, see Tewdwr-Jones, 1995b; Thornley, 1995). Thus, as Hayton (1997: 281) comments:

> . . . faced with this amount of national guidance there is a danger that planning is
> becoming a tick box activity with the scope for formulating policy that reflects local
> priorities being increasingly constrained.

For instance, in the context of guidance concerning planning powers in relation to facilitating disabled people's access in the built environment, central government directives, throughout the 1990s, have guarded against anything other than the use of pro-development voluntary codes of conduct or weakly worded statements in local plans. Indeed, in seeking to minimise restraint on developers, government directives and circulars have made it clear that prescriptive policies on access will be deleted by planning inspectors. Moreover, Planning Policy Guidance 1 (DoE, 1992a) reinforces the conception that planning should only be concerned with physical land use matters in dealing with access matters. Thus, as PPG 1 states:

> . . . where the public are to have access to the building, the local planning authority should consider the extent to which the securing of provision for disabled people can be justified on planning grounds. The sphere of planning control is limited in this context, conditions attached to planning permissions which have no relevance to planning matters will be ultra vires.

For planners, the problems with central guidance of this type are its negative and vague tones, while providing little or no definition as to what 'planning grounds' or 'planning matters' might constitute. Moreover, as MacDonald (1995) notes, the wording in PPG 1 gives few indications to planners as to how access provisions might be enforced. Such situations are evident in a range of other planning practices too. For example, the submission of unitary development plans (UDPs) by local authorities to planning inspectors illustrates the emphasis on facilitating the market and/or business or commercial interests over alternate concerns. Thus, where submitted plans have referred to disabled people's access to buildings and the wider built environment, planning inspectors have been keen to delete any form of prescriptive or binding phrases or terms. Thus, in the London Borough of Newham (1996: 2), policy H9 of the UDP, on accessible housing, was challenged by the inspector for seeking to tie developers to prescribed commitments. The original draft deposit statement read as

> . . . the council will, through entering into legal agreements with developers and attaching conditions to planning permissions, seek to ensure that normally all new houses, ground floor flats, and flats with lift access, are built to mobility standards . . . the council will seek to ensure that units created by conversion are also designed to conform, as far as it is practicable, to mobility standards.

On inspection, the planning inspector recommended the following substitution:

> . . . where the local planning authority considers residential land suitable to accommodate housing accessible to disabled people, it will negotiate with the intention of securing an element of the development to mobility standard.

The contrast between the statements is that the latter provides developers with the latitude and power to pursue most forms of development regardless of planners' views concerning access. There is nothing mandatory or binding while the use of phrases such as 'with the intention of', and 'an element of' do little to guide and/or define what is permissible from what is not. In short, such illustrative material hints at the possibilities for planning to be reduced to not much more than a servicing (or process) function for the development industry.

Others also conceive of planning as (increasingly) a series of routinised, process-based functions bereft of substantive policy development and/or engagement (Hayton, 1997; Healey, 1997; Morphet, 1997). Such observations concur with Clarke and Newman's (1997: 144) analysis, that 'a strong thread in the restructuring of the state has been the attempt to depoliticise decision making by making it a matter of operational management'. This is particularly evident through the dispersal of governance functions to a range of extra-governmental organisations, a process which, in turn, has implications for the implementation of planning policies. Indeed, as Hayton (1997) suggests, the extent to which the policies and programmes in development plans can be implemented is increasingly being constrained by the multiplicity of new agencies involved in aspects of land use development. In the Scottish context, for instance, Hayton (1997) identifies a plethora of agencies, from Scottish National Heritage to the Environmental Protection Agency, with stakes in various aspects of land use development. In this sense, planning and planners may well be reduced to the scenario whereby they seek to resolve a series of single issues rather than interlocking, strategic, concerns.

The competitive ethos of the new local governance, underpinning the emergence of a multi-agency network, is also implicated in the changing organisational nature of the planning system with the development of what Morphet (1997) has characterised as a two-tier planning system operating side by side. For Morphet (1997: 122), there is the land use planning system 'which is increasingly process-oriented . . . formulaic and unimaginative', sitting alongside 'the whole raft of government-generated activities designed primarily to promote the use of . . . competitive funding' (Morphet, 1997: 122). Indeed, the planning system was originally conceived in a period (post-1947) when it was thought that public finance and land would be available to carry through development schemes defined in and through the planning system. Yet, this has rarely been the case and is less so today whereby planning is critically dependent on the newly funded organisations and/or individual private sector investment decisions in facilitating development objectives.

Indeed, for Thomas (1998), and others, the changing nature of local governance is implicated in planners redefining aspects of their work, and of seeking to transform planning discourses about who planners are and what it is they should do (also, see Healey, 1996, 1997; Hillier, 1995). Thus, planners have been at the forefront in working for many of the new local governance institutions since the early 1980s, and many of the urban and regional policy initiatives over the last 10 years, like City Challenge, the urban development corporations and City Pride have been underpinned by planners' involvement in the key positions. While planners could not claim to have a (substantive) knowledge of the respective fields underpinning the different initiatives, what they did do was to present themselves as being able to get things done (Thomas, 1997). In this sense, the resultant discourse, of 'those who do', is a reaffirmation of planners' deeply rooted concerns with process and procedure, and a conception of the profession as enabling. In a context of a centralising, pro-development, agenda perhaps this is the best that planning and planners can do?

FROM CONSUMERISM TO CIVIL EMPOWERMENT AND CITIZENSHIP

In recent times a range of authors have referred to the socio-economic and political fragmentation and differentiation of places or what Offe (1996: 172) refers to as 'society-wide destructuration processes'. For Offe (1996: 172), this is characterised by 'the disorganisation of broad, relatively stable and encompassing commonalities of economic interest, associational affiliation, or cultural values and lifestyles' as a consequence of destabilising forces emanating from transformations in socio-spatial scale relationships. Increasingly, communities are dissolving into fragmented interest groups which do not necessarily correspond with traditional class or ethnic divisions, but often with other social categories such as lifestyle, age and sexuality. In turn, the basis for collective action seems to have dissipated, while new social divisions cut across each other in complex, often contradictory, ways. For planners, identifying collective concerns, and planning on the basis of a collective, are, therefore, a significant, and possibly misplaced, challenge in an era where such collectivities may be difficult to find.

In particular, in a context, post 1947, whereby planning was originally con- ceived within a collectivist tradition, seeking to develop plans and policies for some (mythical) public good, changes in social relations and patterns beg the question of who and/or what are planners now planning for? Moreover, the dispersal of a range of spatial and/or planning functions into a myriad of agencies, has, in Clarke and Newman's (1997: 155) terms, 'multiplied the number of organ- isations, groups and agencies which claim to speak for the public – and produced them in fragmented forms as our customers, patients, parents, communities, etc.'. In this sense, planning seems to be competing for its public. In particular, the managerialist agenda in planning, and elsewhere, is increasingly premised on the development of a consumerist ethos based on a model of citizenship whereby the consumer has the right to choose whether and how to meet his or her welfare and/ or service requirements. For Prior (1996: 93), the overall effect is the increasing dominance of commercial models of organisation and management through a system of management by contracts rather than control via hierarchy.

The drive by governance systems towards commercial or consumer-oriented conceptions of the public has a number of potential implications for planning practice, both positive and negative. Foremost, the consumer analogy is premised on a person expressing a preference in a market place for a specific service and/or good. Yet, public access to a planning, or related, service is premised upon a resource (for example, money) which is the means by which a preference is to be expressed. Yet, resources, or the means by which access to the service is to be gained, are not evenly distributed in society. Thus, while planning may be attentive to social difference, the consumerist conception of the public seems, as Clarke and Newman (1997: 129) note, inattentive 'to issues of inequality of access to the public realm'. In this sense, public participation in planning, along consumerist lines, has the capacity to reinforce social exclusions by doing little more than maintaining the power of the professionals to design, develop and implement the range of planning services (albeit, a process which is influenced by powerful, sectional, interests).

Moreover, as Potter (1994), and others, have argued, there are also conceptual and practice-based limitations in adopting a consumerist logic for planning policy development and implementation (also, see Cochrane, 1993; Flynn, 1990; Rhodes, 1987). In particular, Potter refers to the process orientation of consumerism, with its primary focus on methods and mechanisms of delivering services rather than with, in Clarke and Newman's (1997: 108) terms, 'the decisions about which services should be provided'. The focus of consumerism on individual rather than collective choices also seems to be a challenge to the wider public ethos of planners and planning in seeking to sustain a broader public (or collective) interest in the development and use of land. There is then, I would argue, a potential crisis at the heart of planning which is how to justify and maintain (or even repackage) its collectivist heritage and traditions in an emergent socio-political framework which is anti-collectivist, fragmented and single-issue oriented.

However, aligning the design and development of planning policy alongside a logic of market consumerism is also potentially positive because, theoretically, 'it offers the possibility of services being more attentive to the issues of social diversity in the challenge that it makes to service-led structures of provision' (Clarke and Newman, 1997: 111). Indeed, the debate on consumerism and public services has focused, in part, on the notion that the specific needs of users (or customers) should be paramount. Moreover, it has focused, as Clarke and Newman (1997: 111) note, professional and 'organisational attention on service delivery and the interaction with users'. In this sense, consumerism, potentially, seeks to overturn the bureau-professional conception of the user as passive to one whereby consumers are conceived of as core to defining their specific needs. This is all the more welcome because planning practice has never been particularly opaque or open to scrutiny and, for many, has always been underpinned by a legacy of professional planners paying lip-service to public participation (see, for example, Cockburn, 1977; Saunders, 1980).

In particular, managerialist governance seems to have positioned planners between their perennial concern with, on the one hand, seeking to define who they should be planning for, while, on the other hand, responding to development imperatives to get on with the (primary) task of processing planning applications. For instance, as Thomas (1995) suggests, the pressures on local planning authorities to streamline procedures and reduce delays in plan preparation and development control have diminished the time devoted to public participation in planning processes. For Thomas (1995), efficiency and management are stressed as the keys to good practice, while public participation in processes of plan making is openly discouraged by central government. Thus, as Thomas (1995: 169) notes, the DoE's (1992b) advice on the preparation of development plans 'contains no requirement for public consultation prior to the preparation of the version of the plan that is to be placed on deposit'. As Thomas recounts, government advice in PPG 12 notes that:

> . . . authorities will wish to bear in mind the desirability of resolving points at an early stage of plan preparation and of minimising objections once the plan is on deposit.

While the democratic credentials of local planning have never been great, what remains appears to be under threat from the wider managerialist discourses premised on promoting efficiency in decision-making. This is particularly evident through the system of national policy guidance. For instance, revised Planning Policy Guidance 1 (DoE, 1996a) is revealing for its lack of emphasis on the role of the public interest in planning. As Bell (1997: 67) notes, 'all reference to public interest has been deleted from the opening key paragraphs'. Likewise, Hayton (1997), in the Scottish context, observes how consultations over the contents of the NPPGs have been restricted to a number of key actors and agencies, with little involvement of the general public. Such evidence, of a truncation of public involvement in planning processes, is also evident with PPG 12 (DoE, 1992b) in England which, as Thomas (1995: para. 4.7) indicates, was issued with a directive stating that:

> Authorities will wish to bear in mind the desirability of resolving points at an early stage of plan preparation and of minimising objections once the plan is on deposit.

Moreover, where consultation is encouraged it tends to reflect a form of elitism with the prioritisation of commercial sector organisations and business interests. Thus, as Thomas (1995: para. 4.8) notes, PPG 12 reinforces a partiality in processes of public consultation in that:

> . . . authorities should consult organisations with a particular interest in the plan proposals, including conservation and amenity groups, and business, development and infrastructure interests.

Similar sentiments are conveyed by a good practice guide (ADC/AMA, 1994) on local plan preparation which says nothing about public participation. Moreover the turnaround period of eight weeks for planning applications is, as Thomas (1995) suggests, problematical in that it 'places at a disadvantage those unfamiliar with planning processes and procedures'. Yet, compared to, for example, urban development corporations, or the Scottish local enterprise companies, local planning authorities are bound by statutory public consultation concerning the form and content of their plans. In this sense, there is still a core of democratic procedures and accountability in the statutory planning process which is seemingly being lost to the wider consumerist ethos pervading the emergent systems of local governance in the UK and beyond.

RESISTING COLLABORATIVE PLANNING?

Planning theory and practice beyond the millennium are more than likely to be framed within a managerialist logic and set of related discourses. Such discourses are gaining some ascendancy in planning circles and reflect, in part, Amin and Thomas's (1997) notion that the tide has turned against neo-liberalism while also rejecting any move back to statist forms of governance. Rather, for Amin and Thomas (1997: 255), a third mode of governance is emerging beyond the market or plan involving 'democratisation, decentralisation of decision making, preservation of collective solidarities, and an emphasis on inter-institutional dialogue'. Others concur with this in pointing towards what Amin and Thomas (1997: 255) characterise as 'the development of relations of reciprocity and trust between governance institutions' (also, see Healey, 1996, 1997; Healey *et al.*, 1995). Such perspectives, on urban governance, emphasise the importance of 'local institutional capacity and its role in mobilising interconnections between the relational webs which coexist within and beyond an urban region through encouraging network building, and through discourse' (Healey *et al.*, 1995: 283). The key is consensus seeking, collaboration and communication between diverse and disparate actors at interconnecting spatial scales.

Moreover, for Healey (1996, 1997), the generation of, what she terms, a collaborative cultural community is connected to a wider agenda of helping to re-create a public realm which, seemingly, has disappeared (although it is questionable whether any public realm, whatever it is, ever existed). Others concur with this and, as Carmichael (1994: 251) suggests, 'local authorities should see themselves as leading actors in a pluralistic institutional environment' seeking to bind (together) disparate actors with shared interests (in the land market). In particular, such ideas are something of an emergent orthodoxy in planning studies yet seem to me to be problematical as a way of understanding the methods and mechanisms by which planners and policy-makers can seek to restructure the fortunes of urban and regional economies. Foremost, they are premised on idealist conceptions of power best illustrated by concepts such as 'shared power worlds' (a term coined by Bryson and Crosby, 1992 and adopted by Healey, 1996). Yet, in what senses are power worlds (whatever these are) shared, and shared by whom and on what terms?

In particular, how far can planners influence the powerful to release resources to those without power and/or the requisite means to influence urban and regional development? Indeed, how might planners seek to persuade sharing when to share is to relinquish a resource base and/or the command over land and particular spaces? To what extent will employers, for example, wish to provide strategic decision-making powers to employees, and how might it be possible to bind together ethnic differences in regions characterised by ethnic violence? Moreover, what is it to be 'collaborative' and with whom and for what ends? Indeed, it seems to me that there are significant problems about how the generation of collaborative social relations will occur and also about how collaboration is understood by different interest groups and/or actors (see Imrie and Raco, 1998). In particular, collaboration, and related concepts, are underpinned by an unjustifiable reductionism into pluralist theories of social action which, in Fainstein's (1994) terms, are based on a benign view of social power.

Moreover, Healey (1996, 1997), and others, problematically prioritise communicative interaction and discourse as the means to connect actors, people and places to each other. While this is a necessary condition in developing plans and policies, it is not sufficient and there is no guarantee that communication *per se* will provide and/or enhance understanding (of whatever type). Indeed, the reverse might well occur. In particular, part of the problem with communicative interaction, as a perspective on planning, is its apparent abrogation for seeking to take action on the basis of existing substantive knowledge of urban and regional dynamics. Thus, for Healey *et al.* (1995: 288), the world is so diverse and full of differences, too complex to act, or, as they state, 'we still know so little about how urban life and urban economies are evolving, and how this relates to governance activity'. This, to me, is an astonishing statement because we do know much about the worlds we inhabit, about class, gender, ethnicity and of the power structures which perpetuate inequalities. In this sense, appealing for communicative interaction in order to respond to difference seems to be a diversion. However, the communicative or collaborative approach, as one might term it, is a powerful conception in legitimising a managerialist approach to the problems confronting the planner. If the problems for planning to resolve are conceived of as 'managerial', that is, for example, organising networks, forging partnerships and developing processual mechanisms, then seeking to develop the means to collaborate and co-operate seems an appropriate strategy. Yet, for planners in practice, the managerialist logic is a double-edged sword. On the one hand, it has the potential to redefine the legitimate sphere of planning practice as operational or implementation-based and, in doing so, to provide a core focus for the practices of planners and planning (i.e. a legitimation for their *raison d'être*). Yet, in doing so, it potentially weakens planners' claims to a substantive knowledge base and series of related professional practices while simultaneously abrogating a responsibility for seeking,

120

in a purposive and self-conscious way, to transform the substance of urban and regional systems. In this sense, it constitutes a denial of planners' roles in processes of spatial development.

Such scenarios proffer the possibilities for reaffirming reductive and marginal roles for planning practice and practitioners beyond the millennium; reductive in the sense that planners' core tasks will be organisational, technical and administrative, marginal in that their circumscribed legal powers will have little capacity to produce anything much more than a reactive system. Indeed, managerialist thinking seems set to legitimise a task-centred approach to policy, espousing the virtues of organisation. In this sense, it has the capacity to reinforce the disjuncture between means and ends while denying the value-laden and ideological nature of planning and policy processes. Yet, planning practice in the UK is enmeshed within a series of socio-legal relations underpinned by a particular conception of rights, dealing with challenges arising from the rights of property owners to the enjoyment of their possessions. This is an arena of values, contestation and power, where planning is an active (recursive) shaper of social structures (see Giddens, 1991). A recognition of this should underpin what planning ought to be. Planning practice into the millennium must be considered as an integral or constitutive component of socio-political relations, not as a matter of alternative technologies.

ACKNOWLEDGEMENTS

I would like to thank the Economic and Social Research Council (grant number: R000235833) for providing me with the financial resources to generate some of the information contained within this chapter. I would also like to thank Huw Thomas for providing me with some information and materials for this chapter and for talking through some of the issues raised by the changing nature of planning practice into the millennium.

NOTE

1. As Allmendinger and Tewdwr-Jones (1997) note, central government sees the NPPG system as a vital part of the planning framework with the understanding that local planning authorities have to take them into account in reaching a development decision. Indeed, some research shows that planners regard the policy guidance system as 'the last word' and will fall in line with whatever directives emanate from central government (Hayton, 1997; Imrie, 1996).

CHAPTER 8

REASSERTING TOWN PLANNING: CHALLENGING THE REPRESENTATION AND IMAGE OF THE PLANNING PROFESSION

Mark Tewdwr-Jones

INTRODUCTION

This chapter explores the position of town planning, planning's image and pro-fessionalism, predominantly in the UK at the end of the twentieth century. It is essentially a polemic. It is intended to facilitate a wide-ranging debate on these subjects as we enter into a new millennium, and one which has been lacking over the last 10 years or so. From a personal perspective, although I had always intended to work in practice after leaving university and achieving my two degrees in planning, I found these aspects of the land use process – the definition of town planning and its status, the role of politics in decision-making and policy-making, the values and ethics associated with being a member of a professional body, and the role of the individual in decision settings and in organisational contexts – the most interesting and challenging, and the most difficult, to comprehend.

The fact that my dilemmas and uncertainties about these issues still exist today perhaps lie at the root of the problem of planning itself. My uncertainties with planning correspond to questions of planning as a self-perpetuating activity, devoid of any theoretical basis, devoid of any unique professional skills, and a continual source of jokes. I have not suddenly developed these uncertainties, and other commentators over the years have debated these questions far more effectively. But the opportunity to provide a critical viewpoint of planning and professionalism as part of an edited volume intended to be both reflective and forward-looking, has necessitated an analytical scrutiny of the subject matter I have immersed myself in since the mid 1980s.

In a previous paper, I portrayed the role of the town planner in the UK in a rather negative light, criticising planners as individuals for their apparent embracement of all things technical and their contentment not to be more visionary in their duties (Tewdwr-Jones, 1996). I wish to continue the debate within this chapter by additionally considering the position of the professional institute, but by taking a more positive approach of how we may start to challenge town planning's poor public image and the associated 'intellectual abdication' within planning practice in the new millennium. I might appear patronising in my discussion of town planners as those most at fault, by appearing to distance myself as an academic from practitioners. I will also discuss aspects of planning that will no doubt prove to be exceptionally unpopular, even offensive, to certain sections of the planning profession. This debate is intended to be inclusive of all planners, public sector, private sector and academics, and I certainly have no desire in placing academic discussions of planning on some pedestal. Furthermore, I do not seek to create controversy for controversy's sake by my writing; I simply feel that it is time for a frank and open discussion of some of these issues.

My critical perspective for this chapter has emanated from a growing frustration with planning, particularly with planning professionalism, with some planners' inability to consider planning as an inherently political and powerful activity, and with planners' content not to reassert their position in broader socio-economic and environmental change. As planners we also seemed to have forgotten the early twentieth-century visionary planning ideals, and how town planning can actually not only contribute towards but shape social and economic restructuring. At the present time, planning as a legislative and professional activity is becoming increasingly commodified, a series of checklists, league tables and manual books. The planning process is becoming devoid of intellectual discourse concerning broader spatial or strategic questions, and rather is concentrating on its successful role as very little more than a neighbourhood protection service. There is debate, of course, on sustainability issues, on transport planning and regional economic growth. But when allied to the statutory planning process, they seem to take on an air of rhetoric.

Strategic planning for transport, economic development and environmental protection are fundamental matters for town and country planning and have been since the creation of legislative town planning in the pre-war period. They are also some of the core modules of planning degree programmes taught at university planning schools. But we should not fool students into thinking that planning in the UK can and still does deliver on these matters *per se*. The murky world of planning practice is now inextricably bound up in the political and powerful nuances of governance, and we really need to reassess planning's contribution in socio-economic and environmental change as part of a political reaction, not as some self-standing panacea that is 'worthy'. In reflecting on planning's contribution to both local and strategic change, we also require a reassessment of the particular contribution planning makes as a professional activity, a subsidiary but interlinked area of discussion and one upon which little debate seems to have occurred over the last 10 years.

There is a noticeable lack of research evidence in the area of planning, politics and professionalism in the UK, unusually so for a subject matter that today is at the heart of the very continuation of 'town planning'. Very few studies have looked at the subject of decision-making dilemmas as a political, professional and open process in the past, not least because it is such a difficult area to assess effectively. These are broad issues for discussion, and in the following pages I shall restrict my discussion to four interrelated arguments:

1. Town planning is suffering from a severe albeit outdated image problem, identified by planners and the public, that needs to be tackled positively.
2. Planning's distinct role as a regulatory process in the UK has been reduced to one of a local protectionist force and it has become commodified by successive central government policies, to the extent that it is nothing more than a series of checklists.
3. Public sector planning practice is becoming increasingly devoid of unique skills (normally the attributes of a professional activity) as part of the dominance of a 'new proceduralism' within planning.
4. The status of planning in the 1990s as 'new proceduralism' is being bolstered by the profession's inability to consider broader intellectual discourse on planning's strategic contribution, on planning's professional status, and on planning's position in UK transitionary politics and governance.

It is time for the town planning process to reassert itself as a central facilitating component of socio-economic restructuring, and for public sector planners themselves to be less apathetic towards their tasks. This reassertion needs to occur to bolster the image of town planning, as a deliberate reaction against the domination of proceduralism in planners' activities, and as a way of averting a potential crisis of legitimation associated with planning professionalism. If these negative issues find footing within the planning profession, the danger for town planning at the start of the new millennium is that it could become a second-rate professional activity, devoid of visionary zeal, and placed outside political discussions on future socio-economic and environmental change. We are already seeing this happen to some extent in economic growth and inward investment decisions. Town planning has reached a crossroads: planners can either accept the continuing political and procedural changes to planning to assert administration and technicality (for this seems to be the direction planning is heading towards), or else planners can take up the challenge of fighting their corner, by reasserting themselves, their image and their roles in twenty-first-century Britain.

Before going on to consider these issues in more detail, I wish to commence the debate by discussing the image and representation of town planning by the media and the public and in popular culture since 1945, for this appears to be one reason for what might be termed a professional retrenchment.

Town Planning's Representation and Imagery

The phrase 'town planning' unfortunately possesses negative connotations. Town planning in the public's eye conjures up images of concrete tower blocks, flyovers,

Milton Keynes, change and newness, the abandonment of the past. This is possibly because the public's perception of town planning is, quite naturally, the planning of new towns, a function we rarely perform in the profession these days. The new towns of Britain developed after 1945 are undoubtedly visionary in their design and layouts but this legacy for the planning profession is also the root of public discontentment. 'Town planning' in the public's eye is simply the building of new towns; the only other work planners seem to do is giving out (or more likely refusing) planning permission for householders to build their garage extension, extra bedroom or new house in the countryside. As the scourge of public hatred, town planners are continually lambasted for their overt bureaucracy, their 'toy town' outlook, and for their destruction of Britain's heritage.

This tendency for the public to criticise town planners for the state of the nation is not a particularly recent phenomenon. If anything, it is an ongoing love–hate relationship between planners and the public; it has become, to all intents and purposes, a national pastime. The origins of this criticism go way back to the post-war period, and it is worth briefly revisiting this time to place the birth of town planning in a historical and cultural context, in order to identify how the phenomenon developed.

'INEXPENSIVE PROGRESS'? PRO-COMMUNITY AND ANTI-CHANGE SENTIMENT

The poor image of 'town planning' commenced in Britain as soon as the new legislation had been passed by Parliament in 1947. This was a time, of course, when the post-war Labour government was elected with a landslide electoral majority to rebuild the country, and to implement a radical socialist programme of renewal. This renewal included, *inter alia*, the creation of a National Health Service, a national education programme, the establishment of the nationalised industries, the continued decentralisation of manufacturing industry to the regions and the legislative birth of town and country planning as we know it today. This radical agenda was necessary for a country emerging from the destructive trauma of world war, and certainly emphasises newness and rebirth. But it is also associated with the loss of the old, a recognition on the public's part that things would never be quite the same again. This loss-of-something view seems to have been widespread among the literati at the time, and since town planning was at the centre of facilitating this newness, it was the one profession most readily identifiable in causing physical change. As such, the public's mistrust at town planning started to occur both as a reaction against inevitable change but also as a recognition that planning was also the process that was sweeping the old away. In reality, it was the German bombing of British cities, the need to revitalise British manufacturing and the immense population changes of the post-war period that proved to be the catalyst for change. But since town planning was the force charged with co-ordinating restructuring at this time, the public became more interested in venting their protests at town planning for the state's rebuilding, the perceived loss of community and for the development of visionary high-rise flats and tower blocks that, as centres of community life, failed dismally (Jacobs, 1961).

The writings, poetry and cinema of some of Britain's most respected cultural icons reflect this lament at the loss of the pre-war existence, the perceived loss of community, and the birth of state planning. Between the 1940s and the 1970s, for example, John Betjeman, poet and champion of Victorian Britain, ridiculed town planners fairly successfully for their creation of what he viewed as a New Order in several poems, including 'The Planster's Vision', 'Inexpensive Progress', 'Slough', and 'The Town Clerk's Views'. In the latter, the late Poet Laureate encapsulates his frustration with visionary town planning and the concomitant growth of bureaucracy:

> In a few years this country will be looking
> As uniform and tasty as its cooking.
> Hamlets which fail to pass the planners' test
> Will be demolished. We'll build the rest
> To look like Welwyn mixed with Middle West.
> All fields we'll turn to sports grounds, lit at night
> From concrete standards by fluorescent light:
> And all over the land, instead of trees,
> Clean poles and wire will whisper in the breeze.
> (John Betjeman, excerpt from 'The Town Clerk's Views', 1988: 146,
> with permission from John Murray (Publishers) Ltd)

In a later poem, 'Inexpensive Progress', he revisits the debate by criticising the way the country was moving in the 1960s and 1970s, but seems to channel his *Angst* against town planners specifically:

> Let no provincial High Street
> Which might be your or my street
> Look as it used to do,
> But let the chain stores place here
> Their miles of black glass facia
> And traffic thunder through.
>
> And if there is some scenery,
> Some unpretentious greenery,
> Surviving anywhere,
> It does not need protecting
> For soon we'll be erecting
> A Power Station there.
>
> When all our roads are lighted
> By concrete monsters sited
> Like gallows overhead,
> Bathed in the yellow vomit

Each monster belches from it,
We'll know that we are dead.
(John Betjeman, excerpt from 'Inexpensive Progress', 1988: 287,
with permission from John Murray (Publishers) Ltd)

Putting aside debate over the merit of his poetry, Betjeman was a favourite with the people of Britain, and through his poetry, writings and television documentaries usefully managed to awaken a conservation movement at the grass-roots level in the 1960s and 1970s while simultaneously criticising the loss of Britain's heritage and the onset of change (the town planners' responsibility) in the built and natural environment.

Author and playwright J. B. Priestley was not so tinted by a desire to 'preserve and conserve'. In fact Priestley was a socialist committed to common ownership of land and industrial resources, but nevertheless identifies the emergence of the 'two nations' of Britain, between the pre-war 'thatched cottage, cricket pitch and village green' community and the industrialised, planned and modern image associated with restructuring and development. In his *English Journey* (1979), for example, he portrays a Britain of

> . . . arterial and by-pass roads, of filling stations and factories that look like exhibition buildings, of giant cinemas and dance-halls and cafes, bungalows with tiny garages, cocktail bars, Woolworths, motor-coaches, wireless, hiking, factory girls looking like actresses, greyhound racing and dirt tracks, swimming pools, and everything given away for cigarette coupons.

The author George Orwell in 1941 attempts to pin down the particular sense of the spirit of Britain (more as a propaganda pamphlet than an academic discussion of town planning) where, in an essay entitled 'England, Your England', he remarks about the 'privateness' of British life and the people's aversion to erosion of their local communities through inevitable change (Orwell, 1941). Both Priestley and Orwell differ from Betjeman in their identification of a new nationhood in the post-war period; Betjeman specifically pinpointed town planners as the root cause of a loss of community, whereas Priestley and Orwell were more interested in identifying how a community copes with change. This is an important distinction to make, for an implied criticism of town planners may, in actuality, be nothing more than a lament at the loss of pre-existing community living, and the two are clearly separate matters.

Some of the celebrated British Ealing Studios' films of the 1940s and 1950s are similar to Betjeman's poems in feeling a desire to look backwards for comfort during immense socio-economic change. Many of the most successful Ealing comedy films possessed one particular common characteristic: a story of one small community's desire to break free from overt bureaucratic control. The 1949 film, *Passport to Pimlico*, bases its whole plot within a small London residential area and the people's desire to escape post-war restrictions while coping with physical change and the loss of community. Within the film, the people are divided in deciding on what sort of development to permit to be built on a derelict bomb-site in the heart of their community: a commercial centre (progressive, economic and necessary but portrayed as 'harsh') and a swimming pool 'for the local kids' (social, community-centred and 'nice'). The dilemmas of choosing which type of development for the area reflect the two nations phenomenon identified in Priestley's writings; both are intended to be pro-community and the people's attempt to get on with their lives by creating something new. But the swimming pool dream is portrayed as the more heartfelt response, because it is something the whole community can become involved in.

Ealing's 1953 film, *The Titfield Thunderbolt*, uses a similar theme in telling the story of a rural community's protest at the closure of their local railway line (the community's lifeline) and their attempt to take over the railway themselves to avert the operation of a rival bus service (the operators, 'Pearce and Crump', are portrayed in the film as shifty, corrupt, greedy and anti-community, eager to turn the village of 'Titfield' into 'Pearcetown'). In one interesting scene – a public inquiry into the community's application to run the local rail service – the lead character turns to the assembled public gallery and pleas with the audience for support against Pearce and Crump:

> Don't you realise you're condemning our village to death. Open it up to buses and lorries and what's it going to be like in five years time? Our lanes will be concrete roads, our houses will have numbers instead of names, there'll be traffic lights and zebra crossing. And that will be twice as dangerous.

Charles Barr's authoritative work on the Ealing films excellently portrays this almost pro-community/anti-change sentiment in the film-scripts of T. E. B. Clarke, by referring to the 'polarisation' displayed in the films 'between recreated past and threatening future, between the dynamism of acquisitiveness and the static nature of community' (Barr, 1993: 106), and a tendency to increasingly portray 'something nice and wholesome and harmless, quaint and static and timeless' (Barr, 1993: 159) in the films as change unfolded at the time.

TOWN PLANNING AS THE PERPETUATION OF NEWNESS

There is no doubt that Britain during the 1940s and 1950s did comprise 'two nations': one of a people looking backwards for community stability, and one of a people searching enthusiastically for improved conditions, economic prosperity and better housing. For many, including members of the literati, these two nations were viewed as being at opposite ends of the spectrum; unfortunately, town planning was caught in the middle. What is of concern in some media at the time is the portrayal of town planning as a force against communitarianism, when clearly planners themselves were attempting to co-ordinate change for the benefit of

_____

community-building. This is possibly the fault of planning at this time; instead of planners ensuring community spirit-fostering (through the recognition of the importance people attached to their immediate lifestyles, environments and neighbours), planners pigeonholed community into something that could equally be built up from scratch. It was never going to work in quite this way.

These discussions are useful for they place the birth of statutory town planning in historical context. We identify the alienation some of the people of Britain felt towards the onset of radical change promoted through a new town and country planning process, but simultaneously recognise the need to organise such a process in post-war restructuring. But the debate is also necessary to understand how the British desire to continually criticise town planning has always existed. It emerged in the austerity years of the 1940s and the people's anger with the loss of their pre-war communities (more directly through the ravages of war than planning) and continued through into the 1950s and 1960s as the public continually lamented at the loss of their pre-war existence and vented their frustrations with the professionals who were charged with the task of physical rebuilding. The dream of improved housing, economic prosperity and planned communities was realised but not in the way people had imagined. Young and Willmot's well-known (1957) account of the Bethnal Green community, for example, usefully illustrates the expectations and frustrations communities felt towards this newness, by expressing their sense of loss towards their pre-war and wartime existence and environment and the unhappiness with their new housing in clinical environments. In cinematic representations, the British film industry eagerly portrayed the changing conditions of the country, but was tarnished by a desire to continue the wartime machinery of reasserting the (pre-war) spirit of Britain (Murphy, 1989).

This tendency to cope with physical change by re-creating a golden era image of pre-war Britain only served to fuel the public's dismay at the post-war town planning developments. One doubts whether the sort of romanticised images of Britain portrayed in films of the 1940s and 1950s actually existed in the pre-war era (they are certainly middle-class visions of a Britain comprising (to be tongue-in-cheek): cricket, the village green, warm beer, old ladies walking to evensong, and midwives on bicycles) but the public certainly felt more comfortable with those images of their environments than the visionary new developments being provided in rebuilt towns and cities across the country.

Other books, films and television programmes over the last 30 years have built on this preconceived image of town planning as a 'threat' to community and heritage. Innumerable film and television documentaries by Betjeman, for example, devoted to capturing physical change in historical towns in the 1960s and 1970s were intended to halt town planning in its tracks by encouraging professionals to consider a more 'humane' form of physical restructuring.

In the BBC television series *Bird's Eye View* (an aerial view of Britain accompanied by Betjeman narrating his own verse), a great deal of footage is given over to new housing developments. For example, in one part of the film *An Englishman's Home*, Betjeman mocks town planners for their visionary perspective of new housing. The images move away from English villages, Bath, Clifton and Brighton and the music of Elgar and Vaughan Williams to a depiction of the massive tower blocks of London's East End and Essex accompanied by the more contemporary instrumental music of Stravinsky, leading Betjeman to say:

> Oh the planners did their best.
> Oh yes, they gave it all a lot of thought.
> Putting in trees and grassy rides
> And splendid views across to Richmond Park
> And landscaped streets and abstract sculpture.
> Oh Roehampton won the prizes.
> It was all so well laid out.
> Just so much space from one block to the next.
> Perhaps this is the way we ought to live?
>
> But where can be the heart that sends a family
> To the twentieth floor of such a slab as this?
> It can't be right,
> However fine the views across to Greenwich and the Isle of Dogs.
> It can't be right,
> Caged half way up the sky, not knowing your neighbour
> Frightened of the lift and who'll be in it
> And who's down below.
> And are the children safe?
>
> New towns, new housing estates,
> New homes, new streets, new neighbours,
> New standards of living,
> New financial commitments,
> New jobs, new schools, new shops.
> New loneliness, new restlessness,
> New pressures, new tension.
> And people.
> People who have to cope with all this newness.
> People who cannot afford old irrelevances.
> People who have to find a God who fits in.
> (John Betjeman, excerpt from *An Englishman's Home*, BBC Television, 1971,
> reproduced with permission)

To say that this is sensationalism, rather than prose, would be an understatement. Nevertheless, thanks to Betjeman and others who captured (or perhaps led?) the public imagination, town planners did emerge at this time as truly stigmatised professionals. From a community perspective, of course, Betjeman was – with hindsight – correct. But it only reinforced a myth that town planners were more interested in physical rebuilding rather than with the people who use the buildings. Planning as a community instrument had failed spectacularly, encouraging professionals to reconsider their brief and indirectly to determine that the future of town planning lay in local, pragmatic land use considerations and not as a visionary ideal.

Planning as a public service did change almost immediately after this period, thanks to both the Skeffington report and the introduction of public consultation in the statutory planning process, and to academic and policy accounts of the dangers of ignoring community desires and treating planning as a clinical techno-cratic process (e.g. Jacobs, 1961; Gans, 1972). But town planning as a professional occupation has never really recovered from this sort of attack.

BUREAUCRACY, JOKES AND THE RESPONSE OF THE PLANNING PROFESSION

In addition to the loss-of-community image that town planning perpetuates, the media have also become obsessed with identifying town planning as an overt bureaucratic and administrative machine of local government, especially by con-centrating on examples of corruption, malpractice and shady property deals. The author Tom Sharpe, for example, in his comedy *Blott on the Landscape*, portrays the town planner as corrupt and downtrodden, susceptible to greed and politics. In recent television documentaries, planners have been portrayed (perhaps unfairly) as bungling administrators (British Channel Four's *Cream Teas and Concrete* of 1991) and overt bureaucrats (British Channel Four's *An Inspector Calls* of 1996). Altogether, the portrayal and representation of town planning by the media are not a happy picture, and it is possible to identify a shift in the representation of town planning away from the 'threat to community' portrayal of the the 1950s to 1970s to one of town planning as a 'pusher of paperclips' in the 1980s and 1990s, the overt bureaucrat strictly following laws and policies. The British comedian and author Ben Elton lambasted town planners on one of his television shows by portraying planners as a group of long-haired 'flower-power' hippies standing around a development model and deciding to place traffic roundabouts every-where, for the simple reason that, 'Hey man, they just go round and round and round. Wow!' Comedy sketches aside, the public's perceptions of town planning are stereotypical and at least 25 years out of date.

This imagery and representation have done little to boost the confidence of planning practitioners, who additionally in their day-to-day work suffer the unenviable task of mediating in public displeasure, unrest and argumentation. It is little wonder that practitioners themselves are also starting to abandon using the phrase 'town planners' in their job titles, by preferring to call themselves simply 'planners', 'consultants', 'environmentalists' or 'local authority officers'. As a planning student from Heriot-Watt University, Edinburgh, recently remarked to me, 'Yeah, being a "town planner" is a bit embarrassing with your mates. You just try to call yourself something else.' Craig McLaren has also referred to the inevit-able moment at a party when someone asks 'the dreaded question', 'So, what do you do for a living?', and the response 'Oh, I'm a town planner' which generally is a cue for comic abuse and anger from the other people present (McLaren, 1997). If the phrase 'town planning' is starting to appear as an embarrassment to planning professionals and maybe is totally irrelevant for the type of planning work we now undertake in practice, it is not surprising to find town planning becoming something of a joke.

Planning as a process suffers from a legacy of past images, poor decisions, visionary planning mistakes, 'bureaucracy gone mad', and a perception that it is anti-community. But as planning professionals we have been very intent on accepting the abuse. We have not faced up to the poor images, we have been careful not to admit our mistakes too readily and we may have not taken sufficient account of the community aspect.

One would normally have expected the professional institute to take up the challenge of planning's public image and reassertion. The Royal Institute of British Architects, for example, has responded positively and thoroughly following the public criticisms levelled by the Prince of Wales (1988) towards perceived poor modern architecture (town planners, incidentally, emerged from this haranguing without the same level of stigma for some reason). But the Royal Town Planning Institute (RTPI) has shown little interest in championing a public campaign. It almost makes one wish for the Prince of Wales to have turned his attentions on town planning, for at least it would have initiated a high-profile debate. Even individual presidents of the institute have been largely ineffectual in portraying planning more positively to a sceptical public. The late Francis Tibbalds was an exception in recent presidents in being prepared to reassert town planning more broadly. Other presidencies (for example, the offices of Hazel Mckay in 1993 and Tony Struthers in 1997) are noted, in my view, for their passiveness. Even when one thought that there was an opportunity for more academic discourse on the intellectual development of planning thought within the RTPI through the election of a planning academic as president (Cliff Hague in 1996), the optimism was ill-founded.

The public criticism and ridicule, the roundabout jokes and the political bashing planning received in the 1980s, have all led the planning profession to retrench into a non-controversial, balancing act-based activity, devoid of visionary zeal, as a way of coping with adverse public criticism of previous mistakes that we, as planners, have been responsible for. The RTPI's Press Officer has recently, admittedly, attempted to make planning 'sexy', by 'dressing up' planning in the eyes of the media (Taylor, 1997) and with some success in national and regional newspapers and broadcasts. But part of the problem rests with planners' own inability to reassert their profession. As Taylor (1997: 18) remarks, 'Planners must be prepared to stand up and trumpet their achievements.'

The image of town planning with the public, the popular press and in culture needs improving. Planners are once again undertaking a range of important tasks in socio-economic restructuring and environmental change, but these new roles have not been trumpeted sufficiently to alter the preconceived images. We need to pause for a moment and start to tackle this dilemma. Planning as a political process and governmental activity is at the centre of the state's co-ordination of change. The pressures on the British planning system and the expectations by clients of planning for it to be able to deliver will increase in the next few years as the country undergoes further change. The next section considers the pressures and expectations on town planning today as a prelude to a discussion of the form planning presently takes.

TOWN PLANNING AS THE MEDIATION BETWEEN CONFLICTING PRESSURES AND EXPECTATIONS

The period since 1947 has witnessed many different expectations of what planning as a state process can, should and does deliver, and it is worth briefly considering the fundamental contextual changes that have occurred within which planning operates. There is no doubt that the Attlee post-war Labour government of the 1940s viewed planning as a social good, the state's responsibility to physically rebuild, to protect the best of our landscapes and to regulate physical and economic change. The 1950s, 1960s and early 1970s saw planning become a comprehensive redevelopment activity, particularly in inner-city locations, through road-building programmes, by slum clearance and new town development, and with it the development of a professional stigma. The 1980s decade was characterised by planning's market orientation, a clear move away from state control over physical and economic development and a complete ideological reversal of the Attlee government's stance towards town planning. The 1990s have witnessed the emergence of environmentalism, and in the latter 1990s by the Major and Blair governments attempting to achieve a market and environmental balance in the planning process. The election in May 1997 of a New Labour administration committed towards more openness in government, constitutional reform and possibly a great role for communitarianism as an underlying ideology for government policy, could well place further pressures on an already stretched town and country planning process.

At the time of writing (October 1997), the planning profession is commemorating the fiftieth anniversary of the passing of the Town and Country Planning Act 1947. The 50 years' celebration is, actually, a commemoration of the advent of proceduralism and rule books in planning, the cementation of the professional with the procedural. The 1947 Act had been truly visionary; not only did the legislation implement the development plan system, but additionally legitimised planning control, and set land use change within broader property and state regulation questions concerning compensation and betterment. The abandonment of the compensation and betterment aspect of the trilogy of legislative initiatives has only caused planning's visionary weakness in the 50 years since and its set course as an overt administrative function. Instead of the planning profession celebrating the 1947 Act by talking about the next 50 years (for example, the appropriateness of the current system of planning, the conflicting pressures on planning socio-economically, environmentally and politically, and the birth of a new planning vision), planners are looking backwards and there is little debate being fostered within the UK to consider the future. Patsy Healey's latest book *Collaborative Planning* (Healey, 1997), is a noticeable exception, although even this planning academic guru has not grasped the fundamental problems associated with translating visions into hard realities within a sceptical, content and largely pragmatic planning profession.

The retrenchment of planning as a professional occupation following the criticisms and ridicule associated with 'true town planning' in the 1950s and 1960s is alive and well today. Planners are content to go on working as administrators in fairly narrow contexts, but the world has changed drastically since not only the 1970s but also the 1980s. The continuing pressure for inward investment and economic growth, the concern over the environment and in providing for a sustainable future, the restrictions on the use of the private motor car, and questions on how to utilise town planning to achieve aspects of social justice, are all significant issues for the planning profession to grasp. Planners are aware of these pressures and conflicts, and of the need to integrate these broad strategic policies into planning practice. But the planning profession's response, indeed the government's response, has been to amend, alter or 'fit in' changes to the 50-year-old statutory planning system. In the case of inward investment decisions and urban redevelopments, these have occurred virtually outside the statutory planning framework. The questions we all need to ask are:

- Has the present British town and country planning process served its course?
- How should we adopt a new town planning process in recognition of a changed agenda?
- How, as planning professionals, can we reassert our roles, image and expectations in meeting the challenge of a new planning process?

These questions need addressing, but can look rather academic when placed in the context of the operation of the current planning system. Why? Because the planning process itself over the last 20 years has retrenched into an overt procedural process.

TOWN PLANNING'S 'NEW PROCEDURALISM' AT THE END OF THE TWENTIETH CENTURY

COMMODIFICATION AND STANDARDISATION

It has been acknowledged elsewhere that Thatcherite reforms to the planning system and to planning policy in particular in the 1980s were profound (Brindley *et al.*, 1989; Thornley, 1991; Allmendinger and Tewdwr-Jones, 1997). Uniquely, the statutory planning process *as a local government function* was not altered to any great extent. At a time when local government services were becoming centralised in Whitehall (Rhodes, 1988), the localised planning service was left largely unaltered in the sense that, today, decisions are still made by local government. Some decision-making for planning and economic development projects was determined by central government through the appeals mechanism and by Secretary of State call-ins, as part of the so-called 'appeal-led' system. Additionally, the democratic planning control service was dented in urban areas with the creation of urban development corporations, enterprise zones and simplified planning zones, that either removed planning control functions from local government or else severely curtailed them. But the nature of the localised decision-making process as one of administrative and political discretion remains in place today, and has altered little since its inception 50 years ago.

Exactly why the Thatcher governments did not abolish or radically alter the structure or nature of the planning process into a privatised operation (despite the governments' mauling of every other aspect of local government) has never really been assessed. Could it have been because planning, especially planning control, as primarily a local function was viewed as a popular device by the natural allies of the Conservative Party – the shire voters? In this sense, if the government could legitimise town and country planning for the benefit of local communities, it would become politically non-threatening. Therefore, as nothing more than a neigh-bourhood protection service at the local level, planning would be acceptable as the force for the protection of individual's property rights. However, at the regional and subregional levels (or rather with regard to development proposals with significant regional or subregional implications), central government took a strong interest in reorientating town planning to the centre (Booth, 1996), either through call-in applications, the emphasis on the market or by placing the planning agenda into the hands of local democratically unaccountable quangos such as urban development corporations. What was left for local government to operate was a rump of a statutory planning system, to be used to legitimise strategic decisions taken elsewhere.

For the most part, the statutory planning rump was also made more efficient. For example, planning control as a neighbourhood protection service has received greater attention since 1991 or so through enhanced media reporting and the interest by the Major and Blair governments in public service standards. But note the two rationales for this heightened interest: well-publicised cases of local authorities not conforming to central government's planning policy agenda (Cloke, 1996); and the release at the central level of development control performance criteria to which local authorities are required to conform (Tewdwr-Jones, 1995b). In other words, and as discussed in work by Tewdwr-Jones and Harris (1998), the New Right's impact on statutory town planning since the late 1980s has been essentially one of 'commodification'.

The standardisation of planning has been ensured by the realignment of the process to one of league tables, performance standards and checklists, aspects of the planning function that central government ministers of both Conservative and Labour administrations have been only too eager to heighten to expose relatively poor performances on the part of local government in facilitating both the market and citizens' desires. When local planning authorities have been exposed for their inadequacies, or else when planning departments and committees in certain areas of the country have failed to conform to the planning control standards, central government has intervened by pointing out 'malpractice'. Explanations for the idiosyncratic nature of planning control decision-making – the impact of the political and of values in local areas – derives from rational selection and from prejudice and preference among the decision-makers themselves. It may be difficult, therefore, to generalise a model of planning policy- and decision-making with national standards and checklists when the process is truly localised. We consequently possess a planning control service that, as a function of government, is in limbo. It has survived 1980s Thatcherite reforms to exist as primarily a local activity. However, it has been subject to 1990s Major–Blair reforms of national commodifcation and standardisation as a function of government. The rub is clear to identify for local planning authority officers: conform to national standards or else face intervention from central government.

As Rob Imrie outlines elsewhere in this book, the institutions of governance in Britain have restructured in the 1990s in a manner that can best be described as a 'new managerialism' (Clarke and Newman, 1997). But when allied to the planning process this new managerialism takes on added significance, since planning as a professional activity in itself has long been dogged by a derogatory administrative label. Planning theorists have bemoaned the enthusiasm with which planning practitioners have embraced proceduralism and rationality as a justification for their interventions in property development and environmental change. The preparation of plans, especially in the 1960s and 1970s, and the adoption of rational planning methods by planners at the time (Faludi, 1973), led reactionary theoreticians to criticise planning for its attempt to avert politics within day-to-day land use regulation (e.g. see Scott and Roweis, 1977).

The 1980s was a period characterised by strong central political direction and the ascendancy of the market. Plan preparation was viewed as inadequate and cumbersome; planners were accused by the Environment Secretary, Michael Heseltine, at the time of 'locking jobs away in filing cabinets'. The Thatcher governments reorientated planning as a market-facilitating activity where there was less reliance on statutory policies, plans and frameworks (Thornley, 1991). Planning as a rational and procedural process had, to all intents and purposes, been killed off.

PLANNING'S NEW PROCEDURALISM

The post-Thatcherite New Right's commodification of planning control has served to create a 'new proceduralism' in planning in the 1990s, as local authorities and professional planning officers strive continually to ensure efficient means, following the reassertion of plan-making and the government's legitimation of planning as a state function. In taking account of this restructuring of the planning process, it should also be borne in mind that public sector planners have also retrenched into thinking of town planning more administratively and in a less visionary way over the last 20 years following the adverse public criticisms of their efforts, as previously discussed. Planning has reverted to its overt procedural basis, and planning control to nothing more than an administrative service. While these changes have occurred to public sector town planning, forward planning (the promotion of development planning) has largely been operated successfully by a combination of quangos and the private sector during the 1980s and 1990s. What remains of statutory planning as we enter into the new millennium is a local authority planning function resting largely on development control.

This is a noteworthy situation given the fact that the development control process developed in piecemeal fashion over the last 70 years and was originally not part of the state intervention sought by early planning reformers. Stephen Crow, in an interesting paper on the early twentieth-century birth of the development control function, refers to the origins of planning control as 'the child that grew up in the cold' (Crow, 1996: 399). It is ironic that, at the end of the twentieth century, development control is now regarded as the very essence of planning; the child has not only grown up and matured, but is in danger of taking over the whole house. There is nothing inherently wrong with this restructuring; if anything, it is inevitable. But we are in danger of slipping into a groove by believing that planning control *is* planning.

Planning officers are more than content to follow central government policy and Audit Commission guidance in ensuring the continuation of planning control as a professional function. As Houghton (1997) states, this acceptance by planners of performance indicators is consistent with 'planners' long-standing focus on the planning "process" rather than on the outcomes and impacts of planning decisions' (Houghton, 1997: 1). Local politicians are also supportive of these features of planning control since it ensures the ongoing process of local decision-making and one justification for local government. Members of the public are equally extremely supportive of land use control, since it is one of the few areas of planning which they may have heard of. They can also have their livelihoods affected by planning control, by being materially affected by neighbours' developments, by being refused planning permission, or by a local authority taking enforcement action against unauthorised development. Some residents may additionally discover that planning control indirectly contributes to the protection of their individual property rights or enhances the price of their properties, through conservation area status and listed building control (Larkham, 1996).

In addition to the commodification of planning control nationally, the local political process of decision-making in planning has also been affected by an increase in the amount of officer delegation that is occurring in local planning authorities (Fleming and Short, 1984; Harris, 1996). Officer delegation has the purpose of:

1. Increasing the commodification of planning locally.
2. Ensuring improved league table ratings as a public service along the lines promoted by the Citizen's Charter.
3. Reducing members' roles in the determination process.
4. Increasing the technocratic perspective of development control.

The commodification of planning control has therefore retained local discretionary judgement, but this has occurred within a framework that has increasingly been determined centrally on the one hand and through the marginalisation of politicians on the other (Allmendinger, 1996; Tewdwr-Jones, 1997; Thornley, 1996). The attitude of the public, politicians and local authority planners towards planning has been narrowed to awareness of performance criteria, efficient management and regulation of other people's actions.

The position of town planning as a political tool in the mediation of socio-economic restructuring and environmental awareness is a nettle that has not been grasped in Britain since the Thatcher governments' mauling in the 1980s. Planning has been reduced to a bureaucratic regulatory process in which the political has been downplayed in the interests of organisational efficiency. The 'vision thing', the concept that gave birth to town and country planning as a professional activity in the early years of the twentieth century, has been lost, partly as a consequence of legislative fiat, a New Right determination to standardise and commodify planning as a public service, and individual planners' recalcitrance. Town planning is no longer a political and professional activity: it is rampant technocracy, shared between the public and private sectors.

PERCEPTIONS OF PUBLIC SECTOR AND PRIVATE SECTOR TOWN PLANNING

RECOGNITION AND FRUSTRATIONS

Planning as a professional activity has been the child in the middle of an amicable divorce settlement. The public sector parent of town planning has been stripped by successive governments to become a regulatory, procedural and bureaucratic activity. In planning control, this restructuring has occurred through commodification and standardisation. In plan-making, the restructuring has led to a renaissance in development planning activity, but this process too has taken place according to a series of checklists, national and regional planning 'guidance', and standardised good practice guides, all intended to create consistency.

The private sector parent of planning, meanwhile, has asserted itself as a pro-motional, visionary and forward-looking development activity, through its involve-ment in significant local, subregional and regional building projects. The regeneration of inner-city areas, the completion of town-centre retailing outlets, the building of civic projects funded through the UK National Lottery or Millen-nium Commission, have provided planning with a new impetus. But public sector planning has not received public accolade for these developments. Many of these projects have occurred as a result of joint partnerships between the public and private sectors. But most members of the public, I contend, have yet to be con-vinced of this aspect of a local planning authority's work. When they are asked to think of a planner working for their local council, they relate only to development controllers.

The author undertook a crude analysis of preferred career destinations of planning students enrolled on the planning programme at the Department of City and Regional Planning at Cardiff University, where over three-quarters of the students stated an intention to work in the private sector. Reasons given for this preference included: more exciting work in consultancies; perceived higher salaries than the public sector; a stigma attached to local government; and overt bureaucracy and 'dullness' of development control. Some students also identified a perceived inability to promote and implement environmental agendas (the reason why they chose to study town planning) within local planning authorities. The public sector side of planning is thus no longer viewed as a particularly interesting place within which to work; nor does it possess varied, challenging or exciting planning tasks.

Although these results are crude, it does give rise to a distinct perceived split within the planning profession, and one might even go further by suggesting that new planners are starting to indirectly choose between those planning jobs that they regard as more or less professional in their activities. Planners already employed within local planning authorities may not recognise this distinction; public sector planning may not be as sexy as its private sector counterpart. But does it really matter? After all, it remains a professional activity. The danger of the distinction is related more to future recruitment patterns, planning's position as a public (as opposed to private) service and its retention of a degree of esteem. Whether the opinions of Cardiff's students represent beliefs held more widely or not, there is no doubt that the aura attached to both wings of the profession has changed drastically over the last 10 years. Public sector town planning – particu-larly the development control function – needs to be bolstered if it does not want to be castigated as a second-rate activity. If private sector planning consultancies are regarded as the Premier League, local planning authority town planning is becoming viewed by the planners of the future as the Second Division.

There is no likelihood of public sector town planning reverting to its 1960s/1970s comprehensive development position; it has become a commodified service, a facilitator of the market. But if the planning profession and individual planners have accepted this redefined role with alacrity, then it really is time to reflect on planning's professional status and, indeed, on its uniqueness, as some commentators are already advocating (e.g. Evans, 1995; Evans and Rydin, 1997). My concern at this point is that, given existing public sector planners' apathy towards reasserting planning as something more than just rules and regulations (perhaps as an environmental protectionist force or as a process of social justice, for example), new planning graduates will either become frustrated by an ever-increasing growth within local planning authorities towards technical skills, or else be duped into believing that working according to preconceived manuals and technical criteria is town planning *per se* with little opportunity to consider implementing (or indeed promoting) more innovative planning styles.

Public Disquiet, Planners' Response

The view of planning practice as a technical non-political activity operating within the constraints of rule books and regulations has unfortunately been perpetuated by sections of the professional institute itself. A former president of the RTPI, Martin Bradshaw, actively sought to persuade the government to introduce legislation in the early 1990s to protect planners from the maldecisions of elected politicians, at a time when the decisions of certain local planning authorities were giving cause for concern. Fortunately, this campaign was never endorsed by the government. But it does illustrate how planning control and planning controllers are regarded by the professional institute as independent and 'worthy', virtually devoid of politics and technical in outlook. This tendency towards identifying public sector planning practice as a technical professional activity independent of local political discourse does not accurately reflect the true operation of town and country planning. It also says a great deal about how planning might (not) be viewed by the institute as a legitimate democratic process, resting on public opinion, but instead as a cold activity that should not be affected by social, environmental or political emotion.

At a recent seminar of practitioners in Edinburgh, at which we were discussing the future of planning, I asked the participants' views towards enhancing public participation in the process, by adopting more innovative planning measures centred on communities, by developing true public participation rather than public consultation strategies. Their comments illustrated a technocracy outlook. The vast majority were not in favour of increasing public involvement, and comments included: 'The public aren't interested in getting involved'; 'It's a waste of time'; 'We have elected politicians for that, there's no need for the public to be involved.' If these views reflect the opinions of the profession more widely (and they might not), then town planners firmly believe in representative democracy, but not participatory democracy. Planning is undoubtedly political and rests on a partnership between professionals, politicians and the public. But we are in danger of advancing a 'self-perpetuation' argument, by public sector planners ring-fencing themselves and their duties from the rest of society in splendid isolation. The opportunities for advancing more innovative collaborative forms of planning for the public (Healey, 1997) are not going to be realised until these sorts of views within the planning profession are altered.

Since planning control exposes the differing perceptions of the relevant decision actors, both the administrative, political *and* community context of statutory planning needs to be taken into account in discussions about the future format and delivery of the process. Without taking this more politically realistic and democratic perspective of public sector planning, the technocratic dominance of town planning is likely to be enhanced further, to the disappointment of the public, environmentalists and politicians locally. The further standardisation of local planning control might only reinforce the generation of locally divergent political strategies on the part of 'non-conformist' local planning authorities as they attempt to 'do their own thing', and satisfy the demands of their ward residents (Cloke, 1996; Tewdwr-Jones, 1995; Tewdwr-Jones and Harris, 1998). It could also generate an increase in the amount of 'direct-action' lobbying by the public and environmental action groups as they refuse to be pigeonholed within a strict public consultation timetable and seek to have their voices heard more assertively through other channels.

Whether or not one supported the actions of 'Swampy', the environmentalist who barricaded himself in self-built tunnels below the route of the Newbury bypass in Berkshire in the mid 1990s as a protest against road-building and environmental destruction, the direct action caught the media's attention and the interest of the public and politicians. One doubts whether more formalised written representations on the public's part as part of a public consultation exercise would have generated just as much interest. If town planners retreat further behind this technocratic and professional veil, the image of planners' roles will be damaged further.

There are many planners in practice who are committed to innovative public participation schemes (for example, the attempts by Brecon Beacons National Park, South Somerset District Council and Taunton Deane District Council). There are also many local planning authorities committed to environmental measures (for example, Bristol City Council, Edinburgh City Council and Kirklees Metropolitan Borough). But in these cases, the initiatives have emanated from individuals and individual local authorities; there has been no directive from on high enforcing planners to operate in this way, nor have the planners been convinced by a special professional need to respond. They have rather developed as isolated – though welcome – local attempts to become more innovative, thanks to a partnership between planners, politicians and the public. In many other authorities, individual planners are interested but have not been able to realise their visions, thanks to political direction and an inability to change colleagues' perceptions of their work tasks. And with both the government and the professional institute

advocating a 'minimum necessary' style of public consultation in planning, the
extension of innovative schemes to more local planning authorities across Britain
will not be met, despite the potential existing for this to occur.

TOWN PLANNING AND PROFESSIONALISM: THE INTELLECTUAL ABDICATION

VISIONS AND PROFESSIONAL INTELLECTUALISM

The existing literature on the planning process is devoid of discussions on the
motivation, conduct and perceptions of individual planning officers. British
academics and policy analysts, it seems, have determined that the individualistic
component of planning decision-making is not a subject worthy of attention, save
for one or two excellent accounts (e.g. Reade, 1987; Thomas and Healey, 1991).
This is in marked contrast to the situation in the United States where both academics and practitioners have written extensively on the dilemmas facing planning
as individuals (see, for example, Forester, 1989; Hoch, 1984). In Britain we have
not recognised the fact that not all planners will want to operate according to a
standardised pattern, and some may want to act more innovatively than the
current planning process encourages. But with little debate on the subject, and the
realisation that planning in the UK has become commodified, the standardisation
of the motivation and perception of individual planning officers (particularly the
younger members of the service) is an obvious outcome, as they conform to
national checklists, standardised plans and policies, and legal precedent. In effect,
it is not so much a determined standardisation ritual, but rather an apathetic
attitude on the part of professional planning officers towards thinking about the
role they are undertaking, and how 'the local question' (i.e. local circumstances,
that may include local environmental initiatives) may require a different approach
to the national agenda. As McConnell (1981: 74) remarked in his book *Theories of
Planning*:

> The problem between planning theory and planning practice, of which development
> control is an excellent example, is that well-experienced planning officers seldom
> have to ask themselves what the reason is for what they're doing.

Both Reade (1987) and Houghton (1997) highlight planners' lack of intellectual
curiosity and interest in the relationship between planning decisions and their
outcomes. The commodification of planning control is encouraging planners to
take the easy route out, by concentrating on performance criteria, by being less
visionary and by being more pragmatic and administrative. In the meantime, the
continuation of planning control as a professional entity is occurring largely
without question. Members of the planning profession, and the professional

institute itself, are all suggesting that by its very continuation, planning must offer something creative. In reality of course, planning is nothing more than the imposition of a set of prescriptive ideas. It is the imposition of regulation and the control of space by a set of rule books or manuals. Once versed in these manuals, any individual can implement a series of decisions or policies or act in a specific way accordingly. However, this implementation action does not in itself conform to a particular professional skill. Few analysts are questioning this centrally led restructuring, not least because it is not in anyone's interest to 'rock the boat'. Planning has survived the uncertainties of the 1980s, and the profession seems not to be in the mood to push the limits of planning further for fear of being undermined politically. This is understandable and, indeed, laudable, but it has simultaneously stifled debate. As Eric Reade (1987: 115) points out:

> If the formulation and interpretation of public policy is entrusted to a self-perpetuating occupational group, I conclude, and especially if that group regards itself as a 'profession', the result is likely to be the development of a closed intellectual climate, in which only those perceptions which further the interests of that group will be allowed to prevail.

Over the last 10 years in the UK, the RTPI could be accused of an 'intellectual abdication'. It has shown no interest in developing planning thought, nor has it shown any interest in furthering debate on the big questions and broad objectives of planning; it has merely acted pragmatically and incrementally by commenting on 'the latest policy advice', 'the current initiative', or 'the proposed agenda'. Following the political–planning relationship turmoil of the 1980s, the RTPI retrenched into a non-threatening position. It has even gone so far as to abandon its more conceptual journal, *The Planner*, in which members of the RTPI had been invited to comment in some detail about the future position of planning in the state and in society. That opportunity for the membership to visualise the strategic position of planning ended in 1993 when the journal of the RTPI was removed from the shelves on the grounds of financial expediency, and replaced with a weekly newsletter. Over the last four years, there have been few opportunities for members of this professional institute to make serious and critical comments about the future position and direction of planning in the UK at a time, uniquely, when there has been radical change politically, socio-economically, environmentally and constitutionally. The RTPI itself seems little interested in performing this task, an unusual situation given its supposed desire to secure the advancement of 'the art and science of town planning'.

A profession does not continue unabated unless intellectual debate is fostered to discuss its future. We have entered a period of transition in the UK when planning as a professional occupation needs to be seriously reconsidered. If the RTPI and other senior planning figures do not start addressing these broader questions about the role of planning in the UK, as we enter the new millennium, then more members of the professional institute, particularly the younger generation of planners – the graduates coming out of university and those students currently at university – will start to question in increasing numbers the value of being a member of a professional institution.

Those planning students who are intellectuals, who do enjoy planning to a great extent, who are very enthusiastic to practise and learn about planning and who choose their planning degrees at university in order to make a distinct contribution to environmental change and to regulate and control the environment for the benefit of the community, can end up very disappointed by the process once they have experienced the nuances of planning practice at first hand: '. . . the more gifted, the more ideas based, find planning disappointing and possibly leave' (Reade, 1987). Reade wrote that over 10 years ago and the same applies today. Once they experience the bureaucratic nightmare that can be local government, within which the planning profession is situated, the complex bureaucratic and administrative machinery of government, then for these more intellectually driven individuals disappointment is more evident than success. They find that their personal visions of environmental protection and community development cannot be realised in practice because of a retrenchment on the part of the RTPI, the lack of intellectual discussion and a refusal on the part of existing planners to acknowledge and debate change.

FUTURE CHANGE AND THE DEVELOPMENT OF PLANNING VISION

A review of the planning system in 1990s Britain only adds substance to the view of planning as procedurally dominated. Greater concern with performance indicators in decision-making, for speedy and efficient administration, for the generation of 'league tables' of the most efficient planning authorities nationally, for the publication of 'Planning Charters' showing the public and businesses the rights they should expect from the administration of planning locally, and for ensuring that planning decisions are made in accordance with plans and policies, are all issues relating to technical competence and administrative discretion. The technocratic dominance of planning in Major–Blair's 1990s Britain should be regarded as a new proceduralism; it is nothing more than the continued commodification of planning control without broader debate on the strategic objectives of planning in socio-economic and environmental change (Tewdwr-Jones and Harris, 1998).

Nadin and Doak (1991: 3) writing at the start of the 1990s summarised these dilemmas quite well:

> The role of professionals and the authority of professional expertise . . . has been challenged, and with some success. The result for town planners has been a decade characterised by uncertainty about both the organisation of their profession and the substantive problems with which it deals.

The same is true today as we enter a new millennium. The difference is one of self-identity. The threat and uncertainty in the 1980s emanated from a government eager to reduce the role of the state and with it the red tape of planning. The 1990s have witnessed a renaissance in planning's fortunes with a legitimate role to play in controlling development and producing plans. The threat and uncertainty over the last eight years have been the intellectual void created by little or no discussion of planning's strategic objectives in socio-economic change, and its apparent contentment to transform itself into nothing more than a bureaucratic, pragmatic and low-skills-based activity, masquerading behind a professional label.

Britain is about to undergo an immense period of change. An increasingly environmentally aware public will demand protectionist policies for our green fields and landscapes. The current opportunities to permit the public to have their say on the environment within town planning processes cannot stand still, as they have done for 25 years. If public sector town planning is to remain as the means through which the environment is protected and development regulated, we need to address change within our practices.

Constitutional reform is also a very important change that will affect the British planning system, with the possibility (or even likelihood) of the fragmentation of a national planning process through the establishment of a Scottish Parliament and a Welsh Assembly in 1999, and the creation of regional assemblies in the English regions beyond the millennium. Additionally, the prospect of a more integrated Europe in spatial planning terms (and the development of a European Spatial Development Perspective) could also enforce consideration of the continuation, adaptation or abolition of the form of Britain's planning system in the light of our European partners' planning regimes and the European funding mechanisms that have been drawn up on boundaries very dissimilar to our traditional administrative boundaries.

Town planning in the UK is currently in a very curious position. As a policy tool, it seems to be used by the government to solve three conflicting dilemmas – economic development, environmental protection and social justice. As a procedural tool, the 'British' planning process is at meltdown; it is fragmenting between different and very distinct regions of the country, while nationally coercing with (or becoming coerced by) the EU. Our present system of town and country planning will not be able to resist these pressures for much longer. But, somewhat worryingly, there is little debate occurring presently on what impact these immense changes will have on a town and country planning system that is 50 years out of date. As Janice Morphet (1996: 55) remarked recently,

> The rate of change in the development of views on the future of the spatial planning system in the last year is challenging. However, the coming year seems likely to provide even more change. The issues for the UK system are fundamental and need to be discussed. At present, there seems to be very little awareness of these proposals or indeed much consideration of their implications.

This is an opportunity for town planners to reassert themselves and their tasks in broader intellectual discussion concerning the future strategic direction of the country. I make no prescription here to insist that planners do this, merely to encourage planners to consider whether they want to alter their roles, and to debate the advantages and disadvantages of change.

In my view, planners will no longer be able to 'sit on the fence'. The restructuring of governance and constitutional change mean that they have a chance to determine the future framework of town planning, its role and, indirectly, its status with the public. In fact, the public and the politicians will expect planners to react to change. Public sector planning has become bogged down with bureaucracy and commodification and has lost some visionary ideal. The environmental agenda, a renaissance in the interest of the public towards planning, development and environmental matters, could prove to be the catalyst for local authority planners taking the initiative and responding positively to assert themselves as guardians of the environment and as protectors of community interests.

This is also an opportunity for town planning to reassert itself in the eyes of the public, the media and popular culture, after a 40-year period of criticism and ridicule. Whether this means the abandonment of the 'town planning' term and its replacement with something more relevant for the work we do as planners today, is a matter for the wider membership of the RTPI to determine. A change in roles, however, might also be an opportunity to reconsider the stigma attached to town planning as a phrase.

Town planning will always imply economic development, of course, in addition to environmental protection. Given the changes occurring and about to occur constitutionally, with respect to governance in the UK, and the prominence of the private sector in promoting development and forward planning, should public sector town planning abandon its neutrality and positively discriminate for social justice, of which environmental protection could form a part? After all, in many ways, planning control and environmental protection are forms (albeit weak forms) of social justice. It would not take too much for this social justice remit to be written into policy and codes of ethics more prominently. Public sector town planning as the implementation of inward investment, development of city centres, building of roads and promotion of civic projects, is dead. These activities occur outside statutory planning thanks to the funding mechanisms and their short time-scales, the availability of grants, and the enthusiasm and remit of the private sector. Such schemes are 'legitimised' by statutory planning only in the sense that projects are 'advertised' in development plans and approved or modified in the planning control process.

The reorientation of public sector town planning towards social justice and the environment (reflecting the need to protect the interests of a broader set of people) is distinctly possible. To what extent such a changed remit would encourage local authorities to operate a system of positive discrimination in favour of the disadvantaged in society is a matter for individual planners and politicians to contend with. But the reorientation would have the benefit of broadening the definition of planning away from its narrow and legal land use form towards a definition that encompasses the environment, the economy and society, and is also more reminiscent of our European partners' concern with 'spatial planning'. If public sector planners are unhappy with a switch to environment and community, perhaps because they favour the market or economic development, then they could simply choose to work in the private sector, where these interests are more accurately reflected.

The reassertion of town planning in the interests of community might encourage planners to reflect, 'Look what happened last time in the 1950s and 1960s!' I am not considering community planning as comprehensive development (as planners attempted to instigate unsuccessfully 40 years ago). I am considering planning as a localised community-caring activity, in which the community's interests are placed at the centre of debate and discourse, and upon which policies and decisions rest, rather than pigeonholing community into a minor, inconvenient process along the road to development, the view 'the planner knows best'. Debate on improvements to the planning process to achieve this form of participation is already well under way, thanks to the writings of Patsy Healey and others on forms of 'collaborative planning' (Healey, 1997). But these debates, to date, have been occurring in isolation from the professional and political world of planning practice. Participatory planning may necessitate the restructuring of the whole planning process and consideration of the role of the public in the process. In effect, it would lead to the development of a participatory, rather than a consultative, form of planning, in which all sections of a community (including the private sector) are actively encouraged to become involved.

If we are to operate a truly plan-led system, a participatory process would determine the principle of where there would be scope for further development and on the form that development would take, and from which policies could then be developed. The consultative public process in planning could be retained within the planning control process for the community to have their say on the details of the scheme. The private sector could retain their right to be heard at this stage, but the fact that policies within the plan would have emerged from the open community discourse arena would be a strong material consideration for them to attempt to overturn. This, of course, would also require a weakening of the current strong form of intervention central government takes in local planning policy formulation and implementation; that remit would be removed, and the government would be required only to provide national direction and objectives, a role it always should have provided, to enable local authorities to determine how they wish to operate planning locally. The RTPI would also need to consider how its code of ethics could be changed to reflect this communicative remit of local authority planners.

These, and other subject matters devoted to reconsidering the planning system in Britain, require a great deal of debate, not least by the government, the RTPI and planners themselves. I am not advocating the adoption of my own sketchy ideas as a panacea for planning, nor am I arguing for a change to the process if planners determine that change is not required. But at least let us have some debate on these broader strategic questions. Some readers may take issue with my writing; if people disagree, then please say so. If other planners possess some planning vision, then let the wider planning community hear about it. But let us not progress planning as an intellectual void without any discussion of the future position, role and status of town planning in Britain beyond the millennium.

ACKNOWLEDGEMENTS

The author expresses thanks to Robert Upton for his comments on an earlier draft of this chapter. Opinions expressed in the chapter are those of the author alone.

CHAPTER 9

TRANSPORT POLICY

Julian Hine

INTRODUCTION

The aim of this chapter is to address the prospects for the future integration of transport policy and land use planning over the next 10–15 years. A key failure of UK planning to date has been the way in which land use planning and transport policy have not been integrated. The chapter also seeks to identify what kinds of planning and transport policy instruments are likely to emerge in order to facilitate a greater policy co-ordination in a period of rapid social and economic change. The focus is one which is concerned with the responses of national and local governments to the continued growth in car use. The discussion of land use planning in this chapter is therefore directed at the role of land use planning in managing future increases in transport demand, which is increasingly car-based. Combined with the predictions of future household growth (for England), for the period 1991–2016 that 4.4 million additional households will need to be accommodated (DoE, 1995c), the future growth in transport demand and personal mobility represents a major challenge to policy-makers, especially in terms of encouraging sustainable development.

UK transport policy in the late twentieth century has not only been characterised by a growth in car dependence and significant declines in the modal share by public transport, walking and cycling, but also by a realisation that existing and future patterns of transport and travel should be matched to existing levels of supply. The emerging view in the 1980s and 1990s has been one of developing a consensus around the concept of 'new realism', a

> comprehensive or integrated approach which includes: a planned transfer from car use to improved and expanded public transport systems; better provision for pedestrians, cyclists and other environmentally friendly forms of transport; traffic calming, pedestrianisation, traffic restraint, and traffic management aimed at reduced speed and increased reliability of journey times rather than maximising the throughput of vehicles; the use of land use planning and development control to reduce journey length and unnecessary car travel wherever possible (House of Commons Transport Committee, 1995: xxi).

This view has been given re-emphasis by the recent publication of the Labour Government's White Paper on the future of transport (DETR, 1998e). During this period, the UK transport system has been characterised by market failure.

Currently individuals' transport decisions do not relate to the environmental and social costs that such transport decisions produce (Department of Transport, 1996a), even though there has been a move towards adopting pricing mechanisms which reflect these wider concerns.

The growth in road traffic levels has resulted in a failure to reconcile the movement needs of different user groups and their competing demands for movement space. The movement needs of pedestrians and cyclists are currently subordinate to the movement needs of motor traffic (Cleary and Hillman, 1992; Hillman *et al.*, 1991). Planning has become a key policy tool not only concerned with making a contribution to managing transport demand, through new locational policies aimed at reducing the need to travel by car, but also through the promotion of policy innovations aimed at shifting space towards other non-motorised modes of transport. Planners have also found themselves working with other specialists in developing local environmental management programmes, such as Local Agenda 21 (LA21). Planning and the skills of planners are likely to make a major contribution to the realignment of transport policy that will occur over coming decades as the environmental imperative and demands for sustainable development become stronger.

TRENDS FOR THE TWENTY-FIRST CENTURY

Over the last 40 years, the growth in travel has taken the form of a considerable increase in the distances travelled by private car, the car now accounting for a substantial share of all journey types. Public transport use, walking and cycling have declined. The growth in car use has permitted a continuing trend towards the trip chaining of journeys to serve a number of purposes in succession (OECD/ECMT, 1995; RCEP, 1994). Paradoxically, the increase in car dependence has been accompanied by a heightened sensitivity to the environmental impact of traffic and congestion in many urban areas (Bell, 1995). In the future, demand for travel will continue to grow as will car ownership and use. The current use and dominance of fossil fuels in petrol and diesel engines may be less by the middle of the twenty-first century with the development of alternative fuel cells and energy-storing hybrid vehicles, while continued developments in engine technology will result in improvements in fuel efficiency. Pollution generated per vehicle kilometre may be less, but overall levels of pollution will depend on volumes of traffic (RCEP, 1994; IHT, 1997).

Continued economic growth and rises in levels of personal wealth and prosperity, although likely to continue, may be shared by fewer people. Rising wealth, combined with increased personal mobility levels, will provide a greater choice of locations on where to live, work and shop; the distribution of such choices and levels of personal mobility will, however, be unevenly distributed. Travel patterns for the wealthier groups of society may well become more dispersed geographically

(IHT, 1997). These new lifestyles will not be shared by everyone. Households which do not have access to a car will experience a reduction in the number of goods and services available to them unless provision for locally accessible retailing and services are made. Many new retail developments are currently not easily reached on foot or by public transport (Headicar, 1995; Hall, 1992). The existing transport system is characterised by constraint and non-choice for those without adequate public transport services locally and who are, as a result, forced into car ownership as the only alternative. Other groups such as the disabled, elderly and children are confined to special needs transport services, poor public transport systems and substandard street environments. Lack of an accessible transport system has been shown to affect employment opportunities and levels of independence enjoyed by other individuals. Unless systems are made accessible then vulnerable groups may become more reliant on the state and voluntary sector for access to goods and services.

In the absence of effective demand management policies, including land use policies, congestion will worsen if no additional highway capacity is provided. It is, however, likely that moves made during the 1990s towards demand management and a move away from providing additional road capacity will continue. Herein lies the policy challenge for the twenty-first century: finding publicly acceptable ways of reducing the growth in transport demand and altering household travel behaviour in such a way as to curb car use, and maybe even ownership in particularly constrained locations such as city centres and designated air quality management areas (Office of Science and Technology, 1995; IHT, 1997).

During the 1990s, there has been a move towards road pricing in the UK, partly in response to concerns about intervention failures and the need for private car users to realise the full costs of car use. Increasingly this has also been due to the need to generate revenue to pay for new transport infrastructure (Department of Transport, 1993). Ultimately these goals may be incompatible. Future technological advances are likely to make pricing more efficient and feasible (Hepworth and Ducatel, 1992; Graham and Marvin, 1996). The current reality of road pricing is one of non-implementation, though the introduction of road pricing schemes in England and Scotland is currently being explored (DETR, 1998e; Scottish Office, 1998a). In 1996, the Conservative Government stated an intention that environmental costs should be brought more into investment and policy decisions. In an ideal world: 'the way individuals pay for transport should enable their transport decisions to be related as closely as possible to the costs that such decisions produce' (Department of Transport, 1996a: 51). This corresponds to a wider acceptance of the need for an economically efficient pricing system in transport (European Commission, 1996c). In the context of a level playing field between public and private transport, there is a commitment to set transport prices so that, where possible, transport users pay for the costs, including environmental costs. The previous UK government also stressed that it favoured the use of economic instruments rather than direct regulations to influence travel behaviour, although at the local level, direct regulations are to be used to promote a balanced approach between traffic restraint, better management of roads and encouraging alternatives to the car (Department of Transport, 1996a: 93). The perceived advantages of economic instruments are: cost effectiveness, innovation, flexibility and revenue.

New technologies may result in travel substitution, although at present it is unknown to what extent people regard social interaction as being important. Teleworking and the Internet may result in fewer people needing to travel to town and city centres to work. As computer technology becomes cheaper and available to more people, significant changes in travel-to-work patterns may occur. Employees within the information-based sector of the economy can enjoy more flexible lifestyles, including working variable hours from home (Hepworth and Ducatel, 1992; Graham and Marvin, 1996; IHT, 1997). Peak period congestion and commuting may, as a result of technological advances, become less of a problem. Technological change in the form of teleshopping may also affect shopping behaviour. Customers will be able to inspect and order goods from home. Deliveries could in turn be made to the door using small, environmentally friendly goods distribution vehicles or by providing local goods redistribution points (Office of Science and Technology, 1995). Such trends will result in the need for greater attention being paid to the provision of neighbourhood or local facilities by planners – a skill that was previously used so enthusiastically in the design of new towns over 50 years ago.

In the medium to long term, land use patterns will change. Currently land use planning and development control are increasingly seen as a form of regulatory activity through which urban form and hence travel behaviour and energy use, can be influenced (RCEP, 1994; OECD/ECMT, 1995; Banister, 1996). The 'new realism' or emerging consensus on traffic growth has also influenced the operation of land use planning and development control systems (Goodwin, 1996). Studies have indicated that land use policies can influence not only the need for travel but also the choice of mode (TEST, 1991; DoE, 1993c; Shaw, 1992; Curtis, 1996). New settlements are being encouraged around public transport nodes, while locations along radial routes into city centres and city centres themselves will be developed to encourage public transport use. In many urban centres all 'non-essential' vehicles will be banned. Access in these centres will be restricted to low emission vehicles and public transport. The problems of diverting through traffic will need to be dealt with, but could cause political problems where a bypass passes through an environmentally sensitive area. In the UK, 'clear zones' have been identified as a potentially useful concept around which to manage and create liveable neighbourhoods and urban centres (Office of Science and Technology, 1995). This is a vision based around the use of new technology and policy innovation, but it also suggests a spatial coherence for policy mechanisms. For example, in a wider traffic restraint framework, land use planning in the UK is likely to become more stringent in order to facilitate a modal shift. It is possible that this combined with other policy measures will result in specifically legally enforceable targets for well-defined planning areas with land use, air quality and modal split targets to be reached.

The planned transfer of journeys from private to public transport will need to be accommodated in the form of enhanced and improved public transport system capacity. As in the case of new highway infrastructure, it may only be achievable with private sector funding and support (Department of Transport, 1996a). In the twenty-first century, the local and national state will be forced to enter into public and private sector partnerships in order to provide the financial support and expertise. Not all the journeys transferred from cars could be accommodated on public transport (Hillman, 1996). New technology will, however, enable public transport services to be more effectively managed. In addition, better designed public transport will improve interchanges between different modes of transport, particularly between rail and bus-based public transport systems and walking and cycling. New ticketing systems enabling transfer between public transport modes, often controlled by different operators, will promote public transport as a viable mode of transport for intra- and inter-urban trips. In rural areas and outer sub-urban areas, areas poorly served by public transport, car dependence is likely to continue.

The twenty-first century will also herald the planned reallocation of street space to green modes of transport (environmentally benign) such as walking and cycling. Evidence suggests that the elderly, children and women are likely to benefit from such measures. Local and national planning and transport authorities will be responsible for the development of safe networks (Department of Transport, 1996b). Many cities have already adopted quite extensive pedestrian areas in their centres; the twenty-first century will see the expansion of these pedestrian and cycling networks into the surrounding inner and outer suburbs and eventually into the surrounding hinterlands of larger settlements. Previously this has been under-taken on a much more *ad hoc* basis, usually cities with historic environments, centres well served by public systems allowing easy access and which have the benefit of inner ring roads due to historical investment decisions (TEST, 1988; Hall and Hass-Klau, 1985).

EXISTING APPROACHES AND PROSPECTS FOR CHANGE

Social and technological changes are likely to create a number of pressures for change in the way the existing transport policy and land use planning system currently operate. The previous discussion of trends and their implications highlighted a number of areas where land use planning currently operates, and is likely to continue to do so. However, future trends do highlight the need for a new approach where land use planning decisions are more integrated with transport policy. This section reviews existing approaches to managing transport demand and the contribution and role of land use planning in meeting this objective currently and in the future. The discussion draws the reader's attention to future developments and policy tools that are likely to emerge over the next 10–15 years.

THE ADMINISTRATION OF LAND USE PLANNING AND TRANSPORT POLICY

The developing consensus surrounding 'new realism' (Goodwin *et al.*, 1991) and the wider recognition of the need for demand management suggest that integrated land use and transport strategy will become embedded in national and local decision-making structures in the future. In August 1997, the Labour government published a Green Paper, *Developing an Integrated Transport Policy* (DETR, 1997e). This was followed in July 1998 by the White Paper, *A New Deal for Transport: Better for Everyone* (DETR, 1998e). The White Paper, among other concerns, addressed the question of how to integrate land use planning and transport more effectively. The Paper advocates within existing local government structures the production of local transport plans, regional transport strategies and better planning through a review of existing planning guidance for transport and the incorporation of regional transport strategies in regional planning guidance. The next 10–15 years will herald new forms of democratically accountable regional planning bodies with a remit to develop and pursue integrated transport strategies. In Scotland there is the possibility of Regional Transport Authorities being established, whilst the interim grouping of local authorities will be encouraged. In England, regional planning conferences or groupings at local authorities will be responsible for the development of regional strategies. At the time of writing the current question in relation to UK transport policy is – do we have the appropriate institutional frameworks to oversee the management of transport demand?

The Institute of Highways and Transportation has recently produced guidance on the development of urban transport strategies. This explicitly recognises the connection between land use and transport planning strategy and stresses the importance of vision for the area as the context for strategy development (IHT, 1996). In England and Wales, local authorities are encouraged to submit package bids for the funding of their transport strategies from central government. This has encouraged a re-emphasis within the Transport Policies and Programme (TPP) process on producing an integrated transport system (IHT, 1997). The TPP document is submitted annually by all highway authorities in England and Wales. Despite such a positive approach in England and Wales, in Scotland the TPP process is no longer formally in existence. Instead local authorities are forced to compete with each other for challenge funding from the Scottish Office.

Devolution in Scotland and a new assembly in Wales may result in the development of more rigorous approaches to integrated transport and land use strategies as both Welsh and Scottish Offices become responsible for aspects of transport policy and funding. Many commentators in Scotland have, for example, argued that a new Scottish Parliament with tax-varying powers could herald new forms of taxation, such as a green tax. Such approaches may enhance the viability and opportunities for integrated transport and land use planning strategies backed up by fiscal measures. In May 1997, the new Labour government merged the departments of Environment and Transport, the new department – the Department of Environment, Transport and the Regions (DETR) is now responsible for land use and transport policy. This reflects what had already occurred at the regional level in England with the formation of integrated government offices for the regions with responsibilities for the departments of Environment, Transport and the Regions, Employment and Education, Trade and Industry. These regional offices will play an important role in developing regional planning guidance.

Successive reorganisations of local government in England, Wales and Scotland during the 1980s and 1990s have dealt successive blows to strategic policy development by locally elected government. The picture in many parts of the UK has been one of a fragmentation of planning powers between different agencies (Cullingworth and Nadin, 1997; Hayton, 1996). For example, in areas formerly governed by a county strategic planning authority there are now several visions of planning strategy displayed in unitary development plans. In Scotland, the abolition of the regions has undermined the coherence of the locally developed strategic policy that existed previously for a strategic policy that is no longer consistent with local government boundaries. A strategic plan area may now include part of an authority area or more than one local authority area. Where reorganisation has occurred there are now serious questions for managing transport systems and organising the strategic location of new development. Issues frequently cited are a loss of policy co-ordination (indications are that many strategic issues are affected by the size of the travel-to-work area and consequent patterns of housing demand can occur across several plan areas) and greater central government involvement in policy development through regional and national planning guidance. Additionally, the problem is that not all local authorities are highways authorities. There is some support for the formation and extension of the Passenger Transport Authorities (PTAs) and Passenger Transport Executives (PTEs) model to other parts of the UK, or the voluntary planning conference model consisting of representation from constituent local authorities as in the partnership model advocated in the Scottish version of the transport White Paper (Scottish Office, 1998a). For example, following abolition of the Strathclyde Regional Council constituent local authorities have established a Clyde Valley Structure Planning Team. Both these options are based on significant travel-to-work areas. The problem of potential conflict, or lack of integration in the existing UK framework, is also well illustrated by the lack of controls surrounding the trunk roads programme. Funded by central government, it may run counter to local authority strategic planning objectives. Similar arguments have been raised in relation to the role of Private Finance Initiative (PFI) and land use planning strategy.

Many local authorities in the UK are now involved in Local Agenda 21 (LA21) environmental management initiatives (UNCED, 1992b). LA21s are a community-based approach to setting the agenda for sustainable development. In the UK, these are co-ordinated by the Local Government Management Board which, by 1996, had aimed to establish a framework to promote sustainable development within communities. A major element of the programme has been the development of sustainability indicators, yet it remains to be seen how such measurements and indicators are likely to be used in managing transport demand through land use planning apart from confirming existing trends in the absence of a coherent pricing policy and an enforceable set of legal targets.

Targets have been identified as a useful tool for policy development and analysis (RCEP, 1994; IHT, 1997). The question for future practice over the next 10–15 years is how these can be incorporated into practice in a meaningful way. The requirement has to be for the provision of effective workable legislation, passed by central government, to provide a framework for local authorities to adhere to and additional powers for local authorities to fulfil those targets. The danger is that unless this process occurs then targets are likely to lose their credibility and suffer from a lack of political support as a consequence. Targets for transport policy should be set within the context of effective integrated forms of government at national, regional and local levels where, following a bargaining process, local targets should broadly follow national targets. This process needs to be legally enforced through a system of penalties and guidance, and may not necessarily be restrictive in terms of other goals such as reducing unemployment.

Current UK government is characterised by a fragmentation of decision-making structures at local and national levels. For example, many local authorities see bus-based public transport as a major tool to manage transport demand and encourage modal shift, in combination with land use planning. The reality is that the bus industry in any one local authority area may be under the control of more than one operator in an extremely competitive market, and not under the influence of local authority land use and transport policy. The Road Traffic Reduction Act 1997 is a case in point. The Act requires highways authorities to publish reports on road traffic growth in their areas on local roads, not trunk roads as controlled and funded by central government, and publish targets for reductions in local road traffic growth or targets to reduce rates of growth. Chisholm (1997) has noted that the Act makes no mention of the powers of principal authorities or anybody else to take action on the targets set. There are no new powers associated with the legislation. The Act establishes the duty of central government to specify targets, though does not indicate how targets are to be met. The assumption is that local authorities will be required to use existing powers under existing legislation to meet targets. Clearly this is problematic, given current institutional frameworks. Similarly, the Environment Act 1995 requires local authorities to set targets for air quality, and in areas where air targets are not being met, local authorities can designate air quality management areas. Yet the power to ban vehicles from certain areas is subject to the provision that no vehicle may be stopped by any person other than a policeman in uniform. In addition the Act allows for Traffic Regulation Orders to be made in the pursuit of air quality management objectives,

yet the Road Traffic Regulation Act 1984 confers no powers in relation to the
banning of traffic that may have an adverse impact on the atmospheric environment (Chisholm, 1997). Clearly the next 10–15 years should herald a new legislative programme in the UK aimed at consolidating existing legislation and
introducing a new regulatory framework focused around managing transport
demand and traffic reduction. Using existing legislation and regulation, often
designed for a different purpose, is clearly undesirable if the goals of traffic reduction and environmental improvement are to be met both locally and nationally.

TRUNK ROADS AND THE PLANNING SYSTEM

Regulatory activity, in connection with the provision of roads in the UK, occurs
through the land use planning system controlled by local planning and highways
authorities and through the trunk roads programme as controlled by central
government. Essentially, the provision of trunk roads and motorways occurs outside the land use planning system as controlled by local planning authorities
(RCEP, 1994; Farrington and Ryder, 1993). The Royal Commission on Environmental Pollution (RCEP) suggested that if a system of trunk roads were retained
then all trunk road schemes should be considered initially as an intrinsic part of
the local authority structure plans and integrated fully into the development
control system (RCEP, 1994: 154). This problem has been recognised and there
have been moves towards closer integration (Department of Transport, 1996a;
DETR, 1998). The vehicle identified in pursuance of closer integration is the
regional planning guidance issued by central government. This guidance is seen as
informing the structure planning process for those local authority areas covered by
the guidance. The emphasis in the guidance is traditionally narrowly defined
around land use (Alden and Offord, 1996) so the future inclusion of trunk roads in
these documents raises questions about the future content of regional planning
guidance notes. It seems likely that the content will be wider than has hitherto
been the case.

Although this represents a move in line with a 'new realism', there are still some
concerns. The Department of Transport (1996a) has stated that such a process will
still have an overwhelming emphasis on the national interest as opposed to regional
and local interests. The reality in any case is that regional planning guidance does
not cover the whole of the UK; current coverage has a tendency to extend to those
areas where successive local government reorganisations have increased the
number of local authorities responsible for strategic planning across metropolitan
areas in England (Alden and Offord, 1996). By comparison, in Scotland, no regional
planning guidance is in existence despite a recent local government reorganisation
which is perceived to have weakened strategic planning, as undertaken by local
authorities, and placed the key decisions for such activity in the hands of central
government (Hayton, 1996). It therefore remains to be seen how the trunk road

———

programme, through regional planning guidance, is likely to impact on the planning goals of managing transport demand at the local level where there has been a fragmentation of responsibility and a loss of policy co-ordination between constituent local authorities. Added pressures to this system may arise from PFI funded trunk roads with the recent relaxation of charges payable by developers for accesses on to trunk roads (Department of Transport, 1996c).

PRIVATE FINANCE, ROADS AND LAND USE PLANNING

The present infrastructure crisis – the need for maintenance and provision of transport systems – combined with a tight Treasury control of public investment have resulted in successive UK governments, since 1979, seeking to encourage private sector participation in the development of road and other inter-urban transport projects. It is anticipated that the introduction of private sector expertise and competition will provide better value for money for the taxpayer based on a belief that: 'the private sector is usually in the best position to promote and manage transport services most efficiently ensuring best value for the resources used' (Department of Transport, 1996a: 48). This approach has been made possible under the New Roads and Streetworks Act 1991. The primary use of the PFI has been the funding of major roads by private consortia with repayments from government over 30 years depending on traffic levels (Hoare, 1997). Early schemes under these proposals include the Queen Elizabeth II bridge at Dartford which carries the M25 London orbital motorway across the River Thames. It was built on the basis of a design, build and partial finance contract by Trafalgar House in return for a concession to levy tolls on both bridge and adjacent tunnel for a period of 25 years. The new second Severn crossing, opened in June 1996, is another example where the contractor will recoup the outlay by charging tolls. The Birmingham northern relief road is also currently being negotiated on this basis. The PFI initiative is not just confined to road investment. The Channel Tunnel rail link is being taken forward under the PFI scheme to provide 104 km of new railway line between St Pancras Station in London and the Channel Tunnel.

More recently, debate has been based around the provision of roads by local authorities in partnership with the private sector which represents an extension of the 30-year design, build, finance and operation aimed at the transference of large sectors of the roads programme into private sector consortia. The use of the PFI for roads has provoked criticism (Beal, 1996; *Economist*, 1996; *Local Transport Today*, 1996). Evidence suggests a scepticism about the higher costs to the taxpayer of shadow tolls than if the roads were built with public money. Traditionally, there have been restrictions on local authorities to use private finance for local authority capital projects such as roads, schools and public buildings. Councils wishing to use private finance for projects have had to set aside the full cost of the scheme from their capital resources in order to cover the financial risk.

Under new arrangements, the private sector could be invited to shoulder a greater share of the risk. It is likely that there will in the future be a re-emphasis on public–private partnership to overcome the problems associated with full risk transfer (Labour Party, 1995; *Building*, 1995). Initial evidence suggests that local authorities will respond positively to the new regime, and recent cuts in funding may make this approach more attractive to local authorities (*Local Transport Today*, 1996).

The PFI raises a number of important issues which represent a major challenge to an emerging consensus on the need for controlling road traffic growth and the level playing field approach to transport investment. The buy now, pay later approach commits local authorities to a programme of repayments over an extended future period of possibly 30 years. Local authorities will be constrained by what they can afford in terms of repayments. Critics have argued that this form of hire purchase has created an enormous long-term cost for the taxpayer, and secondly that because repayments are linked to traffic levels there is a concern that PFI roads will lead to traffic growth at a time when consensus is increasingly for traffic reduction (Transport 2000, 1997).

PFI may represent a challenge to the integrity of the land use planning system. It is possible that the planning system could be used to package a scheme and make it more attractive. For example, a local authority which is both the local highways and planning authority for an area could approach a consortium who are asked to provide a road. In order to make this more attractive, land adjacent to the scheme could be offered or used by partners within the consortium to build new housing, thereby making the scheme more attractive. Alternatively, a consortium could, in order to maximise revenue, exert pressure on a local authority in a similar way to establish a partnership. This clearly raises questions of monitoring and what local authority policy objectives are likely to be and the safeguards that need to be in place. The Metropolitan Transport Research Unit (1996) has esti-mated that the controversial Salisbury bypass in Wiltshire would have cost about twice as much to build under shadow tolling than as an ordinary public funded scheme. Evidence of rerouting roads to take them closer to a planned development site, and the downgrading of a road adjacent to a PFI road in order to enhance and generate traffic have also been uncovered. Hoare (1997), in a wide-ranging discussion of the impact of privatisation in Bristol, raised the issue of dual interest for Bristol City Council surrounding proposals for a new access point on the M49 link through Severnside to the second Severn crossing, a PFI scheme using shadow tolls. As the planning authority, Bristol City Council is responsible for guiding development in the Severn coastal zone, but as a landowner in the area has a strong commercial interest in unlocking Severnside's bank of land. Subsequent discussions among planning authorities and the Department of Transport brought support for the junction opening up 300 ha of land for development and employ-ment. Recently, the Department of Transport (1996c) has adopted more flexible guidelines for payments by developers for trunk road improvements. In future, developers will be expected to pay for road improvements necessary to ensure that conditions on the road are no worse than they would have been if the development had not taken place. Previously, developers were required to pay for improvements that would cater for all traffic expected to use the road for 15 years after the full completion of the development. Such a policy change may make it easier to manipulate traffic flows through land use change alongside PFI funded road schemes, despite the continuation of rigorous controls over access requirements on to trunk roads.

While the private sector has been keen to get involved in flagship schemes like river crossings and tram schemes, it remains to be seen whether the same level of interest will be generated by other areas of transport provision such as road improvements and bus priority. A series of questions have recently been raised on this issue relating to the funding of hospitals under PFI. Hospitals are relevant to this discussion, as are bus priority and road improvements, because all are unfamiliar to banks. Banks will need to understand how the different revenue streams will be generated over the 20- or 30-year repayment periods. The PFI hospital sector is competing for funding with PFI roads, property and power projects. Such perceptions could hamper investment patterns which should conform with the idea of a 'level playing field'. There is also the issue for the private sector partner of setting up costs and administering the scheme, so this in turn raises the possibility of a public subsidy being needed to be paid to the contractor. In the context of PFI hospitals, schemes struggling with affordability have been allocated a smoothing mechanism to make some progress. This involves transferring existing money from the National Health Service's capital budget to PFI projects to help meet the initial cost (*Building*, 1997) (Table 1). The packaging of bids, in order to attract private finance, is seen as becoming increasingly important. This approach may also include the added inducement of a revenue stream from a road-pricing cordon or of a parking scheme.

LOCATIONAL POLICIES

The introduction of Planning Policy Guidance Note 13 (PPG 13) on transport in England and Wales (DoE/DOT, 1994) and recent discussions in Scotland surrounding draft guidance on transport and land use planning (Scottish Office, 1996; Scottish Office, 1998b) have done much to raise the profile and role of development control and land use strategies in relation to the need to reduce travel and influence the rate of traffic growth. The guidance, in effect, represents an attempt to guide new development to locations which can be more easily served by public transport, walking and cycling, and to promote development in existing urban locations where people can access a wide range of services without necessarily having to travel a great distance to do so. In addition, the guidance stresses the importance of controlling the amount of car parking provided in new

Table 1 *Problems with PFI and hospital projects*

The complaint	June 1994, NHS Trusts ordered to fund hospital building privately. By January 1997, no privately financed scheme had been approved. Contractors have spent £100 million bidding for 30 PFI schemes. Of these, 25 have reached preferred bidder stage and no final contracts have been signed. Contractors disillusioned and refusing to bid for contracts until first deal is signed
The causes	*Lack of co-ordination.* Unlike PFI roads and prisons which are ordered by government departments, each PFI hospital is commissioned by a separate NHS trust. Contractors' bidding costs have rocketed because all the trusts are devising their own tender rules and contract clauses
	Inexperienced hospital managers. Until the launch of PFI managers never had to commission their own buildings. Many managers have floundered in their negotiations with contractors and their banks
	Over-ambitious trusts. Hospital managers have demanded lavish new hospitals without realising they cannot afford them
	Affordability. Even after cutting out hospital managers' excessive demands, trusts are struggling to afford the schemes. Although the PFI schemes work out cheaper over 30 years than publicly financed hospitals, the charges are higher in the first few years
	Risk. Trusts have attempted to pass excessive and ill-defined risk to the private sector which has been resisted by contractors and their banks
	The financial precariousness of trusts. Banks keen to lend to PFI hospitals are worried that many trusts will not survive the 25- or 30-year lifetime of a PFI contract
	Inadequate support from the Department of Health and the Treasury. Guidance notes to help bidders and contractors are sparse and often contradictory
The cure	*Release a small amount of cash to bridge the affordability gap.* Some trusts need £1 million a year. £25 million extra funding a year would unlock schemes
	Underwrite the trusts' liabilities. If the trust fails there needs to be guarantee that the financial obligations to the PFI consortium will be met
	Trusts need more advice. Contractors want the government to 'parachute' in teams of financial and legal experts to assist hospital managers in negotiations with PFI bidders
	Give trusts better guidance. The Treasury can help trusts by publishing more model clauses. At the moment, these account for only 5% of a PFI contract

Source: *Building*, 1997, 31 January

development and the need to consider complementary transport measures (Table 2). It is recognised that:

> Locational policies in themselves can only provide opportunities for reducing growth in travel demand. If they are to realise their potential, they must be supported by other measures, and in particular by appropriate transport measures. Supporting measures should have three main aims: to promote choice by increasing the relative advantage of means of travel other than the car, especially walking, cycling and public transport; to reduce dependence on the private car; and to increase the competitiveness and attractiveness of urban centres against peripheral development (DoE/DOT, 1994: paragraphs 4.1 and 4.2).

Table 2 *Land use and complementary transport measures*

Location	Development types	Complementary transport measures
Adjacent to major public transport terminus or interchange	Offices – high plot ratios, low parking Hotels Entertainment Convenience shops	Public transport priority Restrained long-term parking Good pedestrian facilities/links Cycle parking/cycle network Traffic management Park and ride along transport access routes
City/town centre	Comparison shop units and small–medium food units Offices – high plot ratio, low parking Housing over shops Restaurants Entertainment/cultural facilities Municipal buildings/central library	
Edge of centre (within easy walking distance)	Bulk purchase retail units, including food superstores – car parks shared with centre Offices – high plot ratio, low parking Dense housing Hotels and restaurants Leisure centre, including multiplex cinemas and car parks shared with other users Hospital School/college/university	
Adjacent to lesser public transport node/corridor	Dense housing Offices Convenience shops Sports/entertainment Park and ride sites	Public transport provision Good pedestrian facilities/links to centre Cycle network Cycle parking Traffic management

Table 2 (*continued*)

Location	Development types	Complementary transport measures
Close to town centre	Dense housing Mixed use employment Light industry (not involving heavy freight)	
Neighbourhood centre	Local food and non-food shopping Housing over shops and dense developments, sheltered accommodation Mixed use employment Schools Local entertainment, restaurants, etc. Local municipal services/health clinics, etc. Parks	
Close to neighbourhood centre	Dense housing Sheltered housing Other services, e.g. medical/ local authority	Public transport provision Good pedestrian facilities Cycle network Cycle parking Traffic management
Adjacent to key highway links	Warehousing and distribution Industrial uses Bulk retail stores only if not suited to other sites	Public transport provision Freight: rail/water access
Adjacent to main rail/water links	Industrial Warehousing and distribution	Freight facilities grant
Village centres	Local shops Mixed employment opportunities Housing School Local services Entertainment	Cycle network Pedestrian facilities Traffic management
Rural communities	Housing Small commercial/industrial/ recreational Tourist attraction Local shops	Cycle and walk provision Public transport provision Tourist park and ride

Source: DoE/DOT (1995: 25).

Critics of a demand management approach focused around land use planning argue that it is imprecise and long term and does not challenge patterns of production and consumption which promote unsustainable traffic growth (Owens, 1995). The fundamental objective of land use planning should be to create liveable settlement patterns where there is less of a requirement to travel greater distances. The extent to which populations make travel and location choices consistent with travel reduction objectives clearly depends on the extent of integration between aspects of fiscal, social and transport policy (James and Pharoah, 1992). It is certainly recognised that land use planning alone without recourse to a wider pricing policy and framework of traffic restraint, concerned with promoting economic growth which is based on a low intensity of road traffic growth, is likely to be ineffective. While much has been said about PPG 13 in England and Wales, its impact on the ground has been much less obvious due to the time lag associated with existing permissions for out-of-town development which pre-date the guidance (Hillier Parker, 1995). The guidance has been incorporated into many local authority policy documents and since it came into force, a high number of high-profile peripheral developments have been called in and (some) rejected by the DoE (Ove Arup Partners, 1995; DoE/DOT, 1995; Earp, 1995; Pharoah, 1996). By comparison, in Scotland, no such guidance exists, although there are plans to introduce some in the future. In a recent survey of reorganised Scottish local planning authorities, it was found that although travel reduction was regarded as an important consideration when assessing planning applications for new development, other considerations tended to dominate. The survey found that economic development was regarded as the most important planning consideration (Hine and Rye, 1997). There is, however, wide recognition of the role which planning policy can play in terms of influencing the links between public transport provision and locational policy, but local planning authorities are frustrated in this task due to limited powers over deregulated bus services.

A variety of land use policies stemming from UK planning guidance and also visible in other European countries can be identified (IHT, 1997; OECD/ECMT, 1995; DoE/DOT, 1995). Increasingly, policies are being used to concentrate dense developments near to or within transport corridors where public transport systems can provide a viable alternative to the use of cars. Also policies currently seek to increase development densities on the basis that higher densities will encourage shorter journeys, walking and cycling while also making public transport more viable. Many studies have sought to identify the links between urban form and energy efficiency, and confirm that as density increases, travel and transport energy use fall (Owens, 1986; 1991b; Newman and Kenworthy, 1989). The indications are that in denser areas there is a greater use of public transport at slower speeds, for short journeys, and in less dense areas, there is more car use at higher speeds, for longer journeys (Goodwin, 1978; RCEP, 1994). Other research, however, suggests that income and car ownership are more important determinants of travel demand than population density, while studies dispute the extent to which density is an independent variable. The RCEP concluded that increasing densities and altering the urban form can reduce journey distances, but it is possible that it is unlikely to have a significant impact on transport demand (RCEP, 1994: 149). What seems likely is that the patterns of travel behaviour and demand now exhibited generally, particularly that of car users, are so complex that in some situations there may be weak links with urban form.

From this debate on urban form, however, the compact city model has emerged as a potentially energy-efficient pattern of urban development. In 1990, the EU Green Paper on urban environment advocated the benefits of high-density compact cities (CEC, 1990). Rickaby (1987) and ECOTEC (1993) have suggested that centralised patterns of growth around free-standing towns are likely to be more energy efficient. Simulations have found that the most effective land use and transport strategy in a metropolitan subregion was a combination of extended public transport provision, limited additional highway capacity and the regeneration of existing centres. Urban containment policies – measures to limit low-density sprawl – have come to be seen as an essential part of a policy package designed to create a compact urban form. Reuse of vacant or derelict land within existing urban areas is a key part of current UK planning strategy despite no formal commitment to the compact city model, although there is a commitment to protect the vitality and viability of existing centres in existing guidance (OECD/ECMT, 1995; DoE, 1996).

The mix of development types has also been identified as a measure that can improve accessibility and reduce the need to travel (DoE/DOT, 1995). Single-use office developments are more likely to generate car trips than mixed developments which include hotels, shops and leisure facilities. Similarly, studies have shown that large areas of housing will generate more car trips than areas where employment, shopping and education are more integrated (James and Pharoah, 1992). Parking controls have also become a focus of activity. The move towards maximum or reduced parking standards as opposed to minimum standards represents an impact on trip end restraint. Under existing guidance, a local authority can require commuted payments (a form of developer contribution) in which the normal requirements for private parking provision are waived in return for payment to a local authority of a charge per space, so that the local authority can make more provision for public car parks or promote park and ride schemes. Voluntary company transport plans could also be developed in the UK, although in the USA and the Netherlands, where travel reduction ordinances exist, there are requirements for developers to stipulate specific ways in which car use to their development can be reduced. Flexible working hours, a land use measure, which can reduce peak period demand for travel at certain locations, is an area of policy that has been encouraged in the UK (IHT, 1997). These types of policies have become fairly well established during the 1990s, but what future direction is policy likely to move in over the next 10–15 years?

Development control activities and decisions, while basically reflecting these concerns, are also prone to matters of interpretation and other planning considerations (for example practical planning considerations, strategic planning considerations, precedent and impact on existing occupants of the site or other nearby sites) (Davies, 1989). The RCEP (1994) for example argued that permitted development rights and the Town and Country Planning (Use Classes) Order ought to be reviewed to ensure that new uses which generate appreciably higher levels of traffic cannot take place without a fresh grant of planning permission. Chisholm (1997) has similarly argued once a planning permission has been given the objective circumstances may change as may the public perception of policies. Clearly, there needs to be some consideration in the future around the issue of under what circumstances should planning permission be modified. The system needs to allow for this through effective monitoring. Basically, planning permission is given on the basis of certain assumptions/limits about the type of activity, the traffic generated and types of travel behaviour occurring on and around the site. The question is what happens when these assumptions are tested or broken. Applications for planning permission and modification of that permission should contain an analysis of the transport implications, including pedestrian, cycling and public transport access and freight movements in the case of industrial developments (National Consumer Council, 1987; RCEP, 1994).

Future land use policy, if it is to succeed in making a contribution to the reduction of car dependence and ameliorating attendant problems, needs to be radically refocused. Most importantly, the spatial organisation of policy at national, regional and local levels needs to be reviewed. In 1994, the Royal Commission suggested that targets for specific planning areas (within the context of air quality these might relate to emissions and traffic growth as well as cycle routes built or bus lanes designated) needed to be defined and adopted (RCEP, 1994). The current land use planning framework based on plan-led planning, national planning guidance, structure plans and local plans is certainly a model that could be widened to include legally enforceable targets relating to other areas of policy. Such integrated planning documentation could have distinct advantages over the current fragmented system. Historically, planning has strengths in neighbourhood design. The adoption of an urban villages approach in many planning circles represents an extension to this tradition. That the implications of future reductions in car use will mean a refocusing of lifestyles away from dormitory settlements and suburbs to liveable and vibrant neighbourhoods should come as no surprise. There is therefore likely to be a future requirement to adopt neighbourhood planning strategies which seek to create independent communities, protect local facilities and incorporate fiscal measures which support such strategies.

COMPLEMENTARY TRANSPORT MEASURES – THE DIRECT REGULATION OF STREET SPACE

The direct regulation of street space is currently favoured at the local level and is seen as an alternative to producing restraints on car ownership and less contentious than the implementation of road pricing (Headicar, 1995; Department of Transport, 1996a). It is widely recognised that the direct regulation of road space, combined with investment in public transport, cycling and walking infrastructure will make a significant contribution to reducing the dominance of motor traffic (Cleary and Hillman, 1992; Potter and Cole, 1992). The direct regulation of street space is undertaken by a variety of policy measures (Goodwin, 1996; OECD/ECMT, 1995; Cullinane, 1997). These include: parking control, pedestrianisation, traffic calming and the prioritisation of public transport. There is a growing amount of evidence to suggest that measures which directly regulate road space *vis-à-vis* reducing traffic flows and speeds can encourage pedestrian activity. Many cities are now seeking to increase the amounts of space provided for walking, cycling and street functions other than traffic (Appleyard, 1981; Engwicht, 1993; TEST, 1990).

PARKING CONTROL

Parking controls covering publicly controlled spaces are generally targeted at the journey to work and peak periods. A recent study of five cities has indicated that parking provision and price are the two most powerful tools of congestion control (Dasgupta, 1994). This is usually done through a combination of high parking charges for long-stay spaces, and/or peak periods, which often account for a small proportion of central area parking supply. Many urban centres adopt a more flexible approach when it comes to short-stay parking. This element of the parking supply is aimed at short-stay visitors who contribute significantly to the economy of central areas. This is currently viewed as essential in light of the competition offered to existing urban centres by retail centres at out of town or outer suburb locations where parking controls are minimal (OECD/ECMT, 1995). Evidence indicates that controls on public parking spaces have had some effect in influencing the use of spaces in prime locations and, when adequate enforcement is available, have contributed to maintaining capacity of the road system (Association of County Councils, 1991). Although this has made limited space available to a larger number of users who contribute to the commercial viability of the city, it is at the cost of a higher number of journeys, which may not have otherwise been made, and of higher off-peak traffic levels. This may conflict with other, wider, environmental objectives in urban areas. Evidence also indicates that parking policy may be undermined if cross-city journeys are too easy and if private parking remains uncontrolled (Goodwin, 1996; Cairns, 1995). Suggestions have recently been made to levy a charge on private non-residential spaces and that this could be used to discourage potential users from driving, while using the revenue to encourage public transport (RCEP, 1994; DETR, 1998).

Parking provision within new developments can be controlled and limited through the operation of the planning system, although it is likely to have a longer-term impact due to the pace of redevelopment. In the UK, there is an emphasis on finding alternative uses for parking space in such developments and restricting the amount of parking available, and revising parking standards downwards to a maximum, as opposed to a statement of minimum provision. Increasingly in the UK, developers are making commuted payments to local planning authorities, where retail schemes cannot provide sufficient parking on site, so that the public provision of parking can be enhanced, or enter into agreements where a developer contribution, following the granting of planning permission, is made for new facilities for pedestrians, cyclists and public transport (York City Council, 1995; DoE/DOT, 1994). Controlling existing private parking spaces is more problematic, however. More than half the off-street parking provision in most large towns is privately owned and controlled (Association of County Councils, 1991). The effectiveness of on-street parking controls has suffered due to the lack of effective enforcement. In London, following implementation of the Road Traffic Act 1991, the enforcement of parking restrictions has passed to the London boroughs which now consider on-street parking as part of a borough-wide strategic parking plan encompassing both private and public (on-street and off-street) parking (Parking Committee for London, 1995). The potential exists for a wider integration of parking controls across planning areas than has been the case in the past.

PEDESTRIANISATION

Pedestrianisation is viewed as a form of traffic restraint measure, although it is often not promoted in this way. Instead, it is often used as a device to remove traffic from historic or retail areas, to provide a more pleasant environment for pedestrians (Tolley and Turton, 1995). Traditionally, pedestrian provision has focused on pedestrian areas in the centre of towns and cities; compared to experience elsewhere in Europe little has been done in the UK to link central area schemes with surrounding areas through pedestrian priority networks (Roberts, 1981; TEST, 1988). The typical model of town centre pedestrianisation is one where the inner area is surrounded by an inner ring road, or combination of roads which could act as such following the implementation of the scheme (Goodwin, 1996). In the UK, many cities and towns have implemented quite successful schemes, the most notable of these being the city of York which can lay claim to having one of the largest pedestrian street networks (York City Council, 1995). Often, however, these extreme forms of traffic regulation are often the subject of controversy, i.e. extreme in the sense that vehicular access is restricted to deliveries in many cases, but they are now more readily accepted by retailers and inhabitants. There is, however, a growing emphasis on the requirement to produce pedestrian networks which are not confined to central areas (Department of Transport, 1996b). It is likely that pedestrian networks (or networks for green modes) will be improved. The challenge for planning has to be to seek their integration with other modes of transport and to incorporate their design and planning into strategic policy. Targets could be readily applied to assess the extent and quality of their implementation.

Traffic Calming

The general requirements within a wider speed management/restraint framework are to reduce the level of priority given to road vehicles and encourage space sharing, including walking and cycling. The objectives of traffic calming are frequently stated as: to improve road safety; to reclaim space for pedestrian and non-traffic activities; to improve pedestrian mobility and reduce traffic barriers; to promote greater security, in particular among residents, pedestrians and cyclists; and to create an improved environment (Pharoah and Russell, 1989). Objectives of speed management and other improvements to the traffic environment could be incorporated into targets for the particular neighbourhood or planning area. Recently revived interest in pedestrian road safety (Department of Transport, 1989) has been further marked by the UK government's target to reduce road casualties by one-third by the year 2000 (Department of Transport, 1987). The elderly and young who account for substantial numbers of pedestrian casualties, have been identified and targeted (Department of Transport, 1990, 1991). Traffic calming has been widely embraced to help in attaining this target. Obviously traffic calming on its own does not necessarily imply a particularly radical departure from traditional traffic management schemes in the sense that it can operate either within a 'do nothing' policy environment or within a wider traffic restraint framework.

Prioritising Public Transport

Within a wider demand management framework of attracting trips away from cars, improvements to public transport can play a vital role in the transfer of longer trips. In the context of the direct regulation of street space, bus priority lanes and park and ride schemes have been widely used. Bus priority lanes involve the allocation of road space from general use for bus use within a specified time period and the reduction in space available for private cars during those periods. Protected space, in a similar format but of a more permanent nature, has also been provided for rapid transit systems running on-street; again this has reduced the circulation space available for cars. Park and ride, often associated with the prioritisation of public transport, represents an innovative form of transport interchange (Tolley and Turton, 1995; RCEP, 1994). Usually such provision occurs on the edge of the built-up urban area or in a suburban location. Drivers are encouraged to park at these locations due to the frequent and fast public transport services available. They are most effective when combined with other measures to dissuade car use in towns. Evidence indicates that these schemes are popular and can complement the restraint of road space and parking to prevent traffic growth. None the less, several disadvantages have been identified. They can generate additional traffic to the park and ride facility, from journeys which would otherwise have been made entirely by public transport or not made at all, reduce the level of amenity in the neighbouring area and unless associated with counteracting measures, do little to reduce overall traffic in the city itself, due to the suppressed demand (Goodwin, 1996; Parkhurst, 1994).

CONCLUSIONS

As the new millennium approaches radical changes will be required to the way in which the land use planning system and transport policy operate. Presently the indications are that there are moves towards an integrated approach where the relationship between land use and transport demand management is recognised.

INTEGRATION OF SOCIAL, FISCAL AND TRANSPORT POLICIES

Pricing mechanisms and taxation measures need to focus holistically on lifestyles and transport demand. For example, the continuation of a policy of non-taxation on private non-residential parking is clearly counter to strategies aimed at reducing car dependence. There are strong arguments for treating such parking provision as income in kind. At the local level, taxation policies could be implemented; on a ratio of parking spaces to employees a tax could be implemented. Hypothecation of taxes may be easier locally than nationally, funds being redirected to fund public transport infrastructure. The extent to which populations make travel and locational choices consistent with travel reduction objectives depends on the extent of integration between fiscal, social and transport policy. Income levels, as well as household location decisions, are important determinants of travel behaviour; however, debates about pricing have focused on road pricing and not on other forms of fiscal policy, for example a tax on house prices or a development charge.

FRAGMENTATION OF DECISION-MAKING STRUCTURES

Current decision-making structures are fragmented at both local and national levels. In the context of existing planning guidance on transport, many local authorities currently see bus-based public transport as a tool of demand management. The problem is that they have little or no control over the operation of these systems which are under the influence and control of one or more private operators. Other new pieces of legislation have been highlighted as problematic: the Environment Act 1995 and Road Traffic Reduction Act 1997 both seek to use existing regulations under other pieces of legislation for them to be enforced.

OLD REGULATIONS, NEW CHALLENGES

Existing legislation such as the Town and Country Planning Acts are based on a particular context and vision. This vision does not include demand management. The next 10–15 years should herald a new legislative programme aimed at consolidating existing legislation and implementing new regulatory frameworks. A possible model would include the integration of land use planning, air quality and road safety targets for specific plan areas. The UK planning system's track record of plan production, both strategic and local, is a useful prerequisite in terms of the future integration of transport and land use policy. The requirement has to be for the provision of workable and enforceable target-driven strategies that can be spatially organised locally in a way to conform with regional and national targets. Ideally, the regional level would be based on significant travel-to-work areas.

PRIVATE FINANCE

Private finance is likely to become an important stream of funding both nationally and locally. Future transport and land use strategies are therefore likely to be heavily influenced by the views of private sector investors, particularly in situations where schemes are unlikely to be flagship schemes for which it is easy to attract funding. Issues surrounding the future integrity of land use and transport decisions need to be addressed and decisions monitored. Work has uncovered evidence of roads being rerouted to take them closer to a planned redevelopment site and the downgrading of a road adjacent to a privately financed road in order to enhance traffic levels and fees which are recouped by the private sector through the operation of shadow tolls.

TAKING THE CAR OUT OF THE EQUATION

In reducing car dependence, integrated land use and transport strategies over the next 10–15 years will need to be focused around the neighbourhood. A policy framework seeking to shift transport demand to a mix of public transport, walking and cycling may mean that household location decisions will strongly favour neighbourhoods within a reasonable travel distance/time from places of work. Neighbourhoods will not only therefore require to be planned around public transport nodes or interchanges, but fiscal policies (local government taxation or developer contributions) will need to offer incentives to developers, households and retailers in order to maintain the viability of such a settlement pattern where competition from out of town retailing, for example, is prevalent.

CHAPTER 10

LOCAL ECONOMIC DEVELOPMENT

Colin C. Williams

INTRODUCTION

The aim of this chapter is to chart the transformations in the theory and practice of local economic development so as to uncover a major paradigm shift which is taking place. To display this, an examination is undertaken of how 'economic base theory', a principal conceptual tool used to define the nature and scope of local economic development, has been variously interpreted over time. This reveals four distinct waves of thought and action. Assuming that an economy needs to generate external income in order to grow, the first three waves all perceived any economy as composed of two sectors: 'basic' sector industries which generate external income and act as the engine of growth, and 'dependent' sector industries which merely circulate income within a locality and thus live off the endeavours of these export-oriented industries. In the first wave, from the Industrial Revolution up until the 1970s, manufacturing comprised the basic sector and services the dependent sector. This was followed by a second wave from the 1980s which realised that producer services fulfilled the same basic sector function as manufacturing and incorporated them into the basic sector, while the third wave from the early 1990s, recognised that consumer services such as sport, tourism, higher education and the cultural industries also generated income for localities and thus viewed them in the same way as other basic sector activities.

In contrast to these previous approaches, the currently emerging fourth wave argues that the incorporation of the last remaining 'dependent' activity into the basic sector not only calls into question the very notion of a 'basic/dependent' sector dualism but also the view that external income generation alone is sufficient to cause economic development. Instead, this new approach, here termed the 'new localism', asserts that preventing the leakage of income out of an area is just as important as generating external income. Here, the economic, environmental and social justice rationales of this new approach towards local economic development are outlined along with the strategies and initiatives adopted. Following this, and to show how such an approach is set to change the nature and scope of local economic development, we take a case study of a pioneering initiative to implement the 'new localism'. Examining Forum for the Future's 'Reinvigorating the Local Economy' project based at the Royal Society of the Arts northern headquarters in Halifax, the 'new localism' is revealed to offer an opportunity for local economic development to not only integrate the goals of sustainable development and social justice which are being pursued in other fields of planning, but to recapture what can and should be its aim: making localities a better place in which to live, work and do business.

The Evolution of Local Economic Development Theory and Practice

For most of the twentieth century, the principal conceptual tool used to formulate local economic policy and theorise local economic development has been 'economic (or export) base theory' (Haggett *et al.*, 1977; Glickman, 1977; Wilson, 1974). Assuming that an economy needs to earn external income so as to grow, this theory, to repeat, has conventionally perceived any economy as composed of two sectors: 'basic' sector industries which generate external income and act as the 'engines of growth'; and 'dependent' sector activities which merely circulate income within the area and are thus seen as 'parasitic' activities feeding off the wealth created in these other industries. Grounded in this theorisation of an economy, local economic development has traditionally sought to develop those industries which can sell their goods and services outside of the locality.

Nevertheless, there have been a number of waves of thought concerning which economic activities are engines of growth and which are parasitic. In the first wave, from the Industrial Revolution up until the 1970s, the view was that manufacturing comprised the basic sector and services were residual or dependent activities. The result was that much of the focus in economic development was placed on developing and promoting manufacturing industry. Services, meanwhile, were regarded as 'lollipop' jobs and of no real value to economic development. Indeed, this view is by no means defunct in economic development circles. As Bachtler and Davies (1989: 168) point out, 'the view that the economy is solely manufacturing-driven still has widespread currency. This view is that services are wholly dependent on manufacturing and that service jobs are not "real" jobs'. In many local government economic development strategies, for example, statements are still found such as 'most services in the district are of an essentially local nature' (Kirklees Metropolitan Borough Council, 1991: 6). Similarly, in the groves of academe, manufacturing 'die hards' are still to be found. Campbell (1996: 49), for example, claims that '"service activities" depend on [manufacturing] for their survival and growth', while Peck and Tickell (1991: 36) argue that 'service industries are essentially "parasitic" in that they do not actually add to wealth in the economy, although they can help to realise the value of wealth created elsewhere'.

From the 1980s, however, this simplistic dominant/subservient view of the relationship between manufacturing and services came under increasing scrutiny, not least due to the rapid and severe restructuring of many advanced economies. The twin trends of deindustrialisation and tertiarisation in the advanced economies and the accompanying new international division of labour (e.g. Cohen, 1981; Dicken, 1992; Sassen, 1991), with control and command functions located in a network of global cities in developed nations and physical production increasingly dispersed into developing nations, resulted in a re-evaluation of the role of services in economic development. This second wave focused upon retheorising the role of producer services (services sold to other businesses) in local economic development and revealed a wealth of evidence that such services export (Beyers and Alvine, 1985; Coffey, 1995a, b; Daniels, 1993; Goe, 1994; Harrington, 1995a, b; Moulaert and Todtling, 1995a, b; O'Farrell, 1993). The result was that producer services have been widely recognised as contributing to external income generation and incorporated into the basic sector. Many economic development strategies, therefore, now sought producer services as keenly as they chased manufacturing industry. Consequently, the old 'manufacturing as engine of growth' versus 'services as dependent' dualism of the first wave was replaced by a 'manufacturing and producer services as engines of growth' versus 'consumer services as dependent activity' dichotomy in the second wave. Remaining largely intact, however, was first, the view of the economy as consisting of both a basic and dependent sector and second, the notion that an economy can be structured according to a 'hierarchy of sectors' prioritised by their ability to export.

The third wave of thought and action, since the start of the 1990s, has shown that consumer services, the major sector remaining entrenched in the dependent category, also fulfil an external income-generating function (e.g. Bale, 1993; Law, 1993; Williams, 1996a, 1997a, b). At first, proponents of this third wave confined themselves to studying specific consumer services in isolation such as tourism (e.g. Law, 1993), universities (e.g. Goddard *et al.*, 1994), sports facilities and events (e.g. Bale, 1993; Burgan and Mules, 1992), cultural industries (e.g. Myerscough, 1988), retailing (Williams, 1997b) and medical services (e.g. Gross, 1995; Vaughan *et al.*, 1994). This meant that although individual consumer service industries were shown to be functioning as basic sector activities, without a re-evaluation of consumer services as a whole, the basic/dependent sector dualism itself went unchallenged. Later analyses, however, showing that the consumer services sector as a whole functions as a basic industry, have contested the very notion of a basic/dependent sector dualism (e.g. Williams, 1996a, 1997a). Between 1981 and 1991 in Britain, for example, while the number of all employees in employment rose by just 2%, consumer services employment increased by 26% (to 40% of the total labour force). Indeed, 3.44 consumer service jobs were created for every producer service job (Williams, 1997a). It has become increasingly difficult to accept, therefore, that consumer service employment is simply a by-product of other supposed engines of growth.

So far as the practice of local economic development is concerned, this third-wave approach has been most popular in those local economies witnessing heavy deindustrialisation coupled with weak producer services growth (e.g. Glasgow, Sheffield). In these localities, consumer services have been adopted as a principal motor of growth in their economic development strategies. However, in cities more successful at retaining and attracting other sectors, such as Leeds, London and Bristol, consumer services have at best, been perceived as making a supportive contribution by bolstering the attractiveness of the city to producer service and manufacturing companies. Consumer services, therefore, although increasingly recognised as having an external income-generating role to play in economic development, are only embraced as a lead sector by localities when other possibilities have been ruled out. Much local economy policy, in other words, has continued to focus on developing and attracting export-oriented activity in the form of manufacturing and producer services (Persky *et al.*, 1993; Williams, 1997a). 'Basic consumer services' which attract consumers into the area in order to spend their money, and which fulfil the same basic sector function as export-oriented industry, have often received little attention.

Therefore, this third-wave approach, by recognising the external income-generating function of the last remaining supposedly dependent activity, has brought into question the very notion of a basic-/dependent-sector dualism. Remaining at the heart of much local economic development theory and practice, however, is the view that sectors should be prioritised according to their ability to export, meaning that there is a 'hierarchy of sectors'. In this view, manufacturing is seen to be at the top of this hierarchy, followed by producer services and only then consumer services. Nevertheless, the fourth wave, as will now be shown, has voiced serious misgivings about this 'hierarchy of sectors' approach.

THE 'NEW LOCALISM': FROM OUTWARD- TO INWARD-LOOKING STRATEGIES

Drawing upon earlier research (Giaratani and McNelis, 1980; McNulty, 1977; Mandelbaum and Chicoine, 1986), a fourth wave of retheorising the economic base, here termed the 'new localism', has displayed that economic development and growth are not so strongly correlated with income-inducing activity as the first three waves assumed. This asserts that for an economy to grow, it is not a rise in external income *per se* which is needed but, rather, an increase in net income. Net income, to explain, is determined by total external income, times a multiplier (which is larger the more self-reliant the economy), minus total external spending. The growth of any economy is thus dependent on not only attracting external income but also preventing the leakage of money out of an area (Persky *et al.*, 1993; Williams, 1997a). As Power (1988) asserts, the only reason to export is to pay for imports. If imported goods and services can be produced locally, then net income will increase without a rise in exports. The variety of economic activity then increases, as does the interconnectedness of the local economy.

The problem in local economic development at present, nevertheless, is that the practice has not caught up with the theory. The positive role that locally oriented activities play in economic development as leakage preventers is normally ignored in economic development practice. Many development agencies continue to pursue export-led development policies by cultivating basic industries according to the 'sectoral hierarchies' approach described above with little regard for the extent to which seepage of income is taking place (Persky *et al.*, 1993). The outcome is that many local economies leak like a sieve. Indeed, so rarely is such an idea considered important that data on the extent to which local economies leak are very rare. One exception is the work of Polese (1982), who finds that over half of regional service demand in a rural area of Quebec is satisfied by imports.

Accordingly, locally oriented activities, far from being dependent or parasitic activities as suggested by the first three waves of economic base theory, have been recognised to be as important to economic development as externally oriented activity. In their role of preventing the seepage of income out of the local economy, they contribute to economic development in two ways. First, locally oriented activities prevent money from draining out of a locality by supplying facilities which negate the need for the local population to either travel outside the area to obtain the good or service, or acquire externally produced goods and services. Second, locally oriented activities can change the expenditure patterns of local businesses by raising the share of their expenditure spent in the locality. To understand the full contribution of any economic activity to local economic development, it is thus useful to envisage them as performing two functions in local economies. On the one hand, they can function as basic activities, drawing income into the economy from outside and, on the other hand, they can operate as leakage preventers, serving the local market and thus retaining and circulating money within the local economy. These two features can be seen as equally important in the economic development of a locality as both are required to increase net income.

The rationale for pursuing leakage prevention and thus the localisation of economies, however, is not only economic. There are also strong environmental and social justice rationales. The increasing globalisation of trade is seen not only to create environmentally degrading and resource-inefficient supply chains but result in production for external wants rather than local needs (e.g. Douthwaite, 1996; Ekins and Max-Neef, 1992; Waters, 1995). As Elkin *et al.* (1991: 217) assert, sustainable urban development can only arise 'through support of locally self-reliant, smaller, co-operative and community businesses. Currently, community life is unsustainable because of imports of labour and materials which significantly reduce local independence. Sustainable urban development needs, wherever possible, to make use of the available local resources, especially human resources, and consume local products.' The rise of environmental awareness and the pursuit of sustainable development, therefore, is causing the notion of localisation to be discussed more widely. Localisation, however, with its focus upon mobilising local resources to meet local needs, also refocuses attention more directly on the ulti-mate social justice goal of local economic development: to meet the needs and wants of the local population. It not only empowers citizens to identify local needs which are currently unfulfilled and develop the means by which they can be met but also enables those who are currently excluded from the global economy to improve both their individual quality of life and that of their community (Porritt, 1996).

Given these economic, environmental and social justice rationales for promoting the new localism, the key issue that remains is how such an approach can be implemented. What are the principles which a locality seeking to imple-ment such a strategy should follow? Here, it is proposed that there are four principal interlocking goals: encouraging local ownership; increasing import substitution; improving the local control of money; and localising work to meet local demand. All are interrelated, but are here considered in turn. The suggestion, moreover, is that the consumer services sector is perhaps the most appropriate place to start in implementing such an approach because it is perhaps easier to localise than manufacturing. This is not because it is already more locally oriented. Rather, it is because there is currently more consensus that consumer services should be localised activities among the various stakeholders engaged in formulating and implementing local economic policy.

Encouraging Local Ownership

In the export-oriented paradigm, simply encouraging activity which generates external income is sufficient reason for supporting an industry. The outcome is that many local economies encourage externally owned large corporations to relocate in their area with little regard for their overall impacts on the local economy. Given that these corporations frequently source their inputs from outside the area, the only benefit for the locality can be the wages and the multiplier effects resulting from employees' expenditure (e.g. Foley *et al.*, 1996). In the new localism, however, where emphasis is placed as much on leakage preven-tion as external income generation, locally owned businesses are encouraged. This is because these firms are asserted to be more likely to retain income within the local economy by recirculating profits and assets locally, and to purchase local services and products, as displayed in the Fens (Williams, 1996a). They also increase jobs at a faster rate than externally controlled firms and tend not to cut back jobs to the same degree as their non-local counterparts during downturns (Bluestone and Harrison, 1982). Therefore, developing locally owned small retailers and guest houses, for example, is seen as preferable to the imposition of food superstores and hotel chains owned by the major corporations, which source their goods to a greater extent externally.

INCREASING IMPORT SUBSTITUTION

Running alongside this principle of encouraging local ownership is that of facilitating the local production of goods and services which are currently imported so as to decrease the reliance of a locality on imports. This reduces leakages and increases the local economic multiplier effects. How, nevertheless, can this shift from an outward-looking orientation to an inward-looking trajectory be achieved in local economic development strategies? The first and most obvious method is for economic development agencies to identify the types of imported products and services that can be replaced by local production, inform local firms of these opportunities, encourage them to compete for this business and provide the necessary technical and marketing assistance. Some of the mechanisms to do this already exist so far as intermediate demand is concerned such as Better Business Opportunities' (formerly Better Made in Britain's) Regional Audit of Industry (REGAIN) initiative (see Williams, 1994a). This seeks to identify on a sector-by-sector basis the current imports into a locality and, following this, to target the potential local suppliers of these goods and services and put them in touch with each other.

A further initiative specifically addressing the reduction of food imports is community-supported agriculture (CSA). This was born in Germany and Switzerland in the 1970s, became a popular movement in North America in the early 1990s and has now spread to Britain in the mid 1990s. Co-ordinated by the Soil Association, their 'Local Food Links' scheme aims to put consumers in touch with local food sources by developing local food distribution systems. Some 250 Local Food Links projects are listed in the 1996 Soil Association directory and 20 000 households participate in these schemes (Booth, 1996; Delow, 1996; Soil Association, 1996).

Finally, and again in terms of final rather than intermediate demand, 'use it or lose it' campaigns to encourage consumers to buy more local products are another possible strategy. This method, however, is not only largely unsuccessful in facilitating local purchasing, but even if people do buy locally, the business may often be owned externally and/or the goods and services sourced from external suppliers, so a share of the profits and income will quickly leak out of the area. It will not be recirculated within the economy. The result is a low multiplier effect (see Williams, 1996b). Such problems can be overcome by improving the local control of money.

ENCOURAGING LOCAL CONTROL OF MONEY

One of the principal problems in local economies, and recognised as early as the 1960s (Jacobs, 1969), is that income leaks out of localities since it is not locally controlled. There are several ways to overcome this. First, cities could invest portions of the municipal pension funds in local projects so that fiscal resources which might otherwise escape the locality can be retained (Keating, 1991; Leatherwood, 1983; Rifkin and Barber, 1978). Second, credit unions could be used to invest money locally (Leyshon and Thrift, 1995; McKillop *et al.*, 1995) or third, localities could create their own local currencies to enable local people both to provide local work and to buy local goods and services, thus retaining income and wealth within the area. To do this, local exchange and trading systems (LETS) can be employed. These are local associations whose members make offers of, and requests for, goods and services in a directory and then exchange them priced in a local unit of currency. In theory, these overcome many of the problems with existing policy instruments for local purchasing. Conventional approaches to local purchasing, to repeat, have low multiplier effects because even if a person purchases locally, either the business is often externally owned so some of the money will leave the area, or the income will be used to purchase further inputs which are themselves produced outside the area. In a LETS, however, the local currency can be used only to purchase further goods and services within the system. None of it can leave the locality, nor can it be used to purchase goods and services outside the area since it has no 'value' external to the local association. The effect is that it creates a 'closed system' so that none of the local money leaks out of the area (Davis and Davis, 1987; Williams, 1996b). In consequence, LETS have been widely advocated as a means by which local purchasing can be encouraged (e.g. Dobson, 1993; Greco, 1994; Lang, 1994; Offe and Heinze, 1992; Williams, 1996b). During the 1990s, moreover, they are taking the UK by storm. As Williams (1996c) reveals, in 1992 there were just 4 LETS but by 1995, some 350 were trading with 30 000 members. All of the signs, moreover, are that they are continuing to develop.

LOCALISING WORK TO MEET LOCAL DEMAND

A fourth and final principle for implementing this more locally oriented economic development strategy is to localise work so that it meets local demand. To achieve this, first, a policy of localising employment could be pursued so as to maximise the number of local people obtaining jobs in the locality, although this is sometimes problematic such as in the realm of EU-funded projects and competitive tendering. Such a policy, nevertheless, is a relatively simple tool which can be integrated into a wide range of tenders and contracts by interested parties.

Second, and more widely, a policy of encouraging informal economic activity could be pursued. Although there are many instances in a Third World context where such a policy has been adopted to create work to meet local needs (ILO, 1996), examples in the advanced economies are notable by their absence. At present, the only known exception is Hackney Council in London which is considering harnessing informal work on some of its most deprived estates. Such an approach, however, is in its infancy and few have begun to think through how informal work can be harnessed to meet local needs and wants. Instead, the myth which pervades much academic and practitioner discourse is that informal work is a leftover from a previous economic era and that economies as they advance shift activity from their informal to their formal sector. Neither proposition has yet been seriously investigated. Until such time as they are proven, there is a need to maintain an open mind about harnessing informal activity as a way of localising work and promoting local economic development.

To evaluate whether these principles of local ownership, import substitution, local control of money and localising work to meet local demand promote local revitalisation in practice is difficult. Unfortunately, some people will feel a 'knee-jerk' opposition to the creation of stronger, more localised economies. This occurs for a variety of reasons. Some, for instance, will perceive the aim of the 'new localism' as total self-sufficiency and have visions of being encouraged to return to some past age of toil and strife. However, localisation does not mean everything being produced locally, nor does it mean an end to trade. It simply means forging a better balance between local, regional, national and international markets (Douthwaite, 1996; Porritt, 1996). It also means gaining greater control over what is produced, where, when and how, so that localities are less dependent upon the foibles of the global economic system for their future well-being. Far from reducing living standards, it makes economic sense for a locality to seek to increase its net income and thus wealth, environmental sense to reduce unnecessary degradation and resource consumption and social and political sense to consider more directly meeting the needs and wants of one's citizens.

Moreover, although there are disparate examples across the advanced economies of attempts to facilitate localisation in a piecemeal manner and where all of these initiatives and institutions have gone beyond the purely experimental phase, no one locality has yet set out to combine a range of these institutions with local empowerment to create a substantial and varied nexus of local economic activity that stands out from the main stream of the global market and is recognisably different from it. The 'localised economy' *in toto* remains largely a concept, with only marginal and fragmented practical expressions. Although the Saint Paul's Homegrown Economy Project (HEP) in Minnesota (Imbroscio, 1995; Judd and Ready, 1986) attempted to shift from a reliance on imports to greater self-reliance, as Imbroscio (1995: 858) concludes, this 'never matured beyond the status of a symbolic gesture'. The current proposal by Forum for the Future, nevertheless, to use West Yorkshire as a crucible for such an approach will provide a much richer source of information over the coming years for those wishing to evaluate this more holistic approach towards local economic development. In the next section, therefore, the reader is briefly introduced to this project.

IMPLEMENTING THE NEW LOCALISM: REINVIGORATING THE LOCAL ECONOMY IN WEST YORKSHIRE

With the global shift in manufacturing towards the newly industrialising countries, and insufficient growth in services to compensate for this decline, areas such as West Yorkshire have found themselves marginalised and essentially peripheral to the wider economic development process. Despite the relative success of Leeds (Haughton and Williams, 1996), producer service employment, especially the headquarters functions, remains overwhelmingly concentrated in the south-east of England (Daniels, 1995a, b) and the vast majority of overseas tourism, major sporting events and higher-value cultural tourism remain heavily concentrated in the southern core regions (Williams, 1997a). The result is that regions such as West Yorkshire have found themselves not only under-represented in service employment but competing with other similar peripheral regions for the back office developments and lower-order consumer service functions (see Haughton and Whitney, 1994; Williams, 1997a).

For peripheral regions such as West Yorkshire, therefore, the spatial division of labour emerging in the UK, Europe and beyond is problematic. It has to compete with cheaper labour locations for routine production functions. High value-adding industries, meanwhile, along with the high-status well-paid core jobs, are emerging far away from the old industrial regions and old collectivisms. The consequence is that there are thus three policy options for peripheral areas such as West Yorkshire so far as economic development is concerned:

- Choose to remain a peripheral region and thus relatively poor
- Attempt to become a 'new core' region
- Pursue a path of 'localised development'

Assuming that West Yorkshire does not wish to remain a peripheral region, it is only the latter two options which are open to such regions. Whichever is chosen, localisation is a central and essential feature of the resulting economic development strategy. If the option of turning West Yorkshire into a 'new core' is pursued, then as Cooke (1990: 164) writes, the lesson from throughout Europe and the Americas is that this requires the creation of the present-day equivalent to the 'nineteenth century industrial district, as described by Alfred Marshall, [These] were systems of small craft-based companies specialised in the production of a particular set of products, inter-linked by tight networks of sub-contractors, capable of producing customised products, often for a luxury market.' Thus, if West Yorkshire were to decide to try to turn itself into a 'new core' area, localisation would be a prerequisite of its economic strategy. It depends upon creating the 'synergies' between local firms so as to facilitate the transformation of the area into a new core. If, alternatively, the 'localised development' pathway is chosen, then again and as shown, localisation will be the core feature of its economic development strategy. Hence, whether either a 'new core' or a 'localised' approach is adopted towards local economic development, localisation has to be a central feature if successful economic regeneration is to result.

Based on this understanding, in August 1996 a survey was conducted of localisation strategies and practices in West Yorkshire. On the one hand, this involved a review of the economic development strategies (as well as the Local Agenda 21 (LA21) approaches) of around 30 of the major public sector authorities and partnership agencies in this region so as to identify the extent to which localisation strategies and initiatives fit into existing local economy policy and LA21 strategies. On the other hand, some 75 semi-structured telephone interviews were conducted with local authorities, TECs, third sector organisations and individuals to identify the magnitude and character of the disparate localisation initiatives already under way. The results of this survey are reported in Williams (1996d). This reveals that the vast majority of existing strategies adopted by economic development agencies provide opportunities for localisation practices to be pursued and that there are a wide range of innovative localisation initiatives occurring at a grass-roots level which can be further developed and promoted. It appeared that all that was lacking was a co-ordinating agency to promote a coherent vision of localisation for the subregion and to disseminate best practice.

Following this baseline study, therefore, support has been sought from the principal private and public sector agencies and stakeholders in this subregion and funding raised to set up a project team to implement this vision. Based at the Royal Society of the Arts northern headquarters in Halifax, the aim of Forum for the Future's 'Reinvigorating the Local Economy' project is to change the notion of a localised economy from being perceived largely as an impractical, nostalgic, backward-looking approach, to take its place as the logical and necessary complement and counterweight, in a modern and progressive society, to involvement in world markets. The aims of this 'Reinvigorating the Local Economy' project are threefold:

1. *Conceptual*. The project will create a vision of a functioning local economy that is intellectually coherent and economically viable in a modern open industrial economy.
2. *Practical*. The project will show how such a vision may be put into practice in the West Yorkshire area. A further practical objective is to show how LA21 activities can reinforce local development initiatives and vice versa.
3. *Pedagogical*. Based on both the vision and the practical local experience, an operational 'tool kit' on how best to reinvigorate local economies in different circumstances will be developed.

At the time of writing, in late 1997, this project remains in its developmental stages with the staff only just having been appointed. Based on the belief that at present there are no examples of a fully functioning 'localised economy', the intention is that West Yorkshire will provide both an exemplar of a localised economy for others to follow and that a 'tool kit' will be developed of best practice in fostering and developing locally oriented initiatives (Porritt, 1996). To commence, therefore, the focus will be upon developing the following initiatives and institutions so as to achieve the four interlocking goals of the new localism identified above: community land trusts (for retaining community control over land), credit unions (for retaining control over credit), LETS (for retaining control over currency), community-supported agriculture (for retaining a community-focused agricultural base), neighbourhood energy groups (for reducing demand on outside sources of energy and, where possible, increasing the local supply of especially renewable energy), community work (whereby local people give their labour to some scheme of local community benefit) and community shops (through which local people retain the value of retail services within the community). At present, it is obviously too early to engage in any evaluation of this pioneering initiative to promote the 'new localism'. That will have to wait for at least several years. All that can be said at present is that this project represents a coherent and strategic attempt to put the theory of the new localism into practice in a way which will provide both a crucible for experiments in how to implement this approach and hopefully, an exemplar of the way forward for local economic policy.

CONCLUSIONS

This chapter has revealed that during the final decades of the twentieth century, local economic development theory and practice have undergone a sea change. For much of the century, the view which predominated was that manufacturing was the engine of growth because it exported its products and that services were dependent or parasitic activities merely circulating money within the area. From the 1980s, however, a large number of academic commentators put much effort into elevating producer services to a basic sector status and changing the perception of practitioners concerning their role in local economic development. During the 1990s, moreover, a similar drive has occurred with consumer services from academics working disparately on individual consumer service industries such as sport, tourism, the cultural industries and higher education. By revealing that such consumer services are also basic activities in the sense that they generate external income, this brought into focus the inherent weakness of not only the basic/dependent sector dualism which lies at the heart of economic base theory but also the view that there is a hierarchy of sectors based upon the ability of sectors to export. The outcome has been a fourth wave of theorising and practice, the 'new localism', which asserts that it is not external income generation *per se* which causes local economic development but also leakage prevention.

Based upon the strategies of import substitution, local ownership, local control of money and localising work to meet local demand, this approach is fundamentally reconceptualising the nature and function of local economic development. It is to be hoped, therefore, that the turn of the millennium will see more research and practice from this inward-looking approach of the 'new localism'. If this is achieved, then local economic development will surely regain what can and should be its aim: making localities a better place in which to live, work and do business.

ACKNOWLEDGEMENTS

My thanks go to Anita Seymour who provided research assistance on the West Yorkshire study, collecting information on both economic development strategies and localisation initiatives. I am also indebted to Jonathan Porritt, Paul Ekins and Sara Parkin, directors of Forum for the Future, who instigated and funded the study of the potential for localisation in West Yorkshire. Nevertheless, the usual disclaimers apply. These are my own views, not necessarily those of Forum for the Future, and any faults or omissions are mine alone.

CHAPTER 11

PLANNING CITIES FOR THE TWENTY-FIRST CENTURY: THE NEED FOR A NEW WELFARE MODEL?

David Etherington and Michael Chapman

INTRODUCTION

One of the most important challenges confronting both central and local government, policy and planning professionals concerns the economic and sustainable future of our cities. Cities provide wealth- and employment-creating opportunities and are important drivers of national economies. As centres of economic development, innovation, cultural activity and social progress, it is not unexpected that there exists a clear link between the performance of urban areas and the performance of the economy as a whole (Oately, 1998: 3). Cities not only have national significance but are increasingly part of the expanding global economy (Castells, 1992). Global forces are transforming the economic and social base of urban areas and as a consequence has engendered changes in the land use system (Fainstien *et al.*, 1992). Borja and Castells (1996) view the new frontier for urban management as one which consists in preparing the city to be ready to face global competition as economic prosperity and the welfare of its citizens depend on that reality. Urban authorities now endeavour to implement strategies which come to terms with the pressures and outcomes of global economic change on the urban economy while, on the other hand, ensuring economic and social cohesion. Yet, it is important to note that urban economies are an integral part of the global/regional economy – they are not separate entities. Planners and policy-makers are not responding to external influences – they are key actors in key processes of urban restructuring (Lovering, 1997: 78).

Borja and Castells argue that without a solid economic, social and environmental platform cities are unable to compete effectively in global markets and function in global networks. In this sense, the local and the global are complementary rather than being antagonistic (Borja and Castells, 1996: 14). The role of cities as a vehicle for attracting globally mobile capital is understood by Porter (1990, cited in Duffy, 1995: 2) who suggests that urban and regional authorities have an increasingly important role to play in fostering a local environment where businesses can grow and remain competitive. Internationally successful industries would:

frequently concentrate in a city or region, and the bases for advantage are often intensely local. Geographic concentration is important to the genesis of competitive advantage and it amplifies the forces that upgrade and sustain advantage. While the national government has a role in upgrading industry, the role of the state and local government is potentially as great or greater.

Indeed, the notion of city government (and urban planning) as grounds for enhancing competitiveness and attracting capital investment underpins what we term the European Union (EU) neo-liberal agenda with regards to urban policy, a theme which we will explore in this chapter. Cities are complex physical, social and economic structures, and as we approach the new millennium urban planning regimes will be confronted with challenges and change of international competition, local social and political forces operating within a framework of national regulation and institutional circumstances (Newman and Thornely, 1996: 5).

However, the impact of economic restructuring is spatially uneven. Cities dominated by traditional 'core' manufacturing industries (engineering, steel, coal, etc.) and once the very centres of economic growth and prosperity have now become associated with the negative outcomes of economic restructuring, physical decline, the rapid suburbanisation of the 'better off' to the outer city and the continued residualisation and marginalisation of the poor, unemployed and excluded. Economic competitiveness and the successful transformation of cities may well rest with the performance of the business, commerce and cultural sectors, but sustainable economic and social development is dependent on how urban authorities address the social and political consequences of poverty, deprivation and exclusion through the provisions of public services and the management of regeneration initiatives. The aim of this chapter is to discuss the future of cities in the next millennium by examining the impact of the social dimension of European polices with respect to urban change.

DIMENSIONS OF URBAN RESTRUCTURING

It has been long recognised that cities are constantly responding to a variety of social and economic pressures. Urban restructuring involves the interaction of complex and often contradictory processes of urban development. Danschat (1992: 24) defines these processes as follows:

> Urban restructuring as defined here embraces aspects of economic restructuring, flexibilisation and deregulation strategies of national and local states (regulation) social polarisation and diversification, as well as polarisation of urban space . . . new divisions between state and local policies, de-regulation; urban management and entrepreneurialism, individualisation, new gender roles; polarisation of space, including gentrification versus the spatial concentration of the urban poor.

It is possible, therefore, to highlight some of the key elements of this restructuring process and its impact on European cities.

- Geographically uneven development is profoundly important to the economic well-being of cities. Spatial inequalities are exploited by capital, in particular multinational corporations which exploit different localities in terms of their endowments and advantages. Cities are thus vulnerable to global economic restructuring as capital searches for new and profitable locations. Some cities and city regions are more vulnerable than others, depending upon the abandonment and rationalisation which occur in specific core industries.
- The impact of restructuring on labour markets and class structure. Deindustrialisation and ensuing reduction in demand for labour in core manufacturing industries, the switch of investment from manufacturing to services, the changing nature of work and representation in the labour process have generated increasingly segmented labour markets reflecting changing occupations and skills, growth in casualisation of labour, part-time work and occupational segregation based on race and gender (Peck, 1996). This process of change in class structures accounts for the dramatic increase in urban poverty and social polarisation and exclusion in Europe's cities. Mandel (1995: 87) argues that these aspects of social changes are an outcome of increasing unequal power relations between labour and capital.

As Hyman (1992) notes, neo-liberal policies have reinforced the changing 'balance of class forces' as they have weakened the bargaining power of labour. A significant component of change in state intervention since the 1960s has been in industrial relations regulation, involving deregulation and the move away from national to plant/sector and individual bargaining systems. The outcome of this intervention is weakened forms of social solidarity formerly engendered through traditional collective bargaining systems. Mass unemployment and changing work practices have reinforced and underpinned these changes in the distribution of class and social power.

- The ending of the political consensus associated with the construction of the post-war welfare state in advanced West European capitalist countries is mirrored by the way individual cities have experienced changes in forms of governance and local policy – i.e. changing modes of political representation with the tendency to adopt 'entrepreneurial' strategies which improve the conditions for capital restructuring while imposing fiscal austerity measures as a response to national welfare state restructuring. The development of 'growth coalitions' with business elites playing a pivotal role in decision-making and policy implementation is an example of this trend.
- Mass immigration in the post-war period has had substantial impacts on class structure and social and political mobilisation within Europe's cities. Occupational segregation has emerged upon racial lines as immigrants have tended to become concentrated in unskilled lower-income occupations, and immigrant communities have experienced racism and hostility from indigenous

communities. These combined processes have led to physical as well as social isolation for ethnic minorities.

- An important dimension and outcome of the 'logic' of capital restructuring is that ecological and environmental degradation is becoming a major social and political issue in all cities. Environmental problems tend to impact disproportionately on working-class communities (Harvey, 1997: 91) and in areas with the highest levels of social and economic deprivation. Any attempt to tackle the problems of run-down, decaying inner cities or peripheral estates has to address environmental issues as much as economic and social problems.

It is our view that, in order to appreciate and fully comprehend the 'social' state of the urban environment it is also necessary to understand how welfare models have changed as a consequence of global, national and local factors. In a recent report for the Joseph Rowntree Foundation, Hirsch (1997: 3), explains why, in the case of the UK, there is a desire to search for a new strategy for protecting the vulnerable in society:

> Its (UK) government wants to promote social welfare and cohesion within tight fiscal constraints, and ways that encourage active participation in society rather than passive dependency. These goals are common to most European countries.

The UK, as with many European countries, is confronted with the political question whether the state can or cannot afford to maintain a generous systems of social security. Hirsch identifies five key factors which have influenced the UK's position which are particularly striking:

1. A rapid growth in the number of households that lack access to income from work.
2. A relatively modest growth in the biggest of these categories, retired people, over the next 20 years compared with other European countries.
3. A decline in the relative incomes of those depending on state benefits in the UK over the past 20 years, together with an increased amount of means testing.
4. A growing amount of inequality both before and after redistribution.
5. A stabilising of the proportion of national income taken in taxation in the UK, at a time when in other countries it has been rising.

The issue of social protection is a major topic of debate for European governments as slow economic growth in the European economy, persistent high levels of unemployment, an ageing population and the problems of controlling the rapid growth of health expenditure combine to impose strong pressures on an already weakened system. As a report on social protection in Europe for the European Commission states:

there are fundamental questions about the role and purpose of social protection in European societies. On the one hand, social insurance is regarded as being too costly for our economies, imposing a heavy burden on labour costs especially. On the other hand, the unquestionable success of systems in combating poverty is considered insufficient and there is a demand to do more, to be a force for integrating those threatened by exclusion into society and in particular, into the labour market (CEC, 1995c: 46).

The debate on social exclusion is one part of the broader issue of social protection and alternative models of welfare provision. Where this debate has made limited impact is on the relationships between the need for new welfare models to support the functioning of the urban economy. In many European countries the worst examples and concentrations of poverty and exclusion can be found in urban areas. To remain competitive, innovative and dynamic cities cannot afford to allow inequalities to widen or for social exclusion as experienced by a small but growing minority within society, who are marginalised and excluded from the mainstream opportunities that ordinary urban citizens often take for granted (a job, a wage, a house, the ability to shop, to travel and enjoy the cultural and entertaining opportunities found in any city), to continue in the long term.

To understand these processes and to shed light on the important policy implications that confront key urban policy decision-makers the chapter highlights the redefining of the European social model in two main ways; firstly the strategy and power at the supranational level, and secondly the role of geopolitics and urban class and social movements as an overlooked but important part of this redefining process. For far too long the UK has looked towards the USA as a source of ideas and policy responses in urban regeneration and social policy. This trend did not change with the election, in May 1997, of a new Labour government. Tackling welfare reform has been at the very centre of the second Clinton administration and the Blair government has adopted many features of the American-style welfare to work in its New Deal programme. As the UK is a member of the EU and that closer European integration is already scheduled for the start of the new millennium, it would seem more than appropriate to learn the lessons from a European perspective on these issues and assess what significance the European debate on welfare provision has for the future management and planning of UK cities.

EMERGING EUROPEAN SOCIAL POLICY – COMPETING AND CONFLICTING AGENDAS

THE SOCIAL AGENDA

How do we characterise the European welfare model? It is an eclectic mix of the diverse European welfare regimes as described by Esping-Andersen (1990) comprising liberal welfare states (primarily based upon market-based social insurance and means testing with a major role for private provision), social democratic, characterised by strong social rights and universal benefits, and conservative, with minimum social services provision, a major role for the voluntary sector and social benefits based on employment status.

The origins of European social policy can be traced back to the actual creation of the European Economic Community (EEC) with the signing of the Treaty of Rome in 1957. At this early stage European social policy was essentially supplementary and corrective. Its aim was to make more acceptable the adverse effects of this new economic community in Europe (Moxon-Browne, 1993). But it was with the introduction of the Single European Act (SEA) in 1987 that the inclusion of social policy was argued as an integral part of the process of completing a fair and even single European market. A strong lead on social policy developed in the aftermath of the SEA and culminated in the formulation of the Community Charter of the Fundamental Social Rights of Workers. The charter was accepted by all member states except Britain in December 1989. The then European Commissioner responsible for social affairs and employment, Mrs Vano Papandreou, was quick to insist that the charter was not a means to impose a uniform social order in the community, but instead it was seen as a main component of the completion of the single market.

Social policy was seen by the Commission as a means to gain not hamper economic efficiency. It was argued that social stability along with market competition, was a critical element of sustained economic growth and job creation. This approach clashed with the basic tenets of right-wing economists who blamed the relative economic stagnation and lack of competitiveness during the 1970s and 1980s on the systems of social protection and labour organisation associated with the growth of post-war welfare states (Wise and Gibb, 1993: 161). The Maastricht Treaty, signed in 1993, created conditions for harmonisation of social protection as well as extending the scope for EU action in the social field and covered areas like education, vocational training, youth culture and public health. The Maastricht social protocol involves two aspects in relation to employment rights. One is about freedom of association and rights to collective bargaining which includes rights to form, and be represented by, a trade union. The second aspect involves rights to information and consultation of the workforce about future company plans (Hantaris, 1995: 191). The key principle of social policy is to ensure individual rights and entitlements for those in employment.

THE SPATIAL AGENDA

If the Social Charter was creating some minimum rights at work in order to create a 'level playing field' throughout the community to avoid 'social dumping' and to provide some element of protection against the worst excesses of the free market, at the same time Maastricht was strengthening the other arm of social policy, the

Structural Funds. Recognising that the process of economic integration and the single market could exacerbate regional inequalities, the Commission gave priority to regional development policies through the European Regional Development Fund (ERDF) in addition to the European Social Fund (ESF) which supports unemployment and labour market initiatives. Since the Maastricht Treaty these funds are managed within a regional/territorial policy framework through community support frameworks (CSFs) for assisted areas drawn up by the European Commission. Another area where the Commission has become increasingly interested is spatial policy instruments. Here the role of the supranational tier of governance is more concerned with the administration of spatial and social cohesion with the territory of the EU. This aspect of policy is likely to become more predominant as the EU expands to incorporate the countries of central and eastern Europe and completes the process towards Economic and Monetary Union (EMU). The Commission has published a series of supranational planning studies such as the Europe 2000 and Europe 2000+ reports and more recently the publication of the European Spatial Development Perspective as well as supporting cross-border planning initiatives under the INTERREG IIc programme.

Although the ERDF and ESF strategies are clearly based upon enhancing regional competitiveness, both from a business and urban perspective, a number of programmes have evolved which comprise social objectives. Under Article 10 of the ERDF regulations, trans-European networks between local and regional authorities and small-scale social projects are promoted (for example, the Quartier en Crise network, the URBAN Community Initiative and the Employment Community Initiative which has four different policy strands: HORIZON, YOUTH-START, NOW and INTEGRA) which are aimed at tackling social problems in cities. The URBAN Community Initiative, for example, was created in recognition of 'growing tensions within European Society evident particularly at the serious level of social exclusion in an increasing number of inner city or peripheral urban areas' (CEC, 1994a: 96) and involves projects which include social and health facilities and positive action targeting ethnic minorities. Thus a handful of 'human capital' type projects have emerged over the last five years to deal with Europe's intensifying urban crisis which has fuelled a debate about the changing nature of spatially targeted programmes towards a more entitlement-based policy regime, and potential for a co-ordinated approach to a European-wide urban policy.

The Social and Spatial — Conflicts and Contradictions

The difference between EU spatial and social policies is that spatial policies define eligible policy beneficiaries while social policies define individual entitlements. Social policies underpin the EU's conception of social citizenship, and the Structural Funds confer eligibility in terms of specific functional actors such as

196

local and regional government, businesses, labour as seen in the collective sense. Andersen (1995) considers that social and spatial policies have possible interactions. The Structural Funds may 'spill over' into areas of social policy and develop elements of entitlement-based policies (as is the case with some of the smaller Article 10 projects), or may hinder such policies as territorial policies are seen as pivotal in counteracting regional uneven development and urban problems. Here perhaps lies the nub of the contradiction between the two policy regimes. Andersen (1995: 150) argues that the 'territorial principle' of EU economic and social policy is paramount:

> Given that a powerful territorial principle lies at the heart of the EU it follows naturally that members have chosen to define a certain class of economic problems, which they see as intimately bound up with the integration process, as territorial in nature. Economic integration produces net efficiency gains for the Union as a whole, but the gains and losses are distributed unevenly across the EU space. Existing and anticipated inequities are more likely to be addressed through policies that offer clear territorial gains to the main protagonists: the member states. The decisions to employ and to expand upon the structural funds resonate with the overarching ideology, preferred policy instruments, and institutional interests of the main actors in the European Union. Once in place, the structural funds exerted powerful interpretative feedback effect on the preferences and goals of EU policy makers and domestic actors.

The impact of the Structural Funds are creating contradictory pressures upon social policy. One is a powerful constituency of local regional interests which seeks to maintain Structural Fund policies and programmes, but their capacity to directly tackle social inequality is constrained by both the level of funding (less than 1% of EU public expenditure) and the fact that they are specifically area based in their orientation. At the same time, the implementation of locally based programmes can mobilise interests around the nature of local problems which could lead to pressures upon the Commission demanding and lobbying for more targeted programmes which meet the needs of disadvantaged groups and increase the scope for policies based on citizen entitlements. A case in point are the groups which have been involved with the Third Poverty Programme which have articulated specific actions in relation to EU social policy (CEC, 1995b; Geddes and Martin, 1997). The other main constraint upon Structural Fund programmes in dealing with urban problems is their orientation towards infrastructure projects at the expense of initiatives which have a more direct job creation aspect. Furthermore, as a major Commission report on urban development acknowledged, spatial concentration of funds will exclude areas and therefore sections of the population which can lead to severe policy gaps (CEC, 1992b: 204):

> For many cities the most problematic aspect of regional policy is the extent to which it fails to target many areas which experience severe economic, social and environmental problems or particularly acute urban problems within eligible areas. The eligibility criteria for current EC programmes, whilst consistent with the aim of

reducing inter regional imbalances across Europe, mean that urban areas experiencing similar problems are treated differently according to their geographical location.

Cities and urban areas experiencing social inequality and polarisation can be excluded from Structural Fund policies. As the report emphasises, regional policy does not have competencies in areas of social policy such as housing and tackling problems of immigration and minority communities which are common in Europe's cities. As Andersen (1995) argues, this awareness of policy gaps may create demands by relevant interest groups to modify and/or extend national welfare state and EU policies.

FUTURE DIRECTIONS FOR SOCIAL POLICIES AND EUROPE'S CITIES – HARMONISATION OR DISINTEGRATION

CITIES, COMPETITIVENESS AND COHESION

Certain sections of the EU political process argue that the European social model can become the key to European economic competitiveness, while at the same time recognising that competitiveness cannot be improved by dismantling the welfare state or by reducing minimum social standards (CEC, 1996b: 14). This view is interesting in the context of EU requirements for deflationary policies in order to meet the public spending conditions for economic and monetary union. The future prosperity of Europe's cities lies with the current phase of economic and monetary integration. To understand the direction of social policies as they relate to urban development and change in Europe, we need to turn towards an assessment of the political economy of integration for a wider frame of reference and context.

Wolfgang Streeck (1995) provides some insights into contemporary developments of integration in relation to social policy. He recognises the importance of class interests in shaping political and policy agendas. The original ideological underpinning of the integration project is strongly neo-liberal (a point also central to the arguments by Williams, 1994). This means that creating conditions for the operation of the free market must be paramount – a key aspect of the Cecchini report. However, how and why the neo-liberal agenda has become dominant should not be taken for granted. For Streeck social policy was doomed to take a low priority because powerful business interests influence the centres of power in the Commission and they have successfully blocked any moves towards comprehensive social policies. Pierson and Liebfried (1995: 450) go as far as to argue that the nature of past and current policies arises out of 'the emergence of an anti social democratic consensus on economic policy with the major member states'.

Thus the integration process underlines and reinforces power relations between capital (i.e. the broad interests of the private sector) and labour (broad interests of the organised labour movement – political parties of labour and trade unions). This tendency towards unequal power relations in favour of capital has been important in maintaining a relatively weak bargaining strength of labour through blocking common collective bargaining and social policies and regulations. Therefore, the biggest question mark around European-based social programmes and harmonisation of social protection policies is that whatever is agreed upon, standards and regulations will be minimal. Liebfried (1993: 145) argues that the few EU rules on welfare are only operational in national welfare contexts. Furthermore, he argues that there are parallels with the US welfare model in that Europe was founded on the four freedoms – free movement of persons, goods, capital and services. Political and social citizenship has become marginal in the process of European unification. For the USA, political citizenship was complemented by social citizenship only since the 1930s, if at all (Liebfried, 1993: 150).

The outcome of a private sector dominated policy regime(s) has been significant for the way cities have managed and responded to EU social policies. Most European urban strategies have been formulated through the process of partnerships encouraged by the Commission which has given rise to 'entrepreneurial cities'. The Commission report on urban development highlights the outcomes as follows:

> However, any of the problems faced in cities remain essentially social in nature. The successful, city based pursuit of economic growth has rarely addressed the interconnections and contradictions between these two sets of issues. In our case studies, economic growth has not resolved many of the social problems identified earlier in this report. Indeed, with limited exceptions, the politics of growth have increased inequalities within those cities (CEC, 1992b: 184).

The dynamic for EU-engendered local strategies emanates from 'regime competition' (Streeck, 1995: 420) which arises from a market-based competitive political environment. The implication of regime competition for cities is that prosperity depends upon being able to compete within the broader framework of a free market environment. Urban elites have mobilised and united interests around entrepreneurial strategies, and local-based partnership building has been formed around policy priorities towards enhancing business competitiveness. Policy priorities often override social and distributional issues. Some studies suggest that the entrepreneurial strategies have positively contributed to creating a dual city effect because access to decision-making by working-class and minority communities is so limited (Danschat, 1994). This has raised wider questions about how these agendas are impacting upon local democracy (Geddes and Martin, 1996).

It is recognised that this analysis is one-dimensional to some extent. While capital's interests are pivotal to driving EMU and social and spatial policies, these interests do not always coincide or are harmonious. In certain cases, business interests will be compatible with strong social protection policies. The Danish government, backed by both the Danish TUC and employers, have consistently lobbied for stronger minimum social standards (Wise and Gibbs, 1994). UNICE, the employers' federation, has not always been united in its response to social policies and industrial relations. Similarly, labour movements have been involved with conflicting campaigns. The European TUC is campaigning for stronger social policies, while at the same time many local-based movements have aligned themselves with local governments to lobby for enhanced Structural Funds.

Furthermore, policies are being contested by a variety of interests. Opposition against the likely impacts of monetary union on national welfare policies has led to intense mobilisation in cities in France, Belgium and Germany. Different forms and models of partnerships and mobilisation vary within and between member states. In some countries partnerships are strongly tripartite or corporatist in nature including trade unions, local government and employers where labour movement interests tend to have some influence, for example, Denmark (Etherington, 1997, 1998), or where business interests dominate as in the UK. Thus partnerships will take on different forms depending upon national and local contexts (central local relations, social and political traditions) and will be influenced by wider social movement mobilisation. They represent different dimensions of class and social mobilisation which tend to be top-down – established by the local state and/or para-state organisations, which provide the legitimation for involvement and consultation with the local population. As noted above, the source of tensions and conflict lies with the nature of partnership formation and decision-making – i.e. its exclusionary nature of disadvantaged groups to the extent that they become the focal point of mobilisation by 'excluded groups'. Cities comprising substantial ethnic minority communities experiencing intense discrimination, oppression and disadvantage are bypassed to a large extent by EU Structural Fund programmes.

The point to emphasise here is that EU policies, as they are intertwined with national urban strategies, are being contested through different social movements. But the nature of this mobilisation in terms of its impact upon different policy communities is difficult to assess. Urban social movements will constitute pressure from below where demands will filter into the Euro-based networks' lobbying and campaigning around social policy. There is no doubt that these networks play a significant role in challenging established power and policy agendas. However, transnational networks are diffuse and fragmented, tending to be based on a single issue. Furthermore, as labour and trade union organisations are weak at the European level in shaping the social agendas, it is unlikely that they will have a major influence upon the current direction of the integration process. In many respects urban and national mobilisation within member states will (as has been in the case of France through national organised protests against EMU) have a more effective influence upon EU as well as national policy processes.

The future of 'social Europe' can be assessed as a continuation of current orthodoxies and ideologies. It is possible to argue that building a strong European welfare state was illusory from the outset because social agendas are narrowly focused upon labour markets, aimed at facilitating the mobility of labour in the same way as capital. As Streeck (1995) argues, it is more appropriate to talk of the collapse of the social dimension under the weight of free market orthodoxies and the pursuit of a more deregulatory environment. The implications of this for Europe's cities needs to be assessed, but it is unlikely that social and spatial distribution will be a strong dimension of local strategies. The Structural Funds provide the key to distributing benefits to Europe's cities, but within a framework of 'trickle down' politics. In any case, other policies, such as the single market, EMU and the promotion of multinational economic expansion act in contradiction to regional policies (Begg, 1995; Dunford and Perrons, 1994).

CONCLUSIONS

Towns and cities in Europe still remain the primary source of wealth creation and act as the centres of social and cultural development. However, as cities adjust to the global economy they are confronted by problems related to unemployment, environmental conditions and traffic congestion, poverty, poor housing, crime and drug abuse (CEC, 1997b). Increasingly cities not only offer new opportunities for economic development but they simultaneously represent some of the worst examples and acute concentrations of spatial deprivation and economic and social exclusion. This duality in the structure of the city has changed the attitudes of both central and local government towards urban policy and the need for economic and social cohesion.

The chapter has alluded to several key factors which have been influential in changing the way that cities function and in the way that policy is now implemented. These factors include:

- *Changing employment patterns*. These include the loss of traditional manufacturing employment and the rise of the service sector and the entry of more women in the labour market, and increasing numbers of part-time and temporary employment. These trends have created a situation where many, especially men, have been excluded from the labour market as their skills have become increasingly obsolete. This situation has helped to perpetuate the growing income divide between those in work and those without a job. Growing income inequalities have strengthened the view held by many who are without work that they have no hope and little chance to participate in the wider urban labour market.
- *Economic exclusion and social problems*. Persistent and long-term unemployment and effective barriers to entry into the labour market for the most vulnerable in society have contributed to the escalation of urban social

problems. High levels of unemployment intensify social problems as the most deprived communities also suffer from low educational attainment, higher levels of homelessness, ill health and crime. The concept of social exclusion, however, goes beyond the lack of financial resources and is concerned with the way that reinforcing processes of exclusion influence the attitudes and values of individuals who experience them. Social exclusion in its broadest sense therefore implies the lack of access to opportunities, as individuals or communities are marginalised and excluded from mainstream activities of day-to-day life that we all take for granted.

• *Spatial concentration of exclusion.* Communities, groups and individuals who suffer from exclusion tend to be geographically concentrated and the worst examples of exclusion and poverty occur in parts of the city characterised by high levels of public sector intervention, poor housing lacking any alternative choice, inadequate local services and retail facilities, poor environmental quality and for residents a negative stigma associated with the neighbourhood.

The 1980s were a period when regeneration policy in European cities emphasised the importance of physical renewal and property-led regeneration in deprived urban areas. One lesson learnt from the experience of cities, and in particular in the case of the UK during the 1980s, was that physical redevelopment is only one part of the solution to a much bigger problem. It is therefore the task of central government, in partnership with local authorities, the community and the private and voluntary sectors, to ensure that by the start of the new millennium a sustainable regeneration framework is established. Such a framework needs to take into account economic, social and environmental considerations and is one which provides local communities the opportunities for sustained, comprehensive and long-term regeneration.

Competitiveness and the economic and social cohesion of cities depend on how urban administrators, decision-makers and professionals come to terms with how best to integrate evolving social protection systems and new models of urban social welfare with existing and future urban policy, where all citizens have equal opportunity and access to the opportunities and benefits which the urban environment provides. This goal may seem to be unachievable and political 'pie in the sky' in the short term. However, the creation of the Social Exclusion Unit on 8 December 1997 by the Prime Minister, Tony Blair, is seen as a positive step towards a new social agenda for Britain and on the future economic, social and spatial development of our cities. The task that confronts both local and central government, urban managers and planners, is how to integrate economic, social and environmental priorities successfully at the local level. As has been the argument throughout this chapter, the first step towards such an approach is to recognise that social cohesion underpins economic efficiency and competitiveness, and mechanisms which address the unequal distribution of resources and opportunities also tackle issues of economic efficiency.

Even in Europe the social policy debate has been characterised by a rift between liberal capitalists and social welfarists (Carter, 1996). In reality the situation is less than straightforward and involves a series of arguments and debates on the relationship between social policy and economic processes. What has happened is the realisation that social and economic policy operate in the same sphere and that rather than being antagonistic, economic and social policy are moving closer together and becoming complementary. This approach is increasingly being reflected at the European level in the way that the European Commission in agreement with the member states of the EU has started to address the important issues of employment flexibility, unemployment and social and economic cohesion.

CHAPTER 12

PLANNING, EUROPE AND THE TWENTY-FIRST CENTURY

Michael Chapman

INTRODUCTION

The impact of the EU on the UK town and country planning system is a subject which typically fails to excite the average planning professional. Since the introduction of the 1947 Town and Country Planning Act, land use planning and spatial policy in the UK has been dominated by a combination of local, regional and national interests. For the majority of practitioners and from the experience of the general public, who come into contact with the day-to-day planning process, this is how the planning system has functioned and evolved over time. However, external forces including global economic change and the process of European integration are increasingly influencing the context in which planning operates. As Newman and Thornely (1996) argue, global forces have a major impact on the operation of local urban land markets and planning responses, and Demaziere and Wilson (1996) also note that global economic restructuring has been a critical factor in the rejuvenation of local economic development strategies in both Europe and North America. While global trends impact on the planning system in many ways the importance of European integration is less well understood, in terms of its impacts on the planning policy. As this chapter will discuss, the process of European economic and political integration implies that national and local government can no longer execute spatial policy objects in complete isolation and as Williams (1996: vi–vii) observes:

> Following the 1992 single market programme and the Maastricht Treaty, the prospect of 'ever closer union' suggests that there will be many more ways in which the EU level of government will matter in the domestic practice in planning as in many other walks of life.

Any review of planning policy and practice into the next millennium must include a review of Europe's role and function in shaping the context in which land use and spatial policy decisions are made. The need to assess the impact of the EU on UK land use and spatial policy is all the more important as the EU is in a period of rapid change. The implications of change at the European level will ultimately influence the way in which spatial policy and planning are undertaken in the UK.

The next century offers the EU important new challenges in terms of improving the economic performance and competitiveness of the European economy:

- Completing the next stage of EMU with the introduction of the single currency
- Tackling unemployment and contributing to economic and social cohesion
- Strengthening the democratic processes at every level of European decision-making and enhancing a citizens' Europe
- Implementing institutions change to improve accountability and efficiency within the EU to allow it to take on board new agendas and deal with an enlarged Europe
- To work towards achieving a sustainable Europe and to complete the next phase of EU expansion to incorporate the former socialist countries of central and eastern Europe

The importance of this interrelationship between Europe and planning system was confirmed in the recent Department of Environment, Transport and the Regions (DETR) publication *Modernising Planning: A Policy Statement by the Minister for the Regions, Regeneration and Planning* (1998b). The statement makes explicit reference to the impact of the EU on the planning system and argues that (DETR, 1998b: 6):

> The European context for planning has been missing from the planning system in England. It has been kept alive by Members and professionals in local government who understand the self-interest of European co-operation. In general, however, for far too long, there has been a tendency to ignore cross-border and transnational planning issues.

The notion that the EU will have an even greater role in the development of planning and spatial policy is reflected in the consultation paper on regional planning guidance from the DETR. This paper issued at the same time as the statement *Modernising Planning*, argues for future regional planning guidance in England should provide a sufficiently broad framework to assist the regions prepare Structural Fund bids to the European Commission and to be 'in tune' with EU developments in spatial planning (*Planning*, 5 June 1998). Given this level of policy interest, is the British planning system really ready for Europe?

CONTEXT

Compared to our European counterparts, we British have often reluctantly accepted the activities and interests of the EU. In the past we have viewed 'Brussels' and the institutions of the EU with a sense of distance and with little real enthusiasm unless Europe somehow infringes on our own national interest, sovereignty or sense of 'fair play'. This adversarial style of relationship is not confined only to the UK, but over time and especially during the 1980s and early 1990s, Britain was perceived to be the reluctant European partner. This is not to say that Britain has always pursued an anti-European position, in fact British governments have been vocal and supportive of several European policy initiatives, including the single European market (SEM) and the enlargement of the EU to incorporate the countries of central and eastern Europe. However, Britain has been less than supportive of other major policy developments including the single currency or moves towards strengthening European social policy. While there is no space in this chapter to rehearse all the arguments for and against issues, it is worth noting that, even if the UK is not part of the next phase of EMU, or is not convinced of the merits of broadening the scope of EU involvement in social policy, nevertheless, actions undertaken at the pan-European level will ultimately impact on the future pattern of economic, social, environmental and spatial development in the UK. As a consequence of this 'Europeanisation' of public policy a new generation of planners not only have to come to grips with a changing national spatial and land use planning system but also how effectively such a system will come to terms with an emerging European agenda and help to advance the European goals of competitiveness, balanced growth, economic and social cohesion and sustainable development.

The importance of impact of the EU on land use planning and spatial policy in the UK has received growing attention from academics, the planning profession and key government departments (Davies and Gosling, 1994; Ratcliffe and Stubbs, 1996; Williams, 1996; Nadin and Shaw, 1988; Roberts, 1998; DETR, 1998f). The professional body which represents planning practitioners, the Royal Town Planning Institute (RTPI), is an active member of the Council of European Town Planners (ECTP), which recently agreed a new Charter of Athens which aims to be a template for urban development in the next century. This document represents a bottom-up approach to planning and covers a diverse range of topics, including transport, leisure and economic development (*Planning*, 5 June 1998). In an attempt to keep up with current European trends, the RTPI has contracted a team of consultants (ECOTEC Research and Constancy Ltd) to provide briefing notes on European policy developments which influence and impact on UK planning practice. The same team of consultants have also worked in collaboration with government departments to organise a series of seminars for planning practitioners as part of the UK consultation exercise on the first official draft of the European Spatial Development Perspective (ESDP). The publication of the ESDP is a the latest stage in a process which began back in 1993 when the informal meeting of European planning ministers at Liège agreed to go ahead with the idea for an ESDP.

One problem with the notion of a European spatial policy is that it can mean different things to different people. Some believe that any discussion of a pan-

European framework for spatial development will ultimately lead to the harmonisation and standardisation of all member state planning systems and represents a weakening of national control over the planning system. Alternatively, it has been argued that the need for an integrated spatial perspective to the sectoral polices of the EU is considered to be a welcome addition to local and national planning systems. Given the level of the debate on the 'Europeanisation of planning policy' there exists, even within the circles of planning education a reluctance, by a few academics, to accept the significance of Europe on planning policy and practice. This introverted and sceptical view on the role of the EU in planning and spatial matters is founded on the argument that the EU has no direct competence in land use planning matters. Under the subsidiarity principle, as laid down in the Maastricht Treaty, decision-making should involve the ordinary citizen as much as possible and the EU does not take any action (except in the areas which fall within its exclusive competence) unless it is more effective to do so than either at the national, regional or local level. This is one of the main arguments against a common European approach to spatial planning, and reflects a certain unease from UK planners in particular when one takes into account the range and diversity of planning systems of the member states. Similarly, concern has been expressed that the continued process of European integration will lead to the 'institutional deepening' of the EU, whereby power is concentrated in the European institutions and results in an unacceptable transfer of decision-making and sovereignty away from the member state. While there is limited evidence to support such a scenario, there is a anxiety, especially from within national governments, that continued involvement of the EU in spatial development matters will open up a new route for regional and metropolitan government to directly negotiate with Brussels while circumventing national government departments.

It is not that surprising that government officials and leading members of the planning profession support the view that the member state and/or the appropriate regional or local authority is the preferred level at which land use planning should be undertaken. While this still remains the same, British planners, like other European planners, have to come to terms with the fact that spatial planning is increasingly recognised as a multi-level activity and that many planning issues cannot be effectively resolved purely on a national basis (CEC, 1994c: 9).

NEW LABOUR, NEW EUROPE

The election of the Labour government under the leadership of Tony Blair in May 1997 considerably altered Britain's outlook towards Europe and Europe's perception of Britain as a reluctant European partner. Under New Labour, the government has been quick to welcome the opportunities that membership of the EU brings. This change in political emphasis towards Europe has been timely as Britain took over the presidency of the EU in January 1998. As Tony Blair comments in the foreword to the publication *Britain in Europe* which accompanied Britain's presidency of the EU:

> January 1998 marks the beginning of the United Kingdom's Presidency of the European Union. It is fitting that our Presidency should start on the 25th anniversary of our membership of the European Community. That membership has registered real successes, but it has been a story of missed opportunities. For far too long we gave the impression that we were less than fully committed to the success of Europe's leading enterprise. We never made up ground we had lost by failing to join the European Community at its inception. Our influence suffered accordingly, with real damage to our national interest. This is set to change. Our presidency of the European Union is a unique opportunity to rebuild Britain's standing. We want to channel more of Europe's energies into those things which most matter to ordinary people, like jobs, crime, the war on drugs, and the quality of the environment. At the same time, we will use our Presidency to make sure that the Single European Currency is built on solid foundations. And we want to make sure that the next round of EU enlargement gets off to a flying start (foreword to *Britain in Europe*, 1998).

As Nadin (1998: 60) observes, the UK priorities for the presidency of the EU, focused on monetary union, job creation, enlargement, crime and the environment, but these agendas happened to coincide with a surge of planning related activity during the presidency which included:

> the draft European Spatial Development Perspective (ESDP); the new Community Initiative on transnational planning, INTERREG IIc; application of the Kyoto greenhouse gas emissions reduction agreements; stricter enforcement of Community environmental legislation; the Commission's urban policy initiative; Agenda 2000's proposals for the reform of the EU regional policy in the context of enlargement; and the introduction of sustainable development as a Community objective through the Amsterdam Treaty.

The importance of the European agenda has been significantly heightened as a consequence of the outcomes of the referenda in Scotland and Wales and the pledge by the government to bring devolution to Scotland and Wales. May 1999 will see the first elections for a Scottish Parliament in Edinburgh and a directly elected Welsh Assembly in Cardiff. A new structure of governance in England is emerging as well with the establishment of nine regional development agencies (RDAs). All these events only add to the growing demands for a more strategic and integrated approach towards the co-ordination of European and UK-wide spatial policies. As Roberts (1998) observes, a renewed sense of regionalism can have longer-term implications on any future relationship with the EU. What will stop Scotland and Wales gaining the same rights as the existing German *Länder* to comment on and influence impending European policy developments? Would this result in a powerful shift in the balance of decision-making away from Westminster to Edinburgh and Cardiff or to the RDAs in England? While European matters still remain a reserved matter for national government, it is not inconceivable that

Brussels will increasingly look towards the Scottish Parliament, the Welsh Assembly or even proposed regional assemblies in England as democratic institutions more closely identifiable with the needs and aspirations of ordinary citizens for consultation on issues including sustainable regional development and economic and social cohesion in urban and rural localities.

Given the publicity over the UK presidency and Britain's new working relationship with its European partners, how far Britain really adopts a 'European' outlook is still less than certain. There remains a degree of hesitancy when Europe is mentioned in the context of the UK planning system. The DETR endorses this perspective and reaffirms the view that planning is fundamentally a local action (1988f: 6):

> The European context is important but most planning issues will be decided locally. For the most part, this Government has a strong preference for decentralising so that decisions can be taken by democratic bodies elected by the people most closely affected by those decisions.

It is interesting to note that both the UK government and the EU are trying to achieve the same goal, namely, bring decision-making as closely as possible to the level of the ordinary citizen. The idea that the European level is inappropriate for such action is understandable given that we are an island community and we have less experience of cross-border co-operation or transnational planning agreements, unlike some of our European counterparts. But the lack of exposure to other forms of planning systems and to alternative planning methodologies can be harmful to our own interests in the long term. While there are clear advantages to the way the planning system functions in the UK, planning professionals should be open to alternative points of view and to best practice elsewhere in Europe. Increasingly, we live in a complex world, and while the problems of congestion, urban sprawl, social exclusion, urban and rural deprivation may be considered to be the same, multidimensional problems require multidimensional solutions and planners across the EU can learn from each other's experiences on what does and what does not work. If we do not take this opportunity then we can end up with an over-inflated view of our system and it becomes all too easy to become fixed in the opinion that Europe is of little or no importance. As Davies (1994: 236) comments:

> The logic of spatial planning at a transnational scale is too strong for the UK's planners to remain isolated and inward-looking. . . . At one level, local planning, with its emphasis on day-to-day development control, will remain largely unchanged in its present form. . . . The real challenge from Europe for planning in the UK is at the wider, regional level, whether it is in environmentalism or in economic development and urban regeneration, that is, in spatial planning in the emerging European sense of the term.

To understand to the importance of the European perspective to spatial policy and planning and its impact on UK planning practice, one first has to understand

the key policy trends which have influenced the overall direction of the EU. By
understanding these objectives and by appreciating what Europe is actually trying
to achieve, one can begin to appreciate how and why the European spatial development framework has emerged and what it means for planning practice in the UK.
The European policy agenda has nothing which planning practitioners should be
afraid of; on the contrary, planning practice in the UK has a lot to offer in shaping
the future development of spatial policy and practice in Europe.

KEY EUROPEAN POLICY TRENDS

THE ECONOMIC OBJECTIVE OF THE EUROPEAN COMMUNITY

Europe has undergone significant political, socio-economic and spatial changes
since the signing of the Treaty of Rome in 1957 which established the European
Economic Community (EEC). Moves towards European integration began in the
aftermath of the Second World War in an attempt to ensure both political and
economic stability for mainland Europe. To begin with the countries of France, the
Netherlands, Italy, Luxembourg, Belgium and the then Federal Republic of
Germany formed the European Coal and Steel Community (ECSC) under the
Treaty of Paris in 1952. The idea was that by 'pooling' the interests of each
countries output in key heavy industries, like coal and steel and production, would
safeguard them from any future conflict or disagreement which could lead to
another European conflict. At the Messina Conference of June 1955 the Foreign
Ministers of the six ECSC countries then launched the idea of a European common
market in which goods, services, people and capital could move about as freely as
within one country. On 25 March 1957 treaties establishing the EEC and the
European Atomic Energy Community (Euratom) were signed in Rome. Since the
inception of the EEC the motive behind the development of an integrated Europe
has overwhelmingly been economic. Even in the context of the debate on the
future spatial development of Europe, it is the economic agenda which is still at
the forefront of any major decision and is the backbone of current European policy
developments.

    In the early years of the EEC the need for further enlargement was considered
part of the process to create the conditions for a genuine European common
market. As part of this process the negotiations for the accession of the UK and
three other countries (Denmark, Ireland and Norway) proved to be long and
arduous. After being suspended twice, they finally led to the Treaty of Accession
which was signed in Brussels in January 1972. After a referendum, Norway finally
rejected the idea of membership, so the first enlargement took effect on 1 January
1973 and increased the Community from its original six to nine member states. As
the process of enlargement continued during the 1980s and 1990s so too did the
need for the EEC and subsequently the EU (the term 'European Union' replaced

the EEC after the signing of the Maastricht Treaty) to take on new roles and responsibilities as a consequence of the expansion of its geographical boundaries. The second enlargement of the Community involved three Mediterranean countries which applied in 1975 and 1977, and after the restoration of democracy Greece joined the EEC on 1 January 1981, followed by Portugal and Spain on 1 January 1986. The accession of poorer southern European countries saw a shift in the redistribution of resources away from the older traditional manufacturing areas of northern Europe to these less developed and agriculture-dependent economies. Enlargement and agreement to establish the SEM involved a radical rethink of the operation of several of the common European policies which command significant levels of financial support. The most important being moves to revise the operation of the Common Agricultural Policy (CAP) and the Structural Funds which support regional policy in the Community.

After the completion of the SEM and agreement to move forward with the next steps to EMU, the countries of Austria, Finland and Sweden joined the EU in 1995. Membership of the EU stands at 15 member states; the need to reform the institutions of the EU is critical in that they were established to cope with a membership of six countries, but following the collapse of communism in eastern Europe and the reunification of Germany, the next phase of European enlargement has taken on a new dimension as expansion into central and eastern Europe could result in the EU growing to 20 or 30 member states. The Treaty of Rome which established the EEC did not envisage nor was it designed to cope with such a large number of member countries. Revisions to the Treaty of Rome (the SEM, the Maastricht Treaty and the Treaty of Amsterdam) have gone some way to reform of the institutions of the EU, but there still remains significant obstacles to the creation of an integrated Europe.

The Single Market, Globalisation and Economic and Monetary Union

The Maastricht Treaty on European Union took effect on 1 November 1993 and most notably prepared the way for the next stages of EMU. The Maastricht Treaty introduced a number of key policy changes which would have both direct and indirect implications for the future spatial development of the EU. Policy changes included: reform of the CAP, implementation of measures to complete the single market; integration of environmental considerations into EU policy, the development of a citizens' Europe and the expansion of the EU both in the Baltic with the accession of Finland and Sweden and in central Europe with the accession of Austria. The Maastricht Treaty strengthened of the powers of the European Parliament, especially in terms of negotiation of the overall budget of the EU and established a new consultative Committee of the Regions. The latter consists of 222 representatives of local and regional authorities who are appointed by the

Council of Ministers (the main decision-making body in the Community), on proposals from individual member states. The Committee of the Regions is consulted
by the Council or the European Commission in areas which affect regional issues
like education, youth, culture, health, social and economic cohesion. The outcome
of the Amsterdam Intergovernmental Conference in 1997 (the Amsterdam Treaty)
further consolidates the role of the Committee. When the Treaty of Amsterdam is
in force the Committee of the Regions will be required to be consulted on a wide
range of new policy areas including, environmental issues, the operation of the
Social Fund, issues relating to vocational training, cross-border co-operation and
transport policy. British planners should be in a position to take the opportunity to
work with and 'lobby' the Committee of the Regions on issues which are of direct
relevance to them, including spatial planning, transportation and regional
development.

INTEGRATION AND COHESION

Achieving economic and social cohesion between the member states and between
the territories of the member states is considered to be a precondition for the
successful implementation of the single European currency, from 1 January 1999.
A commitment to reduce regional disparities across Europe has been in place since
the mid 1970s, but the process of economic integration places the challenge of
reducing regional inequalities as a priority for economic and social cohesion in the
EU (Begg, 1996: 186). A European-wide regional policy was introduced in 1975
with the establishment of the European Regional Development Fund (ERDF). This
fund was created in response to the second enlargement of the EEC with the
accession of Ireland, Denmark and the UK to the Community. All these countries
had existing regional disparities and the limited amount of support provided,
reflected the concern that the performance of these regions would be hampered by
membership of the Community. The Spaak report which suggested the creation of
the EEC did not anticipate that any long-term economic and social imbalances
would result from the introduction of the customs union in 1968. It was presumed
that market forces would correct any significant regional disparities that occurred
in a homogeneous economic space. By the time of the accession of the UK to the
EEC it was clear that the activities of the EEC did in fact contribute to the
continuation of regional inequalities.

The collective name given to the funding mechanisms to support regional
development are the Structural Funds. These include: ERDF which supports
environmental projects, investment in infrastructure and assistance to small and
medium-sized enterprises; the European Social Fund (ESF) which supports
training, retraining and vocational guidance with particular emphasis on young
people and the long-term unemployed and the European Agricultural Guidance
and Guarantee Fund (EAGGF) which is designed to assist measures to speed up the

adjustment of agricultural structures with a view to the reform of the CAP (Chapman, 1994: 79). Between 1989 and 1993, as part of a reform package designed to accompany the implementation of the single market, regional policy assistance was revised and its budget doubled in real terms (Armstrong, 1996) and a key feature of the reform was the requirement for ERDF to be co-ordinated with the other Structural Fund mechanisms mentioned above. In 1993 the Structural Funds were again reformed with a programming period set to start from 1994 to last until 1999. Resources allocated to the Structural Funds for this period amounted to 141 471 million ecu of which 70% would be allocated to the least advantageous regions within the EU. As part of this revision to the Structural Funds a new instrument was introduced, the Financial Instrument for Fisheries Guidance (FIFG), which was designed to help adjustment to the Common Fisheries Policy. In addition to these main funding programmes there are several smaller programmes designed to support particular Community initiatives, support for pilot and demonstration projects and assistance for the establishment of networks within the EU.

The diversity of the regional problem has tended to grow with each successive enlargement of the Community, while this has led to the expansion of resources committed to regional policy it was the introduction of the single market which acted as the catalyst for strengthening the EU's response to regional divergence. This is why the Single European Act of 1986 introduced a new Title V into the Treaty of Rome called 'Economic and Social Cohesion'. Economic and social cohesion means balanced, sustainable development, the narrowing of structural disparities between the regions and countries and the promotion of equal opportunities for individuals. The Maastricht Treaty laid the foundations for achieving EMU; also it was agreed that the EU had to address the risk that EMU could worsen regional disparities. The treaty's requirement that budget deficits of the member states be limited to a maximum of 3% of gross domestic product (GDP) would limit the possibilities of poorer states increasing investments to catch up with their richer partners. As a response to this economic criterion which could disadvantage the poorer economies in the EU, the treaty established a new Cohesion Fund which would channel financial assistance to the four poorest states with a per capita GDP of less than 90% of the EU's average (Ireland, Spain, Portugal and Greece).

ENLARGEMENT AND AGENDA 2000

Agenda 2000 represents the European Commission's blueprint for the future of the EU in the period up to the year 2006. Introduced by Jacques Santer, President of the Commission, to the European Parliament in July 1997, Agenda 2000 is the first step by the European Commission to begin discussions on the future operation of the Structural Funds with member states. The Agenda 2000 includes proposals for reform of the Structural Funds and transitional arrangements, reform of the CAP, the Community initiatives and an assessment of the preparation of central and eastern European countries for entry into the EU. The current programming period for the Structural Funds, which began in 1994, is planned to end in 1999, and unlike the previous reviews of the Structural Funds an important factor taken into consideration in this revision is the financial impact of enlargement of the EU into eastern Europe. The collapse of communism by the end of the 1980s and early 1990s provided the opportunity for the complete integration of mainland Europe. Unexpected as it was, the sudden collapse of former Soviet domination of the region and the rush for newly independent states to introduce market-based economies, only quickened the political pace for integration. Criteria used to decide on which countries from eastern Europe would be eligible for negotiation with the European Commission for accession to the EU were established at the Copenhagen Summit in 1993. The criteria used required that any candidate countries should:

- Achieve stability of institutions guaranteeing democracy, the rule of law, human rights and respect for protection of minorities
- Have a functioning market economy as well as the capacity to cope with competitive pressure and market forces within the union
- Be able to take on the obligations of membership

On the basis of the criteria defined, the European Commission recommended that negotiations would begin with the following countries: Poland, Hungary, Estonia, the Czech Republic and Slovenia. In addition to the enlargement eastwards, the Commission has already established an agreement with Cyprus to start its negotiations for membership of the EU. The enlargement of the EU eastwards seems a distant and less tangible objective of the EU and one which is hardly relevant to spatial policy in the UK. However, this phase of enlargement, probably more than any other previous one, has significant implications for financial support for regional development in the UK, and on the whole spatial development of the EU (Shutt and Colwell, 1997). The European Commission proposes that the coverage for the Structural Funds be reduced from its current level of 50% of the EU population to 35–40% of the population, and that areas with an economic performance above set thresholds should lose their existing eligibility. The loss of eligibility should be phased out and those regions which lose any European assistance would not experience any sudden loss of support. The Commission recognises that France, the Netherlands, Portugal, Ireland and the UK would be the likely countries to see a reduction in regional aid. Such an impact might be particularly important for rural and industrial regions in the UK whose economic performance would be significantly higher than regions in the new accession countries from central and eastern Europe and would therefore lose regional assistance as an outcome of these reforms. The Commission also proposed to reduce the current number of Community initiatives down from 14 to 3 and concentrate on transnational and inter-regional co-operation, rural development and human resources, in particular equal opportunities.

In more detail these reforms would have a particular impact on the main objective areas covered by the Structural Funds as set out in the 1993 reform package. New Objective 1 (includes available funding from ERDF, ESF, EAGGF):

- Strict application of GDP per capita at 75% below EU average
- Special treatment for outmost regions (French overseas departments, Azores, Canary Islands, Madeira) and current Objective 6 (Sweden and Finland) which would otherwise not qualify for Objective 1
- Consistency between Objective 1 areas and areas of regional state aids
- Transitional arrangements for current Objective 1 areas no longer eligible under new arrangements

New Objective 2 (support from ERDF, ESF, FIFG):

- Industrial rural and urban areas facing restructuring, including current Objectives 2 and 5b
- Socio-economic criteria, rate of unemployment, level of industrial unemployment (1985 as reference year), level and development of activity in agriculture and fishing areas, degraded environment, high crime rate, low educational attainment

New Objective 3 (ESF):

- Development of human resources including current Objectives 3 and 4
- Applies across all EU including new Objective 1 and 2 areas.

It would appear that the EU was not prepared to enlarge the Structural Fund budget as was the case with the introduction of the Single Act or the Maastricht Treaty. The concentration of resources on areas in most need has implications for the level of financial support received in the UK. This might result in the loss of the Highlands and Islands Objective 1 status and the consolidation of both Objectives 2 (industrial regions) and 5b (rural regions). An important addition to the reform package is the proposal that there should be a single programming document for each region which covers all EU programmes which operate in that region. This is different from what happens now as each individual objective has its own single document. This has particular importance for the introduction of the RDAs in England and how Scotland and Wales co-ordinate their own programming documents with Brussels. This could provide an ideal opportunity for planners to be interactive with strategic and comprehensive regional plans which link needs with funding with a holistic policy approach.

THE EUROPEAN DEMOCRATIC DEFICIT

One of the most pressing agendas for the EU is to improve what is termed the European democratic deficit. The democratic deficit is a concept used to describe the view that the EU suffers from a lack of democracy and is becoming remote from the ordinary citizen. Part of the process of enlargement and the institutional 'deepening' of the EU has meant that the decisions taken by European institutions are now far removed from the people of Europe. The Maastricht Treaty moved towards an understanding of a citizens' Europe with the establishment of the Committee of the Regions, as an institution which brought decision-making closer to the regions. This issue was to be addressed further at the Amsterdam Inter-governmental Conference, but no real agreement on the reform of the institutions of the EU was achieved. Any changes to the institutions of the EU, and in particular the role of the European Parliament and the Committee of the Regions are likely to overlap with moves towards decentralisation here in the UK with the establishment of the Scottish Parliament, the Welsh Assembly and the RDAs in England. Attempts to democratise the EU and its decision-making are a difficult and complex task, but increasingly the Commission and the European Parliament are interested in regional development, transport policy, urban issues and the environmental problems which confront the EU. There is a clear link here between the emphasis that the European Commission has placed on the need for local capacity building as a way forward for communities which suffer from deprivation and exclusion to establish routes back into the activities of mainstream life, a job, decent housing, access to affordable transport, access to services, etc. Current intentions to further decentralise the planning system and strengthen the role of community planning and the role of local consultation is in keeping with the principles that are being adopted at the European level.

EUROPEAN SPATIAL DEVELOPMENT POLICY

If the EU is to achieve its goals and objectives for the twenty-first century, con-tributing to economic and social cohesion, sustainable development and a balanced competitive economy, a lot will depend on how well the EU in collabora-tion with individual member states can co-ordinate European sectoral polices with a common spatial development framework. During the late 1980s and early 1990s a series of strategic planning documents were implemented by the European Commission (1990, 1991, 1994c). These documents represent the first attempts to establish common frameworks and a European context for planners at the national, regional and local levels to operate and help co-ordinate spatial policies and develop long-term decision-making and planning. There is anxiety that the process of integration has gone too far and that a further deepening of power of the EU would result in unacceptable transfers of sovereignty away from the member states. From a European perspective, a common approach to spatial planning, which would complement rather than replace the local, regional and national approaches, would result in a more efficient use of Community and national resources and help decision-makers understand how the activities of the EU influence the spatial development of its own territories.

Since the publication of the documents, *Europe 2000* and *Europe 2000+* and the implementation of the European Fifth Environmental Action Programme, the basic principles upon which a European spatial planning framework could operate have begun to emerge. At the Liège meeting of the Council of Ministers responsible for spatial planning in November 1993, it was decided then that the EU should prepare a European Spatial Development Perspective (ESDP). Since then, successive EU presidencies have contributed to the developing ideas on the content and status of the ESDP. At the Noordwijk informal meeting of planning ministers in June 1997 the first official draft of the ESDP was launched. As the first official draft states:

> It is intended to be the expression of a shared vision of the European territory as a whole, a common reference framework for action, and to guide relevant authorities in policy formulation and implementation. It is also intended to be a positive step towards commitment to, and participation in, on-going political process of discussion and guidance for decision-making at the European level. (CEC 1997e: 5)

The last meeting of ministers responsible for spatial planning was held in Glasgow, under the UK presidency, in June 1998. It is now expected that the ESDP will be agreed in 1999 under the German presidency; this version should reflect (*Inforegio News* No. 54, July 1998):

- The wide range of national consultations now taking place, as well as the views of the European institutions
- The results of the seminars the Commission is organising on spatial development in Europe
- The initial lessons from the series of studies the Commission launched on the trends and issues in regional development planning
- New aspects of the spatial development impact of the EU

The ESDP has been developing over a number of years and has been in a regular state of flux. To some national governments it is still seen as a threat to sovereignty or as an irrelevance to the wider objectives of the EU. But moves to encourage Europe's cities and regions to co-operate more widely on regional and land use planning issues have gathered pace. As identified by the DETR report (1998f: 7):

> EU activity in the area of spatial planning has accelerated since the early 1990s. In recent years, a number of reports on the subject have been published, most notably Europe 2000 and Europe 2000+ issued by the European Commission, and more

recently the draft European Spatial Development Perspective, produced by the Member States. The Commission is now also making the Interreg IIc Community Initiative, and Article 10 of the European Regional Development Fund.

While there has been a debate on the content of the ESDP, less attention has been placed on the role and purpose of a common approach to European spatial policy and whether its aims and objectives match the aspirations and needs of individual member states. The ESDP will be important at the European level because it provides a context for the horizontal co-ordination between existing spatially relevant policies, but as yet there have to be more tangible signs on how it will be of use to policy-makers in individual countries and regions. However, the benefits of the ESDP can be seen to be that it:

- Acts as a common reference point for policy-makers
- Will help to guide future decision-making, but key implementation principles have yet to be decided
- Provides a useful, visual identification of the spatial issues that confront the EU

On the other hand, there are still fundamental issues that need to be resolved. These, put simply, include the following:

- If it is difficult to implement the ESDP across the EU, why do we need it?
- Given the diversity of spatial planning systems in the EU, can a common approach be achieved when each country has a different system at different stages of development?
- There are the issues of competence and subsidiarity; most people would agree that the best level of competence for spatial planning rests with national and or appropriate regional or local authorities, so why should an extra (European) level be introduced to make the system overly complex?
- Do we have the right structures of governance for this approach to work effectively?
- Is the spatial scale ineffective, is it too big for the job in hand?

The more optimistic view on the proposed ESDP would be to say that:

- The ESDP plans for greater harmonisation, not convergence of each member state's planning system.
- The ESDP can act as an important spatial reference document which will make policy-makers begin to think at different spatial scales and about the impacts of policies at different spatial scales.
- It will help to promote innovative action through the integration of top-down and bottom-up approaches.

- The ESDP identifies the need to balance different policy objectives. Too many contradictions exist in EU policy, these need to be more closely integrated with the policy objectives of the member states or the relevant regional or local authority.

In terms of spatial planning terms the two most important influences that are likely to become important as a consequence of the current debate on the future prospect of a common ESDP are urban issues and the environment. Cities and city regions are important and these will be part of any European spatial development framework. Some cities have been the focus of economic growth and activity, but cities are also places where people live and there is an important social dimension to the development of the EU as the worst examples of deprivation and social exclusion can be found in European cities. The Commission realises that its own activities, the promotion of economic growth and competitiveness, have contributed towards the breakdown in the social fabric in the urban environment, and as such a range of EU activities which impact on urban areas have been identified and which will act as a potential platform for the bases of a new European urban policy. This does not seem to be that controversial except that the EU has no competence in urban matters and, like spatial planning, is subject to the principle of subsidiarity. The reality is, however, that European polices and programmes directly and indirectly impact on the urban environment which has resulted in a call for greater involvement from the EU in urban policy.

The importance of achieving sustainable development and developing the environmental agenda at the European level is likely to have a significant impact on the planning system. As Roberts (1996) states, the Treaty of Rome in 1957 did not mention environmental policy and it was not until the late 1960s that legislation to regulate the negative environmental impacts of economic growth first appeared. But it was the Single European Act and the Maastricht Treaty which gave the EU a firm mandate to intervene in both regional and environmental policies (Davies, 1994). In March 1992 the EC adopted the fifth of its environmental action programmes designed to protect and enhance the quality of the environment in the EU. The SEM has for the first time given the Community a constitutional mandate to take environmental protection measures. The fifth action programme is based on the thesis of 'sustainable development' as proposed by the 1987 Bruntland report and recognises that the full economic benefits of the single market are limited by environmental constraints. The strategy behind the action programme is based on the realisation that environmental damage will never be halted unless behavioural patterns of producers and consumers, governments and citizens are altered to take the environment more into account. A spatial dimension to EU policy will assist in this process and as Roberts (1998: 10) concludes:

> The sustainable development debate is a matter of immense significance and it cannot be resisted or ignored. Sustainable development is likely to be most important driver

of strategic planning, from the supernational to the parish level, over the coming decades and it is no longer a matter of choice as to whether or not a strategic plan meets the test of sustainability. Strategic planning that is not in accord with international, European Union and national planning conventions on sustainable development stands little or no chance of making progress.

CONCLUSIONS

The challenge for the UK planning profession, during the next phase of economic, political and spatial development in the EU, is how best to take on board the importance of European policy and its implications for UK spatial policy and land use planning. It can be argued that there is a growing awareness that EU policies and actions influence the planning systems as the DETR (1998: 64) states:

> There are a large number of measures that currently influence the UK planning system, in a wide variety of ways. The overwhelming majority of these measures are not focused explicitly on planning. Rather they derive from EU polices in such areas as environment, transport, regional development, agriculture, fisheries and climate change, and their impact on the planning system is often indirect, and sometimes subtle.

However, there exists a degree of suspicion from academics, practitioners and policy-makers over what the EU is trying to achieve through collaborative spatial initiatives like the ESDP and the INTEREG IIc and TERA programmes. The lack of any formal or legally binding competence in spatial planning matters reflects a wider problem, at a European level, in agreeing to a common notion of what spatial policy and planning mean in practice. All too often planning professionals prefer to dwell on the threatening advance of European legislation on their own policy backyard. However, European policy trends actually promote the role of the planner and provide greater opportunities for planning professionals to engage in these debates.

The government's devolution proposals for Scotland and Wales, and the intro-duction of the RDAs in England and the establishment of a new Greater London Authority and a Mayor of London, add a new dimension to the governance of the UK and its relationship with Europe. The UK is still one of the more centralised countries in Europe and while other member states have decentralised, moving power to the regions and local government, the UK has been slow to follow. This could be a long-term obstacle for the UK as other European cities and regions develop both informal and formal networks with the European Commission and other European institutions. A European approach to spatial planning thereby necessitates a fundamental change in thinking for planning professionals. As has been argued in this chapter, the impact of the EU goes beyond the confines of the ESDP, but is something which is much broader in its scope and influence. Above all, UK planners need to participate in European policy-making. While this is occurring in some areas of policy and in some regions, it is not comprehensive across the country. As yet the final outcome of the negotiations over the ESDP has yet to be agreed. What is clear is that the UK should be active in these discussions. For far too long we have acted as the reluctant partner to European business, only supporting what we see to be in our own interests while ignoring everything else. We can learn from the experience of other European countries and we offer Europe a great deal of knowledge and experience of spatial and land use planning. The British plan-led system provides the British with an implementation-led experience of planning, what we lack is the integrated and long-term strategic viewpoint.

CHAPTER 13

SOCIAL HOUSING AND EXCLUSION

Jane Kettle and Celia Moran

INTRODUCTION

Descriptions of the state of social housing at the millennium do not make cheerful reading. In 1997, over 110 000 households were accommodated in the sector because they were homeless, and there was an estimated shortfall of over half a million affordable homes for rent. Over two-thirds of those tenants who rent from residential social landlords (RSLs) in the form of local authorities, housing associations or local housing companies are either wholly or partly dependent on state benefits, and over 30% of newly built RSL homes fail the National Housing Federation affordability test (Maclennan, 1998). Over £2 billion is required to carry out essential repairs and maintenance to RSL stock and one in 13 council homes are unfit (Stationery Office, 1998).

On 14 August 1997 the British Prime Minister, Tony Blair, announced the establishment of a special unit to tackle problems of 'social exclusion' in Britain. Housing policy and practice are at the very heart of the debate on increasing poverty and polarisation, for it is estimated that over 3 million Britons are living in what are described as the worst 1300 social housing estates (DETR, 1997f). In September 1997, Peter Mandelson, Minister without Portfolio in the new Labour government, declared that the social exclusion facing residents of Britain's worst estates was the 'greatest social crisis of our time' (*Housing Today*, 18 June 1997). This focus on social rented housing was extended by the Minister for Local Government and Housing, Hilary Armstrong, who recently declared that housing is at the centre of the government's social policy (*Housing Today*, 14 May 1998).

So what processes have led to this unacceptable and inequitable situation where the residents of Britain are divided sharply according to their housing situation? Surely the problems associated with disrepair, poverty and social exclusion are unintended consequences of strategic housing policy? This chapter examines crucial issues emerging in the development and management of social housing in England, using the experiences reported across one city, Leeds, as a case study. It reviews the evidence elicited from local qualitative research in the context of contemporary housing policy to identify significant and intensified problems faced by housing professionals involved in the management of new, and often problematic, housing schemes. These schemes are all owned and managed by RSLs, most usually those in the housing association sector. It assesses the impact of development-driven policies intended to widen consumer *choice* of both land-lord and tenure. It reviews initiatives whose imperative was to instil competition in the production of social housing, and *diversity* in the ownership and management of social housing. It argues that these twin goals of diversity and choice have produced unintended outcomes, including increased social exclusion and area-based deprivation which cannot be addressed by housing investment alone. It comments on the context which has led to a reduced emphasis on *development* and an increased focus on *sustainability* and all that this entails as we approach the millennium. It concludes with comments on opportunities for change and improvement over the next two decades.

HOUSING POLICY IN BRITAIN, THE CONTEXT

Housing policy in Britain has been declared the 'wobbly pillar' of the welfare state (Lund, 1996). In the formative years of both council and philanthropic housing, it was never envisaged that the homes provided were there as a 'safety net', only for those who had no alternative choice. With the exception of a small amount of property built by nineteenth-century philanthropists such as Joseph Rowntree and George Peabody, the earliest social housing in England was built and managed by local authorities. Indeed, local authorities dominated the sector throughout the inter-war and post-war period, and by the mid 1970s were providing more than 30% of dwellings in this country. However, the golden era of council housebuilding declined throughout the 1950s, 1960s and early 1970s as massive slum clearance combined with the introduction of prefabricated system-built and high-rise homes brought state housing into disrepute, being labelled as a 'great British failure' at the beginning of the 1970s (Berry, 1972).

Housing policy has, over the last 30 years, been subjected to scrutiny and criticism more than any other form of welfare provision. Indeed the notion of house and home as a vehicle for expanding personal wealth has underpinned and informed policies throughout the second half of the century. There have also been hotly contested debates and tensions about the role of local elected and politically accountable authorities as landlords: should they supply general needs housing to those who choose not to purchase, should they fulfil a welfare role, providing for the less able financially, or should they not be in the business of housing provision at all? Certainly Conservative governments between 1979 and 1997 adopted housing policies which were informed by New Right theorists' attacks on local authority domination of social rented housing, arguing that 'the restriction of choice . . . both denies a fundamental aspect of human dignity and makes for services which lack the innovatory spur of competition' (George and Wilding, 1994: 25). As with other areas of public policy, government-driven housing policy has over recent years focused upon inculcating market disciplines and compe-tition, ostensibly to improve efficiency, value for money and consumer choice and to establish 'conditions which encourage more managers and professional people to return to the cities' (Cabinet Office, 1988: 19–20). In practice this has been effected by the mass privatisation of council housing via the right to buy; and the further break-up of the so-called local authority monopolies with the introduction of tenants' choice of landlord through stock transfers. The overall effect of this has been to render access to social housing based solely on *need,* with the resulting concentration of people with less economic and political power into social housing estates.

Housing associations have been seen as central to the effectiveness of this policy in recent years as part of the diversification and choice process. Housing associations, known collectively as the voluntary housing movement, are non-profit-making organisations, usually with charitable status. They provide housing, sometimes part funded with central government grants which are administered via the Housing Corporation. There are over 2500 associations operating in the UK, varying in size from over 20 000 units, to a few hundred. In 1986 only 38% of these associations provided general needs housing (Balchin, 1995), but since then they have developed rapidly. This has been due partly to political ideology, but it is crucial to note that they now house some of the poorest households in England, with over 75% of tenants currently eligible for assistance in paying the rent through housing benefit. This rapid expansion has not been without its problems and is the focus of this discussion.

Housing associations have experienced rapid growth in their provision of social rented and low-cost ownership housing, with government policy effectively reducing the activities of local authorities in this field, leaving the bulk of provision in the sector to be made by housing associations. This is either in the form of the construction of new homes, or in the acquisition and rehabilitation of existing stock. Because of the complexities of the allocation and funding regime for social housing, more recently the construction of new housing association homes has been on brownfield sites, often in the middle of a large council estate where the worst properties have been subjected to selective demolition. A perusal through those British newspapers and journals carrying advertisements for vacancies within housing organisations shows that, in the recent past, 'development workers' were much in demand in these housing associations. However, these rapidly growing organisations are increasingly concerned not simply with physical expansion of the affordable rented housing stock but also with managing the underlying area-based social problems which confront them as they move into the new (for them) territory of large-scale housing management. Those associations which have been sucked into rapid expansion by both their own ambitions and central government policies to lure them into this scale of development, have now found themselves confronted by the realities of trying to 'manage' housing in socially marginalised communities; a challenge which requires more than the mere provision of better quality housing, but one which demands more work opportunities, and better education and leisure facilities. The new breed of housing association workers are finding themselves trying to retro-engineer community development with limited and ring-fenced monies in areas stuck in a long-term vortex of economic and social decline. This context makes their much vaunted better management skills and tenure diversification strategies inadequate to bring about sustainable changes in housing stock, tenure and quality at the local level. Increasingly, housing associations have had to adopt a whole area perspective or to be more selective in where and how they invest and develop, since they have neither the powers nor the broad mandate of local authorities to bring about long-term economic regeneration: housing regeneration in isolation is not enough, as the 1960s taught us!

So despite the almost frenzied development activities of housing associations, it could be argued that between 1979 and 1997, and more especially since 1988, housing policy was, in fact, *tenure* policy with most initiatives being intended to promote homeownership over all other forms of tenure. This has led to a situation where, as we approach the millennium, public or social sector landlords in the form of housing associations and local authorities own and manage around only 25% of the housing stock in England and Wales. It is, however, clusters within this 25% that the Social Exclusion Unit is so concerned about. For those people excluded from the house purchase market are those housed by the RSLs, and they are increasingly subjected to close scrutiny and analysis from all parts of the political spectrum. The apparent process of social housing marginalisation is closely associated with the debates surrounding the 'underclass'. While there is lively academic argument about the reality of the underclass (Dean, 1991), physical manifestations of the phenomenon are now part of the everyday working life of housing professionals. Research on the underclass, much of it with a New Right perspective (Barnett, 1986; Murray, 1990, 1994), suggests that although it is not spatially determined, many candidates for membership live in social rented housing. This places the sector firmly in the public and political spotlight as government policy is perceived to be driving people with particular characteristics, based on need, into social housing: in consequence place, underclass and deprivation become inextricably linked in popular urban consciousness (Power, 1996). It will be argued that, as income groups become increasingly segregated spatially, and only those who can afford nothing else are allocated homes in the social housing sector, the underclass debate has transformed what used to be merely a 'sociological concern about the emergent class structure into a wider topic for public and personal debate' (Fainstein *et al.*, 1992: 7). So the recent political triumph of Conservative regimes has resulted in an approach to development which has had negative social costs in terms of individuals and neighbourhoods. Contemporary British housing policy has been driven by attempts to withdraw the 'nanny state' and to undermine the influence of local government, with the effect that there has been intensified social polarisation within the housing stock. This has led to the re-emergence of debates about the so-called underclass and renewed concern about problem estates (Malpass, 1993).

SOCIAL HOUSING IN LEEDS, A PYRRHIC VICTORY?

We now examine the Leeds experience, and consider issues which are likely to be of relevance as housing management focuses more widely. It draws on monitoring data collected by social housing organisations and primary evidence gathered from interviews with senior housing professionals. For the purposes of this research, in-depth interviews of up to two hours' duration were held with eight senior housing managers involved with development from the local authority (Leeds City Council), and from those housing associations which are active in Leeds having developed their stock under the provisions of Leeds Partnership Homes. Together these organisations are currently responsible for the provision of around 80% of the social housing stock in the city and the combination of qualitative and quantitative information provides a useful sense of insight into how processes of social exclusion are impacting on housing provision and management in the city. (The remaining stock pertains to a national housing association which provides accommodation for elderly people: the specialist function and all that goes with this are beyond the parameters of this chapter.) The open-ended interviews were carried out with the assurance that confidentiality would be maintained. This is because the views of the housing professionals were their own, rather than a repetition of their organisations' policy statements.

With a population of 717 400 in 1991 (Campbell, 1996: 43), Leeds is the second largest city in England outside London. The recent history of Leeds has been characterised by a dramatic turn around in economic fortune, associated with a decline in traditional industries such as textiles and engineering and a growth in business, financial, administrative and others services. In this respect, Leeds is hailed as a national success story, with an 'increasingly prosperous city centre based upon a successful integration into the national and global economy' (Haughton and Williams, 1996: 14). At city level, Leeds also fares well when social indicators such as car ownership, employment and rates of lone parenthood are compared to other provincial cities such as Birmingham, Manchester, Liverpool, Sheffield and Newcastle upon Tyne (Stillwell and Leigh, 1996). However, beneath this outward image of good fortune, there exists the typical social divisions and tensions which are a feature of so many large Western cities. High levels of unemployment, material deprivation, crime and disaffected youth are concentrated spatially into the inner-city area and peripheral council estates. For the basic features of housing provision in Leeds are broadly similar to those of other older English cities. An examination of the tenure structure of the 296 100 dwellings in the city reveals that approximately 70% are privately owned (either owner-occupied or privately rented), 27% are council owned, and 3.5% belong to housing associations. Comparison with national figures demonstrates a slight bias in favour of the local authority at the expense of the private sector, with housing associations reflecting national representation (Moran, 1996).

Around the periphery of the older central area are many of the city's 80 000 council stock which were built in the post-war era as large estates of medium and low-rise dwellings, and tower blocks. Among these estates are typical 'problem' areas characterised by multiple deprivation, physical dilapidation and a stigma associated with high levels of crime, vandalism and other forms of antisocial behaviour.

This provides evidence of the continued residualisation of social housing. Stillwell and Leigh's study of the geographies of social polarisation in Leeds found a statistically significant correlation between unemployment and the areas containing large peripheral council estates (Stillwell and Leigh, 1996). While it is true that the distribution of council housing is a function of past investment decisions, what is significant here is that there are distinct areas with high proportions of local authority housing, often in and around the inner city, and these correlate closely with other indicators of disadvantage.

> I think there is a group of people, I can't precisely define or quantify them, who are just not totally isolated, but maybe cast adrift is a better phrase, becoming more and more separate from the proportion of society that is reasonably well resourced . . .
> (Leeds City Council Housing Officer, June 1996).

This spatial analysis of tenure and social disadvantage is supported by other evidence which demonstrates that the social profile of both housing association and council tenants is changing rapidly, and that tenants in this sector are increasingly unlikely to possess political and economic power (Lee *et al.*, 1995).

Fears are growing that sections of cities 'seem to be slipping out of control, dominated by unemployment, violence and fear of crime, and ignored by the good citizens who drive through them, just as godly men of property once ignored the Victorian poor' (Ravetz, 1991: 323). Leeds is no exception. Where earlier conceptualisations of urban poverty were most associated with high densities of private rented properties, contemporary concentrations of poverty are most frequently associated with the social housing stock which was intended to replace the former areas of 'squalor'.

This context becomes more significant when recent local housing policies are considered. In Leeds, the provision of social housing throughout the 1990s has been driven by the creation of an innovative, development-focused initiative, namely Leeds Partnership Homes in 1991. This partnership between five housing associations and the local authority effectively acted as a mechanism for transferring land, channelling resources and stretching public subsidy in the Leeds area, thereby maximising development activity in the city. By 1995, over 2400 rented or low-cost homes for sale had been completed and this had increased to over 4000 by 1998. The initiative was certainly very effective in terms of hard outputs, and indeed became a role model for similar initiatives to increase development output across the country.

DEVELOPMENT AND DIVERSIFICATION: WHERE SHOULD WE BUILD?

Although the provision of homes by RSLs in Leeds during the 1990s could be declared an overwhelming success in terms of units of production, there is a down side, acknowledged by local key players, and now achieving national recognition. The emergent problems associated with large-scale development have had a particularly significant impact on the working practices and policies of housing associations. For it could be argued that the ongoing process of social polarisation has not only been largely ignored by mainstream housing policy, but has also been marginalised by housing organisations in their eagerness to sustain development activities. Many housing associations in the 1990s became sucked into a development vortex in which financial considerations dominated and they soon became 'wedded to an almost unshakeable belief that only by continuing an expensive development programme for meeting general housing needs [could] they demonstrate their virility . . .' (Wadhams, 1995: 58).

However, the operation of Leeds Partnership Homes in conjunction with the prevailing national policy environment did have a profound effect upon the location and type of social development in Leeds. By the early 1990s intensified competition for social housing grant (SHG) and the requirement to work with the local authority in the identification of need, combined locally with the land deals associated with Leeds Partnership Homes, and resulted in a refocusing of attention on rehabilitation and infill development on peripheral and often problematic local authority estates in an attempt to diversify landlords and tenure groups. This was done by introducing the partner associations to developments in selected locations across the city. Overall, there has been muted support for the idea of diversification on the grounds that it 'avoids the large monolithic estates of the past, and brings variety into an area' (Housing Association Manager). However, there are complex issues about the tension created by a desire to preserve autonomy and identity which have yet to be resolved. Although Leeds pursued a collaborative, partnership approach rather than a fiercely competitive one, the process involved a less hands-on approach to the provision of housing by the local authority and an element of competition between the partner associations for development land.

DIVERSIFICATION, DEMAND AND CHOICE: MUTUALLY EXCLUSIVE?

We have described how central government policy has been to diversify landlords in the social rented sector by encouraging multi-agency developments, often in areas with large tracts of existing local authority housing. While this can be explained as a mechanism to encourage choice and competition, it could also be argued that issues of governance and local accountability are central to the project. The provision of social housing in Leeds, as elsewhere, has become contested terrain. Certainly the constraints placed on local authorities were not accidental: it has been the government's aim to 'transform authorities from "providers" of new subsidised rented housing . . . into "enablers" who help other landlords to meet this need' (Fraser, 1991: 9). In practice this has led to many social landlords operating in areas where previously there was usually only one, the local authority itself. The grass-roots response to the rhetoric has been one of weary realism:

> The Department of the Environment put a really generous gloss on what was really a more direct political challenge which was to break the power of the local authorities. I don't think that the Government ever had any intention that diversifying tenure would ease social problems, I don't think there was any research to support the opposite premise (Leeds City Council Housing Officer).

Choice, in this context, is a nebulous concept to grasp. To what extent does choice apply to those who are not able to exercise it through purchasing power? Choice implies selecting from a range of options, but most new entrants to social housing have little or no choice, either of landlord, or of geographical area, or of property type. As noted by Cole and Windle (1992: 37), 'the public are only being given the illusion of choice, through a dogmatic commitment to market principles, in a situation of social polarisation and reducing investment'. In this context, therefore, the question of demand in terms of housing and area popularity is considered. Despite a high level of identified need for affordable housing in Leeds (Leeds City Council, 1994), development in existing stigmatised areas has meant that many of the schemes under discussion have not been popular with potential tenants and have therefore become areas of last resort for the most desperate cases:

> I've spoken to quite a few Council housing contract managers and they've repeated that they're amazed that schemes were developed in particular areas and that there wasn't enough foresight to predict what the demand might be relating to the popularity of the areas . . . really the associations end up fighting with the local authority over the low demand cases for the properties (Leeds City Council Housing Officer).

The new areas of poverty may be less physically squalid, with much local authority and housing association stock of high quality, but they remain locked into processes of economic and social deprivation which 'root' people into them and lead cumulatively to processes of downward spirals of area-based social exclusion. One crucial reason for this is that

> a more narrowly composed group in society is applying for public sector housing. The strict allocation according to need in the circumstances of excess demand ensures

that the group gaining possession of those homes is ever more narrowly composed to reflect the most disadvantaged (CIH, 1996: 3).

It would appear that there is in some areas a continuing downward spiral of desirability. This starts with an ordinary local authority street which gradually becomes unpopular and then hard to let. The most desperate people then take up this low-demand housing because no one else on the list will accept it. A housing association takes over the houses in an attempt to turn the street around, but because wider social and community issues are not able to be tackled, the net result is that there are new or refurbished homes in certain schemes where 30% are standing empty at any one time and the housing associations are advertising in the local press for tenants. This is because

> not enough assessment was made into what a kind of gamble was taken because the associations wanted to develop, the biggest issue was 'let's have a go'. It was just naïvely assumed that 'management' would solve the problem (Leeds City Council Housing Officer).

That low demand has been a major issue is indisputable, particularly where the new development backs on to old, poor-quality, municipal housing. This is backed up by research which suggests that

> many households live in dwellings which are modern and well equipped but which are located in neighbourhoods which offer only poor local resources for residents. As certain areas and parts of the market . . . represent poor social environments, those with choice in the housing system are less likely to move to such areas (NFHA, 1995: 30–31).

BALANCED, MIXED OR SUSTAINABLE COMMUNITIES?

Widening housing choice for people in cities carries an implicit message of social engineering, for the government felt this would result in a 'better balanced, more mobile and economically stronger society' (DoE, 1988: 22). So the government's vision for the future of social rented housing is to

> encourage the development of mixed communities . . . to break down the barriers between the old estates and the rest of the community and help construct sustainable communities where a balanced mix of households, young and old, low income and better off, home owners and renters, live alongside each other. (DoE, 1995b: 35).

One way of trying to achieve this in Leeds yielded unwelcome and unexpected results. This involves schemes which have mixed properties for sale (under low-cost homeownership schemes) with those for rent. For instance, in a scheme in a large peripheral estate in Leeds, despite a name change, only a small proportion of properties were sold to people wishing to purchase property. Many of those who bought are now desperately trying to sell their properties on. A substantial number of derelict properties earmarked for improvement for sale have been abandoned by the private construction company which acquired them from the local authority. The form of diversification being pushed politically has, for its detractors, merely

> supported a political drive, not housing need. In terms of breaking up tenure or providing mixed communities, locations have been badly picked . . . money has been pumped into schemes that maybe should have been provided for rent in the first place. It hasn't balanced communities at all and in some places there has been the traditional animosity between owners and renters (Leeds City Council Housing Officer).

Mixing owners and renters was assumed by central government to be a way of achieving a more 'balanced community', encouraging a wider mix of people from different ages and backgrounds. However, there appear to be serious problems in translating this into practice at local level. The *Guardian* ran a feature describing how a couple, who had bought their council home on the city's Halton Moor estate had been burgled on average once every 11 weeks for four years, had put their home valued at £28 000 on the market for £1000. An extreme case but one which highlights the crucial issues of low demand and 'unbalanced communities'. The net result is that

> Local authorities and housing associations house the least resourced people. In the 70s and 80s there was a more balanced range of customers. Increasingly we are dealing with people who are the least resourced, have the least capabilities and options . . . I don't think that there is any doubt that there is an underclass: we've still got a class structure but the labels and strata have changed (Leeds City Council Housing Officer, June 1996).

Socio-economic polarisation between owners and renters has more generally been heightened, especially in the housing association sector. This is because the financial arrangements for developing new homes relies heavily on private money: this impacts on the rent payable by the tenant. This continues within the social rented sector: there is a marked difference between council and housing association rents. This means that 'in some of the rehabilitated schemes, the only difference has been that you have the same property, with significantly improved facilities, managed by a different landlord . . . albeit at a higher rent' (Housing Association Officer). Higher rent levels impact upon prospective tenants in two ways. Firstly, there is an adverse customer reaction which taints attitudes to housing associations more generally:

> Certainly we had to convince people that these associations were not some kind of shady, marginal, profit making organisations . . . in the early days people were saying,

'I don't want one of these properties, I want a council house because I know what a council house is and I know what the council is' (Leeds City Council Housing Officer).

Secondly, new entrants to housing association properties are increasingly likely to be dependent on welfare benefits: those in work would find the rent commitment an impossible burden. So ultimately, large areas of residential properties are occupied only by those who are economically inactive: unemployment becomes the norm for that area.

SOCIAL EXCLUSION: COMPLEXITIES AND CONSEQUENCES

> Life on that estate was just about a crowd of people just drinking and standing in the middle of the street, and police cars coming and going, beer bottles around . . . kids smashing paint pots against the walls. . . . There's a group of people out there at another level to everyone else and they're desperate (Leeds City Council Housing Officer).

In 1993, a national study of new housing association developments provided the first evidence of emergent problems on these estates, and warned that associations were in danger of repeating the mistakes which had been made during the mass building and high-rise eras when council construction dominated (Page, 1993). As Nuttgens noted, of the earlier era, a numerical solution to a numerical problem was being sought when in reality individual and sensitive approaches were needed to address diverse local problems (Nuttgens, 1989).

One of the most significant emerging issues concerning the management of social housing estates which has not, and maybe could not have, been planned for, is the incidence and growth of antisocial behaviour. Definition of this phenomenon is not easy and it ranges from localised incivilities and hostilities through to organised criminal activity. However, while media attention may have distorted and embellished the problem, ultimately unacceptable behaviour is of real and pressing concern to housing agencies. The DoE estimates that up to 20% of the average housing manager's time is spent addressing neighbour disputes, and that the behaviour of between 2 and 10% of the population of any housing estate has been the subject of a complaint (DoE, 1995a).

Antisocial behaviour has become a cause for concern in Leeds with increasing numbers of reported incidents (Kettle and Moran, 1995). An analysis of the effects of the new regime on those at the interface, the professional housing managers who are involved in the day-to-day running of social housing, questions the efficacy of development-led policy. It acknowledges that the prevailing approach to development has had negative social costs in terms of individuals and neighbourhoods. One housing officer considered that antisocial behaviour underpins all aspects of the day-to-day management of estates and is particularly at odds with demands from the central funding body to reduce costs. Another noted that, with respect to crime and antisocial behaviour 'it is a big issue and it starts to cost us a lot of money. We have to consider that if we don't help people we won't be letting schemes because people won't live there . . . funding that is a nightmare' (Housing Association Manager). The problems of incivilities, antisocial and criminal behaviours are becoming increasingly severe for all the respondents:

> . . . anti-social behaviour is certainly a new issue for even Local Authority staff . . . in the old days the housing manager used to go round and say you won't or will do that. Increasingly we are dealing with people who are the least resourced, have the least capabilities and options. There's a greater mix of problems and staff themselves have to develop a greater awareness and skills. One of the common cries that I come out with is that we're asked more and more to be more than a landlord these days. We almost become the hub of a cartwheel of support agencies, social services, probation, education welfare, mediation, we seem to be the agency that first identifies problems and initiates solutions (Leeds City Council Housing Officer).

As they have entered the vortex of providing mass housing for socially excluded people, many housing associations are being exposed to problems and activities that local authorities have had a longer experience in tackling:

> In effect hard to let streets were made available to associations who naively thought that they could solve the problems and who are probably learning about life now . . . realising that there are issues other than providing housing: need is area based and to be quite honest if you provide decent housing in the wrong area you're a loser (Housing Association Manager).

WHAT LESSONS SHOULD BE LEARNED?

It has been shown that there are serious problems associated with some new social housing in Leeds. These relate not to the fabric of these dwellings, but to the wider issues of the management of both the tenancies and the adjacent areas. All respondents identified new and intensified issues in the management of their estates, leading to increasing demands in terms of staff, resources and creativity, and noted the unfortunate juxtaposition of this situation alongside pressure to reduce costs. Problems centred around the 'extreme deprivation' and 'vulnerability' of many tenants, together with increased incidences of antisocial behaviour. This leads to the need to provide support and intervention, either directly or through other agencies, of a type which those outside the profession would see as going beyond the usual remit of housing managers. While these issues are not exclusive to multi-landlord estates, but are common to the social housing sector, this research concludes that the diversifying approach, far from leading to 'improved efficiency in housing management', has ignored these trends and in some cases unwittingly contributed to them.

Such schemes have also provided very salutary lessons for development-led housing. The design, layout and fabric of the dwellings may be excellent, but location and sense of place are overriding. Management considerations have been conspicuous by their absence during the inceptions of these new social rented housing schemes. Because of the pressures to commit funding to schemes, important considerations about client requirements and management views were not taken into account. A most extreme example of this on one development is where the housing managers of the association felt that the potential problems of this scheme were insurmountable, and urged that the scheme was aborted. Pressure from the City Council to develop meant that 'it went ahead, and the scheme was devised on a wing and a prayer . . . the outcome has been a hard-to-let scheme with a vacancy rate of around 25 per cent' (Housing Association Officer).

The evidence from the Leeds experience shows that there is clearly a strong case for longer-term management considerations to be given a substantially higher profile at the stage when development proposals are being shaped. This has already been done to some degree in terms of making properties 'secure by design' and incorporating tenants' views into design. It is also currently being addressed in one housing association where 'internal restructuring based upon a client–contractor chain is strengthening the relative position of management considerations and making issues such as lettability, manageability and long term costs, paramount to development decision-making and risk appraisal' (Housing Association Manager). Whether this aim is translated into reality remains to be seen.

CONCLUSIONS

Although the incoming Labour government instigated a full review of housing policy, to date there is as yet *no* radical change from the focus on investment that 'is and will remain needs-led' (Housing Corporation, 1996: 1). However, notice *is* now being taken of the daily reality of life in the new estates. The then Housing Corporation's Deputy Chief Executive posited that outcomes of policy have been to build estates

> which have simply overloaded services and the neighbourhood spirit . . . it isn't very clever of us to create communities of poor families with large concentrations of children locking them in the poverty trap (Pam Alexander, CIH Conference, June 1996).

More recently, Brenda Dean, the new Chair of the Housing Corporation, asserted that it was no longer feasible or justifiable to continue to direct money into the most unpopular and problematic areas (Housing Corporation/National Housing Federation Conference, Manchester, April 1998). So there are emerging signs of a new and more coherent vision for British housing policy. The Minister for Housing, Hilary Armstrong, sees a 'trinity of aims' for social housing in the next millennium. These include involving tenants and potential tenants in addressing needs and aspirations, introducing 'best value' into housing management and generating the required levels of investment (*Housing Today*, 11 May 1998).

So how can these aims be put into practice? Without economic and political power, people need intensive support in their daily lives, and a framework through which they can engage in the life of the community. However, the continued preoccupation with efficiency and economy in the guise of best value will impact on housing management: managing vulnerable people and offering added value is difficult to achieve in an environment where efficiency, usually in the form of reduced costs, becomes paramount. Recent housing management practices have, rhetorically at least, tended to treat tenants as *consumers*, with a focus on providing customer satisfaction and value for money, rather than addressing the difficulties faced by poor and vulnerable people. There is, however, an emerging awareness of a need to consider how positive housing policies and practices might aim to enhance *citizenship* (*Housing*, Dec./Jan. 1996). This is a reflection of the language of current discourse which is moving away from the notion of rights alone, and instead inserting balancing notions of social duties and parental and moral obligations on societies which 'increasingly present themselves to people as fragmented, divisive and anomic' (Roche, 1992: 245). The workfare agenda is in its ascendancy.

Diversification has not led to greater choice for users of social housing: the future challenge should surely be to make cities and urban areas better places to live. A greater understanding of local markets and the needs of local people over the medium to long term is far more important than the provision of a choice of landlord: *who* delivers assumes far less significance than *what* actually works. Development-led policies have not strengthened the link between RSLs and the local community: the continuing trend of reduced grant, high rents and high benefits, leading to new swathes of benefit-dependent people, cannot enhance involvement.

Development-led activity has failed to account for changes in the profile of the client group. Connections between housing and other social and economic factors have been ignored at both local and national levels, and there now need to be new mechanisms for tackling this (Forrest and Williams, 1997). Housing associations are now beginning to ask not *what* to develop but *whether* to develop: sustainable communities can only be maintained by wider, less intrusive preventive action to stop the spatial separation of owners and renters: new build should be a last resort, especially in the middle of unpopular, run-down areas which surely cannot benefit from the mere injection of money. It has been suggested that some housing agencies may withdraw from problem areas or emerge with new social engineering solutions to antisocial behaviour (ADC/AMA, 1994). While being careful to avoid stereotyping, the Ridings Housing Association is, for instance, reluctantly coming to the conclusion that this trend of providing housing schemes in areas where there is a multiplicity of other problems may only make a relatively minor difference to the quality of life in those areas and such schemes can indeed be jeopardised by the social and economic conditions in that area (Ridings Housing Association, 1996). Physical improvement and/or change of landlord will not in itself make such an area desirable and, as one respondent told us, experience has taught that 'there is little point in regenerating little pockets where there is no wider plan for the area'.

If housing is to be at the heart of the government's social policy, what role should RSLs have in the development of sustainable communities? Under New Labour, issues to do with equality and class differences have become fuzzy, with a new focus on social capital. Certainly for 'Cool Britannia', the focus of social exclusion is more individualised (Pahl, 1998), and in these circumstances to what extent can RSLs become carriers of their own personal communities? Should the role of housing associations be to strengthen the associational behaviour of their residents? If this is to be the case then we really are returning to an era when the management of social housing is more than the management of bricks and mortar, and the responsibilities as well as the rights of residents are paramount. The process of 'squaring the circle', of returning to paternalistic landlordism backed up with sanctions, is firmly in progress. The prevailing view is that the type of behaviour which impacts on the right of others to a peaceful domestic existence is firmly in the domain of the public sector tenant. Irwell Valley Housing Association Ltd is currently drawing on notions of philanthropy, utilitarianism and reciprocity to encourage 'good tenants' by offering a 'Heart of Gold' service for those with no history of antisocial behaviour. Good tenants receive preferential treatment and access to benefits within the wider community.

At the 'Thinking the Unthinkable' conference in Liverpool in November 1997, Professor Ian Cole of Sheffield Hallam University took the bull by the horns, stating that housing associations should be weaned away from the develop or perish idiom, and that half-hearted attempts at gilding the ghetto should make way for long-term area improvement (*Housing Today*, 13 November 1997). This partnership can only work when there is an end to the obsession with numbers and a focus on management issues: partners need to be involved in long-term strategic decision-making and alliances should be built outside housing. Until this is accepted and agreed by all involved in the shaping of housing policy, it shall be doomed to be the great British failure.

CHAPTER 14

PLANNING IN THE FUTURE: TRENDS, PROBLEMS AND POSSIBILITIES

Philip Allmendinger

INTRODUCTION

Before embarking on what will inevitably be an incomplete and highly personal view of where planning is, where it is going and how it should proceed, it will be worth setting out at the beginning my own feelings which will have a bearing on my interpretation. Having worked both in practice and academia I find myself torn in many directions. On the one hand is the need to question what I see as the ineffective, blasé though largely well-intentioned practice of planning, the academic tradition and system that produces this and the relationship (conspiracy is not too strong a word) between the professional body of planners and the state in retaining the status quo. On the other hand there is also the need not to destroy but to encourage change because, for all its faults, the planning system in principle (and I am referring to the abstract and anodyne sentiments of the post-war approach) holds wide public support and rightly so.

Cullingworth (1997) claims that the world has changed during the 50 or so years planning has been in operation. Yet the system itself has largely remained the same. There are two aspects of this quite common view that I would like briefly to discuss. First, it is true that the *system* of planning has largely remained unchanged. But the *processes* of planning have adapted and taken the brunt of change. By processes I do not mean the perfunctory need to draw up plans and submit planning applications but the inputs into the system, the desire for more participation, the depth and expanse of debates and subject matters, etc. The system itself, in its broadest sense, was originally designed to encompass a wide range of views and positions that formed the delicate post-war consensus for planning. As numerous authors have pointed out, the objectives of planning remained so abstract that just about anyone could have signed up to them. As a consequence the *system* of planning (Parliamentary Acts, statutory instruments, etc.) was robust: certainly robust enough to take the pressures and changes of the last 50 years. The focus for change has therefore been on the processes of planning, leaving the system largely unchallenged even in the heady days of the New Right. So while attention has been paid to detailed debates on in-town versus out-of-town development and who gets involved, questions over whether we need a planning system, what it should address and how have largely gone unasked.[1]

My second point is that there are powerful interests in this situation remaining. Seditious though it may be, I believe that planners, property interests, academics, the professional institute and the government all *need* a planning system. Their reasons are different (and I shall come to these later) but their need is common. They are, however, doing themselves and the country a disservice. Not only that, but I believe that future events and the continuation of existing trends and pressures will expose this situation, leading to questions being asked not only about the planning process but the system as well.

That I am critical of the current situation should be in little doubt. We do not need the complex accretion of rules and regulations that form current planning practice which only serve to obfuscate the issues, allow planners to hide behind a veneer of technical expertise and serve to restrict rather than encourage. This is not an argument for *laissez-faire* as will become clear later. Modern societies need some form of land use regulation and intervention to balance the conflicting needs that emerge. But planning comes in many forms, shapes and sizes.

It is all too easy to question, criticise and some might say be cynical. You also need to be constructive and here I come back to the need not to destroy. Following an analysis of trends, pressures and constraints I explore the boundaries of a possible alternative to the current system. These alternatives seek to build upon difference and locality in a way that gives room for expression rather than fruitlessly working towards a stultifying consensus.

This is where I part company from those who continue to think that the response to failures in and of planning and the growing complexity of society, politics and the economy mean that we should apply *more* planning. They have failed to learn the lessons of history. Instead they argue that planning should not only 'map out' the complex personal, social and economic relations that underpin society (as if this were possible and/or desirable) but also mediate these as if land use planning were a panacea for all the ills and issues that face us in the twenty-first century. Like the apocryphal leaves on the line, tower blocks, social exclusion, homelessness and road-choked cities were not caused by planning, just the wrong kind of planning. As most of the world rolls back the stifling constraints of bureaucratic overkill to allow difference and diversity to flourish, planners and academics seem to be seeking a different route. In some ways, one should not be too surprised. After all, there is a powerful professional and academic industry that needs to justify its existence and which precludes any argument other than for more planning.

Space prohibits me from properly exploring the main differences and options that face planning. But the debate should be more than one-dimensional with the same old tired arguments and clichés about environmental protection. Some of the most ardent supporters of planning are those whose property prices depend on its continued control of supply and location. Have we really set up a complex and costly administrative system to placate the shire voters? Planning does not exist by divine right, it does so through popular support and such support is dependent upon results and perception. Both elements are sadly neglected in planning. Monitoring and assessment seem to be either deliberately avoided or taken as read while the perception of planners is still not far off estate agents and tax inspectors. While the environmental lobby has grown and green issues ride high in the public's perception, planning has failed to capitalise on the opportunity for a symbiosis. This is where we find planning at the cusp of the millennium.

The purpose of this chapter is to explore, from a very personal perspective, the trends, influences, contexts, challenges and possibilities for planning in the twenty-first century. Obviously, this is going to be an incomplete and contestable project by any standard, but there are a host of considerations that will make it more so. Like planning, this book is concerned with the future and like planning it must not underestimate the difficulties of futurology. One lesson from the past is that we cannot depend on it for a picture of the future – who could have predicted or forecasted the fall of the Berlin wall in 1989, the collapse of communism or the end of the cold war? Yet these events and many others have profoundly shaped the world today. As Coyle (1997: 77) puts it:

> Only a fool, a charlatan or, possibly, the Chancellor of the Exchequer claims to be able to predict what will happen in the future, yet, despite the evident failures of these attempts there is an abiding interest in the future and what it might hold.

Planning is no exception to difficulties in futurology. From population forecasts for housing to views on the policy directions the term 'planning', at the very least, hints at some glimpse if not expertise in the future. However, what characterises a subject dependent upon such a need to look beyond the horizon is the lack of appreciation of difficulties and approaches to the future.

Regardless of the difficulties and inevitability of failure we *need* to plan and unfortunately, planning involves a stab at the future. But we also need to be aware that the future will not inevitably be like the present. Take the example of the Channel Tunnel. Designed for rail travel, one obvious question that needed to be considered in the design was would the demand for rail travel be the same in 100 years' time? But more fundamentally, by choosing rail, to what extent have we 'locked in' future options or *created* a future based on rail? The decision to make a rail tunnel was as much future *creating* as future *predicting*. The point is that the future is not something that happens to us, it is partly actively constituted by decisions taken in the present, as well as being comprised of large elements of chance and forces that we cannot perceive or know.

With this in mind I have attempted to stake out a future of planning and within which planning will fit. I have no 'crystal ball' or new methodologies to employ and what this inevitably amounts to is little more than a personal view. What I will endeavour to do is make explicit my arguments and assumptions so that it is clear what has constituted them. Indeed, part of my argument is that the future itself is becoming less not more predictable and understandable in our late or postmodern world.

FACTORS OF INFLUENCE

It may be as well to bring these diverse strands together into some form of coherent whole that constitutes the argument of this chapter. It goes something like this: there are five broad factors of influence that will shape the future. These five factors or categories are not crucial themselves and act merely as a basis for discussion. So, what are these factors? First, there is *political will* or the desire of society. Basically, its vision of the future. This can be subdivided between the *Zeitgeist* as well as the formal arenas found in different levels of government where pressure or will can be transformed into policy and action. Such arenas are conflict ridden and the outcome will be a contestable, often vague, changeable product. The political will 'emerges' from a complex accretion of local and national influences. Political will does not discount difference or opposition, but emphasises instead the majority view as expressed through institutions such as Parliament or local authorities.

At a macro level political will could involve whether the country is a liberal democracy or a planned economy. At a more micro level in terms of planning it could involve whether the system is discretionary or zoning based, as well as the aims and objectives of that system, e.g. in-town versus out-of-town development, protection of the countryside versus planned dispersal.

Against this political will or demand is the second factor: the inherited stockpile of ideas/ideals that form the stability of a particular political system. We could term this the atavistic or conservative element of society. This differs from the first factor in terms of its stability and its longer-term nature. But there is obviously a relationship between the two that could be seen as a *difference of time*. Political desire will influence the conservative nature of society in the longer term. Similarly, the conservatism of a system will have a more immediate impact upon this desire. In most countries conservatism would take the form of a constitution or certain 'ethics' of acceptable ideas/behaviour. Freedom of speech and the right to vote are crude examples that are ingrained in the ethos of most Western countries and against which the more ephemeral shifts in public opinion or political power in the form of governments are benchmarked. Such formal 'checks and balances' and the more informal but no less effective veins of opinion that run through societies act as a brake upon the more radical or progressive aspects of political will.

Third, there are the formal and informal channels and *systems of implementation* that are charged with executing political will. Layers of government, agencies, charities, individuals, professional bodies, vested interests, stakeholders, etc. all to greater and lesser degrees have a role in making sure things *happen* (or do not happen). The literature on implementation has stood still since the mid 1980s, but it clearly and rightly points to the iterative nature of implementation where policy is constantly made and remade. Professional groups such as town planners have successfully argued that they should be given special privileges in this respect and have been granted wide discretion to interpret and effectively make policy on a daily basis. This discretion to interpret and formulate policy effectively adds an extra administrative layer to political will that can and has been used to apply centrally directed policies for ends other than those envisaged.

These first three factors are what I would term 'above the line' of 'controllability'. This is a notional point that aims to bring the unexpected and uncontrollable into the equation of influence. This is not to say that factors such as political will or implementation agencies are immune from uncertainty but that, on the whole, they are able to cushion, adapt and overcome aspects of uncertainty. There are two particular influences 'below the line' that I consider important in any future of and for planning; the 'can we?' factor of chaos and complexity and the 'should we?' influence that postmodern and post-structuralist critiques have brought in their wake. While both are influences upon the future they also provide a sound basis for a new approach to planning that can meet the challenges of the twenty-first century.

I will be turning to questions of chaos of complexity later on, but suffice to say here that a greater understanding of both is a necessary prerequisite for a more fundamental understanding of planning. Chaos is concerned with a sensitive dependence upon initial conditions and the complex influences behind seemingly simple phenomena. It has the potential to tell us much about the reasons why, however hard or well we 'plan', things do not turn out as expected. Complexity is a different phenomenon which has the potential to explain the interrelationship of the five factors of influence and the way that planning itself is not only an administrative and legal set of systems and processes but can be viewed as a complex adaptive system. Complex adaptive systems have been shown to exist in all organisations and work in a similar way to the brain. Rather than neurons, organisations have agents or people who interact, 'learn' and adapt. Planning can be seen as such a system with its constituents participants (planners, the public, councillors, developers, etc.) creating a system that is far greater than the sum of its parts. In many ways the planning system could be seen to resemble an organism in the way it learns, grows and responds to the feedback of its environment. Such systems 'emerge' and organise themselves through a combination of evolution and co-operation into more complex structures that become an integral part of a greater system: society.

I reject the arguments of some that complexity and postmodernism are incompatible. Instead I argue that there is a close relationship between the two that potentially provides the basis of a new planning. Two aspects are of concern here. First, the critique that both (from different but complementary standpoints) provide of planning. Questions of consensus, difference, language, power, professionalism, process and objectives are all given a fresh and revealing dimension. Second, both postmodern and post-structuralist critiques provide the basis for a realistic alternative grounded in a plurality of values and lives. Both hint at an alternative that is less focused on control and is more concerned with providing

___

conditions to enable planning to facilitate a future at the 'edge of chaos'. As we shall see, such an approach neatly corresponds to the lessons of complexity and chaos providing a powerful symbiosis of analysis and alternative. This may all sound very fanciful and, no doubt, aspects of it are – but then if a book about the future cannot be fanciful then what can? What I intend to do is examine a number of elements that will impact upon the five factors of influence outlined above. In the case of the two 'below the line' factors it will also be necessary to go into greater detail about their background and significance for planning. Part of the mythology of chaos theory involves the infamous butterfly's flapping wings. The imagery is meant to portray an interconnected world where even small things can have potential significance. Obviously, as far as this work goes we cannot hope to cover more than a handful of elements corresponding to each of the five factors. The choice of what to include and exclude, what emphasis to place and what connections to make is a purely subjective one.

POLITICAL AND SOCIAL WILL

In his 1989 essay 'The end of history?' Francis Fukuyama claimed that the world was converging in its ideological outlooks – from one of diametrically opposed positions as found in the free market economies of the West and the control economies of the former Soviet Union to one of liberal democracy. He went further and celebrated not only the hegemony of Western values but 'the end of history as such; that is, the end point of mankind's ideological evolution and the universalisation of Western liberal democracy as the final form of human government' (1989: 3). Although Fukuyama can be criticised on a number of fronts it is difficult to disagree with his main points. Drawing on Marxist dialectics he proposes that human history has moved down an evolutionary path where competing ideologies (e.g. communism, fascism, liberalism) have been tested and the clear winner now dominates world thinking. Although conflicts can (and still will) arise, liberal democracy is now the only game in town, even in its many varied forms. While we may disagree with some of Fukuyama's analysis, especially regarding the possibility of future ideologies emerging and the conflicts inherent between the liberal and democratic elements of liberal democracy, we will agree with his broad contention for the purposes of this chapter.

Given the likelihood of the world converging on ideological common ground and moving towards one form of liberal democracy or another, what will this imply for political and/or social values? Firstly, it will emphasise the importance of growth: the liberal aspect of liberal democracy. If concerns such as the environment are moving up the political agenda then a more balanced growth encompassing social concerns will be necessary. But this does not detract from the fact that growth will be needed to pay for this concern. The UK in particular has shifted more quickly than most from a manufacturing base to a more service-orientated economy – it was the first country to earn more from invisible exports (services) than visible ones. As other countries make this shift the UK will have to build its comparative advantage in new motors of growth. McRae (1994) argues that the traditional factors of production (land, capital, etc.) are becoming increasingly redundant. The new important factors are qualitative, or adding value, through, for example, organisational quality or motivation. A well-trained workforce is crucial for continued growth. This will involve not only what is *added* but also what is *subtracted*. An aspect of quality will be what people no longer have to do such as actually travel to work, fill in a tax return (or submit a planning application?).

The role of government as a mediator for political and societal pressure and a provider of this growth will increasingly be constrained both by commercial forces and supranational bodies such as the EU. Common approaches to foreign and domestic policies such as agriculture and the economy are limiting autonomous action. Information about the effectiveness of domestic policies is becoming more easily available, further constraining the freedom of governments by pressuring them to adopt approaches which are seen to be successful elsewhere (e.g. privatisation). Further pressure is being applied by enlarged access to world markets where both capital and labour are becoming increasingly mobile, breaking down national barriers and allowing free movement between competitive economies.

As far as the democratic element of liberal democracy is concerned there have been seismic shifts in the demand for greater participation in all aspects of decision-making. As Gyford in his evidence to the Widdicombe Committee on local government stated:

> . . . there has been a move away from a society with a large degree of consensus on interests and values, towards a more diverse and fragmented society within which there are asserted a plurality of sectional interests and values (quoted in Stoker, 1991: 15).

Stoker goes on to note that the emergence of 'single-issue' politics has allowed people to identify common interests and voice them. The terrain of politics is now strewn with an assertive and active public who are less willing to accept authoritarian styles of leadership or to trust the 'all knowledgeable' technocrat. Part of the reason for the emergence of the sceptical and active citizen lies in the decreased autonomy of national governments outlined above. Another reason are the tensions aroused through the need of government to prioritise and allocate increasingly scarce resources for public sector services. But there is undoubtedly a cultural shift in people's attitudes for greater involvement which has complex origins in changing social norms, increased information and even a reaction to the authoritarian style of leadership under the New Right.

So whereas national governments have increasingly seen powers removed to supranational bodies and the discipline of the market there has also been increased subnational pressure both challenging decisions and wanting a greater say in them. The role of national governments will still be one of setting policy on the majority of domestic issues. However, the mechanisms of how this can be achieved are shifting towards regulation not provision and mediating the increasing pressures and tensions of the two elements of liberal democracy. As McRae (1994) puts it, the high-water mark of intervention has been reached, privatisation is sweeping the world and the private provision of services is now likely to be the norm. In addition to the perceived primacy of markets, the concerns of this empowered electorate will also be an important input into political and social will. What are these concerns? They will be multifarious and shifting: health, education, the environment, jobs, etc. In addition to the need for economic growth discussed above I shall focus on two aspects that will have significance for planning.

THE ENVIRONMENT

It seems that sustainability and sustainable development are now the political and social will of most of the world. Notwithstanding the differences between sustainability and sustainable development, both are now becoming almost meta-concepts that are (in their broadest sense) as fundamental to our lives as 'freedom' and 'justice' (Evans, 1997). It appears clear that sustainability emerged as a grass-roots level concern that was forced upon government by popular desire. It is also clear that it has come into conflict with short-term strategies of market economies. The implications of what is or could be meant by sustainability or sustainable development are also unclear, as is the commitment to tackle environmental problems of some of the largest economies and polluters in the world. There is also an emerging weariness and cynicism as everyone from supermarkets to multinationals jump on the bandwagon promoting their 'greenness'. This has been compounded by the use of sustainability as a mask for some single-issue groups. The Campaign for the Protection of Rural England and the Town and Country Planning Association are arguing that it means less development in the countryside and more development in the countryside respectively. The truth is, nobody really knows.

Notwithstanding these debates the environment will remain a dominant influence upon planning. Pollution, urban sprawl, inner-city decay, air and water quality, CO_2 emissions, climate change, etc. are all of concern and are all currently influencing government policy, not only in planning but across other disciplines. The challenge for planning is to integrate these concerns into plans and strategies for an area. But this should not underestimate the need for an integrated approach with other bodies and agencies. Nor must it be forgotten that the environment is one of many pressures and concerns of political and social will. Employment and social improvement are also seen as concerns of sustainability as if in some way they are all compatible and no choices or conflicts exist. While what is actually meant by sustainability and sustainable development remains obscure and

localities increasingly compete for footloose global capital, longer-term strategies
are likely to yield to the shorter-term necessity of jobs. Different strategies are
emerging – the 'deep green' limits to growth, the techno-green fix and the shallow
green-based route. They are emerging within a centralised legal and administrative
framework. Each places different emphases on aspects of sustainability whether it is
'virtuous growth', conservation or preservation. The problem for society and
planning is not only the tensions between the environment and growth but also
between the national and the local. While these tensions persist, real progress is
unlikely.

SERVICE QUALITY

The 'added value' of services and quality in provision has already been identified as
a future engine of growth, but it is also an undoubted political demand. There
have been two aspects that have and will continue to influence planning practice.
First are the changes that have been introduced by previous governments in an
attempt, as they see it, to improve the quality, choice, value and accountability of
public services. Second has been the growing demand generally for improved
services from the public as these services have become increasingly transparent
and open to scrutiny. These changes have been closely allied to the increasing
demand for participation generally and the distrust of professionals discussed
above.

Although Evans (1997) claims that planning is simply another public policy
process like tax collection or waste management there are some important differences. For a start, contrary to many practitioners' own perceptions, planning is not
a technical activity but a political one and as such it is more difficult to set
standards for service provision. It is not simply a case of 'how quickly?' as in the
eight-week figure standard for planning applications. Discretion and day-to-day
policy-making are inherent within the system, as are a complex mediation of
different inputs. As such it is difficult to set qualitative standards for service
delivery as the Conservative governments throughout the 1980s and 1990s found.

However, an important influence on the changing nature of planning practice
has been the introduction in July 1991 of Citizen's Charter indices. Local planning
authorities have for many years been judged on speed of decision-making (the
infamous eight-week figures) and have also had to make quarterly returns to the
DoE, Scottish and Welsh Offices on a wide range of other criteria. In addition, the
National Planning Forum has published its own 'Charter' on development control,
attempting to codify and quantify various aspects of the planning process. The
Citizen's Charter introduced a number of factors that would be published and
Audited nationally comparing speed and 'quality' of service. As Prior (1995: 88)
points out, the Citizen's Charter approach sought to change the way services were
managed, organised and delivered to achieve four main objectives:

- Raise quality
- Increase choice
- Secure better value
- Extend accountability

The mechanisms to achieve this included a range of approaches including:

- Privatisation
- Competition
- Contracting out
- Performance-related pay
- Independent inspectorates
- Published performance targets
- Information on standards
- Complaints procedures
- Redress

There can be little doubt that an emphasis and demand for quality are welcome in a profession and organisational structure that has been moribund for so long. However, there must be concern about the accompanying shift to privatisation that the Conservatives considered synonymous with quality. But this is not simply a legacy for planning: one of the Labour government's first actions in 1997 was to make it clear that they would reverse this trend, adding 'quality' as a further criterion in any future competitive tendering (*Guardian*, 3 June 1997).

The implications of this for planning are significant. Higgins and Allmendinger (forthcoming) have charted the largely unappreciated extent of privatisation within planning and have concluded that the increased demands for transparency, service quality (however defined) and accountability are not problem free. There are potential and existing issues that the profession appears either unwilling or unable to face. As privatisation of planning continues, public planning practice will increasingly be caught between the desire for greater public involvement, the need to take on more aspects of work as the environment (in its broadest sense) becomes more influential and the need to provide a higher quality service including greater speed and involvement. Again, like the environment above, the implications are of a radically different organisation and direction for planning in the twenty-first century.

IMPLEMENTATION AGENCIES AND SOCIETAL CONSERVATISM

I have merged these two factors of influence because of their close relationship, particularly with regard to planning. Owing to the highly centralised nature of the

UK, government is heavily dependent upon others to execute or implement its policies. As studies of the 1980s clearly demonstrate, these agencies, e.g. local authorities, quangos, health boards, were able in some cases to modify or in some cases totally alter this policy (Marsh and Rhodes, 1992; Allmendinger and Thomas, 1998). As such they acted as a 'brake' on national political will and demonstrated a will of their own. The organisations that planners are most obviously associated with are local authorities and they will form the basis of this section. However, two other important factors will also be examined. The first is the body of local opinion that has influence either through formal (i.e. voting) or less formal (e.g. pressure) channels upon the local authority and the role of planners. The second is the planning profession itself.

So what will be the organisational environment for planning in the twenty-first century and what factors will influence the implementation of national political will? There are a number of elements that will have a direct impact.

There will generally be a reduced role for the state as governments across the developed world haul back the frontiers of their influence. Deregulation of direct service provision will continue (as it has under governments of the left and right). This will be for a number of reasons including:

- The need to reduce the proportion of GDP spent (no electorate will vote in a government that now promises to increase taxes to improve services)
- To stabilise if not reduce tax rates in order to encourage increasingly footloose international capital
- Because recent experience has demonstrated that governments and their agencies are not as good at providing cheap, effective services as the private sector

The implications are that the remainder of the public sector will be increasingly left to private and market provision with governments becoming more regulators than providers. These trends have been evident in local government throughout the 1980s and 1990s. As Stewart and Stoker (1995: 3–4) point out, this period has witnessed some key changes including:

- Financial constraint
- Fragmentation of local government
- Commitment to competition
- Separation of responsibility for a service from the act of providing the service
- Development of an enabling role
- Closer relationship between paying for and receiving a service
- Greater emphasis on customer choice
- Greater scope for individual and private provision
- Producer interests within local government being challenged
- Commitment to developing more 'businesslike' management

- Increased emphasis on new forms of accountability to the centre and within the locality
- Challenge to the mechanisms of local representative democracy

These trends will and are having a number of influences upon planning though an important aspect as far as we are concerned is the extent to which they can be seen to be pushing away from a more participative approach. Their emphasis is on efficiency and effectiveness through a greater centralisation and market orientation of services. However, as we mentioned above, there is also a corresponding push for a greater plurality and participation in planning at a local level. As Cullingworth (1997) argues, planning practice is increasingly having to respond to a plurality of interests, most of which seem to be arguing for different means *and* ends. The result has been a sclerosis of action. Not, as Cullingworth (1997) claims, because the system itself is becoming too locally led, but because this pressure for more local solutions has met a centralising tendency in government. Following the introduction of the highly centralised 'plan-led' system, plan preparation time has increased dramatically as the number of observations and objections have mushroomed. There are no reasons why the demand for more participation is likely to reverse and every reason to believe it is likely to continue.

The tensions between the shifts in local government organisation and grass-roots participation are obvious: one or the other will lose out and during the past 18 years or so it has been participation. Planners and other public sector professionals have been caught by these competing demands, but this is not to say that they have been entirely innocent bystanders. Some planners have made conscious decisions to follow either innovative participation techniques (e.g. Planning for Real) or speed of decision-making. These have been in the minority. Most local authorities have tended to 'muddle through' attempting (as usual) to balance irreconcilable differences. Because of the encouragement (through, for example, government guidance and the Royal Town Planning Institute (RTPI)) to reconcile the irreconcilable the majority of planners have taken the attitude (with some relish) that planning is a technical, apolitical exercise and balance can be achieved. As Evans (1997) argues, such an attitude is a prerequisite of professionalism.

Two implications arise from this. First, there is the attitude that accompanies the 'planning as an apolitical profession' – planners know best. Patently, planning is about as political as you can get. But as long as the myth of objectivity continues then planners will continue to feel that they 'know best'. This has been demonstrated clearly through attitudes towards the role of the public. A survey I carried out for my former employer, Mendip District Council, demonstrated that planners and the public had very different conceptions of their respective roles. Of residents and parish councils surveyed, 72% thought they should be involved in planning on the basis of participation (with the local view prevailing), while three-quarters of planners thought they should involve the community on a consultative basis (with them or the planning committee having the final say). This view is not damning itself, but it must be remembered that planners have considerable discretion within the planning process for them to set the agendas for discussion, decide on the *amount* of involvement as well as the *level* (e.g. notification, consultation or participation) as well as weigh the outcome. Even if a more participative approach is taken there is nothing to stop the outcome being ignored.

This brings us to the second point, the assumption that planners are in some way imbued with a liberal conception of society and a common agreement on what is meant by the 'public good'. This is what planners and their professional body, the RTPI, would like everyone to think. As Evans (1993, 1997) and Reade (1987) have shown, it is actually a requirement of achieving professional hegemony and all the benefits that accompany it. The truth is rather different.

> Planners are people like everyone else; they have their own agendas, grudges, desires and idiosyncrasies and these are reflected in day-to-day practice (Allmendinger, 1996: 231).

The main basis for the apolitical and benign view of planners and planning is to be found in the role and attitude of the RTPI. Evans (1993) claims that its predecessor, the Town Planning Institute, sought to establish itself as a technical and apolitical body separate from the architecture and engineering professions that had spawned it. To do this it had to argue that there was such a thing as 'good town planning' in process and ends – something that required technical skill and training. And they were successful in doing so. But no profession can exist without the explicit or implicit support of the state. A state needs professions to carry out its functions and legitimise its power and decisions. In return the state grants autonomy and status to the profession to regulate membership and ensure standards. But it is too simple to lump the professional body (the RTPI) together with its membership. Professional bodies, according to Grant (1995), act as another 'layer' of control in a corporate relationship with the state. It is not the members of the profession that negotiate with the state, but their professional body. And through allegiance to that body (which grants professional status) individual members are bound. Thus the state relinquishes the responsibility and burdens of regulation in return for implementation of policies.

It was the lobbying and 'apolitical' stance of the Town Planning Institute combined with the need for post-war planning and the 1947 Act that ensured planning's future as a profession was secure. (Though as Reade (1987) points out, lobbying for a profession is a highly political act in itself.) Since then it has pursued the classic roles of a profession including:

- Regulation of professional entry through accreditation of courses, continuing professional development requirements and mentoring new members
- Negotiating with government over policy instruments
- Maintaining that problems are 'solvable'

- Distribution and dissemination of 'good practice' through Planning Advice Notes, the Institute's journal and annual summer school
- Maintaining an apolitical stance

So the spectre is raised of planners not being as objective as they either think or portray themselves. But all of this rests on the technical and expert nature of the job itself.

As Healey and Underwood (1979) have pointed out, planners have succeeded in arguing for this status on the basis on a variety of ideals rather than any particular expertise or skill. A number of writers have pointed to the lack of an agreed body of knowledge that constitutes planning (e.g. Davies, 1972; Reade, 1987; Evans, 1993, 1997). Equally, it is difficult to actually identify any specific or unique skills that planners have. Nor do planners have any agreement on what they are aiming at when they plan beyond vague (and comforting) platitudes such as 'sustainability'.

The situation can be summarised thus: planning as a profession is regulated by the RTPI. This body has entered into a corporate relationship with the state where each party benefits. The state has a compliant body to implement its policies while at the same time providing it with some scientific or technical credibility; the professional body gains a monopoly on influence as well as the status and benefits of a profession. Recent changes in central and local government and in the planning system and processes have begun to centralise and commercialise the local state. The planning profession has been almost mute on this (as they have to be apolitical). But, even if planners as individuals wanted to depart from this line, their professional body restricts them. However, it is unlikely, beyond a few cases that they would choose to do so.

Against these changes there has been a growing will for greater involvement and participation – a demand that has not met with much support from central government, the planning profession or planners themselves. It is in all three's interest to resist this. But, as the skills and 'expertise' of planners are at best questionable – why do we need a profession of 'expert' planners at all? On the whole I would argue that the true obstacle to a more local planning is the cabal of planner, profession and state. As George Bernard Shaw wrote in *The Doctor's Dilemma* in 1911, 'All professions are conspiracies against the laity.'

In conclusion, I have argued that planning faces an uncertain future if it remains as it is. The professional, organisational and legislative aspects of planning are increasingly estranged from the issues that they are being asked to address.

CHAOS AND COMPLEXITY

We have now covered the three 'above the line' factors of influence (see Figure 1). In addition to these three is an increasing awareness of the extent to which there are limits to the ability of planners and others to 'know' or perceive. Similarly, it seems that a succession of theories of state and political activity are redundant in an increasingly complex world. This is why we now turn to two different interpretations of planning and society – the 'can we?' of chaos and complexity and the 'should we?' of postmodernity and post-structuralism.

Chaos and complexity go right to the heart of futurology and planning. Although planning as we know it in the UK has been around for nearly 50 years there are certain aspects that still remain a mystery. There are questions that both practitioners and academics have struggled to resolve, questions that seem to have no answer and if asked by a bemused applicant or member of the public would elicit either a variety of responses or a mumbled silence. For example:

- Why is it that however well you 'plan', things turn out differently than expected?
- Why are we left with so many planning 'disasters' from car-choked cities to homeless young people?
- And why, no matter how hard you try or no matter how inclusive a process you attempt, are people left feeling isolated and frustrated at the system?

One answer to all of these questions is that they involve complexity. They are not simple problems or questions and do not have simple solutions or answers. This is not to say that some have not tried to tackle what Bruton and Nicholson (1987: 52) term 'wicked problems'. The recognition that planning is complex is hardly new, especially with regard to strategy formulation. Bruton and Nicholson (1987) identify four main attempts to deal with such complexity; the systems approach (Chadwick, 1971), the organisational theory approach (Higgins, 1980), contingency approaches (Newstrom et al., 1975) and the strategic choice approach (Friend and Jessop, 1969; Christenson, 1985). All of these attempts see planners as experts able to tackle complexity through greater knowledge and control. Their poverty is that we are still wrestling with the same questions. My points of departure are twofold. First, in not treating complexity as an instrumental problem and second, in arguing that elements of chaos and complexity should be welcomed not feared.

This is not the place (nor is there space) to delve into a detailed debate on chaos and complexity. Interested readers should consult Waldrop (1992), Casti (1994), Gleick (1988) and Phelan (1995) who, among others, have pointed out how chaos and complexity theory has the potential to contribute valuable insights into strategy formulation. Complexity developed from chaos – a word that since Genesis has been the antithesis of order and progress. But as numerous authors have pointed out, chaos does not mean disorder, but that it is extremely difficult if not impossible to model certain systems even though the systems themselves are ordered. Chaos is part of the emerging science of complexity and is universally seen as *a sensitive dependence on initial conditions* (Gleick, 1988; Cohen and

Stewart, 1994; Coveney and Highfield, 1995). On the whole chaos theorists now believe that (Gleick, 1988: 303):

- Simple systems do not behave in simple ways
- Complex behaviour does not imply complex causes
- Different systems do not necessarily behave differently

But chaos itself is only a subset of a much more general field termed complexity (Lissack, 1996):

> Chaos tells us that simple laws can have very complicated – indeed, unpredictable – consequences. Simple causes can produce complex effects. Complexity theory tells us the opposite: Complex causes can produce simple effects (Cohen and Stewart, 1994: 2).

Complex systems are characterised by (Waldrop, 1992: 11):

- A great many independent agents interacting with each other in a great many ways
- Spontaneous self-organisation
- Adaptation and (co)evolution
- Dynamism

Complexity is therefore qualitatively different from chaos (though the two terms are often used interchangeably) (Phelan, 1995: 14):

> Complexity refers to the condition of the universe which is integrated and yet too rich and varied for us to understand in simple mechanistic or linear ways. . . . Complexity deals with the nature of emergence, innovation, learning and adaptation.

Compared to a simple linear system, complexity demonstrates clear differences (Table 1).

As Bird (1997) has pointed out, chaos and complexity can be found almost anywhere in nature, science and society. Complexity and chaos have now been investigated for over two decades and a number of findings are now well established. These include:

1. Many dynamical and complex systems do not reach equilibrium.
2. Processes that appear random may be chaotic.
3. Two entities with similar initial states can follow radically divergent paths over time. Behaviour can be sensitive to small differences in initial conditions.
4. Complex patterns can arise from interaction of agents following relatively simple rules – properties are emergent in that they appear at different hierarchical levels.

Table 1 *Characteristics of complex and simple systems*

Complex	Simple
Counter-intuitive, acausal behaviour (i.e. it did not turn out as expected)	Reducible behaviour
Adaptive behaviour through constant and varied feedback	Few interactions or feedback/feedforward loops
Diffusion of power and authority	Centralised decision-making and concentrated power
Irreducible. Breakdown of aspects does not lead to total collapse	Decomposable. Weak interactions among components

Adapted from Casti, 1994: 269.

5. Complex systems may resist reductionist analysis.
6. Time series that seem to be random may actually be fractals.
7. Complex systems can be self-organising (Phelan, 1995).

Forms of Complexity

Some premature conclusions have been reached regarding the implications of chaos and complexity upon strategic planning. Sensitivity to initial conditions implies that long-term forecasting or strategy-making is difficult if not impossible. Certainly if one was to rely on chaos theory as a basis for characterising strategy formulation, futility would be a reasonable conclusion. This could be demonstrated in Figure 1.

If we take a hypothetical example from strategy formulation and assume that the factors that will influence the ability of a strategy to meet its objectives are infinite (as chaos theory invites us to do) and plotted along the x-axis and then give these a y-coordinate to represent their notional complexity we have a ranked order of factors running from the most complex (to the left) and the less complex (to the right).

The list along the x-axis is infinite though I have taken Gleick's butterfly's wings as a notional and metaphoric end point. If we now plot a line across the graph (dotted) above which it is more likely that a strategy will be able to predict and control the factors, and below which it is less likely that control is possible then we can visualise what elements any strategy could hope to be based upon. If we add up the notional areas of factors above the line and compare them to areas of factors below the line we will naturally find that *any* strategy be it land use planning or otherwise is highly unlikely to achieve its aims – in fact, mathematically it will be impossible given the infinite nature of factors along the x-axis. However, we still plan. Why?

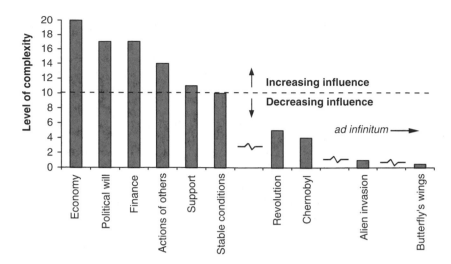

Figure 1 *I realise the drawbacks of this approach that is intended only as an illustration of complexity in strategy formulation. Leaving aside the ability to quantify the complexity of factors (something that cost–benefit analysis has struggled with) the notional line of complexity may vary from factor to factor. So, while finance is less complex than, say, the economy as a whole it may be far easier to control. Nevertheless, the overall point remains. The total area beneath the line will always be greater than the total area above it according to chaos theory. And yet we still plan*

1. The main reason is that not all aspects of systems are complex – large parts of social systems are linear (Bird, 1997). Organisations are composed of intelligent individuals who learn and proactively organise themselves (Lin, 1996). But as Lane and Maxfield (1996) point out, this level of planning depends on a certain kind of situation and foresight. Some situations are clearly and easily controllable; e.g. those with fixed goals, time horizons, resources. In planning this could be development control of, say, a house extension. Lane and Maxfield's other two categories of situations, the 'complicated' and the 'complex', could be seen to include plans in their wider sense. The distinction between the controllable and the complicated/complex is both the time horizon of uncertainty and knowledge of all the possible consequences. The problem for planners is seeing that controllable situations are diminishing and that kinds of planning such as strategic planning may now be located in the complicated or even complex categories. When modern planning was initiated 50-odd years ago this was not the case – strategic planning, as we will see later, was far more controllable. There appears a conservatism within planning in accepting this.
2. One possible (and to some seditious) reason for this could be termed the myth of planning as control. Being in charge or control is the core belief of many

planners who feel technically and morally responsible through what Gabriel (1996) terms quasi-magical rites for the future. To lose such mystique would be to reveal their mortality not only for the planners but for the public. Planning fulfils an important psychological need in the public's mind that 'someone' is in charge if only to provide a scapegoat when things go wrong. Under this view plans are important defensive techniques aimed at exorcising fear of losing control. This is not to say that all planning is groundless as mentioned in point (1) or that it cannot achieve some objectives, but to say that plans themselves have functions beyond achieving their objectives.

3. The ontological nature of chaos and complexity does not preclude a human desire/search for some kind of certainty (i.e. the basis of planning) even in the face of entropy as described above. Planning and plans do achieve some things, but it is notoriously difficult to monitor and mostly avoided (Reade, 1987). Often failure is put down to too *little* rather than too much planning (e.g. Breheny and Congdon, 1989; Healey, 1997) or 'political realities' (Rydin, 1997: 336). As other research has shown, the relationship between policies and decisions is estranged (Bruton and Nicholson, 1987) and the success of strategies has as much to do with the market conditions in the area as the inherent nature of plans themselves (Hall *et al.*, 1973). Little research has been carried out examining the nature of success and failure in planning (or indeed what those terms actually mean), success/failure for whom? In the meantime planners and plans go on. The reason that success and failure are vague are because they are complex. This hints at the next point: is planning complex?

IS LAND USE PLANNING A COMPLEX SYSTEM?

The terms 'complex system' and 'complex adaptive system' (CAS) have been used in relation to many systems including biology, economics and meteorology. It is becoming clear that chaos and complexity will feature to varying degrees in social systems as well as natural ones (Eve *et al.*, 1997). There is no clear definition of a CAS though Waldrop's (1992) four characteristics provide such a framework against which to assess planning:

1. *A great many independent agents interacting with each other in a great many ways.* The UK planning system is highly political in its structure and operations and has been portrayed as an arena for interest mediation (Healey *et al.*, 1988). The number and divergence of agents and interests in the system and processes coupled with the discretionary basis of planning and the different roles of planners and councillors, developers, etc. mean that outcomes cannot be guaranteed or 'read off' from the strategies within which they operate. While the system lacks absolute 'order' (in the sense of a simple

system portrayed in Table 1 or more likely to be found in some European systems) it is also not chaotic. There is a level of stability and complexity evident somewhere between the two extremes.

2. *Spontaneous self-organisation.* Waldrop (1992), Kauffman (1995) and others have mainly explained biological and economic systems in this regard though Phelan (1995) has also applied these ideas to business organisation. In economies Kauffman has stressed the non-linear characteristics – the 'system' 'learns' and reorganises itself through feedback and price signals. Land use planning is not based on price mechanisms, but it does have other types of feedback through exogenous factors such as political and professional routes. The example of the sudden change from *laissez-faire* to plan-led system in the late 1980s is a good example. Pressure through electoral popularity, financial and professional disquiet led the government to make a massive U-turn in the late 1980s back towards a plan-led system. The planning process changed significantly though the system itself changed only slightly when Section 54A was introduced (which is another characteristic of complex systems in Table 1).

3. *Adaption and co-evolution.* In some ways this is related to point (2) especially with regards to land use planning. Specifically it refers to more concrete system-specific feedback/feed forward loops. Such loops proliferate in planning. Its political nature means that it must retain legitimacy. Formally, feedback/feed forward is found in processes such as participation, planning committees of elected members, appeals, policy guidance and hierarchies of systems (central, regional, local). They all serve to diffuse to the locus of planning and make it evolve in response to pressure.

4. *Dynamism.* Complex, non-linear systems change over time. Land use planning has certainly done this in *certain respects.* Although the system as set out in 1947 more or less resembles the current system, the processes, priorities and objectives have changed significantly. From blueprint planning to project planning and back again. From a top-down professionally led process to a more bottom-up publicly led approach. From market leading to trend following. Some elements such as green belts have remained mainly because of public pressure, but the process has shown its ability to adapt over short periods.

Consequently, planning could be regarded as exhibiting elements of chaos and complexity. It also could be defined as a CAS; neither order (e.g. central planning) or chaos (unrestrained market forces) but a point somewhere in between the two. Although there are normative debates about where this point is or should be (e.g. the left arguing it is too near chaos and the right too near order) developments in complexity theory demonstrate that complex adaptive systems emerge to a natural position through evolution and co-operation that they strive to maintain independent of normative considerations and even political interference; the *edge* of chaos. Further, as Stacey (1996b) rightly concludes, planning as a CAS operates in an environment that is for the most part characterised by the four features above (e.g. the economy, society and politics) so as together they form a co-evolving supra system that 'learns' its way to the future. We therefore have a nested approach to CASs:

- The brain as a collection of neurones
- The individual as parts of groups
- Groups and organisations interacting to form societal, economic and political systems which interact to form a global CAS

COMPLEXITY AND CELLULAR AUTOMATA

An area of work closely related to complexity and emergence is the field of cellular automata (CA) (Batty et al., 1997). CA is based on simulations of lifelike conditions in an artificial world run on simple rules. Such rules determine whether a cell is 'alive' or 'dead' through its relation to other cells. Although CA dates back to the beginnings of digital computing its main development and links to complexity were made by Stephen Wolfram (1986). He found that cellular automata rules fall into one of four distinct classes (Wolfram, 1986). Class I situations are when a random pattern of cells are created and after some initial activity all 'die'. Class II situations were little better. Here cells began to form into groups and form patterns, though did little else, and after a short while appeared 'dead' or static. Class III rules went to the other extreme. They followed a chaotic cycle of 'ons' and 'offs' not resembling any pattern. Finally, Class IV situations fell somewhere between Class II and III. They did not produce dead systems, but did not produce chaos either. They formed structures that grew, divided, proposed and developed. Chris Langton built upon Wolfram's findings and drew parallels between the four classes and natural systems such as population. Running various simulations he demonstrated that at a point somewhere between complete order and total chaos was a phase or transitional point(s) where there was a combination of order and chaos that produced dynamic growth – the best of both worlds. Complexity emerges as a combination of evolution and co-operation.

As Waldrop (1992: 293) has summarised, in between chaos and order:

> . . . you . . . find complexity: a class of behaviours in which the components of the system never quite lock into place, yet never quite dissolve into turbulence, either. These are systems that are stable enough to store information, and yet evanescent enough to transmit it. These are the systems that can be organised to perform complex computations, to react to the world, to be spontaneous, adaptive and alive.

From sand piles, to earthquakes to traffic jams, self-organisation and complexity have been identified at the edge of chaos. Traffic will reach gridlock in a city until people begin to look at alternative routes and forms of transport, but the system hardly ever collapses, just teeters on the edge of collapse. Take the examples of the former Soviet Union. A totalitarian regime that was centralised and sclerotic: a 'simple' ordered system as portrayed in Table 1. Or Dickensian London and the resultant horrors at the other extreme: a chaotic system. It is not difficult to see the correspondence between natural CASs and social CASs:

> Every human organisation is a network of individual agents interacting with each other and with agents in other organisations that constitute its environment. That is exactly . . . a CAS . . . (Stacey, 1996b: 16).

It is not making a quantum leap to suggest that somewhere between total chaos and order a more 'healthy' and creative society lies. But where between the two? Traditionally this has been the debate of left and right in politics. But what complexity theory argues is that there is a 'natural' point where the optimum balance between chaos and order space is to be found. This dimension cannot necessarily be seen or planned for as it is constantly changing and possibly unpredictable (as chaos theory warns us). But this does not mean that we cannot plan, only that we should plan differently to take *advantage* of complexity rather than try and avoid or minimise it. Linking this debate through to strategic planning we can see (at a very crude level) how strategy formulation at different times has interacted with these four classes (Phelan, 1995). Class I strategic planning is unnecessary as the system is closed. Class II planning is predictable and could be seen to correspond roughly to a period in the 1950s and early 1960s when Keynesian demand management and top-down government intervention were possible. Strategic planning was relatively easy as predictable patterns emerged and the command and control approach to the economy combined with a largely passive population allowed for strategies to be set and largely met. Class III could be seen to correspond to the aftershock of the 1973 oil crisis, the rise of a more politically aware population and the collapse of blueprint style Class II planning. During the 1970s strategic planning became difficult beyond specifying very broad targets: chaos was the order of the day. Class IV systems showed a return to a more complex but more predictable system in the 1980s and 1990s as the approach to strategic planning took a broader perspective. Rather than specifying targets, the government of the day prescribed that broad conditions were outlined and planning became market enabling rather than leading. This has been termed the 'project-led' approach to planning (Brindley *et al.*, 1996) and was widely seen as an 'attack' (Ambrose, 1986; Thornley, 1993). The ideological approach of the New Right governments during this period represented a sharp shift towards market mechanisms but also a move towards centralisation (a characteristic of a simple system in Table 1). They could therefore not be seen as a conscious response to complexity. In terms of strategic land use planning these moves were seen by many including residents, landowners, developers and planners as a shift too far towards chaos and were followed by a shift back towards greater order in the late 1980s. This corresponds to what Gell-Mann (1994) and others describe as punctuated equilibrium where change may take a time to arise but when it does it is sudden.

Strategic planning in these different classes obviously varies, though it worth stressing here that not all aspects of land use planning will fall clearly into these classes. Out of the four classes strategic planning is only possible in two: Class II (predictable) and Class IV (complexity) and only to a certain degree in the latter class. The concept of co-evolution has been explored to describe the relationship between a system such as planning and a wider system within which it fits such as a liberal economy. The evidence points to the adaptation of the former to the latter in general apart from when a punctuated equilibrium is reached: the sudden collapse of communism in eastern Europe is one example, the fall of Margaret Thatcher is another (Eve *et al.*, 1997). So what does all this have to do with planning? Complexity theory has two lessons to teach. The first is the problem of strategic planning in a chaotic and complex world. The second is the propensity for and advantages of allowing systems to behave as if on the edge of chaos. The two are naturally linked. The implications will be expanded upon later, but first it is necessary to examine another area of thinking that has significance and connections to chaos and complexity.

POSTMODERNITY AND POST-STRUCTURALISM

Like chaos and complexity there is not room here to go into too much detail on postmodernism and post-structuralism. So what I intend to do here is provide a broad landscape and briefly explain its relevance for planning. Many of the changes and influences we have discussed in *political will* could be described as postmodern or a result of New Times. However, what I am more concerned with here are the underlying trends which have led to these pressures.

There has been an academic industry in postmodern writing during the past 15 years or so. It is now extremely uncommon to come across work in any subject that does not make a reference to postmodernism or postmodernity. A highly contested and charged debate has ensued but basically we can identify three broad elements: postmodernity as style, epoch and method (Dear, 1988). The question 'do we live in New Times?' is still no nearer being answered. On one extreme are Lyotard (1984) and Bauman (1988) who consider that there has been a definite break from modernism and term it postmodernism. This new epoch is charac-terised by depthlessness, a consequence weakening of historicity, a fragmentation of the subject, the omnipresence of a pastiche and a prevalence of 'nostalgia mode'. At the other extreme are Marxists such as Callinicos (1989) who consider that postmodernists have exaggerated changes or ignored the links between any devel-opments in society and the underlying influence and logic of capitalism. Any changes that have occurred are termed late rather than postmodern. Habermas (1984, 1987) also criticises from a left-wing though more sympathetic perspective the 'anti-modernisms' of some postmodern writers but concedes that certain negative aspects of modernity (e.g. instrumental rationality) have come to dominate people's 'lifeworlds'.

Richard Rorty takes a more pragmatic line, criticising modernists and postmodernists – modernists for the over-optimistic view of the benefits of the Enlightenment and postmodernists for their readiness to destroy rather than create. The debate is far from resolved, though as Smart (1993) points out, it is alluring to conclude that the present is sufficiently different to enable it to be termed 'new'. It is also worth remembering that not everyone shares the change 'we' may be experiencing – important continuities remain in a society still dominated by power relations of value, class, sexuality and gender (Hebdige, 1989). This caution is reinforced by post-structural analyses. The issues facing people in their everyday lives are real regardless of whether they are termed late or postmodern.

Out of this maelstrom of normative and empirical work there is little of any substance. Smart (1993: 16) probably sums up the situation best, he says that there has been a

> . . . shared sense that significant cultural transformations have been taking place in western societies during the period since the end of the second world war and further that the term 'postmodernism' may be appropriate, for the time being at least, to describe some of the implied shifts in sensibilities, practices and discourse formations.

The debate concerning postmodernism as epoch has been less contested in the field of *method* or post-structuralism. Strohmayer and Hannah (1992) claim that the 'crises of representation' are the real challenge to modernity, particularly the

> . . . fragile and problematic representational character of language, the disarticulation of words and things, and the ways in which meaning is increasingly sustained through mechanisms of self-referentiality (Smart, 1993: 20).

Any kind of independent reality or 'truth' is brought into question because, as Derrida argues, all knowledge (including truth) is a social creation as it is impossible to separate the rhetorical of the text from the context, message or meaning.

This is a broad and simplistic mapping of the terrain of post-structuralism and postmodernism, but it serves to flag up the main elements in relation to planning. Various authors have sought to interpret these debates in relation to planning theory and practice. The starting point for most is the assertion that planning is a thoroughly modern project (e.g. Healey, 1983; Low, 1991) and to similarly characterise the period in which planning now finds itself as postmodern (Fillion,

1996). The postmodern challenge to planning according to Moore-Milroy (1991: 183) is deconstructive (questioning conventional beliefs), anti-foundationalist (dispensing with universal bases of truth), non-dualistic (questioning the gap between truth and opinion) and encouraging a plurality of difference. It is there-fore a radical challenge. It is also a challenge that taps into the *Zeitgeist* as well into sentiments of planning practice. While it is difficult to agree upon and pin down, the broad thrusts of difference, respect, challenge and investigation are evident.

There is naturally a problem. According to Beauregard (1996), planning is modern in that it still attempts to (i) bring reason and democracy to bear on capitalist urbanisation, (ii) guide state decision-making with technical rather than political rationality, (iii) produce a co-ordinated and functional urban form organ-ised around collective goals, and (iv) use economic growth to create a middle-class society. The result is that US planning finds itself suspended between modernity and postmodernity with 'practitioners and theorists having few clues as to how to (re)establish themselves on solid ground' (Beauregard, 1996: 227).

The upshot of this is the claim that planning (modern) has lost touch with society (postmodern). I have argued elsewhere (Allmendinger, forthcoming) that this portrayal is misleading and simplistic. Planning practice is adapting and questioning the master-narratives demonised by postmodernists such as Lyotard. As such it is becoming more sensitive *on the whole* to the local and pursuing difference rather than similarity. The problem is that the system itself (processes, guidance, legislation, etc.) is mostly centrally determined. This is the modern aspect of planning: the centrally directed Whitehall view. And this is what is stopping planning becoming truly postmodern and locally responsive.

The implications of the postmodern challenge to planning could be argued over in the same way that the debate on New Times has, i.e. inconclusively. One route is the much hyped collaborative approach which some have claimed to be the paradigm for the next millennium (Alexander, 1997). My views on this can be found elsewhere, but suffice to say here that I would fundamentally disagree with this (Tewdwr-Jones and Allmendinger, 1998). Another route would be to attempt to construct a planning that is genuinely local. A planning that encourages difference and does not try to stifle it. The postmodern approach would be to leave the options for this open – to attempt to enforce or even suggest a view equates to 'terror'. In the real world, however, options need to be aired to move the situation forward. This is the role of the next section.

A NEW PLANNING?

There has recently been some debate on the crude relationship between chaos, complexity and postmodernism (Eve *et al.*, 1997). Price (1997) argues that chaos and complexity remain grounded in the scientific tradition, whereas postmodernists such as Foucault attempt to 'problematise' science, claiming it is simply another narrative that has been privileged over others. Because power plays an important role in the construction of reality, knowledge and power are inseparable – knowledge is therefore not neutral. Chaos and complexity are truly modernist though manage to obscure it. At a broad level there may be something in this. Clearly, there are some inconsistencies between complexity and postmodernity. But this is only when viewing complexity as applicable to the natural sciences. Its literal and metaphoric use in the social sciences is similar in many ways to postmodernism. As we have seen, it questions the overriding deterministic, linear and reductionist assumptions of much of social science. At the very least it highlights the unpredictable and subjective nature of social science. At its extreme, it provides an alternative set of criteria upon which to build pseudo-scientific disciplines such as planning.

So how can you combine chaos, complexity and postmodernity? How do conflicting pressures upon and within planning practice point to a way forward? Any attempt to construct a planning for the twenty-first century must be built upon a firm assessment of the trends, influences and problems discussed above. Three broad categories emerge. First are those influences that will have a direct and indirect impact upon planning. These include:

- Government as regulator rather than provider
- A decreasing influence upon the power of national government
- A greater questioning of authority
- More local desire for involvement
- Demands for better local services
- Decreasing resources
- Dual concern for economic growth and the environment

Planning can only survive with widespread support and to survive it must meet these challenges. At a macro level this implies:

- Increased localisation of planning control
- A focus on what planning can realistically hope to achieve within scarce resources

The resolution of the environment/economic growth debate is another matter. On the face of it many involved in initiatives such as Local Agenda 21 imply that the two are not mutually incompatible. As I mentioned above, environmental concern must go hand in hand with increased economic growth and social awareness. But it is easy to envisage how difficulties could arise. Would a local authority turn away a multinational company and associated jobs if it meant compromising their green credentials and making a decision contrary to the development plan? I doubt it.

Second are the conservative and institutional influences, or the 'problems' if you like. These include:

- A centralised planning system and procedures
- The RTPI/planner/state cartel
- The technical attitude of planners to planning

If planning is to meet the demands and challenges then all three of the above need to be addressed. The centralisation of planning cannot be reconciled with increasing local desires to express difference. The triad of planner/RTPI/state can no longer be allowed to dominate discourse and limit and prescribe debate. Neither can the continued portrayal of planning as a technical exercise founded on pseudo-scientific principles. The challenge is to 'open up' planning as it is constituted and as it operates.

Finally, we have also touched upon a new critique, interpretation and way forward of and for planning. The analysis of the increasingly unpredictable and eclectic world combined with an organic focus on 'holding the reins' as society and systems evolve provides for a new and fruitful perspective on planning. The post-modern and post-structural concern with difference and diversity taps into this and has a good deal of sympathy with the above critique of planning, providing a basis to 'open up' and challenge the conservative and problematic aspects.

The implications of chaos and complexity are that planning in the conventional 'we want to be here and this is how we will do it' sense is a hopeless task. We can only create the right conditions for systems to emerge through evolution and co-operation. Second, land use planning as a complex adaptive system should aim to recognise and work with complexity in wider society rather than treating all social systems as linear. This can best be achieved through diversity in systems, processes, organisations and outputs.

What therefore are the implications for land use planning? The first point to make of course is that as well as being a natural or behavioural model it is also a normative one, i.e. as well as saying this is how things *are* in certain systems it also says this is how they *should* be. In this respect it is not alone. Collaborative or political economy approaches are similar in this respect. The second point worth stressing is that planning for complexity does not imply a New Right approach or supply-side economics and minimal restraints. Complexity may be at the *edge* of chaos but chaos is not the free market. Emergence is a combination of evolution and co-operation. Complexity implies certain qualitative values such as room or space; space for creativity, for expression, for dissension, for agreement, but most of all space for change. Surrounding this space are frameworks or rules; what Waldrop (1992) describes as bottom-up meeting top-down. The challenge is to find a way of building such a framework that maximises robustness and survivability in the face of an ill-defined future. In doing so we need to avoid the duality of man and nature – complex adaptive systems are *part* of nature and follow similar rules

(Waldrop, 1992: 331); i.e. evolution *and* co-operation. We also need to avoid stultifying consensus that seeks to point towards a future rather than let the future find itself. In doing this we need to understand that mess is good:

> Contrary to some of our most deep seated beliefs, mess is the material from which life and creativity are built and it turns out that they are built, not according to some prior design, but through a process of spontaneous self organisation that produces divergent outcomes (Stacey, 1996b: 14).

The implications for planning are twofold. First, planning with complexity involves looking at the way in which planning relates to the other CASs; i.e. how planning seeks to meet its objectives within a complex world; the balance between certainty and flexibility (I will term this the macro-level interface or 'planning for complexity'). The second is the way that planning organises itself and goes about this, i.e. the processes involved (the micro-level interface or 'planning as complexity').

PLANNING FOR COMPLEXITY

The key here is the reconciliation of a number of competing ideas:

- Order vs chaos
- Certainty vs flexibility
- Conformity vs freedom
- Collective vs individual

The question is, how do we reconcile them? The answer I propose is to let the answer *emerge* locally. Taking the self-organisational basis of complexity theory a dynamic consensus will emerge through political interaction. Planners have no more right or ability to reconcile these ideas than anyone else – to do so would be to impose a consensus or view that is unlikely to lead to the edge of chaos. As Stuart Kauffman (1995: 246) has put it:

> No molecule in the bacterium *E. coli* 'knows' the world *E. coli* lives in, yet *E. coli* makes its way. No single person at IBM, now downsizing and becoming a flatter organisation, knows the world of IBM, yet collectively IBM acts. Organisms, artifacts and organisations are all evolved structures. Even when human agents plan and construct with intention, there is more of the blind watchmaker at work than we usually recognise.

While planners may like to think they have foresight beyond others the fact is that an emergent society or natural consensus is far better placed to identify such a balance that will keep the whole CAS (society) on the edge of chaos. How can planners and planning best achieve this? (Or do we need planning at all?[2]) A clue can be found in the parallels between CAS and postmodernism raised earlier. What is needed is a planning of difference. One that is flexible, resilient, intelligent and adaptive. Such a planning would seek to create a 'fitness landscape' for emergent structures to evolve by:

1. In Lyotard's (1984) words, an incredulity towards metanarratives.
2. The breaking down of the public and the private.
3. A genealogical view of power and history.
4. Planners as agents of disciplinary/normalising power.
5. A suspicion of consensus.[3]
6. An encouragement of conflict, power struggles and opposition.
7. An emphasis and preference for the local over the global.
8. The recognition and encouragement of temporal and spatial agreement.
9. A recognition of ontological difference.
10. A protean perspective on structure and agreement.

Where planning as a CAS differs is in the postmodern and post-structuralist emphasis on empowering the individual: we also need to empower and free the system and processes within a broad framework. As such postmodernism can provide us with some indications of how to empower/free individuals and systems. Central to both individuals and system is the question of power,[4] and in postmodern or post-structuralist analyses power is handled most convincingly by Foucault (Haber, 1994). In Foucault's postmodernism power is good as well as bad – it can construct alternatives and challenge the status quo as well as being perniciously used. Power is centreless. It is everywhere in everyday life, but there are agents of disciplinary/normalising power, e.g. social scientists, social workers and planners. Such people have the opportunity to create truth and knowledge through power, i.e. create situations through language that become accepted as truth whereas they are merely constructed.

In CASs power can be seen as analogous to the feedback/feed forward links necessary for evolution. Certain links will already be in place, i.e. the democratic process of elections. But this is not to say that these are the only links or that they are being used most effectively. Taking Foucault's agents we could project that existing links in systems may have been constructed to the advantage of some and the detriment of others. In planning it has been shown by Healey et al. (1988: 245) that the system favours certain economically powerful interest groups. Feedback/ feed forward loops will reinforce this situation. What Foucault argues and what planning for complexity will require is that such loops or inputs into the system are open to everyone and used by everyone; what Lyotard (1984) calls the law of multiplicity. Foucault could be criticised on two grounds here. First, that those who have created existing truths and knowledge will be happy just to give this up, and second that those who have been marginalised or excluded will reach a consciousness that they have been so treated and subsequently want and become included. Here the role of the planner *is* important. Building on Habermas's ideal speech situation provides a building block for inclusionary discourse (Forester, 1989), i.e. we should aim at comprehensibly, sincerely, legitimately and truthfully (Low, 1991: 251). But we need to go further. This will not free alternative voices as existing truths and knowledge are very powerful. The way to challenge these is through the *creation of opposition*, by processes and systems that do not aim to create consensus (though consensus is not anathema) but to question it. This would imply a far greater emphasis on the temporal and spatial contingency of plans – complexity and postmodern analyses meet.

But as I pointed out earlier we also need a protean approach to structure as well as individuals. Structures can have as much a normalising and a disciplining function as agents and as such should be open to challenge and ready for reconstruction. But structures also need to be sensitive to the ideas of complexity, i.e. to frame directions and processes rather than prescribe them. First, what do I mean by structure? Essentially there are three elements:

1. The scope and function of organisations (e.g. central and local government).
2. What ideas and knowledge are relevant for an organisation in carrying out their functions (i.e. policy).
3. How they go about both of the above (i.e. process).

A protean structure needs to both be ready and able to change and adapt as well as being a loose framework to raise issues while allowing emergence in complex systems to proceed. Thus a protean structure will consist of fluid collections of agents (e.g. planners) and the existence of 'rules' or guidelines of action (or bounded instability as Kauffman, 1995, terms it), i.e. the emergent status quo. Unlike postmodern analysis, complexity points to a hierarchy of rules at different levels of structure. Like postmodernism these structures and rules are spatially and temporally contingent. If a particular locale decides through political feedback that it wants to adapt procedures and rules for its own purposes then this can be done within the existing hierarchy. For example, there will be freedom and discretion to interpret higher-order rules to a certain extent (e.g. in the natural world a higher-order rule could be that humans have two legs, but this does not determine the shape and length. In planning this could be that development in the open countryside is generally unacceptable but this provides the opportunity for local interpretation). The higher-level rules will naturally evolve more slowly than the lower-level rules, but as Casti (1994) has demonstrated, when higher-level rules do change in complex systems it tends to be very dramatic. What is important is that there is scope for these rules to change and that different rules are decided at different levels. What would this mean for planners in practice? This is the second part of the future for planning: planning *as* complexity.

PLANNING AS COMPLEXITY

Complex systems drift from stable attractors to dynamic attractors or bounded instability. The question here is how to facilitate that *within* planning. Organisational and management analysis provide some clues. As Stacey (1996b) concludes, whenever we become a member of an organisation we join its legitimate system *and* its shadow system. Such a system is an informal network that we spontaneously establish among ourselves in a self-organising manner and is built on social links, political and conflictual encounters and personal networks to enable us to do our jobs and advance in the world. Stacey (1996b) suggests that this form of system is play; it is sometimes bizarre, cruel, destructive, exciting and creative. Traditionally such systems have been frowned upon in organisations. The current approach to management stresses participative and consensual decision-making, improving teamwork, etc. But, following Foucault, Stacey (1996a) stresses the positive aspects of dissension and shadow systems. Such systems are not necessarily a brake on the intentions of managers and policy-makers but can also be put to creative uses (Shaw, 1996). Tensions between formal and shadow systems generate new forms of behaviour, break down old patterns of thought and allow the new to emerge. Informal systems (as opposition) are the driving force for change and direction in organisations. But because of their messy, political and non-linear nature we tend to disguise their influence, downplay them and present them as insignificant.

Research on the role of shadow systems by Shaw (1996) has pointed to their valuable role in progress and their importance to Class IV systems. So how can we work towards difference? In another parallel with the debate on postmodernism, Lyotard (1984) has explored the 'terroristic' nature of unified systems that seek to impose and limit through order and exclude the voice of the other. His solution is based on what he terms the 'pagan ideal' or what Haber (1994) terms 'radical pluralism'. While there are significant practical and theoretical problems with Lyotard's relativistic approach he does provide one way of ensuring diversity and encouraging it; the law of multiplicity. The irony is of course that multiplicity is ensured through the prescription of a universal value but this is only a problem if we associate anything but pure pluralism with 'terror'. Such a law of multiplicity seeks to ensure that organisations, systems and processes are constructed in such a way so as to avoid consensus and maximise opposition. In planning there are a number of ways a shadow system could be helpful:

1. Planning is still predominantly a public activity carried out within organisations such as local authorities. As such planning departments could be viewed in the same vein as organisations and seek to facilitate their own shadow organisations in order to encourage opposition, debate, play, destruction and evolution.

2. In the approach to planning there should be constant reflexivity, opposition, questioning and suspicion of consensus. This is important not only within organisations but also in the relation with other actors and interests.

3. Crucial to biological and social evolution is feedback. In planning this is already a part of processes and systems, but as we saw above monitoring and evaluating planning policies and ideas have not been as strong as they might be. Challenging ideas and policies requires information upon which to do this and this can only be provided through evaluation.

4. The democratic imperative – in its widest sense – is central to evolution. The more who are involved the more likely it will be that debates will be generated and opposition ensured. This gives little clue as to *how*, as postmodernists are particularly mute on this. However, one could, for example, follow the ideal speech approach of Habermas or the inclusionary discourse ideas of Dryzek (1991).

5. Flexibility is also required to allow adaptation of complex adaptive systems to reach the edge of chaos. This requires the ability to change as well as the room for manœuvre. Planning should therefore not be prescriptive. This does correspond to the overall approach of UK planning as opposed to its European counterparts. But even so, certain aspects of UK planning are rigid; ideas in particular. Protection of the countryside, segregation of uses, dispersal, urban clearance, etc. are all ideas that have dominated even when opposed. These 'metanarratives' in the UK system usually dominate across the country given the centralised nature of government. So, ideas and policies need to be flexible in terms of their implementation and interpretation (which they currently are to a certain extent) and flexible in terms of space.

6. It is essential for a planning system to encourage difference. Communities (however defined) will be more likely to engage in debate, participate and oppose if it will make a difference and if a process or system can reflect local circumstances.

The micro-politics of how we approach planning and take advantage of complexity are not something that should be prescribed but explored with central ideas such as flexibility, participation, opposition, etc. as guides.

CONCLUSIONS

How will a protean planning take advantage of societal trends, meet the challenges and address the problems outlined at the beginning of this chapter? In line with the 'nested' approach of higher- and lower-level rules there will be different roles and responsibilities for different levels of government. Broad prescriptions of the system with policy indicators will be set at a national level (e.g. allowing locales to establish a planning system and processes within broad limits) along with definitions of national objectives such as the need to encourage diversity and difference *in* and *through* planning (a law of multiplicity). At a regional or county level more defined objectives (though not systems or processes) will be identified (the balance between the environment and the economy, conservation and development). And finally, it will be up to the lower-level units of government to define for themselves or in conjunction with other authorities how to approach planning in their area, what their priorities are and how to go about it.

Information concerning different approaches in different areas could be made available to allow comparisons to be made and different systems to be adopted if desired. The role of different actors in this protean planning will also obviously change. Planners may need to work for areas with whom they find themselves in sympathy (much as in Davidoff's advocacy approach). This will imply a recognition of various 'professional' standards and the need to be open about their views. It must also undermine the need for a professional body. The idea of planning as a political and technical exercise will be finally laid to rest. Instead, we will have a planning of emotion, evolution, argument and coalition. In short, planning will come to terms with its messy nature:

> To remove the mess by inspiring us to follow some vision, to indoctrinate us to share the same culture, to sing off the same hymn sheet and pull together, is to remove the mess that is the very raw material of creative activity (Stacey, 1996b: 21).

Some may see both practical and theoretical problems here and I know I certainly do. There are a number of important questions to be addressed:

1. How do you combine political and complex ends and which should take priority?
2. How do you know when you are taking advantage of complexity and a system is at the edge of chaos?
3. Does this mean we are to live with the anxiety of constant change and if so would we not be happier accepting less creativity and progress for greater certainty?
4. Are chaos, complexity and postmodernism *really* compatible?

It is important to stress that this is not an echo of Peter Hall's call for an 'essay in non-plan' (Banham *et al.*, 1969) though one can see parallels with the work of, say, Jacobs (1965) with its emphasis on diversity. It is persuasive to argue that we should accept political ends as the only tangible or desirable ones, but the edge of chaos is not simply about economic growth but creativity in society including political ideas, freedom, artistic development, etc. It is a plea for a redefinition of 'plan' to become a search, not a map and of 'planner' to be a facilitator and interpreter. It is not only a step back from planning as 'predict and control' but also as planning being wholly about finding consensus and agreement. It is saying that as a whole, interacting together in what may appear messy and uncoordinated ways we can achieve things we could not achieve as well through conscious decisions and actions.

NOTES

1. I do however, acknowledge the contribution of Reade (1987) and Evans (1995) to this debate.
2. A land use planning system would not necessarily be needed and the option of doing without one must always be kept open – such a system must demonstrate benefits over 'pure' emergence. However, if we are situated within a CAS (society) then there is the possibility of sudden change that could disadvantage people. Further, as I have stated earlier, in the short term and under certain conditions planning (in the sense of being able to predict and control) is still possible as well as desirable. Society needs certainty as well as the illusion of certainty. Ontological complexity does not preclude some form of intervention in markets and society which can, for example, make issues such as sustainability important in reaching the edge of chaos.
3. This is a suspicion of consensus only. Ontological difference must not be conflated with the synthetic or political desire for difference. As Haber (1994) reminds us, not all difference is bad. We are already part of many communities within which consensus may be a sign of genuine similarity and not terror.
4. This is something that complexity theory is particularly mute on. Power in natural systems is taken as read – be it high pressure in a weather system or a jaguar in the jungle. Planning cannot accept this 'natural' balance quite as uncritically. If there is to be a meaningful interaction that will help a system emerge at the edge of chaos then as many as possible must be included.

CONTRIBUTORS

Philip Allmendinger, Department of Land Economy, University of Aberdeen

Rob Atkinson, School of Social and Historical Studies, University of Portsmouth

Michael Chapman, School of Planning and Housing, Edinburgh College of Art/ Heriot-Watt University

David Etherington, Centre for Local and Regional Analysis, University of Huddersfield

Donna Heaney, Scottish Consumer Council, Glasgow

Julian Hine, Department of Transport Engineering, Napier University

Rob Imrie, Department of Geography, Royal Holloway University of London

Jane Kettle, School of the Built Environment, Leeds Metropolitan University

Colin Jones, Department of Land Economics, University of Paisley

Roderick Macdonald, Halcrow Fox, Edinburgh

Phil Macnaughton, Centre for Study of Environmental Change, Lancaster University

Celia Moran, School of the Built Environment, Leeds Metropolitan University

Graham Pinfield, Centre for Study of Environmental Change, Lancaster University

Dave Shaw, Department of Civic Design, University of Liverpool

Mark Tewdwr-Jones, Department of Land Economy, University of Aberdeen

Craig Watkins, Centre for Property Research, Department of Land Economy, University of Aberdeen

Colin C. Williams, Department of Geography, University of Leicester

BIBLIOGRAPHY

Abercrombie P. (1933) *Town and Country Planning*, Thornton Butterworth: London

Action for Cities (1988) *Action for Cities*, Cabinet Office: London

Adair A., Berry J. and McGreal W. (1996) Hedonic modelling, housing submarkets, and residential valuation, *Journal of Property Research*, **13**: 1, 67–84

Adam B. (1998) *Timescapes of Modernity*, London: Routledge

ADC/AMA (Association of District Councils/Association of Metropolitan Councils) (1994) *Winning Communities – the Role of Housing in Promoting Community Safety, Executive Summary*, ADC: London

Adriaanse A. (1993) *Environmental Policy Performance Indicator*, Ministry of Housing, Physical Planning and Environment: The Hague

Agyeman J. and Tuxworth B. (1996) The changing face of environmental policy and practice in Britain, in Buckingham-Hatfield S. and Evans B. (eds) *Environmental Planning and Sustainability*, Wiley: London

Alden J. and Offord C. (1996) Regional planning guidance, in Tewdwr-Jones M. (ed.) *British Planning Policy in Transition – Planning in the 1990s*, UCL Press: London

Alexander E.R. (1997) A mile or a millimeter? Measuring the 'planning theory–practice gap', *Environment and Planning B*, **24**, 3–6

Allmendinger P. (1996) Development control and the legitimacy of planning decisions, *Town Planning Review*, **67**: 2, 229–235

Allmendinger P. (1998) Planning in the future. Trends, problems and possibilities, in Allmendinger P. and Chapman M. (eds) *Planning in the Millenium*, John Wiley: Chichester

Allmendinger P. (1998) Planning practice and the postmodern debate, *International Planning Studies*, forthcoming

Allmendinger P. and Tewdwr-Jones M. (1997) Post Thatcherite urban planning and politics, *International Journal of Urban and Regional Research*, **21**: 1, 100–117

Allmendinger P. and Thomas H. (1998) *Urban Planning and the British New Right*, Routledge: London

Ambrose P. (1986) *Whatever Happened to Planning?* Methuen: London

Amin A. and Thomas D. (1997) The negotiated economy: state and civil institutions in Denmark, *Economy and Society*, **25**: 2, 255–281

Andersen J.J. (1995) Structural funds and the social dimension of EU policy: springboard or stumbling block? in Liebfried S. and Pierson P. (eds) *European Social Policy between Fragmentation and Integration*, Brookings Institute: Washington

Anderson P. and Mann N. (1997) *Safety First. The Making of New Labour*, Granta: London

Armstrong, H.W. (1996) European Union Regional Policy Sleepwalking to a Crisis, *International Regional Science Review*, **19**: 3, 193–209

Appleyard D. (1981) *Livable Streets*, University of California Press: Berkeley

Association of County Councils (1991) *Towards a Sustainable Transport Policy*, ACC: London

Atkinson R. and Cope S. (1994) The structures of governance in Britain, in Savage S., Atkinson R. and Robins L. (eds) *Public Policy in Britain*, Macmillan: London

Atkinson R. and Cope S. (1997) Community participation and urban regeneration in Britain, in Hoggett P. (ed.) *Contested Communities*, Policy Press: Bristol

Atkinson R. and Moon G. (1994a) *Urban Policy in Britain. The City, the State and the Market*, Macmillan: London

Atkinson R. and Moon G. (1994b) The city challenge initiative: an overview and preliminary assessment, *Regional Studies*, **28**, 94–97

Audit Commission (1989) *Urban Regeneration and Economic Development*, HMSO: London

Audit Commission (1997) *It's a Small World – Local Governments' Role as Stewards of the Environment*, Audit Commission: London

Bachtler J. and Davies P.L. (1989) Economic restructuring and services policy, in Gibbs D. (ed.) *Government Policy and Industrial Change*, Routledge: London

Baker M. and Wong C. (1997) Planning for housing land in the English regions: a critique of the household projections and regional planning guidance mechanisms, *Environment and Planning C: Government and Policy*, **15**, 73–87

Balchin P. (1995) *Housing Policy. An Introduction*, Routledge: London

Bale J. (1993) *Sport, Space and the City*, Routledge: London

Ball M. and Kirwan R. (1977) Accessibility and supply constraints in the urban housing market, *Urban Studies*, **14**, 11–32

Banham R., Barker P., Hall P. and Price C. (1969) Non-plan: an experiment in freedom, *New Society*, 20 March

Banister D. (1996) Energy, quality of life and the environment: the role of transport, *Transport Reviews*, **16**: 1, 23–35

Barlow J. and Bhatti M. (1997) Environmental performance as a competitive strategy? British speculative house builders in the 1990s, *Planning Practice and Research*, **12**: 1, 33–44

Barlow J., Cocks R. and Parker M. (1994) *Planning for Affordable Housing*, DoE: London

Barnett C. (1986) *The Audit of War*, Macmillan: London

Barr A. (1995) Empowering communities – beyond fashionable rhetoric? Some reflections on Scottish experience, *Community Development Journal*, **30**, 121–132

Barr C. (1993) *Ealing Studios*, 2nd edn, Studio Vista: London

Batty M., Couclelis H. and Eichen M. (1997) Urban systems and cellular automata, *Environment and Planning B: Planning and Design*, **24**, 159–164

Bauman Z. (1988) Is there a postmodern sociology? *Theory, Culture and Society*, **5**: 2, 3

Beal A. (1996) Public is paying for PFI, *New Civil Engineer*, 2 May, pp. 14–15

Beardmore D. (1997) The bad old days of easy answers, *Planning*, 19 September, p. 14

Beauregard B. (1996) *Between Modernity and Postmodernity: The Ambiguous Position of US Planning*, reprinted in Campbell S. and Fainstein S. (eds) *Readings in Planning Theory*, Blackwell: London

Beecham J. (1993) A sceptical view, *Policy Studies*, **14**: 2, 14–18

Begg I. (1995) Threats to cohesion, in Amin A. and Tomaney J. (eds) *Behind the Myth of the European Union Project: Prospects for Cohesion*, Routledge: London

Begg I. (1996) The European Union Structural Funds, in Philippe Barbour (ed.) *The European Union Handbook*. Fitzroy Dearborn: London

Bell G. (1997) The P-shocking PPG and the limits to planning, *Town and Country Planning*, **66**: 3, 67

Bell M.G.H. (1995) Solutions to urban traffic problems: towards new realism, *Traffic Engineering and Control*, February, pp. 78–81

Bennett J. and Patel R. (1995) Sustainable regeneration strategies, *Local Economy*, **10**: 2, 133–148

Berry F. (1972) *The Great British Housing Failure*, Routledge & Kegan Paul: London

Betjeman J. (1988) *Collected Poems*, John Murray: London

Beyers W.B. and Alvine M.J. (1985) Export services in post-industrial society, *Papers of the Regional Science Association*, **57**, 33–45

Bigg T. (1997) *UNED–UK Report on Earth Summit II*, UNED–UK: London

Bina O., Cuff J. and Lake R. (1997) *EU Cohesion and the Environment: A Version for 2000 and Beyond*. A Report for the Birdlife International Regional Task Force. The Royal Society for the Protection of Birds: Bedfordshire

Bird R.J. (1997) Chaos and social reality: an emergent perspective, in Eve R., Horsfall S. and Lee M. (eds) *Chaos, Complexity and Sociology. Myths, Models and Theories*, Sage: London

Blair T. (1998) A modern Britain in a modern Europe, speech at the Annual Friends of Nieuwspoort Dinner, The Ridderzaal, The Hague, 20 January 1998

Blowers A. (ed.) (1993) *Planning for a Sustainable Society*, Earthscan: London

Bluestone S. and Harrison B. (1982) *The Deindustrialization of America*, New York: Basic Books

Booth E. (1996) Think local food links, *Living Earth*, **189**: 8

Borja J. and Castells M. (1996) *Local and Global: The Management of Cities in the Information Age*, Earthscan Publications: London

Bovaird T., Martin S., Tricker M., Gregory D. and Pearce G. *et al.* (1990) *An Evaluation of the Rural Development Programme Process*, Rural Research Report No. 5, Rural Development Commission

Bramley G. (1996) *Housing with Hindsight: Household Growth, Housing Need, and Housing Development in the 1980s*, CPRE: London

Bramley G. and Watkins C. (1995) *Circular Projections: Household Growth, Housing Development and The Household Projections*, Council for the Protection of Rural England: London

Bramley G. and Watkins C. (1996) *Steering the Market: New Housebuilding and the Changing Planning System*, Policy Press: Bristol

Breheny M. and Congdon P. (eds) (1989) *Growth and Change in a Core Region*, Pion: London

Breheny M. and Hall P. (1996) National questions, regional answers, in Breheny M. and Hall P. (eds) *The People – Where Will They Go?* TCPA: London

Breheny M. and Hall P. (1997) *The People – Where Will They Go?* TCPA: London

Brindley T., Rydin Y. and Stoker G. (1996) *Remaking Planning*, Unwin Hyman: London

Britain in Europe (1998) Strategems Publishing Ltd: London

Brooke R. (1989) *Managing the Enabling Authority*, Longman: London

Brown P. and Crompton M. (eds) (1994) *Economic Restructuring and Social Exclusion*, UCL Press: London

Bruton M. and Nicholson D. (1987) *Local Planning in Practice*, Hutchinson: London

Bryson J. and Crosby B. (1992) *Leadership in the Common Good: Tackle Public Problems in a Shared-power World*, Jossey Bass: San Francisco

Buckingham-Hatfield S. and Evans B. (1996) Achieving sustainability through environmental planning, in Buckingham-Hatfield S. and Evans B. (eds) *Environmental Planning and Sustainability*, pp. 1–17. Wiley: London

Building (1995) PFI trailblazers – fellow travellers, *Building*, 20 October, p. 24

Building (1997) Mission inhospitable, *Building*, 31 January, pp. 16–21

Burgan B. and Mules T. (1992) Economic impact of sporting events, *Annals of Tourism Research*, **19**: 700–710

Burke T. (1997) The buck stops everywhere, *New Statesman*, 20 June, pp. 114–116

Cabinet Office (1988) *Action for Cities*, HMSO: London

Caborn R. (1997) Government plans for regional planning and development, speech to the Town and Country Planning Association Conference, 4 November 1997

CAG Consultants (1998) *Sustainability in Development Control – a Research Report*, Local Government Association/Local Government Management Board: London

Cairns S. (1995) Travel for food shopping: the fourth solution, *Traffic Engineering and Control*, July/August, pp. 411–418

Callinicos A. (1989) *Against Postmodernity: A Marxist Critique*, Polity Press: Cambridge

Callinicos A. (1991) *The Revenge of History: Marxism and the East European Revolutions*, Polity Press: Cambridge

Campbell M. (1996) The Leeds economy: trends, prospects and challenges, in Haughton G. and Williams C.C. (eds) *Corporate City? Partnership, Participation and Partition in Urban Development in Leeds*, Avebury Press: Aldershot

Carmichael P. (1994) Analysing political choice in local government: a comparative case study approach, *Public Administration*, **72**, 241–262

Carter C. (1996) The European Union social policy debate, in Philippe Barbour (ed.) *The European Union Handbook*, Fitzroy Dearborn: London

Carter N. and Darlow A. (1997) Local Agenda 21 and developers: are we better equipped to build a consensus in the 1990s? *Planning Practice and Research*, **12**: 1, 45–57

Castells M. (1992) *European Cities, the Informational Society, and the Global Economy*, Centrum voor Grootstedelijk Onderzeok: Amsterdam

Castells M. (1996) *The Rise of the Network Society*, Blackwell: Oxford

Casti J.L. (1994) *Searching for Certainty. What Scientists Can Know About the Future*, Abacus: London

Chapman M. (1995) Urban policy and urban evaluation: the impact of the European Union, in Hambleton R. and Thomas H. (eds) *Urban Policy Evaluation Challenge and Change*, Paul Chapman: London

CEC (Commission of the European Communities) (1990) *Green Paper on the Urban Environment*, CEC: Brussels

CEC (1991) *Europe 2000: Outlook for the Development of the Community's Territory*, Luxembourg

CEC (1992a) *Fifth Environmental Action Programme for the Environment and Sustainable Development*, CEC: Brussels

CEC (1992b) *Urbanisation and the Future of Cities in the European Community*, Brussels

CEC (1994a) *Community Initiatives Concerning Urban Areas (URBAN)*, Com (94) 61 Final 2. Brussels

CEC (1994b) *Competitiveness and Cohesion: Trends in the Regions Fifth Report on the Social and Economic Situation of the Regions in the Community*, EC: Brussels

CEC (1994c) *Europe 2000+: Cooperation for European Territorial Development*, Luxembourg

CEC, Directorate General V. Employment, Social Affairs and Industrial Relations (1995a) *Social Europe Medium-Term Social Action Programme 1995–97*, EC: Brussels

CEC, Directorate General V. Employment, Social Affairs and Industrial Relations (1995b) *The Lessons of the Poverty 3 Programme*, CEC: Brussels

CEC, Directorate General V. Employment, Social Affairs and Industrial Relations (1995c) *Social Protection in Europe*, CEC: Brussels

CEC, Directorate General V. Employment, Social Affairs and Industrial Relations (1996a) *For a Europe of Civic and Social Rights*, A report by the Comité des Sages: Brussels

CEC (1996b) *First Report on Social and Economic Cohesion*, OOPEC: Luxembourg

CEC (1996c) *Towards Fair and Efficient Pricing in Transport: Policy Options for Internalising the External Costs of Transport in the European Union* (COM(950691), February, Brussels

CEC (1997a) *Agenda 2000: For a Stronger and Wider Europe*, OOPEC: Luxembourg

CEC (1997b) *European Cohesion Forum: Speeches and Summaries 28–30 April 1997*, OOPEC: Luxembourg

CEC (1997c) *Towards an Urban Agenda in the European Union*, COM (97) 197 final. Brussels

CEC, Directorate General for Regional Policy and Cohesion (1997d) *The EU Compendium of Spatial Planning Systems and Policies*, CEC: Luxembourg

CEC (1997e) *First Official Draft. European Spatial Development Perspective*. 9 and 10 June, Noordwifk

Chadwick, G. (1971) *Systems View of Planning*, Pergamon: Oxford

Cherry G.E. (1976) *Rural Planning Problems*, Hill: London

Cherry, G. (1992) Green belt and the emergent city, *Property Review*, **1**: 3, 91–101

Chisholm M. (1997) The Road Traffic Reduction Act 1997 lacks teeth, *Traffic Engineering and Control*, September, pp. 454–456

Christenson K.S. (1985) Coping with uncertainty in planning, *Journal of the American Planners Association*, **51**: 11, 63–73

CIH (Chartered Institute of Housing) (1995a) *How Much Housing Investment Do We Need?* CIH: Coventry

CIH (1995b) *Citizenship and Housing: Shaping the Debate*, CIH: Coventry

Clark G. (1995) *The Single Regeneration Handbook*, revised and updated edition. National Council for Voluntary Organisations: London

Clarke J. and Newman J. (1993) The right to manage: a second managerial revolution? *Cultural Studies*, **7**: 3, 427–441

Clark J. and Stewart J. (1997) *The Managerial State*, Sage: London

Cleary, J. and Hillman, M. (1992) A prominent role for walking and cycling in future transport policy, in Roberts J., Cleary J., Hamilton K. and Hanna J. (eds) *Travel Sickness – The Need for Sustainable Transport Policy for Britain*, Lawrence and Wishart: London

Cloke P. (1996) Housing development in the countryside, *Town Planning Review*, **67**: 3

Cloke P.J., Milbourne P. and Thomas C. (1994) *Lifestyles in Rural England*, Rural Research Report No. 18, Rural Development Commission

Cmnd 6845 (1977) *Policy for the Inner Cities*, Cmnd 6845, HMSO: London

Cmnd 3178 (1996) *Government Response to the Environment Committee First Report into the Single Regeneration Budget*, Cmnd 3178, HMSO: London

Cochrane A. (1993) *Whatever Happened to Local Government?* Open University Press: Buckingham

Cockburn C. (1977) *The Local State*, Pluto Press: London

Coffey W.J. (1995a) Producer services research in Canada, *The Professional Geographer*, **47**, 1: 74–81

Coffey W.J. (1995b) Forward and backward linkages of producer service establishments: evidence from the Montreal metropolitan area, paper presented to AAG Annual Meeting session on Producer services in an age of flexibility, Chicago: March

Cohen J. and Stewart I. (1994) *The Collapse of Chaos*, Penguin: London

Cohen R. (1981) The new international division of labour: multinational companies and urban hierarchy, in Scott A.J. and Dear M. (eds) *Urbanization and Planning in Capitalist Society*, Methuen: London

Cole I. and Windle K. (1992) Decentralisation, in Davies C. (ed.) *Housing for Life*, E. & F.N. Spon: London

Cooke P. (1990) *Back to the Future: Modernity, Post-modernity and Locality*, Unwin Hyman: London

Coveney P. and Highfield R. (1995) *Frontiers of Complexity*, Faber and Faber: London

Coyle G. (1997) The nature and value of future studies or do futures have a future? *Futures*, **29**: 1, 77–93

CPOS (County Planners Officers' Society) (1993) *Planning and Sustainability*, available from Peter Bell, Hampshire County Council, Winchester

CPRE (Council for the Protection of Rural England) (1997) *More Homes Welcome*, CPRE: London

Crow S. (1996) The child that grew up in the cold, *Planning Perspectives*, **11**

Cullinane S. (1997) Traffic management in Britain's national parks, *Transport Reviews*, **17**: 3, 267–279

Cullingworth J.B. (1997) British land use planning: a failure to cope with change? *Urban Studies*, **24**: 5–6, 945–960

Cullingworth J.B. and Nadin V. (1997) *Town and Country Planning in Britain*, Routledge: London

Curry N. and Owen S. (eds) (1996) *Changing Rural Policy in Britain; Planning Administration, Agriculture and the Environment*, The Countryside and Community Press

Curtis C. (1996) Can strategic planning contribute to a reduction in car based travel, *Transport Policy*, **3**: 1/2, 55–65

Daniels P.W. (1993) *Service Industries in the World Economy*, Blackwell: Oxford

Daniels P.W. (1995a) The locational geography of advanced producer service firms in the United Kingdom, *Progress in Planning*, **43**: 2–3, 123–138

Daniels P.W. (1995b) Producer services research in the United Kingdom, *The Professional Geographer*, **47**: 1, 82–86

Danschat J. (1992) Conceptualising urban space in Germany, in Mangen S. (ed.) *Polisation and Urban Space*. Cross National Research Papers, University of Loughborough

Dasgupta M. (1994) *Impact of Transport Policies in Five Cities*, Project Report 107, Transport Research Laboratory: Crowthorne

Davidson J. and Wibberley G. (1977) *Planning and the Rural Environment*, Pergamon: Oxford

Davies H.W.E (1989) England, in Davies H.W.E (ed.) *Planning Control in Western Europe*, HMSO: London

Davies, H.W.E. (1994) Towards a European planning system? *Planning Practice and Research*, **9**: 1, 63–69

Davies H.W.E. (1996) Planning and the European question, in Tewdwr-Jones M. (ed.) *British Planning Policy in Transition*, UCL Press: London

Davies H.W.E and Gosling J. (1994) *The Impact of the European Community on Land Use Planning in the United Kingdom*, RTPI: London

Davies J.G. (1972) *The Evangelistic Bureaucrat*, Tavistock: London

Davis H.C. and Davis L.E. (1987) The local exchange trading system: community wealth creation within the informal economy, *Plan Canada*, **20**, 238–245

Davoudi S., Hull A. and Healey P. (1996) Environmental concerns and economic imperatives in strategic plan making, *Town Planning Review*, **67**: 4, 421–435

Deakin N. and Edwards J. (1993) *The Enterprise Culture and the Inner City*, Routledge: London

Dean H. (1991) In search of the underclass, in Brown P. and Scase R. (eds) *Poor Work*, OUP: Oxford

Dear M. (1988) The postmodern challenge: reconstructing human geography, *Transactions of the Institute of British Geographers*, **45**: 262–274

De Groot L. (1992) City challenge: competing in the urban regeneration game, *Local Economy*, **7**, 196–209

Delow E. (1996) Food for thought, *Living Earth*, **189**, 9

Demaziere C. and Wilson, P.A. (eds) (1996) *Local Economic Development in Europe and the Americas*, Mansell: London

Dennis, S. (1997) Keeping the environment on the agenda, *Municipal Journal*, 25 July 1997, pp. 26–27

Department of Transport (1987) *Road Safety: The Next Steps*, Department of Transport: July, London

Department of Transport (1989) *Pedestrian Safety – New Proposals for Making Walking Safer*, Department of Transport: London

Department of Transport (1990) *Children and Roads: A Safer Way*, Department of Transport: May, London

Department of Transport (1991) *The Older Road User*, Department of Transport: June, London

Department of Transport (1993) *Paying for Better Roads*, Cmnd 2200, HMSO: London

Department of Transport (1996a) *Transport the Way Forward – The Government's Response to the Transport Debate*, Cmnd 3234, HMSO: London

Department of Transport (1996b) *Developing a Strategy for Walking*, December, London

Department of Transport (1996c) Watts lifts burden on roadside developers, Press Release Notice 221, 11 July, Department of Transport: London

DETR (Department of the Environment, Transport and the Regions) (1997a) *Building Partnerships for Prosperity*, HMSO: London

DETR (1997b) *Single Regeneration Budget Challenge Fund Round 4: Supplementary Guidance*, HMSO: London

DETR (1997c) *Regional Development Agencies. Issues for Discussion*, HMSO: London

DETR (1997d) *Regeneration Programmes – The Way Forward*, HMSO: London

DETR (1997e) *Developing an Integrated Transport Policy*, Consultation Document, London

DETR (1997f) *Mapping Local Authority Estates*, HMSO: London

DETR (1998a) *Best Value White Paper*, HMSO: London

DETR (1998b) *Modernising Planning*, HMSO: London

DETR (1998c) *Regeneration Programmes: The Way Forward, a Discussion Paper*, HMSO: London

DETR (1998d) *Sustainable Development: Opportunities for Change*, HMSO: London

DETR (1998e) *A New Deal for Transport: Better for Everyone*, HMSO: London

DETR (1998f) *The Impact of the EU on the UK Planning System*, HMSO: London

Dicken P. (1992) *Global Shift: the Internationalization of Economic Activity*, Paul Chapman: London

Dobson R.V.G. (1993) *Bringing the Economy Home from the Market*, Black Rose Books: London

DoE (Department of the Environment) (1977) *Housing Policy: A Consultative Document*, HMSO: London

DoE (1988) *Housing: The Government's Proposals*, HMSO: London

DoE (1992a) *Planning Policy Guidance, No. 1*, HMSO: London

DoE (1992b) *Planning Policy Guidance, No. 12*, HMSO: London

DoE (1992c) *City Challenge Bidding Guidance 1993–94*, HMSO: London

DoE (1992d) *PPG3: Housing*, HMSO: London

DoE (1992e) *PPG12: Development Plans and Regional Planning Guidance*, HMSO: London

DoE (1993a) *Bidding Guidance. A Guide to Funding from the Single Regeneration Budget*, HMSO: London

DoE (1993b) *Merry Hill Impact Study*, HMSO, London

DoE (1993c) *Environmental Appraisal of Development Plans*, HMSO: London

DoE (1994a) *Building on Success*, DoE Information Pack, HMSO: London

DoE (1994b) *Nature Conservation*, Planning Policy Guidance Note 9, HMSO: London

DoE (1995a) *A Consultation Paper on Probationary Tenancies*, HMSO: London

DoE (1995b) *Our Future Homes, Opportunity, Choice, Responsibility*, HMSO: London

DoE (1995c) *Projections of Households in England to 2016*, HMSO: London

DoE (1996a) *Planning Policy Guidance 1 (revised): General Policy and Principles*, HMSO: London

DoE (1996b) *Household Growth: Where Shall We Live*, HMSO: London

DoE (1996c) *Indicators of Sustainable Development for the United Kingdom*, HMSO: London

DoE (1996d) *Town Centres and Retail Development*, Planning Policy Guidance Note 6, HMSO, London

DoE (1997a) *PPG1: General Policy and Principles*, HMSO: London

DoE (1997b) *Planning Policy Guidance Note 7: Countryside: Environmental Quality and Social and Economic Development*, HMSO: London

DoE (1997c) *Department of the Environment Annual Report 1997. The Government's Expenditure Plans 1997–98 to 1999–2000*, Cmnd 3607, HMSO: London

DoE/DoT (1994) *Planning Policy Guidance Note 13 – Transport*, HMSO: London

DoE/DoT (1995) *PPG 13 A Guide to Better Practice*, HMSO: London

DoE and Ministry of Agriculture Food and Fisheries (1995) *Rural England: A Nation Committed to a Living Countryside*, HMSO: London

Douthwaite R. (1996) *Short Circuit: a Practical New Approach to Building More Self-reliant Communities*, Green Books: Dartington

Dryzek J.S. (1991) *Discursive Democracy: Policy, Politics and Political Science*, Cambridge University Press: Cambridge

Duffy H. (1995) *Competitive Cities Succeeding in the Global Economy*, E. & F.N. Spon: London

Dunford M. and Perrons D. (1994) Regional inequality, regimes of accumulation and economic development in contemporary Europe, *Transactions of the Institute of British Geographers*, **19**, 163–182

Earp J.H. (1995) *Reducing the Need to Travel – Some Thoughts on PPG 13*, Occasional Paper 47, Oxford Brookes University, School of Planning

Economist (1996) Peering into the shadow, *The Economist*, 25 May, pp. 40–41

ECOTEC (1993) *Reducing Transport Emissions through Land Use Planning*, Department of Transport, HMSO: London

Ekins P. and Max-Neef M. (eds) (1993) *Real-life Economics: Understanding Wealth-creation*, Routledge: London

Elkin, S.H., McLaren, D. and Hillman, M. (1991) *Reviving the City: Towards Sustainable Development*, Policy Studies Institute: London

Elson M., MacDonald R. and Steenberg C. (1995) *Planning for Rural Diversification*, HMSO: London

Elson M., Walker S. and Macdonald R. (1993) *The Effectiveness of Green Belts*, HMSO: London

Engwicht D. (1993) *Reclaiming Our Cities and Towns – Better Living with Less Traffic*, New Society Publishers: Philadelphia

Enterprise PLC (1998) East Midlands draft rural strategy and action plan, unpublished policy document

Esping-Andersen G. (1990) *Three Worlds of Welfare Capitalism*, Polity Press: Cambridge

Esping-Andersen G. (ed.) (1996) *Welfare States in Transition: National Adaptations in Global Economies*, Sage: London

Etherington D. (1997) Trade unions and local economic development – Lessons from Denmark, *Local Economy*, **12**: 3

Etherington D. (1998) Welfare to work in Denmark: an alternative to free market policies, *Policy and Politics*, **26**, 2: 147–159

Evans B. (1993) Why we no longer need a town planning profession, *Planning Practice and Research*, **8**: 1, 9–15

Evans B. (1995) *Experts and Environmental Planning*, Avebury Press: Aldershot

Evans B. (1997) From town planning to environmental planning, in Blowers A. and Evans B. (eds) *Town Planning in the 21st Century*, Routledge: London

Evans B. and Rydin Y. (1997) Planning, professionalism and sustainability, in Blowers A. and Evans B. (eds) *Town Planning in the 21st Century*, Routledge: London

Eve R., Horsfall S. and Lee M. (1997) *Chaos, Complexity and Sociology. Myths, Models and Theories*, Sage: London

Fainstein S. (1994) *The City Builders: Property, Politics, and Planning in London and New York*, Blackwell: Oxford

Fainstein S., Gordon I. and Harloe M. (1992) *Divided Cities: New York & London in the Contemporary World*, Blackwell: Oxford

Faludi A. (1973) *Planning Theory*, Pergamon: Oxford

Farrington J. and Ryder A (1993) Environmental assessment of transport infrastructure, *Journal of Transport Geography*, **2**: 1, 102–118

Field B. and MacGregor B. (1987) *Forecasting Techniques for Urban and Regional Planning*, Hutchinson: London

Fillion P. (1996) Metropolitan planning objectives and implementation constraints: planning in a post-Fordist and postmodern age, *Environment and Planning A*, **28**: 1637–1660

Finger M. (1993) Politics of the UNCED process, in Sachs W. (ed.) *Global Ecology: a New Arena of Global Conflict*, Zed: London

Fischler F. (1998) A vision for a European agricultural policy, opening speech for International Green Week, Berlin, 15 January 1998

Fleming S. and Short J. (1984) Committee rules OK? *Environment and Planning A*, **16**: 7, 965–973

Flynn N. (1990) *Public Sector Management*, Harvester Wheatsheaf: Hemel Hempstead

Foley P., Hutchinson J., Harbane B. and Tait G. (1996) Impact of Toyota on Derbyshire's local economy and labour market, *Tijdschrift voor Economische en Sociale Geografie*, **87**: 1, 19—31

Forrest R. and Murie A. (1995) From privatisation to commodification: tenure conversion and new zones of transition in the city, *International Journal of Urban and Regional Research*, **10**, 46–65

Forester J. (1989) *Planning in the Face of Power*, University of California Press: California

Forrest R. and Williams P. (1997) Future directions? In Williams P. (ed.) *Directions in Housing Policy: Towards Sustainable Housing Policies for the UK*, Paul Chapman: London

Fothergill S. (1997) The premature death of EU regional policy, a paper presented at the Regional Studies Association Conference, Frankfurt-on-Oder, Germany, September 1997

Fraser R. (1991) *Working Together in the 1990s*, Institute of Housing: Coventry

Freeman C., Littlewood S. and Whitney D. (1996) Local government and emerging models of participation in the Local Agenda 21 process, *Journal of Environmental Planning and Management*, **39**: 1, 65–78

Friend J.K. and Jessop W.M. (1969) *Local Government and Strategic Choice*, Tavistock: London

Fukuyama F. (1989) *The End of History?* Penguin: London

Gabriel Y. (1996) *The Hubris of Management*, Complexity and management papers No. 5, Complexity and Management Centre, University of Hertfordshire

Gans H.J. (1972) *People and Plans: Essays on Urban Problems and Solutions*, Pelican: London

Geddes M. and Martin S. (1997) *Local Partnership for Economic and Social Regeneration: Experience in the UK and the European Union* The Local Government Management Board: London

Gell-Mann M. (1994) *The Quark and the Jaguar*, W.H. Freeman: New York

George V. and Wilding G. (1994) *Welfare and Ideology*, Harvester Wheatsheaf: Hemel Hempstead

Gerald Eve and the Department of Land Economy at Cambridge (1992) *The Relationship between House Prices and Land Supply*, Department of the Environment, HMSO: London

Ghazi P., McKie R. and Narayan N. (1995) Now let the fight for the Pacific begin, *The Observer*, 25 June

Giaratani F. and McNelis P. (1980) Time series evidence bearing on crude theories of regional growth, *Land Economics*, **6**, 238–248

Gibbs D. (1996) On course for a sustainable future? European environmental policy and local economic development? *Local Environment*, **1**: 3, 247–258

Gibbs D., Longhurst J. and Braithwaite C. (1996) Moving towards sustainable development? Integrating economic development and the environment in local authorities, *Journal of Planning and Management*, **39**: 3, 317–332

Giddens A. (1991) *Modernity and Self Identity: Self and Society in the Late Modern Age*, Polity Press: Oxford

Gilg A. (1978) *Countryside Planning*, David and Charles: Newton Abbott

Gilg A. (1996) *Countryside Planning*, 2nd edn, Routledge: London

Glickman N.J. (1977) *Econometric Analysis of Regional Systems: Explorations in Model Building and Policy Analysis*, Academic Press: London

Gleick J. (1988) *Chaos: The Making of a New Science*, Heinemann: London

Goddard J., Charles D., Pike A., Potts G. and Bradley D. (1994) *Universities and Communities*, Committee of Vice-Chancellors and Principals: London

Goe W.R. (1994) The producer services sector and development within the deindustrializing urban community, *Social Forces*, **72**: 4, 971–1009

Goodwin M., Cloke P. and Milbourne P. (1995) Regulation theory and rural research: theorising contemporary rural change, *Environment and Planning A*, **27**, 1245–1260

Goodwin M. and Painter J. (1996) Local governance, the crisis of Fordism and the changing geographers of regulation, *Transactions of the Institute of British Geographers*, **21**: 4, 635–648

Goodwin P.B. (1978) Travel choice and time budgets, in Hensher and Dalvi (eds) *Determinants of Travel Choices*, Saxon House: London

Goodwin P.B. (1996) *The Real Effects of Environmentally Friendly Transport Policies*, Consultation Draft, ESRC Transport and Environment Research Programme

Goodwin P.B., Hallett S., Kenny F. and Stokes G. (1991) *Transport: the New Realism*, Transport Studies Unit, University of Oxford: Oxford

Gordon I. (1997) Densities, urban form and travel behaviour, *Town and Country Planning*, **66**: 9, 239–241

Graham S. and Marvin S. (1996) *Telecommunications and the City – Electronic Spaces, Urban Places*, Routledge: London

Grant W. (ed.) (1995) *The Political Economy of Corporatism*, Macmillan: Basingstoke

Greco T.H. (1994) *New Money for Healthy Communities*, Thomas H Greco: Tucson, Arizona

Green Balance (1994) *The Housing Numbers Game*, CPRE: London

Gross H.T. (1995) The role of health services in metropolitan and central city economic development: the example of Dallas, *Economic Development Quarterly*, **9**, 1: 80–86

Groundwork (1997) *Meeting Local Agenda 21*, Groundwork: Birmingham

Grove-White R. (1992) Land use law and the environment, in Churchill R., Gibson J. and Warren L. (eds) *Law, Policy and the Environment*, Blackwell: Oxford

Grove-White R. (1997a) Environmental sustainability, time and uncertainty, *Time and Society*, **6**, 99–107

Grove-White R. (1997b) Currents of cultural change, *Town and Country Planning*, **66**, 169–171

Guardian (1997) Britain's green lead at UN, *The Guardian*, 24 June 1997

Haber H. (1994) *Beyond Postmodern Politics*, Routledge: London

Habermas J. (1984) *The Theory of Communicative Action* Vol. 1. *Reason and the Rationalisation of Society*, Polity Press: Cambridge

Habermas J. (1987) *The Theory of Communicative Action* Vol. 2. *Lifeworld and System: A Critique of Functionalist Reason*, Polity Press: Cambridge

Hadley R. and Clough R. (1996) *Care in Chaos: Frustration and Challenge in Community Care*, Cassell: London

Haggett P., Cliff A.D. and Frey A.E. (1977) *Locational Analysis in Human Geography*, Edward Arnold: London

Haigh N. (1995) Environmental protection in the DOE (1970–1995) or one and a half cheers for bureaucracy, in Department of the Environment, *A Perspective for Change*, DoE: London

Haigh N. (1997) *Manual of Environmental Policy*, Cartermill: London

Hall M. (1994) Industrial relations and the social dimension of European integration: before and after Maastricht, in Hyman R. and Ferner A. (eds) *New Frontiers in Industrial Relations*, Blackwell: London

Hall P. (1973) The containment of urban Britain, Vol 1. *Urban and Metropolitan Growth Processes*, Allen and Unwin: London

Hall P. (1989) *Urban and Regional Planning*, 2nd edn, Unwin Hyman: London

Hall P. (1992) Transport maker and breaker of cities, in Mannion A.M. and Bowlby S.R. (eds) *Environmental Issues in the 1990s*, John Wiley: Chichester

Hall P. (1997) Who says we have to slum it? *The Guardian*, 5 February, p. 2

Hall P., Gracey H., Drewett R. and Thomas R. (1973) *The Containment of Urban England*, Allen and Unwin: London

Hall P. and Hass-Klau C. (1985) *Can Rail Save the City? The Impacts of Rail Rapid Transit and Pedestrianisation on British and German Cities*, Gower: Aldershot

Hall P. et al. (1996) *The Single Regeneration Budget. A Review of Challenge Fund Round II*, University of Birmingham: Birmingham

Hancock K. et al. (1991) *Housing Subsidies in Glasgow*, Joseph Rowntree Foundation: York

Hantrais L. (1995) *Social Policy in the European Union*, Macmillan Press: London

Harvey D. (1997) Contested cities: social process and spatial form, in Jewson N. and MacGregor S. (eds) *Transforming Cities: Contested Governance and New Spatial Divisions*, Routledge: London

Harrington J.W. (1995a) Empirical research on producer service growth and regional development, *The Professional Geographer*, **47**: 1, 66–69

Harrington J.W. (1995b) Producer services research in U.S. regional studies, *The Professional Geographer*, **47**: 1, 87–96

Harris N. (1996) Officer-Delegation in Development Control, unpublished postgraduate dissertation, Department of City and Regional Planning, University of Wales Cardiff

Harrison C., Burgess J. and Filius P. (1996) Rationalizing environmental responsibilities: a comparison of lay publics in the UK and the Netherlands, *Global Environmental Change*, **6**, 215–234

Hastings A. and McArthur A. (1995) A comparative assessment of government approaches to partnerships with the local community, in Hambleton R. and Thomas H. (eds) *Urban Policy Evaluation*, Paul Chapman: Liverpool

Haughton G. and Whitney D. (eds) (1994) *Reinventing a Region: Restructuring in West Yorkshire*, Avebury Press: Aldershot

Haughton G. and Williams C.C. (eds) (1996) *Corporate City?: Partnership, Participation and Partition in Urban Development in Leeds*, Avebury Press: Aldershot

Hayton K. (1996) Planning policy in Scotland, in Tewdwr-Jones M. (ed.) *British Planning Policy in Transition – Planning in the 1990s*, UCL Press: London

Hayton K. (1997) Planning in a Scottish parliament, *Town and Country Planning*, 66, 208–209

Headicar P. (1995) Future roles for urban public transport, Paper presented at Current Planning Practice Seminar on Priorities for Public Transport, School of Planning and Housing, Edinburgh College of Art/Heriot-Watt University, November

Healey P. (1983) *Local Plans in British Land Use Planning*, Pergamon: Oxford

Healey P. (1996) Consensus-building across difficult divisions: new approaches to collaborative strategy making, *Planning Practice and Research*, 11: 2, 207–216

Healey P. (1997) *Collaborative Planning: Shaping Places in Fragmented Societies*, Macmillan: London

Healey P., Cameron S., Davoudi S., Graham S. and Madanu-Pour A. (eds) (1995) *Managing Cities: The New Urban Context*, Wiley: Chichester

Healey P., McNamara P., Elson M. and Doak J. (1988) *Land Use Planning and the Mediation of Urban Change*, Cambridge University Press: Cambridge

Healey P. and Shaw T. (1994) Changing meanings of 'environment' in the British planning system, *Transactions of the Institute of British Geographers*, 19, 425–438

Healey P. and Underwood J. (1979) Professional ideals and planning practice: a report on research into planners' ideas in practice in London borough planning departments, *Progress in Planning*, 9, 73–127

Hebdige D. (1989) New times: after the masses, *Marxism Today*, January

Held D. (1992) *Liberalism, Marxism and Democracy*, in Hall S., Held D. and McGrew T. (eds) *Modernity and its Futures*, Open University Press: Milton Keynes

Henderson C. (1997) The other big issue, *New Scientist*, 4 January, pp. 12–13

Hepworth M. and Ducatel K. (1992) *Transport in the Information Age: Wheels and Wires*, Belhaven Press: London

Heseltine M. (1991) Speech to Manchester Chamber of Commerce and Industry, 11 March 1991

Higgins J.C. (1980) *Strategic and Operational Planning Systems: Principles and Practice*, Prentice-Hall: London

Higgins M. and Allmendinger P. (forthcoming) *The Changing Nature of Public Planning Practice under the New Right: the Legacies and Implications of Privatisation* (copies available from authors)

Hill D. (1994) *Citizens and Cities: Urban policy in the 1990s*, Harvester Wheatsheaf: Hemel Hempstead

Hillier J. (1995) Deconstructing the discourse of planning, in Mandelbaum S. and Mazza L. (eds) *Planning Theory in the 1990s*, CUPR Press: New Jersey

Hillier Parker (1995) The impact of PPG13, paper presented at University of Westminster/Local Transport Today Conference on Land-use and Transport: Reducing the Need to Travel, Regent's Park Hotel, October

Hillman M. (1996) Curbing car use; the danger of exaggerating the future role public transport, *Traffic Engineering and Control*, 37: 1, 26–29

Hillman M., Adams J.G.U. and Whitelegg J. (1991) *One False Move . . . A Study of Children's Independent Mobility*, Policy Studies Institute: London

Hine J.P. and Rye T. (1997) The theory and practice of using planning to manage transport demand: a survey of Scottish experience, paper presented to Association of European Planning Schools Congress, May, Nijmegen, Netherlands

Hirsch D. (ed.) (1997) *Social Protection and Inclusion: European Challenges for the UK*, Joseph Rowntree Foundation: York

Hoare A. (1997) Privatization comes to town: national policies and local responses – the Bristol case, *Regional Studies*, **31**: 3, 253–265

HoC (House of Commons) (1995a) *Environment Committee. First Report. Single Regeneration Budget*. Vol. I, House of Commons Paper, HCP 26–I, HMSO: London

HoC (1995b) *Environment Committee. First Report. Single Regeneration Budget*. Vol. II, House of Commons Paper, HCP 26–II, HMSO: London

HoCSCE (House of Commons Select Committee on the Environment) (1995) *Housing Need*, Second Report, Vol. 2, HMSO: London

Hoch C. (1984) What Planners Do. *Power, Politics and Persuasion*, American Planning Association: Chicago

Hoggett P. (1991) A new management in the public sector, *Policy and Politics*, **19**: 4, 143–156

Hoggett P. (1996) New modes of control in the public sector, *Public Administration*, **74**, 9–32

Hogwood B. (1995) *The Integrated Regional Offices and the Single Regeneration Budget*, Commission for Local Democracy Research Report No. 13, CLD: London

Holmans A. (1996) Housing demand and need in England to 2011: the national picture, in Breheny M. and Hall P. (eds) *The People – Where Will They Go?* TCPA: London

House of Commons Transport Committee (1995) Urban Road Pricing, Third Report, Vol. 1, Report and Minutes of Proceedings, Transport Committee, HMSO: London

Housing Corporation (1996) *North Eastern Policy Statement 1996/97: Yorkshire and Humberside Programme*, Housing Corporation: London

Hull A. (1997) Restructuring the debate on allocating land for housing growth, *Housing Studies*, **12**, 367–382

Hyman R. (1992) Trade unions and the disaggregation of the working class, in Regin M. (ed.) *The Future of Labour Movements*, Sage: London

Hyman R. and Ferner A. (eds) (1994) *New Frontiers in Industrial Relations*, Blackwell: London

IHT (Institute of Highways and Transportation) (1996) *Guidelines on Developing Urban Transport Strategies*, IHT: London

IHT (1997) *Transport in the Urban Environment*, IHT: London

Ilbery B. and Bowler I. (1998) From agricultural productivism to post productivism, in Ilbery B. (ed.) *The Geography of Rural Change*, Longman: Harlow

ILO (International Labour Organisation) (1996) *World Employment 1996*, ILO: Geneva

Imbroscio D.L. (1995) An alternative approach to urban economic development: exploring the dimensions and prospects of a self-reliance strategy, *Urban Affairs Review*, **30**: 6, 840–867

Imrie R. (1996) *Disability and the City: International Perspectives*, Paul Chapman: London

Imrie R. and Raco M. (1997) Assessing closures in the new local governance, paper presented to the XIth Congress of the Association of European Schools of Planning, University of Nijmegen, Nijmegen, Netherlands, 28–31 May

Imrie R. and Raco M. (1998) Mediating global–local relations through institutional and collaborative governance: a critique, paper presented at the Association of American Geographers Annual Conference, Boston, Massachusetts, USA, 27–31 March

Imrie R. and Thomas H. (1993a) The limits of property-led regeneration, *Environment & Planning C: Government and Policy*, **11**, 87–102

Imrie R. and Thomas H. (eds) (1993) *British Urban Policy and the Urban Development Corporations*, Paul Chapman: London

290

IUCN (International Union for Conservation of Nature) (1991) *Caring for the Earth*, Gland, IUCN, UNEP and WWF: Switzerland

Jacobs J. (1961) *The Death and Life of Great American Cities*, Penguin: London

Jacobs J. (1969) *The Economy of Cities*, Random House: New York

Jacobs M. (1993) *Sense and Sustainability*, CPRE: London

Jacobs M. (1999) Reflections on the discourse and politics of sustainable development. Part II: Assumptions, contradictions, progress, *Political Studies* (forthcoming)

James N. and Pharoah T. (1992) The traffic generation game, in Roberts J., Cleary J., Hamilton K. and Hanna J. (eds) *Travel Sickness – The Need for Sustainable Transport Policy for Britain*, Lawrence and Wishart: London

Jones C. (1979) Population decline in cities, in Jones C. (ed.) *Urban Deprivation and the Inner City*, Croom Helm: London

Jones C. and Mills C. (1996) *The Definition of Housing Market Areas*, Department of Land Economics, University of Paisley

Judd D.R. and Ready R.L. (1986) Entrepreneurial cities and the new politics of economic development, in Peterson G.E. and Lewis C.W. (eds) *Reagan and the Cities*, The Urban Institute Press: Washington DC

Kauffman S.A. (1995) *At Home in the Universe*, Oxford University Press: New York

Keating M. (1991) *Comparative Urban Politics*, Edward Elgar: Aldershot

Kettle J. and Moran C. (1995) Managing mean streets? Housing and anti-social behaviour in Leeds, *Regional Review*, **5**: 3, 16–18

Keyner E. (1997) Sacred cows or dinosaurs? *Planning*, 18 April, p. 14

Kintrea K. (1996) Whose partnership? Community interests in the regeneration of a Scottish housing scheme, *Housing Studies*, **11**, 287–306

Kirklees Metropolitan Borough Council (1991) *Economic Development Strategy*, Kirklees Metropolitan Borough Council: Huddersfield

Labour Party (1995) *Partnership for Investment*, Labour Party: London

Lancashire County Council (1997) Green Audit 2, Lancashire County Council: Preston

Lane D. and Maxfield R. (1996) *Foresight, Complexity and Strategy*. Copies available from the author at maxfield@leland.stanford.edu

Lang P. (1994) *LETS Work: Rebuilding the Local Economy*, Grover Books: Bristol

Larkham P. (1996) *Conservation and the City*, Routledge: London

Law C. (1993) *Urban Tourism: Attracting Visitors to Large Cities*, Mansell: London

Leach S., Davis H. and Associates (1996) *Enabling or Disabling Local Government*, Open University Press: Buckingham

Lean G. (1994) New green army rises up against roads, *The Observer*, 20 February

Leatherwood T. (1983) Pension fund investment, in Jones D. and Webb L. (eds) *America's Cities and Counties: a Citizen's Agenda*, Washington DC: Proceedings of Conference on Alternative State and Local Policies

Lee P. *et al.* (1995) *The Price of Social Exclusion*, NFHA: London

Leeds City Council (1994) *Housing Strategy 1995/96–1997/98*, LCC: Leeds

Le Gales P. and Mawson J. (1994) *Management Innovations in Urban Policy. Lessons from France*, Local Government Management Board: Luton

Leyshon A. and Thrift N. (1995) Geographies of financial exclusion: financial abandonment in Britain and the United States, *Transactions*, **20**, 312–341

LGMB (Local Government Management Board) (1993) *A Framework for Local Sustainability*, LGMB: Luton

LGMB (1995) *Sustainability Indicators Research Project*, LGMB: Luton

LGMB (1997) *Local Agenda 21 in the UK – the First Five Years*, LGMB: Luton

Liebfried S. (1993) Towards a European welfare state? In Jones C. (ed.) *New Perspectives on the Welfare State in Europe*, Routledge: London

Lin Z. (1996) Averting decision chaos under external threats: exploring the roles of organisation structures and decision making rules, copies available from the author at Dept of Management Organisations, Hong Kong University of Science and Technology, Clear Water Bay, Kowloon, Hong Kong. Email: mnlin@usthk.ust.hk

Lissack M. (1996) Complexity metaphors and the management of knowledge based enterprise: an exploration of discovery, copies available from the author at Henley Management Centre, University of Hertfordshire, Hertford, England

Little J., Clements J. and Jones O. (1998) Rural challenge and the changing culture of rural regeneration policy, in Oatley N. (ed.) *Cities, Economic Competition and Urban Policy*, Paul Chapman: London

Local Transport Today (1996) New regime opens the door to 'buy now, pay later' for council transport projects, *Local Transport Today*, 20 June, pp. 12–13

London Borough of Newham (1996) *Draft Unitary Development Plan*, LBN: London

Lovering J. (1997) Global restructuring and local impact, in Pacione M. (ed.) *Britain's Cities: Geography of Division in Urban Britain*, Routledge: London

Low N. (1991) *Planning, Politics and the State: Political Foundations of Planning Thought*, Unwin Hyman: London

Lowe P. (1995) Vision without strategy: The rural White Paper, *Countryside Recreation Network News*, **3**: 3, November, pp. 18–19

Lowe P. and Ward S. (1998) *British Environmental Policy and Europe*, Routledge: London

Lowndes V. (1996) Varieties of new institutionalism: a critical appraisal, *Public Administration*, **74**: 2, 181–197

Lund B. (1996) *Housing Problems and Housing Policy*, Longman: London

Lyotard J.-F. (1984) *The Postmodern Condition*, Manchester University Press: Manchester

McArthur A. (1993) Community partnership – a formula for neighbourhood regeneration in the 1990s? *Community Development Journal*, **28**, 305–315

McConnell S. (1981) *Theories of Planning*, Heinemann: London

MacDonald K. (1997) Mind over matter, *Planning*, 13 June, p. 18

MacDonald R. (1995) Disability and planning policy guidance, paper presented to the Access Sub-committee, Oxford City Council, 7 March

MacFarlane R. (1993) *Community Involvement in City Challenge. A Good Practice Guide*, National for Council Voluntary Organisations: London

MacFarlane R. and Mabbott J. (1993) *City Challenge: Involving Local Communities*, National Council for Voluntary Organisations: London

McKillop D.G., Ferguson C. and Nesbitt C. (1995) The competitive position of credit unions in the United Kingdom: a sectoral analysis, *Local Economy*, **10**, 48–64

Maclennan D. (1992) *Housing Search and Choice in a Regional Housing System: New Housing in Strathclyde*, Report to the Housing Research Foundation, Centre for Housing Research: University of Glasgow

Maclennan D., Munro M. and Wood G. (1989) Housing choice and the structure of urban housing markets, in Turner B., Kemeny J. and Lundquist A. (eds) *Between State and Market Housing in the Post-Industrial Era*, Almquist and Hicksell: Gothenburg

Maclennan D. with Pryce G. (1998) *Missing Links: the Economy, Cities and Housing*, The Housing Corporation/NHF: London

Maclennan D. and Tu Y. (1996) Economic perspectives on the structure of local housing systems, *Housing Studies*, **11**: 3, 387–406

McManus P. (1996) Contested terrains: politics, stories and discourses of sustainability, *Environmental Politics*, **5**, 48–73

Macnaghten P., Grove-White R., Jacobs M. and Wynne B. (1995) *Public Perceptions and Sustainability: Indicators, Institutions, Participation*, Lancashire County Council: Preston

292

Macnaghten P. and Jacobs M. (1997) Public identification with sustainable development: investigating cultural barriers to participation, *Global Environmental Change*, **7**, 1–20

Macnaghten P. and Urry J. (1998) *Contested Natures*, Sage: London

McNulty J.E. (1977) A test of the time dimension in economic base analysis, *Land Economics*, **53**, 358–368

McRae H. (1994) *The World in 2020. Power, Culture and Prosperity: A Vision of the Future*, Harper Collins: London

Malpass P. (1993) Housing management and residualisation, *Housing Review*, **42**: 4, July–August

Malpass P. (1996) Unravelling housing policy in Britain, *Housing Studies*, **11**, 459–470

Malpass P. and Murie A. (1994) *Housing Policy and Practice*, Macmillan: London

Mandel E. (1995) *Long Waves of Capitalist Development*, Verso: London

Mandelbaum T.B. and Chicoine D.L. (1986) The effect of timeframe in the estimation of employment multipliers, *Regional Science Perspectives*, **12**: 37–50

Marsh D. and Rhodes R.A.W. (1992) *Implementing Thatcherite Policies: Audit of an Era*, Buckingham: Open University Press

Marshall J.N. and Wood P.A. (1995) *Services and Space: Key Aspects of Urban and Regional Development*, Longman: Harlow

Marshall T. (1994) British Planning and the new environmentalism, *Planning Practice and Research*, **9**: 1, 21–30

Marshall T. (1996) British land use planning and the European Union, in Buckingham-Hatfield S. and Evans B. (eds) *Environmental Planning and Sustainability*, pp. 125–144, Wiley: London

Mawson J. *et al.* (1995) *The Single Regeneration Budget: The Stocktake*, Birmingham, Centre for Urban and Regional Studies: University of Birmingham

Meen G., Maclennan D. and Stephens M. (1997) Supply and sustainability: home-ownership in Britain, in Wilcox S. (ed.) *Housing Finance Review*, Joseph Rowntree Foundation: York

Metropolitan Transport Research Unit (1996) *For Whom the Shadow Tolls*, London

Milan Report (1996) *Renewing the Regions. Strategies for Regional Economic Development,*. Report of the Regional Policy Commission: Sheffield, Sheffield Hallam University

Ministry of Housing and Local Government (1969) *People and Planning*, HMSO: London

Monk S. and Whitehead C. (1996) Land supply and housing: a case study, *Housing Studies*, **11**: 3, 407–423

Moore V. (1995) *Planning Law*, 5th edn, Blackstone Press: London

Moore-Milroy B. (1991) Into postmodern weightlessness, *Journal of Planning Education and Research*, **10**: 3

Morphet J. (1996) *Lessons from Europe: Town and Country Planning Summer School Proceedings*, 1996. p. 55

Morphet J. (1997) There'll be planning, but not as we know it, *Town and Country Planning*, **66**: 4, 122–123

Morphet J. (1998) Personal communication

Morphet J. and Hams T. (1994) Responding to Rio: a local authority approach, *Journal of Environmental Planning and Management*, **37**: 4, 479–486

Morgan G., Fennell J. and Farrer J. (1993) Authorities struggling to deliver sustainable plans, *Planning 1047*, 3 December, pp. 20–21

Moulaert F. and Todtling F. (1995a) Preface, *Progress in Planning*, **43**: 2–3, 101–106

Moulaert F. and Todtling F. (1995b) Conclusions and prospects, *Progress in Planning*, **43**: 2–3, 261–274

Moxon-Browne E. (1993) Social Europe, in Lodge J. (ed.) *The European Community and the Challenge of the Future*, Pinter: London

Mulgan G. (1997) *Connexity*, Chatto and Windus: London

Murdoch J. and Marsden T. (1994) *Reconstructing Rurality: Class Community and Power in the Development Process*, UCL Press: London

Murray C. (1990) *The Emerging Underclass*, Choice in Welfare Series No 2. Institute for Economic Affairs: London

Murray C. (1994) *Underclass: The Crisis Deepens*, Choice in Welfare Series No. 20. Institute for Economic Affairs: London

Murphy R. (1989) *Realism and Tinsel: Cinema and Society in Britain 1939–49*, Routledge: London

Myers G. and Macnaghten P. (1998) Public rhetorics of environmental sustainability: persuasion, participation, action, *Environment and Planning A*, **30**: 2, 333–353

Myerscough J. (1988) *The Economic Importance of the Arts in Britain*, Policy Studies Institute: London

Myerson G. and Rydin Y. (1996) Sustainable development: the implications of the global debate for land use planning, in Buckingham-Hatfield S. and Evans B. (eds) *Environmental Planning and Sustainability*, Wiley: London

Nadin V. (1998) Planning and the UK presidency, *Town and Country Planning*, **67**: 2, 60–63

Nadin V. and Doak J. (1991) •••

Nadin V. and Shaw M. (1998) Transnational Spatial Planning in Europe: The Role of Interreg IIc in the UK. *Regional Studies*, **32**: 3, 281–299

Naess P. (1993) Can urban development be made environmentally sound? *Journal of Environmental Planning and Management*, **36**: 3, 301–333

National Audit Office (1990) *Regenerating the Inner Cities*, HMSO: London

National Consumer Council (1987) *What's Wrong with Walking?* HMSO: London

Nevin B. and Shiner P. (1994) Behind the chimera of urban funding, *Local Work*, 52

Nevin B. and Shiner P. (1995) The single regeneration budget: urban funding and the future for distressed communities, *Local Work*, 58

Newby H. (1979) *Green and Pleasant Land? Social Change in Rural England*, Hutchinson: London

New Life for Urban Scotland (1988) *New Life for Urban Scotland*, Scottish Office: Edinburgh

Newman P.W.G. and Kenworthy J.R. (1989) Gasoline consumption and cities, *Journal of the American Planning Association*, Winter, pp. 24–37

Newman P. and Thornley A. (1996) *Urban Planning in Europe. International Competition, National Systems and Planning Projects*, Routledge: London

Newstrom J.W., Reif W.E. and Monczka R.M. (1975) *A Contingency Approach to Management Readings*, McGraw-Hill: New York

NFHA (1995) *The Price of Social Exclusion*, NFHA: London

NHTPC (National Housing and Town Planning Council) (1995) *Methodology for Assessing Housing Need*, NHTPC: London

Nocon A. and Qureshi H. (1996) *Outcomes of Community Care for Users and Carers*, Open University Press: Buckingham

Nuttgens P. (1989) *The Home Front*, BBC: London

Oatley N. (1995) Competitive urban policy and the regeneration game, *Town Planning Review*, 66, 1–14

Oatley N. (ed.) (1998) *Cities Economic Competition and Urban Policy*, Paul Chapman: London

OECD (1993) Core set of indicators for environmental performance reviews, *Environment Monographs No. 83*, OECD: Paris

OECD/ECMT (Organisation for Economic Co-operation and Development/European Conference of Ministers of Transport (1995) *Urban Travel and Sustainable Development*, ECMT/OECD: Paris

O'Farrell P.N. (1993) The performance of business service firms in peripheral regions: an international comparison between Scotland and Nova Scotia, *Environment and Planning A*, **25**: 1627–1648

Office of Science and Technology (1995) *Technology Foresight: Progress through Partnership – Transport*, HMSO: London

Offe C. (1996) *Modernity and the State: East, West*, Polity Press: Cambridge

Offe C. and Heinze R.G. (1992) *Beyond Employment: Time, Work and the Informal Economy*, Polity Press: Cambridge

O'Riordan T. and Voisey H. (1997) The political economy of sustainable development, *Environmental Politics*, **6**, 1–23

Orwell G. (1941) England, your England. pamphlet, cited in Barr (1993)

Ove Arup Partners (1995) *Implementation of PPG 13* – Interim Report, DoE: London

Owens S. (1986) *Energy, Planning and Urban Form*, Pion: London

Owens, S. (1991a) *Energy-conscious Planning: The Case for Action*, Council for the Protection of Rural England: London

Owens S. (1991b) Energy efficiency and sustainable land use patterns, *Town and Country Planning*, February, pp. 44–45

Owens S. (1994) Land, limits and sustainability, *Transactions, Institute of British Geographers*, **19**, 439–456

Owens S. (1995) The compact city and energy consumption, a response to Michael Breheny, *Transactions of the Institute of British Geographers*, **20**: 3, 81–384

Owens S. (1997) Giants in the path – planning sustainability and environmental values, *Town Planning Review*, **68**: 3, 293–304

Page D. (1993) *Building for Communities*, Joseph Rowntree Foundation: York

Pahl R. (1998) presentation to Housing Corporation/National Housing Federation conference, Manchester, 22 April

Parkinson M. and Harding A. (1994) European Cities towards 2000: problems and prospects, in Hantrais L. (ed.) *Polarisation and Urban Space Cross National Research Papers*, University of Loughborough: Loughborough

Parkinson M. and Le Gales P. (1995) Urban policy in France and Britain: cross-channel lessons, *Policy Studies*, **16**: 2, 31–42

Parkhurst G. (1994) Park and ride: could it lead to an increase in car traffic? *Transport Policy*, **2**: 1, 5–23

Parking Committee for London (1995) *Annual Report and Accounts 1994/95*, London

Parr J.B. and Jones C. (1983) City size distributions and urban density functions: some inter-relationships, *Journal of Regional Science*, **23**: 3, 283–307

Pawson H. and Watkins C. (1998) Examining spatial patterns in the pace of housing commodification, *Tidjschrift voor Economische en Sociale Geografie*, **89**

Peck J. (1996) *Work Place and the Social Regulation of Labour Markets*, The Guildford Press

Peck J. and Tickell A. (1991) Regulation theory and the geographies of flexible accumulation: transitions in capitalism; transitions in theory, *Spatial Policy Analysis Working Paper 12*, Manchester: School of Geography: University of Manchester

Persky J., Ranney D. and Wiewel W. (1993) Import substitution and local economic development, *Economic Development Quarterly*, **7**, 18–29

Pharoah T. (1996) Reducing the need to travel, *Land Use Policy*, **13**: 1, 23–26

Pharoah T. and Russell J. (1989) *Traffic Calming: Policy and Evaluations in Three European Countries*, Occasional Paper 2/1989, Department of Planning, Housing and Development, South Bank Polytechnic: London

Pierson P. and Liebfried S. (1995) The dynamics of social policy integration, in Pierson P. and Liebfried S. (eds) *European Social Policy between Fragmentation and Integration*, The Brookings Institute: Washington DC

Pilkington C. (1995) *Britain in the European Union Today*, Manchester University Press: Manchester

Pinfield G. (1996) Beyond sustainability indicators, *Local Environment*, **1**, 151–163

Pinfield G. (1997) Sustainability indicators: a new tool for evaluation? in Farthing S. (ed.) *Evaluating Local Environmental Policy*, Avebury Press: Aldershot

Planning (1998) Advisors tell Government to raise brownfield target, *Planning*, 27 March, p. 5

Polese M. (1982) Regional demand for business services and inter-regional service flows in a small Canadian region, *Papers of the Regional Science Association*, **50**, 151–163

Pollitt C. (1993) *Managerialism and the Public Services*, Blackwell: Oxford

Porritt J. (1996) Local jobs depend on local initiative, *Finance North*, September/October, p. 88

Potter C. (1998) Conserving nature: agri-environmental policy development and change in Ilbery B. (ed.) *The Geography of Rural Change*, Longman: Harlow

Potter J. (1994) Consumerism and the public sector: how well does the coat fit? in McKevitt D. and Lawson A. (eds) *Public Sector Management: Theory, Critique, and Practice*, Sage: London

Potter S. and Cole S. (1992) Funding an integrated transport policy, in Roberts J., Cleary J., Hamilton K. and Hanna J. (eds) *Travel Sickness – The Need for Sustainable Transport Policy for Britain*, Lawrence and Wishart: London

Power A. (1996) Area-based poverty and resident empowerment, *Urban Studies*, **33**: 9, 1535–1564

Power A. and Tunstall R. (1995) *Swimming against the Tide*, Joseph Rowntree Foundation: York

Power T.M. (1988) *The Economic Pursuit of Quality*, Sharp Armonk: New York

Price B. (1997) The myth of postmodern science, in Eve R., Horsfall S. and Lee M. (eds) *Chaos, Complexity and Sociology. Myths, Models and Theories*, Sage: London

Priestley J.B. (1979) *English Journey*, Harmondsworth: London

Prince of Wales (1988) *A Vision of Britain*, Doubleday: London

Prior D. (1995) Citizen's Charters, in Stewart J. and Stoker G. (eds) *Local Government in the 1990s*, Macmillan: London

Prior D. (1996) Working the network: local authority strategies in the reticulated local state, *Local Government Studies*, **22**: 2, 92–104

Ravetz A. (1991) The lost promise of the healthy city, *Town and Country Planning*, **60**: 11/12, 323–324

Ratcliffe J. and Stubbs M. (1996) *Urban Planning and Real Estate Development*, UCL Press: London

RCEP (Royal Commission on Environmental Pollution) (1994) Transport and the Environment, Eighteenth Report, HMSO: London

Reade E. (1987) *British Town and Country Planning*, Open University: Milton Keynes

Redclift M. (1992) Sustainable development and global environmental change: implications of a changing agenda, *Global Environmental Change*, **2**, 32–42

Redclift M. (1993) Sustainable development: concepts, contradictions, and conflicts, in Allen P. (ed.) *Food for the Future: Conditions and Contradictions of Sustainability*, John Wiley: London

Redclift M. (1995) The UK and international environmental agenda: Rio and after, in Gray T. (ed.) *UK Environmental Policy in the 1990s*, Macmillan: London

Rhodes R. (1987) Developing the public service orientation, *Local Government Studies*, May–June, pp. 63–73

Rickaby P.A. (1987) Six settlement patterns compared, *Environment and Planning B: Planning and Design*, **14**, 193–223

Ridley N. (1987) *The Local Right*, Centre for Policy Studies: London

Ridings Housing Association Ltd (1996) *Annual Report*

Rifkin J. and Barber R. (1978) *The North Will Rise Again: Pension, Politics and Power in the 1980s*, Beacon: Boston

Roberts J. (1981) *Pedestrian Precincts in Britain*, TEST: London

Roberts P. (1996) European spatial planning and the environment: planning for sustainable development, *European Environment*, 6, 77–84

Roberts P. (1998) Reviving strategic planning: the European and UK context, paper presented to the Royal Town Planning Institute Conference on Strategic Planning Issue, Edinburgh

Robson B. *et al.* (1994) *Assessing the Impact of Urban Policy*, HMSO: London

Roche M. (1992) *Rethinking Citizenship, Welfare, Ideology and Change in Modern Society*, Polity Press: Cambridge

Roger-Machart C. (1997) The sustainable city – myth or reality, *Town and Country Planning*, **66**: 2, 53–55

Rowan-Robinson J., Ross A. and Walton W. (1995) Sustainable development and the development control process, *Town Planning Review*, **66**: 3, 269–286

RTPI (Royal Town Planning Institute) (1997) *Members' Survey*, RTPI: London

Russell H., Dawson J., Garside P. and Parkinson M. (1996) *City Challenge Interim National Evaluation*, DoE: London

Rutland District Council (1996) *Blueprint for Success*, Rutland District Council

Rydin Y. (1997) Planning, Property and the Environment, *Planning Practice and Research*, **120**: 1, 5–7

Sachs W. (ed.) (1993) *Global Ecology: a New Arena of Global Conflict*, Zed Books: London

Sassen S. (1991) *The Global City: New York, London, Tokyo*, Princeton: Princeton University Press: Princeton

Saunders P. (1980) *Urban Politics: A Sociological Interpretation*, Penguin: London

Scott A.J. and Roweis S.T. (1977) Urban planning in theory and practice – a reappraisal, *Environment and Planning A*, 9, 1097–1119

Scottish Consumer Council (1998) *Travel Choices and Behaviour – A Study of Urban Travel Patterns*, Scottish Office Central Research Unit: Edinburgh

Scottish Homes (1993) *Local Market Analysis and Planning in Scottish Homes: A Best Practice Guide*, Scottish Homes: Edinburgh

Scottish Office (1977) *Scottish Housing: A Consultative Document*, HMSO: Edinburgh

Scottish Office (1993) *Progress in Partnership*, Scottish Office: Edinburgh

Scottish Office (1994a) *Programme for Partnership, Announcement of the Scottish Office Review of Urban Regeneration Policy*, Scottish Office: Edinburgh

Scottish Office (1994b) *Programme for Partnership. Guidance for Applying for Urban Programme Funding*, Scottish Office: Edinburgh

Scottish Office (1994c) *The Planning System*, Scottish Office: Edinburgh

Scottish Office (1996a) *NPPG3: Land for Housing*, Scottish Office: Edinburgh

Scottish Office (1996b) *PAN38 – Structure Plans: Housing Land Requirements*, Scottish Office: Edinburgh

Scottish Office (1996c) *Draft National Planning Policy Guideline – Transport and Planning*, Development Department, Edinburgh

Scottish Office (1998a) *Travel Choices for Scotland – The Scottish Integrated Transport White Paper*, Scottish Office, Edinburgh

Scottish office (1998b) *Draft National Planning Policy Guideline (NPPG) Transport and Planning*, Scottish Office, Edinburgh

Selman P. (1995) Local sustainability, *Town Planning Review*, **66**: 3, 287–301

Shaw D. (1992) Traffic impact study for a retail store, paper presented 4th Annual TRICS Conference, September

Shaw D.P. and Hale A. (1996) Realising capital assets: an additional stand to the farm diversification debate, *Journal of Environmental Planning and Management*, **39**: 3, 403–418

Shaw M. (1979) *Rural Deprivation and Planning*, Geobooks: Norwich

Shaw P. (1996) *Intervening in the Shadow Systems of Organisations*, Complexity and Management Papers No. 4, Complexity and Management Centre: University of Hertfordshire

Shutt J. and Colwell A. (1997) *Towards 2006 European Union Regional Policy and UK Local Government*, Local Government Information Unit: London

Skelcher C. (1996) Public service consumerism: some questions of strategy, *Community Development Journal*, **31**: 1, 66–72

Smart B. (1993) *Postmodernity*, Routledge: London

Soil Association (1996) *Directory of Organic Farm Shops and Box Scheme List*, Soil Association: Bristol

Southwood R. (1997) Transport – the crucial basis for sustainability, *Planning*, **66**: 4, 116–118

Stacey R. (1996a) *Complexity and Creativity in Organisations*, Berrett-Koehler: San Francisco

Stacey R. (1996b) *Excitement and Tension at the Edge of Chaos*, Complexity and Management Papers No. 6, Complexity and Management Centre: University of Hertfordshire

Stationery Office (1998) *English House Condition Survey 1996*, HMSO: London

Stewart J. (1997) The great housing debate, *Housebuilder*, Jan/Feb, pp. 10–11

Stewart J. and Ranson S. (1994) *Management for the Public Domain: Enabling the Learning Society*, Macmillan: London

Stewart J. and Stoker G. (1995) *Local Government in the 1990s*, Macmillan: London

Stillwell J. and Leigh C. (1996) Exploring the geographies of social polarisation in Leeds, in Haughton G. and Williams C.C. (eds)

Stoker G. (1991) *The Politics of Local Government*, 2nd edn, Macmillan: London

Streeck W. (1995) From market making to state building? Reflections on the political economy of European social policy, in Liebfried S. and Pierson P. (eds) *European Social Policy Between Fragmentation and Integration*, Brookings Institute: Washington

Strohmayer U. and Hannah M. (1992) Domesticating postmodernism, *Antipode*, **24**, 1

Symes V. (1995) *Unemployment in Europe: Problems and Policies*, Routledge: London

Taylor-Gooby P. and Lawson R. (1993) (eds) *Markets and Managers: New Issues in the Delivery of Welfare*, Open University Press: Buckingham

TCPA (Town and Country Planning Association) (1997) Living within the social city region, *Town and Country Planning*, **66**: 3, 80–82

TEST (1988) *Quality Streets – How Traditional Urban Centres Benefit from Traffic Calming*, Transport and Environment Studies: London

TEST (1990) *Space Sharing – A Study of Bus and Pedestrian Shared Shopping Streets in Eight British Towns*, TEST: London

TEST (1991) *Changed Travel – Better World?* Transport and Environment Studies: London

Tewdwr-Jones M. (1995a) Development control and the legitimacy of planning decision, *Town Planning Review*, **66**: 2 163–181

Tewdwr-Jones M. (1995b) Introduction: land use planning after Thatcher, in Tewdwr-Jones M. (ed.) *British Planning Policy in Transition: Planning in the 1990s*, UCL Press: London

Tewdwr-Jones M. (1996) Reflective planning theorising and professional protectionism, *Town Planning Review*, **67**: 2, 235–245

Tewdwr-Jones M. (1997) Plans, policies and intergovernmental relations: assessing the role of national planning guidance in England and Wales, *Urban Studies*, **34**: 1, 145–166

Tewdwr-Jones M. and Allmendinger P. (1998) Deconstructing communicative rationality: a critique of Habermasian collaborative planning, *Environment and Planning A*, **30**: 1975–1989

Tewdwr-Jones M. and Harris N. (1998) The New Right's commodification of planning control, in Allmendinger P. and Thomas H. (eds) *Planning and the British New Right*, Routledge: London

Therivel R., Wilson E., Thompson S., Heaney D. and Pritchard D. (1992) *Strategic Environmental Assessment*, Earthscan: London

Thomas H. (1995) Public participation in planning, in Tewdwr-Jones M. (ed.) *British Planning Policy in Transition: Planning in the 1990s*, UCL Press: London

Thomas H. (1997) Personal communication, 24 September

Thomas H. (1998) Planning in a post-bureaucratic public sector, in Laffin M. (ed.) *Beyond Bureaucracy: New Approaches in Public Sector Management*, Avebury Press: London

Thomas H. and Healey P. (1991) *Dilemmas of Planning Practice*, Gower: Aldershot

Thomson D. (1997) *The End of Time. Faith and Fear in the Shadow of the Millennium*, Minerva: London

Thornley A. (1991) *Urban Planning under Thatcherism*, Routledge: London

Thornley A. (1993) *Urban Planning under Thatcherism: the Challenge of the Market*, 2nd edn, Routledge: London

Thornley A. (1995) Planning policy and the market, in Tewdwr-Jones M. (ed.) *British Planning Policy in Transition: Planning in the 1990s*, UCL Press: London

Thornley A. (1996) Planning policy and the market, in Tewdwr-Jones M. (ed.) *British Planning Policy in Transition*, UCL Press: London

Tolley R. and Turton B. (1995) *Transport Systems, Policy and Planning: A Geographical Approach*, Longman Scientific and Technical: Harlow

Transport 2000 (1997) Road scandal, *Transport Retort*, April/May, p. 6

Turok I. (1993) Property-led urban regeneration: panacea or placebo? *Environment & Planning A*, **24**, 36–79

Turok I. (1997) Should travel to work areas be replaced? *Working Brief*, March 1997, pp. 77–78

Turok I. and Hopkins N. (1997) *Picking Winners or Passing the Buck? Competition and Area Selection in Scotland's New Urban Policy*, SCVO: Edinburgh

Tyme J. (1978) *Motorways versus Democracy: Public Inquiries into Road Proposals and Their Political Significance*, Macmillan: London

UK Government (1994) *Sustainable Development: The UK Strategy*, HMSO: London

UK Government (1998) *Sustainable Development: The UK Strategy* (consultation edition), HMSO: London

UNA (United Nations Association) and CDF (Community Development Foundation) (1995) *Towards Local Sustainability*, UNA: London

UNCED (United Nations Commission on Environment and Development) (1992) *Agenda 21 – Action Plan for the Next Century*, UNCED: New York

Urban Scotland into the 90s (1990) *Urban Scotland into the 90s*, Scottish Office: Edinburgh

Vaughan M., Hilsenrath P. and Ludke R.L. (1994) The contribution of hospitals to a local economy: a case study in Iowa and Illinois, *Health Care Management Review*, **19**: 3, 34–40

Wadhams C. (1995) Housing, in Atkinson, D. (ed.) *Cities of Pride: rebuilding Community, Refocusing Government*, Cassell: London

Wagle S. (1993) Sustainable development: some interpretations, implications and uses, *Bulletin of Science, Technology and Society*, **13**, 313–323

Waldrop M.M. (1992) *Complexity: The Emerging Science at the Edge of Chaos*, Simon and Schuster: New York

Waters M. (1995) *Globalization*, Routledge: London

Watkins C. (1998) The definition and identification of housing submarkets, *Aberdeen Papers in Land Economy*, 98–04, Department of Land Economy, University of Aberdeen

WCED (World Commission for Environment and Development) (1987) *Our Common Future*, Oxford University Press: Oxford

Whitehead C. (1993) Privatising housing: an assessment of the UK experience, *Housing Policy Debate*, **14**: 1, 101–139

Whitehead C. (1997) Changing needs, changing incentives, in Williams P. (ed.) *Directions in Housing Policy*, Paul Chapman Press: London

Williams A. (1994) *The European Community*, Blackwell: London

Williams C. (1993) Planners carry capacity for sustainable development, *Planning*, **1013**, 18–19

Williams C.C. (1994a) Local sourcing initiatives in West Yorkshire: an evaluation of their effectiveness, in Haughton G. and Whitney D. (eds) *Reinventing a Region: Restructuring in West Yorkshire*, Avebury Press: Aldershot

Williams C.C. (1996a) Understanding the role of consumer services in local economic development: some evidence from the Fens, *Environment and Planning A*, **28**: 3, 555–571

Williams C.C. (1996b) Local purchasing schemes and rural development: an evaluation of Local Exchange and Trading Systems (LETS), *Journal of Rural Studies*, **12**: 3, 231–244

Williams C.C. (1996c) Local Exchange and Trading Systems (LETS): a new source of work and credit for the poor and unemployed? *Environment and Planning A*, **28**: 8, 1395–1415

Williams C.C. (1996d) *Reinvigorating the Local Economy*, Forum for the Future: London

Williams C.C. (1997a) *Consumer Services and Economic Development*, Routledge: London

Williams C.C. (1997b) Rethinking the role of the retail sector in economic development, *Service Industries Journal*, **17**: 2, 205–220

Williams H. (1997) Development plans: time for a change, *Property Journal*, June, **22**: 2, 11

Williams R.H. (1996) *European Union Spatial Policy and Planning*, Paul Chapman: London

Willmott P. and Hutchinson R. (1992) *Urban Trends 1*, Policy Studies Institute: London

Wilson A.G. (1974) *Urban and Regional Models in Geography and Planning*, John Wiley: Chichester

Winter P. (1994) Planning and sustainability: an examination of the role of the planning system as an instrument for the delivery of sustainable development, *Journal of Planning and Environmental Law*, 883–900

Wise M. and Gibb R. (1993) *Single Market to Social Europe. The European Community in the 1990s*, Longman: Harlow

Wolfram S. (1986) Cellular automata as models of complexity, *Physica*, **10D**, 1–35

Wolmar C. (1997) Unelected, unaccountable, and still unchallenged, *The Independent*, 13 June

WWF (World Wildlife Fund for Nature) and NEF (New Economics Foundation) (1994) *Indicators for Sustainable Development*, WWF and NEF: London

Wynne D. (1992) Urban regeneration and the arts, in Wynne D. (ed.) *The Culture Industry: the Arts in Urban Regeneration*, Avebury Press: Aldershot

York City Council (1995) *Local Plan, Deposit Draft*, September, York

Young M. and Willmot P. (1957) *Family and Kinship in East London*, Routledge and Kegan Paul: London

INDEX

Index compiled by Geoffrey Jones